Constitutional Courts in Comparison

Constitutional Courts in Comparison

The U.S. Supreme Court and the German Federal Constitutional Court

New and Revised Second Edition

Edited by
Ralf Rogowski and Thomas Gawron

berghahn
NEW YORK • OXFORD
www.berghahnbooks.com

First published in 2002 by

Berghahn Books
www.berghahnbooks.com

Revised edition published in 2016

Library of Congress Cataloging-in-Publication Data

Names: Rogowski, Ralf, editor, author. | Gawron, Thomas , editor, author.
Title: Constitutional courts in comparison: the U.S. Supreme Court and the German Federal Constitutional Court / edited by Ralf Rogowski and Thomas Gawron.
Description: Revised edition, | New York: Berghahn Books, 2016. | Includes bibliographical references and index.
Identifiers: LCCN 2016024962 | ISBN 9781785332739 (hardback)
Subjects: LCSH: United States. Supreme Court. | Germany. Bundesverfassungsgericht. | Constitutional courts. | Judicial review.
Classification: LCC KF8742 .C655 2016 | DDC 347.73/26—dc23
LC record available at https://lccn.loc.gov/2016024962

British Library Cataloguing in Publication Data

A catalogue record for this book is available from the British Library

ISBN 978-1-78533-273-9 (hardback)
ISBN 978-1-78533-096-4 (ebook)

Contents

Foreword to the Second Edition

It is a great pleasure to present the second edition of *Constitutional Courts in Comparison: The U.S. Supreme Court and the German Federal Constitutional Court.* We are grateful to the publisher, Dr. Marion Berghahn, for inviting us to prepare this new edition. We take it as a sign that the first edition of the book has sold reasonably well and that interest in research on two of the leading constitutional courts and their comparison is undiminished and actually increasing.

We are pleased to welcome seven new authors as contributors to the second edition. Some have replaced authors of the first edition who were no longer able to participate; others cover new aspects or assisted in updating. In particular, the new chapters enrich and deepen the analyses of the two courts with fresh perspectives. All remaining contributors to the first edition have revised and updated their chapters.

The widening of the range of authors and themes has not changed the approach we adopted in the first edition of the book. This approach centers on analysis of the U.S. Supreme Court and the German Federal Constitutional Court from a dispute-processing perspective. We still think that our socio-legal perspective contributes uniquely to the fast-growing literature on comparative constitutionalism.

The dispute-processing approach views litigation as a process that transforms a social or political conflict into a legal dispute, and then back into a social or political conflict. This socio-legal approach pays particular attention to the procedures, personnel, and societal impact of the courts. It distinguishes three phases of dispute processing: mobilization of disputes, decision making in court, and implementation of judicial decisions.

The three phases of dispute processing create the basis for the comparison in the book. In the first part, conditions of mobilization are discussed under the heading of *Access and Case Selection.* The second part, *Decision Making,* contains contributions that look at the internal organization of decision making in the two courts, focusing on specific features of strategic choices and consensus finding, including the role of law clerks and legal assistants at the courts. The third part, *Implementation,* compares postjudicial processes and provides information on research on the impact of the two courts.

We have added a new part, *Comparative Perspectives.* In this part we take up a suggestion made by the eminent comparativist Donald P. Kommers, who, in his 2002 review of the first edition of our book in *Law and Politics Review* 12(10), noticed a lack of genuinely comparative chapters. We have responded to his suggestion, at least in part, by including chapters that compare organizational aspects, especially the choice of personnel at the courts and the impact they have on their respective political systems.

Ralf Rogowski and Thomas Gawron

Ralf Rogowski is a professor of law and the director of the Law and Sociology program at the School of Law of the University of Warwick, Coventry.

Thomas Gawron is a lecturer in law at the Hochschule für Technik und Wirtschaft (HTW), Berlin.

Foreword to the First Edition

The world has recently experienced one of its periodic waves of constitution making. Earlier episodes involved establishing basic substantive principles of liberal democracy and devising various forms of separated powers. The recent wave may be distinctively concerned with creating institutions of constitutional review, typically involving various forms of constitutional litigation. This book's examination of well-established variants of constitutional litigation in the United States and Germany will deepen our understanding of developments elsewhere and may direct our attention to emergent patterns that might otherwise be overlooked. The authors' use of the dispute-processing model in particular gives a coherent overview of the processes of constitutional litigation in the two nations.

The field of comparative constitutional law, although relatively young as a discipline, already has established some patterns. Perhaps the most prominent feature of scholarly works in the field is their highly normative focus. That is, scholars identify a fundamental normative question—free speech rights, or notions of equality—and ask how different constitutional systems resolve that question. One tension in the field is between claims that these normative questions can have universally valid answers, and claims that each constitutional system's resolution of the normative questions can be understood only in the nation's entire social, economic, and institutional context.

A second feature of comparative constitutional study moves the normative inquiry to a slightly more abstract level. Here scholars are less concerned with what resolutions different constitutional systems provide for similar questions than with the ways in which constitutional systems go about resolving the questions. Some systems, for example, seem more attracted to rule-like resolutions of constitutional questions, as in U.S. constitutional law's reliance on "tiers" of "scrutiny" in equal protection cases or its use of sharp distinctions between content-based and content-neutral forms of speech regulation. Others seem more comfortable with analytic approaches that are open to explicit balancing of competing social interests, as in the Canadian Charter's provision that the constitutional rights it guarantees can be limited by law when the limitation is demonstrably justified in a free and democratic society. Again, the methodological inquiry can be directed to discerning which approach—rules or balancing—is better universally, or to accounting for the choices different systems make in selecting their basic analytic approaches.

This collection of essays deepens prior comparative examinations in its focus on constitutional litigation as a social process. The essays here carefully lay out the ways in which each constitutional system is historically specific and develops in conjunction with changes in the economy and society of the country it serves. Perhaps more significant, the essays stress the importance of institutional structure. Some explain how different institutional structures provide different opportunities for judges to develop distinctive judicial agendas, or at least how different structures induce agenda construction at different points in the process. Further, some essays show how different political structures present different opportunities for implementing constitutional change through litigation. These essays offer good models of the direction that comparative constitutional study should take by supplementing the normative principles of constitutional law with attention to the consequences of specific institutional design choices.

Other essays direct attention to questions of culture, both large and small. Taken most broadly, all the essays concern the development and institutionalization of constitutional cultures in Germany and the United States, that is, what it takes to embed constitutionalism in a nation's political and legal culture. But the authors focus on important cultural issues of a narrower sort as well. The essays that direct attention to the culture of constitutionalism that develops within each constitutional court are particularly valuable in this connection.

Readers will benefit from the descriptions provided here of the processes of constitutional litigation in Germany and the United States. But they will benefit even more from being offered the dispute-processing framework as a model for systematic inquiry. Undoubtedly other works will provide alternative frameworks for comparative study, but until then these essays will surely prove models of systematic comparative study.

Mark Tushnet

Mark V. Tushnet is the William Nelson Cromwell professor of law at Harvard Law School.

Figures and Tables

Figures

Tables

Introduction

Constitutional Litigation as Dispute Processing

Comparing the U.S. Supreme Court and the German Federal Constitutional Court

Ralf Rogowski and Thomas Gawron

Generally, constitutional litigation has two functions: to protect fundamental rights of citizens and to supervise the government's legislative activities. The introduction of constitutional litigation is often understood as an important step in the modernization of a country's political and legal systems. From an evolutionary perspective, constitutions and their judicial enforcement are crucial achievements in establishing both autonomous legal orders and democratic political orders based on the notions of checks and balances of central powers, the rule of law, and inalienable individual rights (see Luhmann 1990; see also Luhmann 1993: 468–481; Murphy 1993).

However, constitutions and their enforcement bodies differ significantly among countries. The organization and the tasks of constitutional courts reflect both historical peculiarities and political arrangements within nation-states (Padoa-Schioppa 1997). A comparison of constitutional courts, such as this one between the U.S. Supreme Court and the German Federal Constitutional Court (Bundesverfassungsgericht), can illuminate these differences. It can also point to similarities in the political cultures of Western democracies.

Nevertheless, a comparison of these courts is immediately confronted with a methodological question. Is the U.S. Supreme Court a constitu-

Notes for this chapter begin on page 18.

tional court? Are we comparing like with like? The Federal Constitutional Court deals exclusively with constitutional law and thus is not an appellate court. It is responsible for judicial review of legislation and is open to any citizen who wishes to file a complaint about a violation of a basic right. In contrast, the U.S. Supreme Court is at the top of the federal judicial system and has appellate jurisdiction in all cases arising from federal courts. However, the Supreme Court is also the highest constitutional court in the United States. More than half of its decisions focus on constitutional law issues (see Wieland 1990: 343). It engages in judicial review of legislation and is the institution to which citizens, particularly those with little or no financial means to engage in litigation, turn to claim their constitutional rights. More than two-thirds of all Supreme Court petitions are in forma pauperis, brought by indigent people for whom the fee and the requirement of multiple copies are waived (see Baum 2013: 96–98). Thus, notwithstanding Mauro Cappelletti's (1989: 142) statement that "the Supreme Court should be compared not to the special constitutional courts, but rather to the highest courts of appeal on the continent," the U.S. Supreme Court is, in our understanding, comparable to the German Federal Constitutional Court, particularly when functional and sociological aspects are taken into consideration.

Constitutional courts have been compared in a number of ways. A large part of the existing comparative research focuses on policy making in constitutional courts and their relationship to the legislature (see the special issue of *Comparative Political Studies,* Vol. 26(4), 1994, on constitutional courts; Becker 1987; Schmidhauser 1987: 7–33; Landfried 1988; Jackson, Tate 1992; Stone-Sweet 2000; Hönnige 2007; see also Tate, Vallinder 1995). In addition, there are comparative studies on the judicial behavior of judges (see Schubert, Danelski 1969) and a range of legal comparisons (Mosler 1962; Cappelletti 1971; Favoreu 1986; Stark, Weber 1986; Brünneck 1992; Kau 2007; Hönnige 2008).

The concept of our book differs in some respects from these approaches. We adopt a socio-legal perspective that understands constitutional litigation as dispute processing. This approach focuses on the reality of dealing with cases—the judicial organization and the routines developed in the decision making of the courts. The sociological dispute-processing perspective views litigation as a process in which a social or political conflict is transformed into a legal dispute, and then back into a social or political conflict. It distinguishes three phases of dispute processing: mobilization of disputes, decision making in court, and implementation of judicial decisions.

The book applies the dispute-processing approach to constitutional litigation in Germany and the United States. It is structured accordingly.

Part I, "Access and Case Selection," is concerned with mobilization of cases and questions of procedure and docket control at the two courts. Part II, "Decision Making," comprises analyses of internal ways of case disposal with a special emphasis on the role of personnel, including judges and the legal assistants at the Federal Constitutional Court, respectively justices and the law clerks at the U.S. Supreme Court. Part III, "Implementation," contains discussions of conditions of implementation and some assessments of the impact that decisions of the Federal Constitutional Court and the U.S. Supreme Court have had on the political process. Finally, Part IV, "Comparative Perspectives," is devoted to comparative analyses of the two constitutional courts, with particular foci on functional aspects, composition, and impact on democracy and political culture.

Access, Success, and Case Selection

Both courts enjoy high prestige among the general public. They regularly achieve high scores in public opinion polls and rank above other national political institutions (see Friedman 1975; Beyme 1999; Kommers, Miller 2012: 39–40). Furthermore, both courts adjudicate in disputes over basic rights granted to citizens in their written constitutions (for a comparative overview, see Glendon 1995). Their high prestige and their rights jurisdiction are important factors in explaining the caseload of both courts. The following table shows the caseload development, in five-year averages, at the Supreme Court and the Federal Constitutional Court from 1951 to 2010.

The increase in caseloads reflects the constantly rising popularity of both courts after World War II. Also noteworthy is the dramatic rise in cases in the 1990s, due mainly to an extraordinary increase in petitions in forma pauperis and their equivalents in the form of constitutional complaints in the Federal Constitutional Court (see Kagan, Elinson, in this volume; Grossman, Epp 2002 for the U.S. Supreme Court; Blankenburg, in this volume for the German Federal Constitutional Court). The number of judges or justices has not risen, so the increase has put enormous strain on both courts. Each has reacted with procedures to shape conditions of access and regulate selection of cases for full hearings.

In socio-legal terms it makes sense to distinguish between barriers of access and barriers of success. Access barriers are factors that hinder the filing of a case. Success barriers are related to legal and organizational conditions that prevent a case from being admitted and subsequently won. Access barriers might be financial burdens, litigants' limited legal knowledge, insufficient social competence or support when establishing

Table I.1. Cases Filed in the U.S. Supreme Court and the German Federal Constitutional Court, 1951–2010 (in five-year averages)

	U.S. Supreme Court	*German Federal Constitutional Court*
1951–1955	—	680
1956–1960	1,812	1,090
1961–1966	2,383	1,417
1966–1970	3,191	1,623
1971–1975	3,787	1,590
1976–1980	3,985	2,729
1981–1985	4,249	3,451
1986–1990	4,788	3,543
1991–1995	6,531	5,037
1996–2000	8,157	4,965
2001–2005	9,132	5,041
2006–2010	9,438	6,316

Sources: Numbers for the U.S. Supreme Court are taken from Baum, L. *The Supreme Court*, 6th ed. Washington, 1998 (122, Figure 3.1) for the years 1951–1995 and from our own survey based on data from http://www.uscourts.gov/Statistics/JudicialBusiness/archive.aspx for the years 1996–2010. Numbers for the German Federal Constitutional Court are from our own survey based on data from Statistik des Bundesverfassungsgerichts, Tabelle "Statistik für das Geschäftsjahr 2010, A I 2: Verfahrenseingänge," retrieved from http://www.bundesverfassungsgericht.de/DE/Verfahren/Jahresstatistiken/Archiv/2010/gb2010/A-I-2.html.

contact with the legal system, or the diffuse nature of the interest pursued. Success barriers include the nature of legal rights, judicial policies, and organizational interests guiding the case selection in judicial institutions (on the distinction between access and success barriers, see Rogowski 1996).

The two courts differ significantly in relation to legal and social conditions of access. In the United States, access barriers seem lower than in Germany. In general, given the high density of lawyers in the United States, finding legal representation seems easier. However, bringing a case to the Supreme Court requires specialist lawyers. There is an official Supreme Court Bar comprised of lawyers prepared to handle Supreme Court cases, although experience in arguing a case before the Supreme Court does not seem to be necessary to become a member of this bar (McGuire 1993). Probably more important is the group of specialist lawyers, often former law clerks, who frequently participate in cases before the Supreme Court. Furthermore, the collective organization of diffuse interests is an important factor in the preparation of claims for constitutional litigation in the United States (one of the most active of these interest groups is the National Association for the Advancement of Colored People [NAACP]; see Tushnet 1987). For more than fifty years, privately funded advocacy organizations and government-funded lawyers' offices have organized litigation campaigns and provided legal assistance to overcome access barriers. Interest groups are also major participants in litigation, either as sponsors or through amicus curiae briefs (see Kagan, Elinson, in this volume). They have managed to build up an impressive support structure for rights litigation in the United States (Epp 1998, especially ch. 4).

The role of lawyers and interest groups is different in Germany. The Federal Constitutional Court understands itself as a "citizens' court." A citizen does not need to hire a legal representative to file a constitutional complaint. This contrasts with litigation in all other federal supreme courts, where a citizen is obliged to be represented in court by a member of the small, specially accredited bar for final appeals in Karlsruhe. When the Court began in the 1950s, more than 80 percent of all constitutional complaints were initiated by the parties themselves. Even in 1995, a third of all complaints were still filed by the complainants without attorneys representing them (see Blankenburg, in this volume). Interest groups rarely play a significant role in preparing or assisting constitutional complaints or other forms of constitutional litigation. Generally, the Court is not seen as a platform for advancing causes pursued by social movements.

Given the stark contrast in access conditions, it is remarkable that success rates are similar in the United States and Germany. Success at constitutional courts has to be defined in a twofold manner: the first success is to get the case admitted; the second is to win the case. The actual rate of admitted constitutional complaints in the Federal Constitutional Court is as low as the rate of petitions granting a writ of certiorari in the U.S. Supreme Court: in both courts, only 1 to 2 percent of filed complaints and petitions are admitted for decision on merit (Blankenburg, in this Volume; Baum 2013: 86).

Table I.2 below sheds light on the practice of admittance at the Supreme Court and the Federal Constitutional Court. For the year 2010, it compares decisions on merit and summarily decided cases with cases denied, dismissed, or withdrawn at each court. The data reveal the enormous filter effect. In 2010, only 90 out of 7,828 cases were decided on merit in the Supreme Court, and just 115 out 6,344 cases received a full decision by one of the two senates or the chambers of the Federal Constitutional Court.

The jurisdiction of the U.S. Supreme Court is comprised of two types: original jurisdiction, in which the Court acts as a trial court, and appellate jurisdiction. The vast majority of U.S. Supreme Court cases arise from legal proceedings initiated in lower courts, mostly federal courts. In this appellate jurisdiction, the Court enjoys autonomy in accepting or rejecting cases. The decision on the standard petition for constitutional litigation (writ of certiorari) by which the Court calls up the case from a lower court

Table I.2. Cases Disposed at the Supreme Court and the Federal Constitutional Court in 2010

Cases	*Supreme Court*	*Federal Constitutional Court*
Decided on merit	90	115
Summarily decided	82	25*
Denied, dismissed, or withdrawn	7,656	6,204
Total	7,828	6,344

* Other decisions (Zwischen-/Nebenentscheidungen) of the two Federal Constitutional Court senates, including interim relief.

Sources: "The Supreme Court, 2010 Term," *Harvard Law Review*, Vol. 125(1), 2010, 370, table II (C): "Method of Disposition" http://0-web.ebscohost.com.pugwash.lib.warwick.ac.uk/bsi/pdfviewer/pdfviewer?vid=3&sid=084d34ac-57fc-41a3-b7b1-bad04df4a367%40sessionmgr110&hid=128; Statistik des Bundesverfassungsgerichts, Tabelle "Statistik für das Gesch äftsjahr 2010, A III 2: Erledigungen" http://www.bundesverfassungsgericht.de/DE/Verfahren/Jahresstatistikn/Archiv/2010/gb2010/A-III-2.html.

is entirely discretionary (Rule 10 of the Rules of the Supreme Court). This large autonomy creates difficulties for litigation strategies. The lack of predictability and objective criteria in accepting petitions thus constitutes an enormous success barrier.

In contrast, individual cases can be brought to the Federal Constitutional Court relatively easily. However, they have to meet the strict objective criteria of admittance of either of two procedures, namely, the constitutional complaint and the preliminary ruling or concrete norm control procedure (art. 93 I 4a and 100 I of the Basic Law in conjunction with art. 80 to 82 and 90 to 95 of the Federal Constitutional Court Act). These criteria work both ways: to some extent they generate legal certainty among litigants, or at least among their legal representatives, about how to prepare a case. However, the criteria also create the basis on which the Court can swiftly reject complaints and thus legitimize the high rate of denials and dismissals of constitutional complaints.

The practice of acceptance and rejection reveals the strong concern of both courts to protect themselves from caseload overflow. Selection is thus a mechanism for caseload management. Furthermore, through the selection process, cases not deemed relevant for the development of the law are excluded. Both courts are indeed "fishing for the right cases" and operate with criteria that reveal specific judicial policies. Through the selection of cases, they set their agenda.

However, the courts' agenda-setting processes differ somewhat. The Federal Constitutional Court operates mainly with legal criteria. Only constitutional law questions can be heard, although the criteria ("being constitutionally relevant," "intensity of the infringement of basic rights," and so on—see Heun, in this volume) are deliberately vague and leave enough flexibility to select cases in accordance with the Court's general agenda.

The selection process at the U.S. Supreme Court seems more policy-oriented. It is task- rather than goal-oriented (Grossman, Epp 2002; see also Perry 1994 and Schwartz 1997). Each justice (supported by his or her clerks) usually adopts a specific policy agenda, and the selection process is often the result of internal political negotiation between justices (Provine 1980). Furthermore, the Court follows a rather hybrid agenda influenced by institutional norms and individual preferences. These include considerations of a case being brought too early or too late (and thus not being "ripe") or of pertinent facts or law having changed (the case becoming "moot") (O'Brien 1993: 217–220). Probably the best known among the institutional norms is the so-called "political question" doctrine according to which the Court decides that a particular political branch should resolve the issue and not the Supreme Court (in relation to the judicial restraint and the political question doctrine, see Lamb 1982: 21–22). However, it has to be stressed that the decision to apply the "political question" doctrine is a judicial and not a political decision (Henkin 1976).

The Process of Decision Making

It is well known that the political and ideological preferences of judges and justices influence both case selection and decision making on merit. Research on judicial behavior has provided insights on the voting behavior of justices and judges in decision making (Schubert 1960, 1964; Rottleuthner 1973). Furthermore, the personal backgrounds, education, and professional careers of Supreme Court justices in particular, as well as their attitudes and values, have been foci of empirical research (see Menez 1984; Segal, Spaeth 1993).

However, analyzing the behavior of individual judges or justices is unlikely to fully reveal the reality of the decision-making process at any constitutional court. The eight or nine judges sitting together do not act in isolation. They are a group, and their group interactions are a strong influence on their decision making (Vermeule 2011). They often form coalitions, and in both courts the minority is allowed to publish "dissenting opinions" (in Germany since 1970). Furthermore, analyzing the decision-making process in its entirety entails analysis of not only the voting behavior or interactions of judges and justices in senates and conferences, but also the internal decision-making in the vast majority of routine cases. These include negative decisions on hearing certiorari petitions and constitutional complaints. These cases dominate the day-to-day decision making in the two courts.

The U.S. Supreme Court has a number of procedures designed to screen petitions for hearing. Except for a small number of cases that require a decision (mandatory appeals), the vast majority of cases—a quarter of which are so-called paid cases and three-quarters of which are in forma pauperis cases without payment of fees or other restrictions (on the growth of paupers' petitions, see Baum 2013: 97–98)—are decided on a discretionary basis. The Supreme Court has adopted a standard procedure in handling these cases (see the account of the agenda setting process in Grossman, Epp 2002). Copies of all petitions go to each justice's chamber. The justices and their law clerks then prescreen the cases. Approximately 800 petitions per term are put on the list of cases to be discussed in conference (see Johnson, Sorensen, in this volume). The chief justice creates the discuss list, but cases can be added by each justice (Ward, in this volume).

At the Federal Constitutional Court, in contrast, most cases are first handled in so-called chambers. Each senate annually appoints several chambers consisting of three judges each. The chambers deal with all constitutional complaints and concrete norm controls. They have the power to reject by unanimous vote or admit the complaint or norm control to a full hearing. They even can decide on the merits in case of a prior decision of the Court on the issue (see Kranenpohl, in this volume). Since 2004, important chamber decisions are published in a separate collection of decisions of the Federal Constitutional Court (Kammerentscheidungen des Bundesverfassungsgerichts, BVerfGK, see Massing, in this volume).

The FCC is characterized by a high degree of jurisdictional specialization. Each of the sixteen judges is considered an expert in charge of particular areas of law. Each year at the beginning of the Court's term, the Court adopts an official schedule (*Geschäftsverteilungsplan*) that allocates legal subject areas to specific judges. Based on this schedule, the president and the vice-president decide which judge is to act as rapporteur (see Kranenpohl, in this volume). Case assignment might take the interests and expertise of judges into account (Kommers, Miller 2012, 26). However, the overarching characteristic of the procedures for the handling of cases at the Federal Constitutional Court is high bureaucratization.

In both courts, the responsibility for preparing "routine cases" is delegated to law clerks and legal assistants who prescreen petitions, respectively prepare constitutional complaints to be discussed in chambers. The delegation of these cases to law clerks or assistants relieves the burden on the constitutional judges. It creates space for discussion of "big cases" in a small circle, in the conference of all nine Supreme Court justices or the hearing of the senate at the Federal Constitutional Court. Law clerks and assistants form a crucial part of the decision-making team. The judges or justices rely heavily on these assistants, and in routine cases of constitutional complaints and certiorari petitions the assistants or clerks carry the main burden. In addition to preparatory work on constitutional complaints for the chambers, each of the legal assistants of the Federal Constitutional Court assists in preparing two to three decisions in the senate each year (see Wieland 2002). These are decisions for which his or her judge is the reporter (Massing, in this volume).

Law clerks or legal assistants are assigned to individual judges or justices. In either court judges or justices have four law clerks, with the exception of the chief justice of the U.S Supreme Court, who has five. The judges and justices select their assistants and law clerks personally and observe personal preferences and individual sympathies. The legal assistants are appointed for three to four years, the law clerks for only one year. Whereas legal assistants work in close cooperation with their judge, the law clerks work more often with each other (Ward, in this volume). Eight of the nine Supreme Court justices have combined their clerks in a so-called "certiorari pool" in which petitions and the writing of memoranda are distributed among clerks (Ward, in this volume; see also O'Brien 1993: 173; Perry 1992: 43–51).

The legal assistants of the Federal Constitutional Court are recruited as experts with experience in a specific legal field. Each judge of the Federal Constitutional Court runs his or her own department, which is exclusively responsible for the handling of cases in one or more specific areas of law. With the exception of a few assistants who formerly worked as academic assistants to a then professor of constitutional law who is now their constitutional judge, most legal assistants in the Federal Constitutional Court have been judges at lower specialized courts. Indeed, they are recruited for both their experience in judicial decision-making and their knowledge of a particular field of law.

At the Supreme Court, on the other hand, decisive criteria are that law clerks have graduated from prestigious Ivy League law schools and are from the region favored by the selecting justice. An increasing number of candidates have also clerked for judges on other courts (see Mazor 2002; see also O'Brien 1993: 166–177). They are at the beginning of their professional lives and spend a year at the most prestigious legal institution of the country before embarking on lucrative careers as lawyers. Their attitude to work is often marked by high identification with the Supreme Court and idealism toward the law.

For the assistants and clerks, the period spent at the Constitutional Court forms a significant part of their professional career. Furthermore, through them both constitutional courts influence and contribute to shaping central segments of their respective national legal professions. In the Federal Republic, the former legal assistant typically moves into the higher levels of the judiciary. In the United States the former law clerk typically starts working for a law firm or the government in Washington, D.C. or on Wall Street. These different patterns neatly reflect the differences in the importance each of the two legal cultures attaches to careers in the judiciary and in legal practice.

In both courts the number of cases heard and decided on merit is small (see Table I.2). In admitted cases, oral arguments play a large role in the Supreme Court (Baum 2013: 107–108 and Johnson, Sorenson, in this volume), whereas formal public hearings are a rare event in the Federal Constitutional Court (see Schlaich, Korioth 2012: Rdnr. 69 and Kommers, Miller 2012: 27). A difference between the courts exists in relation to the possibility that external interests may influence the procedure. At the Supreme Court the procedural device of the *amicus curiae* brief allows interested parties to provide information and present their views on their initiative. In Germany, however, third parties have to wait for the Federal Constitutional Court to invite them as participants.

Deliberations among judges differ between the courts. Whereas deliberations in the senates of the Federal Constitutional Court are characterised by discursiveness (Kranenpohl 2010: 133–198 and in this volume) and a drive toward consensus, an argumentative style dominates in the U.S. Supreme Court. Dissensus among Supreme Court justices is evidenced by the fact that a majority of decisions are not unanimous, and that justices commonly disagree in dissenting or concurring opinions (54 percent of decisions with opinions in the 2010 term, Baum 2013: 111, table 4.1). Fewer than 10 percent of the published decisions of the Federal Constitutional Court are issued with a dissenting opinion (*Sondervotum,* see Statistik des Bundesverfassungsgerichts, Tabelle "Statistik für das Geschäftsjahr 2015, A I 7: Entscheidungen mit oder ohne Sondervotum" http://www.bundesver fassungsgericht.de/DE/Verfahren/Jahresstatistiken/2015/gb2015/A-I-7.pdf).

Impact, Implementation, and Evaluation

From a dispute-processing perspective, implementation, the third phase in treating judicial cases, follows mobilization and decision-making. Judicial institutions have only limited means of influencing enforcement of their decisions. Constitutional courts in particular operate in specific social contexts that they cannot ignore. They do not just solve individual disputes but take part in the treatment of social and political problems in society at large. However, a social or political problem underlying constitutional litigation is rarely solved by the decision of the constitutional court.

Neither court can mobilize money or administrative resources (bailiffs, the police, or the military) to ensure the effective implementation of its decisions. Lacking special implementation agencies, the courts are dependent on other institutions to implement their decisions. Sometimes they can encourage other institutions to act favorably. Constitutional judges may use personal contacts with other judges, as well as careful public relations and close contact with the media. Over the past years, judges of the Federal Constitutional Court have frequently commented in newspapers, magazines, or television on certain constitutional interpretations and the tasks of the Constitutional Court, and have actively cultivated contacts with vested interests (Kranenpohl 2010: ch. 8).

Academic awareness of postjudicial events and processes triggered by constitutional decision-making varies between the United States and Germany. Analyses of the impact and implementation of U.S. Supreme Court decisions have been available since the beginning of the 1960s. In Germany, postjudicial processes have only recently caught the attention of social scientists and legal academics.

In general, research on postjudicial processes can be divided into three types of study: impact, implementation, and evaluation research (Gawron, Rogowski 2007: ch. 2). Impact studies analyze the court in its social and political environment. They tend to ask grand questions about social change instigated by court decisions (Rosenberg 1991). Methodologically, however, they are rather narrowly confined to a focus on the addressees or recipients of the decisions (see Wasby 1970; Becker, Feeley 1973). Impact is assessed behavioristically by analyzing communication processes, motivations for resistance, and sanctions for disobedience (see Baum 2013: 196–202). Famous examples of successful impact studies have dealt with Supreme Court decisions on school desegregation, school prayer, and abortion (Keynes, Miller 1989; Epstein, Kobylka 1992; McGuire 2009; see also from a German perspective Heldrich 1972). Comparable examples for the Federal Constitutional Court are cases concerning freedom of speech (Lüth decision), abortion, and classroom crucifixes (Liebl 1990; Henne, Riedlinger 2005; Schaal 2006).

In the United States, there is an extensive body of research on political powers' resistance to Supreme Court decisions. Congress and the president are known for openly criticizing the Supreme Court, ignoring its decisions, or even using political means to restrict the court in the form of legislative initiatives limiting its jurisdiction, verbal attacks, and politicization of selection of justices (Baum 2013: 206–8). In these cases one may speak of a "negative impact" of the Supreme Court in the form of negative reactions in actual politics, although others view this as "positive impact" in terms of strengthening democratic control and republicanism (see, for example, Habermas 1996: ch. 6).

Whereas impact research is mainly interested in the targets of policies, the implementation approach focuses on organizations that administer policies and on the processes that occur during enforcement of these policies (Canon, Johnson 1999). This research perspective assumes that implementation agents enjoy some autonomy in implementing policies. Implementation research has found that political programs are systematically undermined by factors related to the implementation process (Pressman, Wildavsky 1984/1973), and that implementation agents engage in implementation games (Bardach 1977).

The implementation approach views judicial implementation as a form of policy implementation (Baum 1977; see also Schmidhauser, Berg 1972; Baum 1976). It understands judicial decisions as programs that contain both general—and in the case of constitutional courts, often political—statements and behavioral instructions for participants to the dispute. It distinguishes between symbolic and instrumental parts of the program. The instrumental part aims directly at the implementation process. However, judicial implementation is more than policy implementation. We suggest distinguishing five implementation arenas that follow system specific logics. These arenas are courts, legislatures, administration, collective interest groups, and private economic actors (Gawron, Rogowski 2007, ch. 3).

From an implementation perspective, constitutional courts use different steering mechanisms to recognize differences among implementing agents. In their relationship to other courts, a main steering mechanism consists in the shaping of procedures (on interjudicial relationships, see Tarr 1977; Gawron, Rogowski 2007, ch. 4). Regarding administrative agencies, the courts steer via constitutional interpretations that choose between administrative law doctrines, or by limiting the scope of discretion by favoring the position of certain participants in the administrative arena (for the United States see Shapiro 1968; for Germany see Gawron 2013).

In relation to legislation, both constitutional courts generally operate cautiously and exercise some form of judicial self-restraint either as a doctrine or in practice. However, both courts engage in judicial review of legislation and regularly find existing laws unconstitutional. In cases where legislative change is required, the Supreme Court has little means to demand obedience from Congress or the president, as its relationship to these political powers "is one between equals rather than one of hierarchy" (Baum, in this volume). In general, this also holds true for the relationship between the Federal Constitutional Court and the German legislature. However, there is a subtle difference. The Federal Constitutional Court can rely on the assistance of excellently positioned implementation agents. The relevant departments in the Federal Ministry of Justice, especially the so-called constitutional law department, understand themselves as the mouthpiece of the Constitutional Court (Gawron, Rogowski, in this volume).

Evaluation research adopts a broader view than impact and implementation research. It looks at the societal impact of constitutional courts, for example, the impact that interpretations of legal conditions like the rule of law, civil liberties, and freedom of speech have on democratization processes (see Epstein, Knight, Shvetsova 2001; Kneip, in this volume). Such evaluation of the courts can extend to their impact on value structures in society, like the "spirit of equality and harmony" (Lietzmann, in this volume).

Evaluation research looks at all three levels of program, implementation process, and addressees or beneficiaries of constitutional court decisions. By evaluating the positive or negative impact of the implementation of decisions, such research aims to improve the quality of programs mandated by subsequent decisions (Gawron, Rogowski 2007: 43–45). In an evaluation perspective, court judgments are of central concern, as they are the main instruments whereby constitutional courts may shape implementation processes. Evaluation research emphasizes that, in order to guarantee effectiveness, judgments not only need to be clear and precise in their instructions to the implementing agents but must also reflect the social and political consequences of constitutional decision-making.

Evaluation research assumes that new conflicts continuously emerge as a result of a constitutional court's decision. Such research focuses on how decision making at constitutional courts is actually concerned with these self-generated conflicts and with the shortcomings of previous decisions. From an evaluation point of view, it is important to study the form of argumentation (Luhmann 1995) and the techniques each courts uses to consider social, political, and legal consequences during decision making.

Furthermore, evaluation research enables us to ask wider sociological questions, like those posed by social systems theory. These questions can concern the functioning of courts' autonomy and the basis of self-reproduction or autopoiesis of constitutional decision-making (Gawron, Rogowski 2007: ch. 6; Rogowski 2013). The systems theoretical perspective assesses constitutions and constitutional courts as mechanisms of structural coupling of the legal and the political system (Luhmann 1993: 470–481). In fact, systems theory suggests that the U.S. Supreme Court and the Federal Constitutional Court can be viewed as organizations increasingly engaged in a process of reflexive decision-making, in which the role of constitutional litigation as part of dispute processing in society is continuously reevaluated.

Organizational Comparison

The U.S. Supreme Court and the German Federal Constitutional Court differ in age, size, and location. The Supreme Court was introduced in conjunction with the Constitution of the United States of America in 1787. Its competencies are regulated in Article III of the Constitution and in the Judiciary Act of 1789. It is thus 225 years old. The German Federal Constitutional Court was introduced in 1949 by the Basic Law (*Grundgesetz*), in which its competencies and composition are regulated in Articles 93 and 94. The Court itself was established in 1951, and the 1951 Federal Constitutional Court Act (*Bundesverfassungsgerichtsgesetz*) regulates its composition and proceedings. It is thus just over sixty years old.

In size, the Federal Constitutional Court is almost twice as large as the Supreme Court. It now consists of two senates with eight judges each ("twin courts"—the original number of twelve judges per panel was decreased to ten in 1956, and finally to eight in 1963). The sixteen judges are appointed for a maximum of twelve years but not beyond the retirement age of sixty-eight, and they tend to be younger than the Supreme Court justices. The U.S. Supreme Court consists of one panel with nine judges, appointed for life. In the nineteenth century most justices died in office. Even today justices resign or retire voluntarily only if they fall seriously ill or reach a very advanced age (Baum 2013: 59–65).

The seat of the Supreme Court is in the nation's capital, Washington, D.C. It reflects the fact that the Court forms part of the U.S. government and plays a particular role in the balance of powers at the federal level. The seat of the Federal Constitutional Court is in Karlsruhe, that is, not in the capital of the Federal Republic but "outside the political power center" (Rinken 2002). However, Karlsruhe is widely seen as the nation's "legal capital" since it is also the seat of Germany's highest court of appeal for civil and criminal matters, the Federal Supreme Court (Bundesgerichtshof), which is the largest and most important of the federal courts (Lamprecht 2011).

One function of both constitutional courts is to arbitrate between bodies of the state or between states that are part of the federation or federal republic. In this respect, the Federal Constitutional Court takes up the tradition of the Court of the Empire (Reichsgericht) that until 1806 adjudicated disputes among the members of the Holy Roman Empire of the German Nation. During the nineteenth century, there were a number of special courts and procedures for constitutional conflicts, none of them having any great influence (Robbers 1990). Neither did the unification of Germany in 1871 and the formation of the German Empire (Deutsches Reich) lead to the establishment of a separate constitutional court. The first step in this direction was taken after World War I, when the State Court (Staatsgerichtshof) was established for adjudicating conflicts over jurisdictions between a state and the Reich government and for reviewing decisions by the highest state organs (Caldwell 1997: 147 and 160–170). However, the Weimar Constitution of 1919 did not grant this court jurisdiction over fundamental individual rights. These rights became justiciable only after World War II. In conjunction with the adoption of a catalogue of basic rights, the establishment of a Federal Constitutional Court with powers to adjudicate in the two main areas of basic rights and state affairs was announced in the Basic Law of 1949 (Doemming, Füsslein, Matz 1951; see also Laufer 1968; Schiffers 1984; Lhotta 2003; Lembcke 2007; Kneip 2009).

The Federal Constitutional Court and the Supreme Court both played important roles in the formation of their respective nations. In its early period, the Federal Constitutional Court was particularly engaged with problems of federalism in the newly established Federal Republic. Its decisions on the merger of states in the Southwest of Germany (BVerfGE 1, 14, 1951—*Southwest State* case)[1] and the incorporation of the Saar region into the Federal Republic (BVerfGE 4, 157, 1955—*Saar Treaty* case) are leading examples. In this period the Court, initially guided by an antifascist impulse and by recourse to natural law principles, also developed an understanding of basic rights, which allowed for the creation of an extensive common law of the Federal Constitutional Court. A particular topic preoccupying the Court early on was the rights of civil servants employed during the Nazi period: in opposition to all other supreme federal courts, which favored an apolitical assessment of civil service during the Nazi period, the Federal Constitutional Court limited their pension entitlements (BVerfGE 3, 58—*Civil Servant* case and BVerfGE 6, 132—*Gestapo* case; Limbach 2011). Furthermore, the Federal Constitutional Court was able to decisively influence the process of democratization in the new Federal Republic by fostering the end of the autocratic regime, institutionalizing new democratic structures, and consolidating democracy in general (see Kneip, in this volume; Bryde 2006).

The U.S. Supreme Court played a crucial role during the formative years of the United States. In particular its arbitration of interstate conflicts and its endorsement of a national economic policy contributed decisively to the building of the American nation (Hurst 1986; see also Höreth 2008, ch. 4). By developing a particular notion of federalism it strengthened the federal powers. Later, after the Civil War, in the period from 1865 until 1937, the Supreme Court was concerned with developing a liberal-capitalist ideology protecting free markets against state intervention. After 1937, the focus shifted toward the protection of civil rights (Tushnet 2009: 28–34). During the 1980s, most of these rights were again denied and the

Court became increasingly conservative on issues such as labor relations and environmental protection (Pacelle 1991; see also Baum 2013: 175–177).

Since its beginnings, the Supreme Court has struggled over its powers of judicial review of legislation. Indeed, one of the most remarkable aspects of this institution is that it was able to define its own powers of judicial review. In the famous decision *Marbury v. Madison* (5. U.S. [1 Cranch] 137 [1803]) the Supreme Court adopted the doctrine of judicial review and applied it to a congressional statute for the first time. Through judicial review, the Court asserted its authority to determine what the Constitution means. The Court developed this doctrine into a powerful instrument to review federal legislation and decisions of the president. In *Cooper v. Aaron* (358 U.S. 1 [1958]) it expanded the doctrine by declaring that governors and state legislatures were bound to uphold decisions of the Supreme Court and its constitutional interpretations, just as they were bound to uphold the Constitution itself (on *Cooper* and *Marbury,* see Hall 1992: 197–198 and 521–523; see also the assessment of judicial review powers of the Supreme Court by Tushnet 1999 and 2014). In this context it is worth mentioning that the Supreme Court is not the exclusive decision maker in constitutional litigation, as constitutional issues can also be raised in any lower or appellate state or federal court in the United States (see also Kagan, Elinson, in this volume).

The German Federal Constitutional Court was granted powers of judicial review by the Basic Law. From the outset, a major task has been to control federal and other legislative acts. The Federal Constitutional Court extended its influence through generous interpretation of its judicial review powers. In particular, it declared itself competent to control any act of the state as potentially violating basic rights (the leading decision was BVerfGE 6, 32, 1957—*Elfes* case; see Henne, Riedlinger 2005). However, unlike the Supreme Court, it is obliged to decide highly politicized cases and cannot resort to a political doctrine in order to reject decision making (see also Currie 1994: 170–171; Jestaedt et al. 2011 and several contributions in van Ooyen, Möllers 2006).

Both constitutional courts enjoy independence from the political system in their decision making but are at the same time controlled by the political system. Their personnel, that is, the judges, are selected in political procedures, and in both courts the selection of judges and justices is politicized, although in different ways. In Germany, the major political parties nominate candidates to be elected as judges by the Federal Parliament (Bundestag) and the Federal Council (Bundesrat). Each judge is thus nominated by either the government or the opposition of the day, and the parties ensure that there exists political parity among the judges (Stüwe, in this volume; Laufer 1968; Billing 1969). In contrast, in the United States the president nominates the candidates, whom the Senate must confirm as Supreme Court justices. The president's political convictions and personal preferences shape the composition of the Supreme Court (Kagan and Elinson, in this volume; Abraham 1992; Watson, Stookey 1995; Hiesel 2010).

However, it can be demonstrated in relation to dissenting opinions that the politicization of the judicial selection process does not automatically mean politicization of decision making in the courts. The use of dissenting opinions differs significantly between the courts (see the reference to dissenting opinions above in the section "The Process of Decision Making"). The low use of dissenting opinions in the Federal Constitutional Court can be explained by another practice: the Court's legal reasoning reveals a high degree of self-reference, and path dependency lowers the possibility of dissensus (Hoffmann-Riem 2006; Deters, Krämer 2011; Rogowski 2013).

The role of the public differs in the selection of the judges of the two courts. In the United States, each prospective justice has to endure lengthy public hearings of the Senate Judiciary Committee. In Germany, the discussions are less public. Half of the judges are elected in nonpublic, almost secretive meetings of a Judicial Committee (Richterwahlausschuß) consisting of twelve members of the Federal Parliament (see Stüwe, in this volume). The Federal Council elects the other half after nonpublic negotiations between representatives of the German states and leading party officials. Three of the judges in each senate must each have been a judge at one of the other federal supreme courts prior to being appointed a member of the Federal Constitutional Court. Over the last two decades the number of law professors on the bench has tended to increase.

Both constitutional courts enjoy an elevated position in their national political cultures (Jacob 1996; Vanberg 2005; Lembcke 2007). The chief justice of the Supreme Court and the president of the Federal Constitutional Court both perform symbolic political functions. In the United States, these include the swearing-in of the incoming president. In Germany, the president of the Federal Constitutional Court is fifth in line to officially represent the Federal Republic, after the federal president, the president of the Federal Parliament, the president of the Federal Council, and the federal chancellor (see Schlaich, Korioth 2012: 20).

Though they differ in age, size, and location, the U.S. Supreme Court and the German Federal Constitutional Court also show similarities. This is particularly true in relation to the function they fulfill in the political culture of their countries (Schlögel 2015). By successfully serving as ultimate arbiters in fundamental questions concerning their respective political systems, they have been able to pacify their countries, albeit the Federal Constitutional Court more so than the Supreme Court, which reflects the different degrees of the two courts' politicization. Moreover, there is a good chance that the two established constitutional courts might begin to learn from each other. It would indeed be desirable for the courts to find forms of cooperation that benefit their decision-making practices.

Ralf Rogowski is a professor of law and director of the Law and Sociology program at the School of Law of the University of Warwick, Coventry.

Thomas Gawron is a lecturer in law at the Hochschule für Technik und Wirtschaft (HTW), Berlin.

Notes

1. The Official Collection of the Decisions of the Federal Constitutional Court (Amtliche Sammlung der Entscheidungen des Bundesverfassungsgerichts) will, throughout the book, be cited as BVerfGE.

Bibliography

Abraham, H.J. *Justices and Presidents: A Political History of Appointments to the Supreme Court,* 3rd ed. New York, 1992.

Bardach, E. *The Implementation Game: What Happens After a Bill Becomes a Law.* Cambridge, 1977.

Baum, L. "Implementation of Judicial Decisions: An Organizational Analysis." *American Politics Quarterly,* Vol. 4, 1976, 86–114.

Baum, L. "Judicial Impact as a Form of Policy Implementation." In Gardiner, J.A., ed., *Public Law and Public Policy.* New York, London, 1977, 127–144.

Baum, L. *The Supreme Court,* 11th ed. Washington, 2013.

Becker, T.L. *Comparative Judicial Politics: The Political Functioning of Courts.* Lanham, 1987.

Becker, T.L., Feeley, M.M., eds. *The Impact of Supreme Court Decisions,* 2nd ed. New York, 1973.

Beyme, K. von *Das politische System der Bundesrepublik Deutschland.* 9th ed. Opladen, Wiesbaden, 1999.

Billing, W. *Das Problem der Richterwahl zum Bundesverfassungsgericht. Ein Beitrag zum Thema Politik und Verfassungsgerichtsbarkeit.* Berlin, 1969.

Brünneck, A. von *Verfassungsgerichtsbarkeit in den westlichen Demokratien. Ein systematischer Verfassungsvergleich.* Baden-Baden, 1992.

Bryde, B.-O. "Der Beitrag des Bundesverfassungsgerichts zur Demokratisierung der Bundesrepublik." In Ooyen, R. Van, Möllers, M., eds., *Das Bundesverfassungsgericht im politischen Prozess.* Wiesbaden, 2006, 321–331.

Caldwell, P.C. *Popular Sovereignty and the Crisis of German Constitutional Law: The Theory and Practice of Weimar Constitutionalism*. Durham, London, 1997.
Canon, B.C., Johnson, C.A. *Judicial Policies: Implementation and Impact*, 2nd ed. Washington, D.C., 1999.
Cappelletti, M. *The Judicial Process in Comparative Perspective*. Oxford, 1989.
Cappelletti, M., ed. *Judicial Review in the Contemporary World*. Indianapolis, 1971.
Currie, D.P. *The Constitution of the Federal Republic of Germany*. Chicago, 1994.
Deters, H., Krämer, R. "Der steuerpolitische 'Aktivismus' des Bundesverfassungsgerichts als pfadabhängige Entwicklung." *Zeitschrift für Rechtssoziologie*, Vol. 32, 2011, 7–26.
Doemming, K.-B. von, Füsslein, R.W., Matz, W. "Entstehungsgeschichte der Artikel des Grundgesetzes. Abschnitt IX: Die Rechtsprechung." *Jahrbuch für Öffentliches Recht, Neue Folge*, Vol. 1, 1951, 664–747.
Epp, C. *The Rights Revolution: Lawyers, Activists, and Supreme Courts in Comparative Perspective*. New York, London, 1998.
Epstein, L., Knight, J., Shvetsova, O. "The Role of Constitutional Courts in the Establishment and Maintenance of Democratic Systems of Government." *Law and Society Review*, Vol. 35(1), 2001, 117–163.
Epstein, L., Kobylka, J.F. *The Supreme Court and Legal Change: Abortion and the Death Penalty*. Chapel Hill: University of North Carolina, 1992.
Favoreu, I. *Les Cours constitutionnelles*. Paris, 1986.
Friedman, L.M. *The Legal System: A Social Science Perspective*. New York, 1975.
Gawron, T. "Das ferne Gericht–Wirkungsanalysen zum Verhältnis zwischen Bundesverfassungsgericht und Verwaltungsbehörde." In Wrase, M., Boulanger, C., eds., *Die Politik des Verfassungsrechts. Interdisziplinäre und vergleichende Perspektiven auf die Rolle und Funktion von Verfassungsgerichten*. Baden-Baden, 2013, 216–240.
Gawron, T., Rogowski, R. *Die Wirkung des Bundesverfassungsgerichts. Rechtssziologische Analysen*. Baden-Baden, 2007.
Glendon, M.A. "Rights in Twentieth Century Constitutions." In Etzioni, A., ed., *Rights and the Common Good*. New York, 1995, 27–36.
Grossman, J.B., Epp, C.R. "Agenda Formation on the Policy Active U.S. Supreme Court." In Rogowski, R., Gawron, T., eds., *Constitutional Courts in Comparison: The U.S. Supreme Court and the German Federal Constitutional Court*. New York, Oxford, 2002, 103–124.
Habermas, J. *Between Facts and Norms: Contributions to a Discourse Theory of Law and Democracy*. Cambridge, 1996.
Hall, K., ed. *The Oxford Companion to the Supreme Court of the United States*. New York, Oxford, 1992.
Heldrich, A. "Höchstrichterliche Rechtsprechung als Triebfeder sozialen Wandels. Betrachtungen zur Entwicklung und Auswirkung der Judikatur des arnerikanischen Obersten Gerichtshofes in der Rassenfrage." In Rehbinder, M., Schelsky, H., eds., *Zur Effektivität des Rechts. Jahrbuch für Rechtssoziologie uml Rechtstheorie*, Vol. 3. Düsseldorf, 1972, 305–343.
Henkin, L. "Is There a 'Political Question' Doctrine?" *Yale Law Journal*, Vol. 85, 1976, 597–622.
Henne, T., Riedlinger, A., eds. *Das Lüth-Urteil aus (rechts-)historischer Sicht*. Berlin, 2005.
Hiesel, M. "Rechtsprechungskorrektur durch Richterernennung? Über den Einfluss von Präsidenten auf die Entwicklung der Rechtsprechung des U.S. Supreme Court

durch die Ernennung neuer Richter." *Zeitschrift für öffentliches Recht*, Vol. 65, 2010, 177–202.
Hoffmann-Riem, W. "Die Klugheit der Entscheidung ruht in ihrer Herstellung—selbst bei der Anwendung von Recht." In Scherzberg, A., ed., *Kluges Entscheiden: disziplinäre Grundlagen und interdisziplinäre Verknüpfungen*. Tübingen, 2006, 3–23.
Hönnige, C. *Verfassungsgericht, Regierung und Opposition. Die vergleichende Analyse eines Spannungsdreiecks*. Wiesbaden, 2007.
Hönnige, C. "Verfassungsgerichte in den EU-Staaten—Wahlverfahren, Kompetenzen und Organisationsprinzipien." *Zeitschrift für Staats- und Europawissenschaften*, Vol. 6(3), 2008, 524–553.
Höreth, M. *Die Selbstautorisierung des Agenten: der Europäische Gerichtshof im Vergleich zum U.S. Supreme Court*. Baden-Baden, 2008.
Hurst, J.W. *Law and the Conditions of Freedom in the Nineteenth-Century United States*. Madison, 1986.
Jackson, D.W., Tate, C.N., eds. *Comparative Judicial Review and Public Policy*. Westport, 1992.
Jacob, H. "Courts and Politics in the United States." In Jacob, H., et al., *Courts, Law and Politics in Comparative Perspective*. New Haven, London, 1996, 16–80.
Jestaedt, M., Lepsius, O., Möllers, C., Schönberger, C. *Das entgrenzte Gericht*. Frankfurt/Main, 2011.
Kau, M. *United States Supreme Court und Bundesverfassungsgericht*. Berlin et al., 2007.
Keynes, E., Miller, R.K. *The Court v. Congress: Prayer, Bussing and Abortion*. Durham, 1989.
Kneip, S. *Verfassungsgerichte als demokratische Akteure. Der Beitrag des Bundesverfassungsgerichts zur Qualität der bundesdeutschen Demokratie*. Baden-Baden, 2009.
Kommers, D.P., Miller, R.A. *The Constitutional Jurisprudence of the Federal Republic of Germany*, 3rd ed. Durham, London, 2012.
Kranenpohl, U. *Hinter dem Schleier des Beratungsgeheimnisses. Der Willensbildungs- und Entscheidungsprozess des Bundesverfassungsgerichts*. Wiesbaden, 2010.
Lamb, C.M. "Judicial Restraint on the Supreme Court." In Halpern, S., Lamb, C.M., eds., *Supreme Court Activism and Restraint*. Lexington, 1982, 7–38.
Lamprecht, R. *Ich gehe bis nach Karlsruhe. Eine Geschichte des Bundesverfassungsgerichts*. München, 2011.
Landfried, C., ed. *Constitutional Review and Legislation: An International Comparison*. Baden-Baden, 1988.
Laufer, H. *Verfassungsgerichtsbarkeit und politischer Prozeß. Studien zum Bundesverfassungsgericht der Bundesrepublik Deutschland*. Tübingen, 1968.
Lembcke, O. *Hüter der Verfassung. Eine institutionentheoretische Studie zur Autorität des Bundesverfassungsgerichts*. Tübingen, 2007.
Lhotta, R. "Das Bundesverfassungsgericht als politischer Akteur: Plädoyer für eine neoinstitutionalistische Ergänzung der Forschung." *Schweizerische Zeitschrift für Politikwissenschaft*, Vol. 9(3), 2003, 142–153.
Liebl, K.-H. *Ermittlungsverfahren, Strafverfolgungs- und Sanktionspraxis beim Schwangerschaftsabbruch. Materialien zur Implementation des reformierten § 218 StGB*. Freiburg, 1990.
Limbach, J. "Der Konflikt zwischen dem Bundesverfassungsgericht und dem Bundesgerichtshof über den Fortbestand der Beamtenverhältnisse nach 1945." In Mahlmann, M., ed., *Gesellschaft und Gerechtigkeit: Festschrift für Hubert Rottleuthner*. Baden-Baden, 2011, 221–227.

Luhmann, N. "Verfassung als evolutionäre Errungenschaft." *Rechtshistorisches Journal,* Vol. 9, 1990, 176–220.

Luhmann, N. *Das Recht der Gesellschaft.* Frankfurt/Main, 1993.

Luhmann, N. "Legal Argumentation: An Analysis of Its Form." *The Modern Law Review,* Vol. 58, 1995, 285–298.

Mazor, L. "The Law Clerks at the Supreme Court of the United States." In Rogowski, R., Gawron, T., eds., *Constitutional Courts in Comparison: The U.S. Supreme Court and the German Federal Constitutional Court.* New York, Oxford, 2002, 175–195.

McGuire, K.T. *The Supreme Court Bar: Legal Elites in the Washington Community.* Charlottesville, 1993.

McGuire, K.T. "Public Schools, Religious Establishments, and the U.S. Supreme Court: An Examination of Policy Compliance." *American Politics Research,* Vol. 37(1), 2009, 50–74.

Menez, J.F. *Decision Making in the Supreme Court of the United States: A Political and Behavioral View.* Lanham, 1984.

Mosler, H., ed. *Verfassungsgerichtsbarkeit in der Gegenwart.* Cologne, Berlin, 1962.

Murphy, W.F. "Constitutions, Constitutionalism, and Democracy." In Greenberg, D., Katz, S.N., Oliviero, M.B., Wheatley, S.C., eds., *Constitutionalism and Democracy: Transitions in the Contemporary World.* New York, Oxford, 1993, 3–25.

O'Brien, D.M. *Storm Center: The Supreme Court in American Politics,* 3rd ed. New York, London, 1993.

Pacelle, R. *The Transformation of the Supreme Court's Agenda: From the New Deal to the Reagan Administration.* Boston, 1991.

Padoa-Schioppa, A., ed. *Legislation and Justice.* Oxford, 1997.

Perry, H.W., Jr. *Deciding to Decide: Agenda Setting in the United States Supreme Court.* Cambridge, 1992.

Pressman, J.L., Wildavsky, A. *Implementation: How Great Expectations in Washington Are Dashed in Oakland; Or, Why it's Amazing that Federal Programs Work at All,* 3rd ed., 1984. Berkeley, 1973.

Provine, D.M. *Case Selection in the U.S. Supreme Court.* Chicago, 1980.

Rinken, A. "The Federal Constitutional Court and the German Political System." In Rogowski, R., Gawron, T., eds., *Constitutional Courts in Comparison: The U.S. Supreme Court and the German Federal Constitutional Court.* New York, Oxford, 2002, 55–90.

Robbers, G. "Die historische Entwicklung der Verfassungsgerichtsbarkeit." *Juristische Schulung,* 1990, 257–263.

Rogowski, R. "Zugangs- und Erfolgsbarrieren." In *Lexikon des Rechts,* Entry 3/320, 2nd ed. Neuwied, 1996, 1–7.

Rogowski, R. "Constitutional Courts as Autopoietic Organisations." In Wrase, M., Boulanger, C., eds., *Die Politik des Verfassungsrechts: Interdisziplinäre und vergleichende Perspektiven auf die Rolle und Funktion von Verfassungsgerichten.* Baden-Baden, 2013, 117–131.

Rosenberg, G.N. *The Hollow Hope: Can Courts Bring About Social Change?* Chicago, 1991.

Rottleuthner, H. *Richterliches Handeln.* Frankfurt, 1973.

Schaal, G.S. "Crisis! What Crisis? Der 'Kruxifix-Beschluss' und seine Folgen." In Van Ooyen, R.C., Möllers, M.H.W., eds., *Das Bundesverfassungsgericht im politischen System.* Wiesbaden, 2006, 175–186.

Schiffers, R., ed. *Grundlegung der Verfassungsgerichtsbarkeit. Das Gesetz über das Bundesverfassungsgericht vom 12. März 1951.* Düsseldorf, 1984.

Schlaich, K., Korioth, S. *Das Bundesverfassungsgericht — Stellung, Verfahren, Entscheidungen*, 9th ed. Munich, 2012.
Schlögel, M. "Strategen in Roben. Einflussfaktoren auf die Rechtsprechung des U. S. Supreme Court und deren Implikation für das Bundesverfassungsgericht." In Ooyen, R.C. Van, Möllers, M.H.W., eds., *Handbuch Bundesverfassungsgericht im politischen System*, 2nd ed. Wiesbaden, 2015, 889–910.
Schmidhauser, J.R., ed. *Comparative Judicial Systems: Challenging Frontiers in Conceptual and Empirical Analysis*. London, Boston, 1987.
Schmidhauser, J.R., Berg, L.L. *The Supreme Court and Congress: Conflict and Interaction, 1945–1968*. New York, 1972.
Schubert, G.A. *Quantitative Analysis of Judicial Behavior*. Glencoe, 1960.
Schubert, G.A., ed. *Judicial Behavior*. Chicago, 1964.
Schubert, G.A., Danelski, D., eds. *Comparative Judicial Behavior: Cross-Cultural Studies of Political Decision-Making in the East and West*. New York, 1969.
Schwartz, B.A. *Decision: How the Supreme Court Decides Cases*. New York, 1997.
Segal, J.A., Spaeth, H.J. *The Supreme Court and the Attitudinal Model*. New York, 1993.
Shapiro, M. *The Supreme Court and Administrative Agencies*. New York, 1968.
Stark, C., Weber, A., eds. *Verfassungsgerichtsbarkeit in Westeuropa*. Baden-Baden, 1986.
Stone-Sweet, A. *Governing with Judges: Constitutional Politics in Europe*. Oxford, 2000.
Tarr, G.A. *Judicial Impact and State Supreme Courts*. Lexington, Toronto, 1977.
Tate, C.N., Vallinder, T., eds. *The Global Expansion of Judicial Power*. New York, London, 1995.
Tushnet, M.V *The NAACP's Legal Strategy against Segregated Education, 1925–1950*. Chapel Hill, London, 1987.
Tushnet, M.V. *Taking the Constitution away from the Courts*. Princeton, 1999.
Tushnet, M.V. *The Constitution of the United States of America: A Contextual Analysis*. Oxford, Portland, 2009.
Tushnet, M.V. *Advanced Introduction to Comparative Constitutional Law*. Cheltenham, Northampton, 2014.
Vanberg, G. *The Politics of Constitutional Review in Germany*. Cambridge, 2005.
Van Ooyen, R.C., Möllers, M.H.W., eds. *Das Bundesverfassungsgericht im politischen System*. Wiesbaden, 2006.
Vermeule, A. *The System of the Constitution*. New York, 2011.
Vorländer, H., ed. *Die Deutungsmacht der Verfassungsgerichtsbarkeit*. Wiesbaden, 2006.
Wasby, S.L. *The Impact of the United States Supreme Court: Some Perspectives*. Homewood, 1970.
Watson, G.L., Stookey, J.A. *Shaping America: The Politics of Supreme Court Appointments*. New York, 1995.
Wieland, J. "Der Zugang des Bürgers zum Bundesverfassungsgericht und zum U.S. Supreme Court." *Der Staat*, Vol. 29, 1990, 333–353.
Wieland, J. "The Role of the Legal Assistants at the German Federal Constitutional Court." In Rogowski, R., Gawron, T., eds., *Constitutional Courts in Comparison: The U.S. Supreme Court and the German Federal Constitutional Court*. New York, Oxford, 2002, 197–207.

Part I

Access and Case Selection

Chapter 1

Constitutional Litigation in the United States

Robert A. Kagan and Gregory Elinson

Since the establishment of constitutional courts at the national and supranational levels in Europe, European legal scholars have become more interested in studying constitutional courts, such as the German Federal Constitutional Court and the European Court of Justice, in comparative perspective. Their attention, understandably, has been directed to the United States, where courts have long had the power to declare legislative policies and administrative actions unconstitutional. This chapter seeks to advance that comparative effort, using the U.S. experience to analyze the social, political, and legal factors that encourage high rates of constitutional adjudication.

Important decisions of constitutional courts often resemble volcanic eruptions, reshaping the landscape of political and administrative action, usually in small ways but occasionally in large ones. Legal scholars typically focus on the justifications offered for constitutional decisions. Political scientists, in turn, speculate about the political influences on judges' approaches to decision making and how the courts' rulings might affect the conduct of government. Yet a different set of issues might also be addressed. To continue the "volcano" metaphor, what are the geological (i.e., political, economic, or legal) conditions that lead to constitutional eruptions? How do different political and legal structures influence the frequency and nature of constitutional adjudication? These questions, which concern the mobilization of constitutional courts, are the subject of this chapter. In its first section, we provide a rough map of the frequency of

Notes for this chapter begin on page 52.

constitutional litigation in the United States, particularly since the 1960s. Frequent recourse to constitutional litigation, however, does not seem to be an inevitable companion of judicial authority to issue constitutional rulings, for that authority existed in the United States for two centuries before reaching the levels of judicial activism of the last five decades. Therefore, as the rest of the chapter unfolds, we explore the legal, sociological, and political factors that appear to explain the significant increase in constitutional litigation in the United States over the past half century.

We begin in the following section by discussing the malleability of constitutional law in the United States. Theories of how the U.S. Constitution should properly be interpreted are strongly contested by legal scholars, high court judges, and politicians—as is the interpretation of many important provisions and principles in the constitutional text. Not infrequently, changes in the composition of both the U.S. Supreme Court and state supreme courts lead to the rejection or reinterpretation of existing precedents or doctrines. Consequently, lawyers representing ordinary litigants and political interest groups are encouraged to file lawsuits, defenses, and appellate briefs that explicitly challenge existing constitutional law. The malleability of American constitutional law, we go on to argue, stems from three interrelated socio-political factors.

The first of those factors, discussed below, is the American system of judicial selection. Unlike most European judiciaries, American judges are not selected, trained, and promoted through an orderly, bureaucratically controlled system (Damaska 1986). Instead, American appellate judges at both the state and federal levels are selected by overtly political processes. At the state level, despite some degree of variation, most judges are chosen by popular vote.[1]

At the federal level, where judges are nominated by the president and confirmed by the Senate, nominees are appointed largely on political grounds for having served their political party well or demonstrated that they have political values favored by the appointing politician. As levels of political polarization in the United States continue to increase (particularly at the elite level), the partisan nature of judicial selection has only intensified. Indeed, in recent decades, political interest groups and political party leaders often have conducted open campaigns for and against the appointment of particular candidates for the Supreme Court based on those judges' perceived ideological proclivities (Caldeira, Wright 1988). And at the state level, intensely partisan, interest-group-funded elections for judicial positions on state supreme courts—once an extremely rare phenomenon—have become increasingly common (see Gibson 2008 for state supreme court campaign activity and Gann Hall 2001 for state supreme court elections).

The second factor, which we discuss in this chapter's penultimate section, is the diverse army of ideologically motivated advocacy organizations and lawyers that specialize in constitutional litigation to advance their policy goals. The expansion of this "demand side" part of the litigation equation is linked, the chapter shows, to the "opportunity structure" (McAdam 1999) created by the distinctively "instrumentalist" legal and judicial culture of the United States. Much American legal scholarship—and much of the politically experienced American judiciary—values pragmatic problem–solving or "doing justice," even at the expense of uniform and predictable application of law (Atiyah, Summers 1987: 404). In combination with the politicized appointment system, American judges' diverse individual backgrounds, political attitudes, and notions of justice help perpetuate a legal culture that views the Constitution as a politically malleable document, one that can be harnessed to an array of political projects and purposes. Political interest groups and lawyers, faced with politically chosen judges with a flexible set of constitutional precedents and shifting interpretations of key constitutional provisions, remain ever hopeful that the reasoning in a dissenting opinion will grow into the basis for a majority opinion at some later time. Alternatively, they seek to offer the justices a set of creative legal arguments, often built on signals the justices themselves have sent in previous written opinions, which they hope will form the basis of a substantial reassessment of previously settled constitutional doctrine.

In the final section, we consider some of the structural aspects of the U.S. political system that drive groups and individuals into the judicial system in the hope that the flexibility of American constitutional interpretation will work to their benefit. Compared to other advanced industrial democracies, the United States is characterized by a high degree of political fragmentation. Political power under the U.S. Constitution is divided in many different ways: between state and federal governments, among the three branches of government, and even within the legislative branch itself. Because the legislative and executive branches of the national government in Washington do not have direct authority over city mayors, police departments, school boards, magistrates, and correctional officials, reformers often have pushed for judicial rulings that expand the rights of individuals and minority groups to pursue their grievances against local governments in court. In this way, constitutional litigation performs a coordinative function in the American federal system (Kagan 2001). In addition, the difficulty of assembling successful lawmaking coalitions at either the state or federal level means that political winners and losers both look to the courts as an alternative political forum, either for blocking unfavorable policy changes or for enforcing hard-won legislative bargains.

On the Volume of Constitutional Adjudication in American Courts

In many countries, constitutional adjudication is concentrated in specialized constitutional courts, and a significant proportion of constitutional adjudication is triggered by petitions filed by other courts, governments, or political parties (see Tate, Vallinder 1995). In the United States, however, constitutional issues can be raised in any ordinary civil, criminal, or administrative law case, in any lower court—county, state, or federal. Much constitutional adjudication is based on state constitutions rather than the U.S. Constitution. Trial court judges, for example, are legally obligated to decide any properly raised constitutional claim. Any criminal defendant can argue, in any court, that the law or order on which the claim against him or her is based, or the procedure by which it is implemented, violates the state or the federal constitution. Moreover, any individual or organization whose interests are directly and significantly affected by governmental action can assert a defense or bring a lawsuit against the relevant enforcement officials, seeking a declaration that the law or enforcement procedure violates a constitutional provision. Consequently, the U.S. Supreme Court decides only the tip of the iceberg of constitutional litigation—the most intensely controversial and politically contested cases, winnowed from the mass of constitutional decisions in state supreme courts and the lower federal courts.

Because constitutional issues are raised in the course of ordinary litigation in thousands of lower courts, and because court administrators' reports typically do not reveal the incidence of constitutional issues, it is difficult to determine with precision the overall incidence of constitutional adjudication in the United States. At best one may rely on estimates of the volume of constitutional issues in state and federal appellate courts.

State Supreme Courts

"Over the past thirty years, state courts have eclipsed the U.S. Supreme Court in shaping the meaning of constitutional values, both in their home states and throughout the nation.... The volume and import of state supreme court decision-making is truly awesome" (Devins 2010: 1635–1636). In 2009, according to the National Center for State Courts' Court Statistics Project, state appellate courts (including both supreme courts and "intermediate appellate courts," located between trial courts and the supreme court in the state judicial hierarchy) handled more than 273,000 cases (LaFountain et al. 2011). Of these, the fifty American state supreme courts received over just over 82,000 cases (mostly appeals or petitions for review, plus a small number of "original jurisdiction" disputes). The state supreme courts *decided* roughly 10,000—an average of approximately 270 per state (ibid.; see Devins 2010 and Posner 2005 for a similar set of estimates).[2] The number of formal, written state supreme court opinions per year is still smaller—approximately 31 percent of the total number of dispositions.[3] The selectivity of state supreme courts in reviewing cases from intermediate appeals courts, particularly in states with large populations, means that for most constitutional disputes, the final decisions are made by intermediate appellate courts or state trial court judges (Eisenberg, Miller 2009: 1459).[4]

Nevertheless, constitutional adjudication in state supreme courts appears to be increasing. In a representative sample of state supreme court opinions in the 1940–1970 period, 14.6 percent discussed constitutional issues, as compared to 8.7 percent in the 1905–1935 period (Kagan et al. 1977; Kagan et al. 1978). By 1990, this figure had risen to approximately 21 percent, as reflected in a study of seven state supreme courts (California, Massachusetts, New Hampshire, New York, Kansas, Louisiana, and Virginia) (Gardner 1992). If we apply that percentage to the estimated 3,100 annual published opinions in all fifty state supreme courts, they collectively decide roughly 650 constitutional issues per year. A large majority of these opinions involve state, rather than federal, constitutional issues. Although the *proportion* of constitutional cases on state supreme court dockets remains considerably smaller than it is for the U.S. Supreme Court, *cumulatively* the state courts together decide many more constitutional issues. As Devins (2010: 1635) points out, in the year 2005, the California Supreme Court alone issued 37 opinions on state constitutional issues, whereas the U.S. Supreme Court issued only 30 opinions dealing with federal constitutional issues.[5]

The increase in constitutional cases in state supreme courts may reflect changes in court organization (in particular, greater discretion in case selection), a significant rise in criminal cases (which have entailed more constitutional issues since the Warren Court's "due process revolution" in the 1960s) (Brace, Butler 2001; Kritzer et al. 2007), or the simple willingness of state supreme courts to assert themselves more forcefully in a number of important policy domains (Brace, Gann Hall, Langer 2001: 86; Langer 2002).[6] Relatedly, as the federal courts, including the U.S. Supreme Court, have become more politically conservative in the last twenty-five years, advocates asserting individual rights claims have faced greater incentives to make constitutional claims in state courts.[7]

Did these constitutional cases in state supreme courts present "difficult" (rather than frivolously raised, or doctrinally and politically unimportant) constitutional issues? One indicator that they tend to involve serious issues is that in the 1940–1970 period, 19.4 percent of the sampled opinions in which a constitutional issue was discussed resulted in a declaration of unconstitutionality. In state supreme courts that had discretion to select their caseloads, that figure was 30 percent (Kagan et al. 1978) (and as noted above, the number of courts with broad case-selecting discretion has grown since that study was completed). Similarly, and more recently, Emmert (1992) finds that in the period between 1981 and 1985, approximately 20 percent of state statutes that were challenged on constitutional grounds before state supreme courts were struck down. And in 1996, for example, one study found that "each state supreme court decided an average of eleven constitutional challenges to state law … [and] on average, each court invalidated two of these eleven" (Brace et al. 2001: 86).

Finally, in some states and on some controversial issues—same-sex marriage, school finance equity, racial discrimination, voter registration, abortion funding, and religious liberty, to name a few prominent examples—some state supreme courts have asserted constitutional protections that exceed those embodied in U.S. Supreme Court opinions (see, e.g., Reed 1998 concerning school finance litigation at the state level; Williams 1997 and Devins 2010 for broader overviews).

Federal Courts of Appeal

Between 1986 and 2004, the dockets of the eleven federal courts of appeals (to which dissatisfied litigants in federal trial courts, known as U.S. District Courts, may appeal) increased by 82.4%, rising from roughly 30,000 cases per year to close to 60,000 (Posner 2005; Stras 2007). By contrast, in 1959 the federal courts of appeal decided only 3,753 cases (Posner 2005). The records of the federal Administrative Office of the United States Courts do not show how many involved constitutional issues. Nevertheless, as with state supreme courts, it seems clear that both the absolute and relative numbers of constitutional issues considered by federal appeals judges have grown over the past several decades. A study of three circuit courts of appeal (the D.C. Circuit, the Second Circuit, and the Fifth Circuit) for the years 1965–1967 found that these three courts considered constitutional questions in approximately 9 percent of their opinions (Howard 1973). Although Howard's study has not been updated, we can conservatively estimate the number of constitutional questions in recent decades based on a study of federal district courts.[8] Approximately 21 percent of the 121,986 cases filed in federal district courts between 1990 and 1995 raised constitutional claims (Kreimer 1997: 451). Applying this percentage to the 43,426 cases filed in the federal courts of appeal in between March 2010 and March 2011, we can guess that over 9,000 cases (and likely more) in the federal courts of appeal deal with constitutional issues.

Another available estimation technique involves focusing on two categories shown in the administrative records: civil rights and criminal cases, which often involve constitutional issues or are based on statutes that incorporate principles of constitutional law and are used to challenge governmental actions and policies. In one study of cases brought at the federal trial court level, for instance, the authors found that approximately 50 percent of cases coded by the Administrative Office of the United States Courts as civil rights cases actually raised constitutional issues, with over 80 percent of prisoner civil rights cases and 70 percent of cases categorized as "other" civil rights cases involving such claims (Eisenberg and Schwab 1987). In 1980, the federal courts of appeals decided 3,750 civil rights cases and 9,500 criminal cases. By the period from September 1996 to September 1997, federal courts of appeal disposed of 14,505 civil rights cases and 10,466 criminal cases (Krafka, Cecil, Lombard 1995; Administrative Office of the United States Courts 1997). And by the March 2010–March 2011 period, civil rights appeals had decreased to 9,150, whereas criminal appeals had grown to 12,797 (Administrative Office of the United States Courts 2010).[9]

Not all of these cases, of course, raise constitutional issues. If we estimate, based on the Eisenberg and Schwab study, that only two-thirds of them do, we can guess that more than 14,000 such cases each year concern constitutional issues—of which perhaps 2,100 include serious constitutional issues that elicit full court of appeal opinions.[10] Another way to estimate, very roughly, the number of constitutional claims is to consider the number of habeas corpus petitions filed in U.S. federal courts by state prisoners. Since 1996, according to one recent analysis, habeas petitions represent roughly one out of every fourteen civil cases filed in federal court, or approximately 18,000 per year. More than 6,000 of these cases reach the federal courts of appeal (King, Cheesman, Ostrom 2007). In other words, at least 10 percent of the workload of the federal appeals courts is devoted to only one kind of constitutional claim.

U.S. Supreme Court

Of the roughly 15,000 constitutional cases decided each year by state supreme courts and the federal courts of appeals, how many are reviewed by the U.S. Supreme Court? Again, no clear answer appears in published records, but the answer certainly can be stated as "not many." As numerous commentators have pointed out, even as the number of cases the Court is asked to decide continues to increase, the number of cases the Court actually decides continues to decrease (see, e.g., Stras 2007; Cordray, Cordray 2001). The Supreme Court today decides, "on a relative basis, approximately four times fewer federal cases than it did in 1986" (Stras 2007: 967). In its 2010 term, the Supreme Court received 7,868 petitions for review (*Harvard Law Review* 2011)—close to double the number in the 1980 term (*Harvard Law Review* 1985) and approximately seven times the number in 1954 (Casper, Posner 1976). Of these 7,868 petitions, the Court accepted 90 (1.1 percent) and decided 82 of these cases with a full written opinion. Of the cases the Supreme Court decided in its 2010 term, 27, or 33 percent, raised constitutional issues.[11]

Overview

The estimates surveyed above suggest several observations about constitutional adjudication in the United States:

- With regard to its actual decision making, the U.S. Supreme Court is in significant measure a constitutional court. Although the percentage of constitutional cases the Court decides each term has been decreasing over the past few decades (Posner 2005), more than 30 percent of its major decisions each year concern constitutional challenges to state and federal governmental action.[12] In addition, the Court's constitutional cases are more likely than nonconstitutional ones to draw public attention, partly because they result in split decisions more frequently (ibid.), but partly because they often have far-reaching consequences and are politically controversial.
- At the same time, the U.S. Supreme Court decides only a declining proportion of the constantly growing number of constitutional decisions by U.S. courts of appeals and state supreme courts. Of the 57,357 cases terminated in the federal courts of appeal in 2010, only 1,618 even made it to the Supreme Court for consideration, and of these, only 76 were granted review by the Court (*Harvard Law Review* 2011). In short, the Court reviewed only 0.13 percent of the decisions of the federal appeals courts (see Posner 2005 for a similar set of estimates).[13]
- The present Court's purposive decision to grant review in fewer cases—only 4.7 percent of petitions in 2010, compared to 10.6 percent in 1980 and 5.7 percent in 1990 (*Harvard Law Review* 1981, 1991, 2011)—suggests that a constitutional decision rendered by a state supreme court or a federal court of appeals is exceedingly unlikely to be heard by the Supreme Court. Consequently, state supreme courts and federal courts of appeals are very important constitutional courts; their decisions on constitutional issues usually are final.

- The number of constitutional issues decided each year by the state supreme courts and federal courts of appeal suggests a much higher and probably increasing volume of trial-court cases involving constitutional challenges to policy decisions, adjudicative methods, and law enforcement practices of municipal, state, and federal governmental bodies. In 2010, for example, civil rights suits, including prisoner petitions, accounted for 34,388—approximately 10 percent—of the 323,840 cases filed in federal district courts (up from 59,284, or 1 percent, in 1960; Schuck 1983) (Administrative Office of the United States Courts 2010).[14] One study estimated that between June 1990 and June 1996, federal trial courts considered constitutional claims in more than 25,000 published cases; during this period, the Supreme Court considered only 292 (Kreimer 1997).

Constitutional Malleability

Constitutional litigation at the appellate level typically stems from legal uncertainty. It involves a claim that the trial court erred in the interpretation of existing constitutional doctrines or precedents, or that the judge was too cautious in extending previously recognized constitutional rights to new fact situations, governmental policies, or practices. Constitutional litigation thus thrives on belief in the malleability of existing constitutional doctrines or precedents. More specifically, in the United States it is encouraged by the instability of constitutional law and doctrine, which often makes high court outcomes in constitutional cases unpredictable and thereby encourages novel claims or arguments.

The clauses of the U.S. Constitution that stimulate litigation are brief and general statements. They forbid government to deny citizens "due process of law" or "equal protection of the laws," or to undertake "unreasonable searches and seizures" or abridgments of "freedom of speech." Given such vague textual guidance, most constitutional law is judge-made in the common-law case-by-case tradition, and the politically diverse judges' different reactions to the fact patterns in particular cases exacerbate the problem of legal uncertainty.

A crucial feature of constitutional law is the complicated array of "tests" the justices articulate (and debate) as criteria for determining how to interpret and apply constitutional provisions and principles. These "tests" are intended to provide stability and consistency in the adjudication of individual cases, and perhaps they do so to an extent (Richards, Kritzer 2002). Nevertheless, a large body of scholarship has demonstrated that in the most controversial cases, such as those that dominate the docket of the

U.S. Supreme Court, individual justices' votes are more closely predicted by their individual political stances on a left-right political spectrum, as revealed by their decisions in prior cases (Segal, Spaeth 1993, 2002). Moreover, American judges not infrequently disagree, as a matter of principle, about the continued desirability of the particular constitutional "tests" or principles of interpretation.

Thus, despite the formal tradition of following prior precedents in defining the meaning of constitutional provisions, constitutional law has always been subject to change, both incrementally and, especially in periods of major political and ideological conflict, quite radically. For example, during the chief justiceship of Earl Warren (1953–1970), amidst the ideological politics of the Cold War and the Civil Rights movement, the Court overturned principles of constitutional law that for decades had insulated racist policies in southern schools, police departments, and prisons from central government control. In the years since, the instability of constitutional doctrine, if anything, has increased, as political conservatives have mobilized to advocate constitutional interpretations that would limit or reverse Warren Court–era precedents in various fields (Teles 2008; Hollis-Brusky 2015) and to engineer the appointment of politically conservative justices committed to limiting the power of the federal government and the rights of individual litigants.

While constitutional malleability is difficult to measure precisely, it can be illustrated in a variety of ways. One is to observe rates of dissensus among the judges on high courts, which we turn to next. We then provide illustrations of legal malleability and the uncertainty that gives rise to it in particular issue areas.

Constitutional Malleability and Rates of Dissent

The publication of dissenting opinions in appellate court cases is both an indication of legal uncertainty and a promise of the possibility of legal malleability. A dissent signals that at least some qualified judges believe the law governing the case at hand is not, or should not remain, what their brethren contend it should be. Dissenting opinions thus lend hope to the defeated party and others who share that party's interests, by suggesting that if the political composition of the court were to shift, the legal theories advocated by the dissenters might be adopted by a court's new majority. That encouragement, of course, is one of the reasons judges write dissenting opinions. Viewed from this perspective, the high and growing rate of dissenting opinions in American high courts not only signals a growing level of uncertainty about what the law is or should be, but also indicates that the judges themselves more often see and present themselves as agents of legal change.

A study of a representative sample of sixteen state supreme courts found that in 1900, 91 percent of published opinions were unanimous. Many courts had internal norms of promoting the image of consensus: judges who lost a vote were expected to be good sports and join the majority opinion. By the 1960–1970 period, that norm seemed to have eroded a bit. Only 83.5 percent of opinions were unanimous; one in six were not. More significantly, the researchers measured dissent rates for "significant" state supreme court cases, that is, those that were subsequently cited more than twelve times by other courts. Even in this category of cases, 89 percent decided in 1900 were unanimous. In 1960–1970, however, only 71 percent were unanimous: dissents were written in more than one of every four "important" cases. In the influential California Supreme Court, which had full discretion in selecting its caseload from petitions for review—and therefore concentrated on more potentially far-reaching and controversial cases—only 60 percent of such opinions were unanimous (Friedman 1983).

More recently, a study that examined 7,055 state supreme court cases decided with written opinions in 2003 found that the overall rate of dissent was 22 percent. In cases reviewed under mandatory jurisdiction, the rate of dissent was 19 percent, but in cases where the court in question deliberately selected the case for review, that rate of dissent grew to 27 percent.

In the U.S. Supreme Court, with its highly selective focus on divisive and important cases, dissensus has become even more pervasive. A 2001 study notes that for most of the Court's history, the percentage of the Court's cases with at least one dissent hovered between 10 and 20 percent. This rate, however, shot up in the late 1960s and has generally varied between 50 and 80 percent in the years since (Epstein, Segal, Spaeth 2001). The high point was in the 1986 term, where only 19 percent of cases decided with full opinions were unanimous; 30 percent of cases resulted in a 5:4 vote (*Harvard Law Review* 1987).

The retirement of most of the more liberal and moderate justices helped to create a somewhat less fractured Court beginning in the 1990s. Nevertheless, the 2010 term, to focus on just one, saw sixteen 5:4 decisions, or about 20 percent of all opinions, while only 31 percent of the decisions issued by the Court were unanimous (54 percent were issued with dissenting opinions, and 16 percent with separate concurring opinions) (*Harvard Law Review* 2011).[15]

In this climate of splintered opinion, litigants are encouraged to believe that if they can distinguish their claim slightly from an ostensibly adverse precedent, they might be able to win, for they only need to induce a small shift in the alignment of Supreme Court justices. Losers of constitutional arguments might justifiably try again each time a justice retires and a new one is appointed.

Substantive Examples of Constitutional Malleability

One pattern of constitutional instability and change, as mentioned earlier, arises from changes in the personnel on the Court, particularly when new governments take power after promising to make large changes in the role of government that may conflict with existing constitutional law. Thus President Franklin D. Roosevelt, after his famous clash with the U.S. Supreme Court in the mid 1930s, was able to relatively quickly replace conservative justices with political liberals sympathetic to his promised New Deal. Those justices then reinterpreted the constitution, greatly enhancing the regulatory power of the federal government vis-à-vis the states (Kagan 2013).

More commonly in recent American politics, judges themselves have triggered partisan demands for changes in the role of courts, even in the absence of a transformative election. In 1986, political conservatives, complaining that the California Supreme Court had reversed the trial court in 64 of 68 appeals in capital punishment cases, mounted a successful electoral campaign to oust Chief Justice Rose Bird and two liberal colleagues (Wold, Culver 1987). In the next decade, with a new cast of Republican judges, the California court *upheld* most of the death sentences it reviewed—much more often, in fact, than almost every other state supreme court—and did so not by announcing radical changes in the law but via decisions that made seemingly minor technical changes in the application of existing precedents (Kamin 1999).

Similarly, as noted earlier, a succession of Republican presidents, beginning with Richard Nixon in 1968, began a deliberate campaign to appoint conservative justices to the U.S. Supreme Court in order to roll back what they perceived as the inappropriate excesses of the liberal Warren Court. Perhaps the most dramatic manifestation of this conservative legal movement occurred in June 2012, when conservative lawyers and five conservative justices challenged long-standing and seemingly settled interpretations of Congress's delegated powers under the Interstate Commerce Clause.[16] To take a step backward, between the end of the Civil War in 1865 and 1936, the Supreme Court had drawn wavering lines between "interstate" and "intrastate" commerce, as well as between "commerce" and "production" and labor relations, often using restrictive interpretations to limit Congressional power to regulate labor practices and other business activity.[17] During the crisis of the Great Depression, however, when a conservative majority of justices struck down major Congressional laws designed to stabilize economic activity, President Franklin D. Roosevelt mounted a political attack on the Court, arguing that in a modern, tightly integrated economy in which nationwide solutions to economic problems were demanded, the Commerce Clause should be interpreted expansively.

In response, the Court—composed of an increasing number of Roosevelt appointees—held in a series of cases that (1) Congressional regulatory power extended to any economic activity, however local, that in the aggregate had a "substantial effect" on interstate commerce and economic conditions, and (2) that questions concerning the wisdom or efficacy of the particular methods Congress chose to implement its regulatory powers were policy questions to be resolved by Congress, not the Court.[18] This much looser Commerce Clause doctrine bestowed a constitutional imprimatur on the construction of a large federal regulatory and administrative state. The Commerce Clause thus served as the constitutional foundation for Congressional enactment of labor legislation, the 1964 Civil Rights Act (Silverstein 2009), the major federal environmental programs created in the 1970s, and much else.

Nevertheless, after the retirement of Chief Justice Warren in 1968, a series of conservative chief justices sought to limit federal authority. Over the course of a twenty-five year back-and-forth, the Court first upheld (*Maryland v. Wirtz* [1968]), then struck down (*National League of Cities v. Usery* [1976]), then upheld again (*Garcia v. San Antonio Metropolitan Transit Authority* [1985]) the constitutionality of statutes applying federal minimum wage legislation to the states in their capacity as employers. More recently, as the conservative legal movement has grown, the Court has also struck down congressional legislation restricting gun possession near schools (*U.S. v. Lopez* [1995]) and providing federal civil remedies for female victims of violent crimes (*U.S. v. Morrison* [2000]), ruling that the connection of the legislation to the regulation of commercial activity was overly tenuous. Yet none of these rulings appeared to be *significant* restrictions on federal regulatory power.

Consequently, Republican legislators raised no serious constitutional objections (as opposed to policy objections) in 2009–2010 when Congress debated and enacted a law (the Patient Protection and Affordable Care Act) designed to expand access to health care for the many millions of Americans who were not protected by governmental or employer-provided health care insurance programs. In addition to imposing regulatory obligations on health insurance companies, the law required "free riders" who do not currently have health insurance (but probably will need health care someday) to purchase such insurance (with a subsidy for those with limited income). Most constitutional law scholars, referring to the interpretation of the Commerce Clause that had reigned since 1937, saw no constitutional defect in the law. But in June 2012, a 5:4 majority of the justices concluded that Congress's ability to regulate commercial activity—the market for health insurance, in this case—does *not* permit it to require nonparticipants in that interstate market to purchase such insurance (*National Federation of Independent Business v. Sebelius* [2012]; see Barnett 2010 for an academic version of the argument).[19] Writing for the Court, Chief Justice Roberts emphasized that the Commerce Clause was not intended to provide the federal government carte blanche to regulate any problem of sufficiently national scope. "Congress already enjoys vast power to regulate much of what we do," he wrote. Upholding the Affordable Care Act as a legitimate exercise of the government's power under the Commerce Clause "would give Congress the same license to regulate what we do not do, fundamentally changing the relation between the citizen and the Federal Government" (ibid.). Nor could the law be saved—for Commerce Clause purposes—on the ground that Congress could "dictate the conduct of an individual today because of prophesied future activity" (ibid.).

The Chief nevertheless provided the crucial fifth vote in favor of the core provision underlying the health care law. In his view, the Affordable Act could be sustained under Congress's Article I taxing power. Congress chose to punish an individual's failure to purchase health insurance by requiring an "additional payment" to the Internal Revenue Service (ibid.). Though labeled a "penalty" to avoid criticism that the Act raised taxes, the "exaction," Roberts noted, "looks like a tax in many respects" (ibid.). Concluding that the Court has a "duty to construe a statute to save it, if fairly possible," Roberts held that the so-called individual mandate "can be interpreted as a tax," and is therefore constitutional (ibid.). Three years later, Chief Justice Roberts served as the deciding vote in a subsequent dispute over the law's text, once more siding with the Obama Administration (see *King v. Burwell* [2015]).

In light of the significant uncertainty over the Court's direction in the wake of Justice Antonin Scalia's death—and the attendant political struggle over his successor's identity—it is not clear how great a constitutional change *Sebelius* portends. But it clearly introduced a resounding chord of uncertainty into the Commerce Clause symphony that had dominated in the last 70 years. Although it reflects the continuing politicization of the Court's highest-profile cases, *Sebelius* certainly did not check partisan rancor over the Affordable Care Act's legitimacy. Indeed, in the years since the Act's passage, the House of Representatives has voted over forty times to repeal it. At minimum, *Sebelius* illustrates, we think, the perpetual malleability of American constitutional law.

Criminal law also provides evidence of constitutional malleability, with great consequences for defendants, prosecutors, attorneys, and lower-court judges. The 1960s and 1970s witnessed a Court-driven revolution in criminal law, particularly with respect to criminal procedure. The Warren Court extended U.S. constitutional provisions to state courts, most prominently by reading the constitution to require that states provide lawyers for indigent defendants (*Gideon v. Wainwright* [1963]), that criminal suspects be informed of their constitutional rights by arresting officers (*Miranda v. Arizona* [1966]), and that evidence obtained in violation of the Fourth Amendment could not be presented before a jury in a criminal trial (*Mapp v. Ohio* [1961].[20] It also ruled that the death penalty, as administered at the time, violated the Eighth Amendment's prohibition on cruel and unusual punishment (*Furman v. Georgia* [1972]). At the same time, a network of federal district court judges were orchestrating a comprehensive set of reforms in state prisons and mental institutions, particularly in the American South (Feeley, Rubin 1998).

Once the courts have made public policy in such fields a matter of constitutional law, litigation becomes a recurrent method of further policy elaboration and adjustment, for any individual or advocacy organization that is unhappy with measures taken by legislators or the executive branches, at any level of government, can claim they violate the principles set forth in prior constitutional rulings by the courts. Indeed, four short years after its decision in *Furman*, the Court found that a series of state-level procedural reforms had cured the constitutional defects in death penalty administration (*Gregg v. Georgia* [1976]). Since then, the Court has regularly considered an array of incremental death-penalty policy changes, including whether the Eighth Amendment prohibits the application of the death penalty to crimes committed by juveniles or the mentally disabled, and whether the death penalty can be applied for crimes other than murder (Steiker, Steiker 1995; Steiker 2002).

Moreover, those dissatisfied with Warren Court precedents have also sought to roll back some of the landmark criminal procedure rulings of the Warren Court. The Rehnquist Court found particular success in limiting the *Miranda* rights of criminal defendants (Barkow 2006: 1, n. 2); in turn, the Roberts Court has recently considered challenges to the exclusionary rule established in *Mapp*, with four justices suggesting they were potentially ready to overturn it (*Hudson v. Michigan* [2006]). Although the Supreme Court has not overturned these central rulings themselves, they have instead sought to find various exceptions to the broad principles established by the Warren Court (Steiker 1996).

At the same time, however, the Supreme Court has appeared to expand the rights of criminal defendants in several recent cases, finding, for instance, that the Sixth Amendment right to counsel applies to the plea bargaining process (where the vast majority of American criminal cases are resolved) (*Lafler v. Cooper* [2012]). The Court has also recently held that the Sixth Amendment right of a defendant to confront her or his accuser in court means that forensic lab technicians must personally testify in court, rather than simply submitting a written report (*Melendez-Diaz v. Massachusetts* [2009]; see also *Crawford v. Washington* [2004]; *Bullcoming v. New Mexico* [2011]).

On sentencing issues, the Court has also appeared to be favorable to criminal defendants. In 2012, the Court ruled that the mandatory sentencing of juvenile defendants to life imprisonment without the possibility of parole is an unconstitutional violation of the Eighth Amendment (*Miller v. Alabama; Jackson v. Hobbs* [2012]). And, in 2005, the Supreme Court ruled that mandatory federal sentencing guidelines, which had operated for 20 years to limit judicial discretion in sentencing individuals convicted of crimes, were unconstitutional.[21] In the Court's view, the guidelines violated the Sixth Amendment right of a defendant to be sentenced only on the basis of facts that had been proved beyond a reasonable doubt before a jury (*United States v. Booker* [2005]). The guidelines remained advisory (Reynolds 2009).

This propensity of the Supreme Court to make new law—sometimes more conservative, sometimes more liberal—contributes to inconsistencies among lower court rulings and encourages politically attentive groups to bring cases with new constitutional arguments. If the law is unstable, it is foolish not to ask a malleable court to reshape it in ways you think are desirable. This does not mean that constitutional law is infinitely unpredictable or unstable. Important areas of doctrine stand firm and reliable for decades on end. Thousands of disputes emerge each day in which law enforcement officials, legislators, lawyers, and lower court judges have no doubt about what existing constitutional doctrine has to say about the matter and about how the Supreme Court would decide such an issue. The instability we refer to is "at the margin," as economists would say, affecting only "hard cases." But unpredictability at the margin is what produces litigation, especially if the margin is a rather broad and shifting one and lawyers are readily available to probe its dimensions.

Structural Features of the American Judiciary: Discretion and Selection

Constitutional changeability is a symptom, not a cause, of the American approach to constitutional law. The importance of judicial replacement for changes in constitutional policymaking helps to highlight several structural features of both the U.S. Supreme Court and state supreme courts that, in turn, help explain the profusion of constitutional litigation in the United States. These structural features underlie the development of a legal culture that views law as inherently pliable and places a high value on imaginative challenges to existing doctrine. This section identifies three such structural factors in particular: (1) a high degree of discretion in case selection; (2) the difficulty of constitutional amendment; and (3) the resulting incentives for the politically motivated selection of high court judges. Although we focus on the U.S. Supreme Court and the U.S. Constitution, our conclusions also apply to state supreme courts.

"The history of the Supreme Court throughout the twentieth century has been its own largely successful effort to persuade Congress to reduce the number of cases it must hear" (Levinson 2010; see also Perry 1991; Grossman, Epp 2002). Because the process of agenda-setting is crucial for understanding political (and legal) outcomes, this degree of docket control has wide-ranging implications for the malleable nature of American constitutional law. Nevertheless, the logic is relatively straightforward. Given the volume of cases before the Court, the Court's small size, and the limited staff allocated to each justice, full docket control means the Court is likely to identify and consider only those cases the justices believe will have the highest national impact. They are likely to select for decision those cases that carry particular legal weight—for example, when the Court is asked to resolve disagreements between two or more federal appeals courts—cases whose outcomes would have significant social, political, or economic impacts, or cases that raise vital issues of principle or individual rights. All these types of cases, of course, are likely to be politically controversial and attract a good deal of news media attention.

As Grossman and Epp (2002) note, full docket control also brings the justices' policy preferences to the fore, not just with respect to case outcomes, but also with respect to the prior process of agenda-setting. By tradition, the Court takes on cases if four of the nine justices vote to place the case on the Court's docket (see Johnson and Sorenson, in this volume, on the Rule of Four). Much of the strategic interaction among the justices, therefore, concerns not just the process of selecting those cases that the Court will hear, but also the process of keeping certain cases off the Court's docket for fear of creating law that at least some of the justices oppose (Epstein, Knight 2000). Because the justices delegate much of the screening of petitions to their law clerks, petitions from frequent litigants—the U.S. Solicitor General's Office, private attorneys who often appear before the Court, and a select set of legal advocacy groups—are likely to be treated as signals of a case's importance (Caldeira, Wright 1988; Lazarus 2008).

Elected politicians may also take advantage of the Supreme Court's capacity to choose its cases by "inviting" the Court to decide contentious and polarizing political issues whose resolution is likely to alienate a substantial portion of the voting public (Graber 1993). Thus, the political insulation of the judiciary holds out the prospect of turning a wrenching popular political issue into a technocratic, legal one with much lower political salience.

The likelihood of the Supreme Court taking on politically controversial cases is amplified by another institutional feature: the difficulty of successfully amending the federal constitution.[22] The U.S. Constitution has been amended only twenty-seven times since its drafting in 1789. The passage of the first ten amendments was a necessary condition of the ratification process; therefore these amendments, commonly referred to as the Bill of Rights, are more appropriately considered part of the original document, rather than subsequent additions.[23] One result is that constitutional change in the United States, particularly over the past century, has largely taken place in the arena of constitutional interpretation instead of the arena of formal textual revision. The critical twentieth-century constitutional revolution—the Supreme Court's affirmation of a muscular federal intervention into the nation's economy, as discussed earlier—was self-consciously carried out through "a series of transformative [judicial] opinions," rather than through the amendment process laid out in Article V of the U.S. Constitution (Ackerman 1991: 52).

The precedent established by New Deal reformers continued to form the template for constitutional change in the years following, as in the case of the Warren Court's "due process revolution" in the 1960s, through which the Court extended the Bill of Rights to state and local criminal justice systems. Contemporary constitutional reform or revolution is much more likely to be enacted through the process of "partisan entrenchment" (Balkin, Levinson 2001) than through the cumbersome amendment process. Simply put, "When enough members of a particular party are appointed to the federal judiciary, they start to change the understandings of the Constitution that appear in positive law" (Balkin, Levinson 2001: 1067). Political activists and their elected allies look to the composition of the Supreme Court as a political opportunity: only five individuals are required to make durable political change of the kind that legislators can only dream about. For proof, we need only look to the intense partisan battle, beginning in 2016, over Justice Scalia's replacement.

The combination of the structural factors noted above intensifies the politically motivated selection of federal and state supreme judges, itself a deep-rooted American political tradition. Because courts of last resort can choose to hear only the most important, highly charged cases, and because the formal amendment route to constitutional change is generally politically infeasible, the stakes in appointments to state and federal high courts are very high. As levels of political polarization have increased in recent decades, the composition of the Supreme Court (and state supreme courts) has, in turn, become an important locus of partisan political contestation in the United States.

When compared to other economically advanced democracies, the judicial selection system of the United States is distinctive. Judges are appointed, or in some states nominated for election, by elected political leaders (presidents, governors, senators, and party chairmen), who regard the candidate's demonstrated political views or allegiances, as well as his or her legal capacity, as a paramount consideration. A study of state supreme court judges in the twentieth century revealed that when appointed, almost half had either no experience or less than two years' experience as a lower court judge. One-third had held elective political office; another third had been public prosecutors, which also is typically a "political" office (Kagan, Infelise, Detlefsen 1984). A similar pattern holds for U.S. Supreme Court appointments. Since 1930, only about one in four justices has served a lower court apprenticeship of five years or more. Many famous justices, beginning with John Marshall and including Louis Brandeis, Earl Warren, Hugo Black, William Douglas, Felix Frankfurter, and William Rehnquist, had no prior judicial experience.[24]

The American judicial system, in short, recruits judges with political experience and strong policy views. Many agree to enter the judiciary because they see it as an opportunity to put their personal stamp on the development of the law. They are more oriented to doing justice as they see it, or to making policy, than to upholding tradition. A cross-national comparison of styles of statutory interpretation classified the American judiciary as the most freewheeling and creative (Summers, Taruffo 1991). Enjoying considerable discretion to choose which cases to decide, federal and state supreme court judges "can indulge their political instincts and select … those matters that address politically important issues. The resulting judicial potential to make politically 'creative' rather than 'narrowly' legalistic decisions inevitably increases" (Damaska 1986: 234).

There is little doubt that the political affiliations of judges and their ideologies helps to explain both case outcomes and the reasoning on which those outcomes are based (Segal, Cover 1989; Segal, Spaeth 1993; Peretti 1999; Epstein, Knight 2000; Keck 2007). These results have held up in both micro- and macro-level studies. Frank Cross and Emerson Tiller (1998), for instance, find that both Democratic and Republican judges on federal courts of appeal are less likely to rule against federal agencies when the agency in question has issued a regulation that broadly reflects the values of the judge's political party. In addition, they note that panels composed of both Republican and Democratic appointees rule differently than panels composed of only Republicans or only Democrats. Casting a broader net, Mitchell Pickerill and Cornell Clayton (2004) trace the Rehnquist Court's jurisprudence on federal versus state authority back to the longer-term anti-federal-power agenda of Republican Party elites.

Because rulings are malleable and judges political, scholars and lawyers are more likely to think about law as a set of political settlements, rather than a stable, authoritative code. Indeed, beginning in the 1930s, American legal education has reflected the influence of the "legal realists," who argued that judicial opinions often are the product not of legal logic but of individual judges' political attitudes and psychological characteristics, or of the differential litigating capacities of strong and weak parties. From their first day in class, American law students are taught not merely to "learn the law" but to discern and criticize the logical flaws, unstated values, and political allegiances that lie behind statutory rules and judicial decisions. They are rewarded for articulating imaginative challenges to the fairness or validity of existing law. The law reviews, which law students and their teachers write, bristle with arguments for new laws and judicially created rights. As observed by Austin Sarat and William Felstiner (1986), American lawyers describe the judicial system to their clients as unpredictable, personalistic, and yet highly manipulable. And that, in turn, encourages interest groups and political party leaders to lobby for the appointment or election of judges who share their political philosophies and partisan allegiances.

The Role of Interest Groups

Even the most eager partisan judges must wait for transformative constitutional cases to come their way.[25] Although constitutional malleability and the political selection of judges creates important opportunities for politically minded litigants, pushing constitutional litigation up through the hierarchy of courts is a difficult enterprise for the ordinary citizen. It requires specialized knowledge, significant financial resources, and an interest in seeking delayed or public benefits. Individuals are not likely to raise constitutional issues or take them to higher courts without either large subsidies or organized support. The constitutional agenda of American high courts, therefore, tends to be shaped by groups that can best overcome the usual obstacles to collective action (Olson 1965; Wilson 1980) and systematically ask the courts to overturn governmental policies that their members dislike. To continue the volcano metaphor used earlier, there are many constitutional eruptions in the United States because the substructure is pervaded by increasing numbers of politically organized groups busily seeking fissures through which to push their grievances to the surface. They are assisted by an abundant supply of lawyers whose career goals and prestige depend on discovering the constitutional arguments that can propel grievances onto court dockets.

Because constitutional cases do not typically make their way onto the Supreme Court's severely restricted docket on their own, successful constitutional litigation requires an extensive "support structure" (Epp 1998), such as that provided by issue-oriented legal groups like the American Civil Liberties Union (ACLU) and the Legal Defense Fund of the National Association of Colored People (NAACP-LDF, often called the "Inc. Fund"). Such support structures provide the financial and legal resources necessary to select and sustain promising court cases, learn from experience, and choose issues and arguments strategically, as the cases move through the legal system. They help to recruit, and organize the work of, a set of dedicated, issue-oriented lawyers with the specialized experience necessary to successfully litigate complex cases to their conclusion. As public-interest law has become an important part of the American legal landscape, experienced public-interest practitioners return to teach the next generation of lawyers or become high-level judicial decision-makers themselves. Ruth Bader Ginsburg, before becoming a U.S. Supreme Court justice, founded the ACLU Women's Rights Project; Justice Antonin Scalia was an important voice in the development of the politically conservative Federalist Society, which has a significant influence on legal education as well as litigants' arguments (Hollis-Brusky 2011, 2015) and judicial appointments (Teles 2008).

In principle, sustained litigation campaigns are most difficult for diffuse, unorganized interests, such as impoverished citizens charged with criminal activity, political dissenters, and members of socially deviant or marginal minorities (e.g., narcotics users, immigrants, teenagers, welfare recipients). Conversely, organizing litigation campaigns would seem particularly feasible for business firms, which often belong to established trade associations and have a substantial financial stake in resisting costly government regulations and revenue measures. Thus, in the late nineteenth century and first third of the twentieth, a large number of constitutional issues in the U.S. Supreme Court involved challenges to state and federal business regulations and taxes that especially burdened business interests (Epp 1998). Business lawyers were influential in shaping constitutional doctrine concerning "due process of law" and the federal Commerce Clause, arguing for limits on regulation of business and on governmental protection for organized labor (Twiss 1942; Paul 1960). This tradition of outsized business influence has arguably been resuscitated over the past three decades. Trade associations, particularly the U.S. Chamber of Commerce, have successfully established their own legal arms (Rosen 2005, 2008). Business groups and individual firms have also nurtured a network of elite lawyers with experience either litigating before the Supreme Court (often in the Office of the Solicitor General) or clerking for one of the justices (Lazarus 2008). In recent years, they have succeeded in inducing a conservative Supreme Court majority to issue numerous rulings on issues of civil procedure and statutory interpretation that have steadily made it more difficult for individuals or liberal advocacy groups to successfully sue large corporations and government officials.

On the other hand, throughout the last century more and more diffuse or marginal interests have achieved the capacity for organized litigation efforts, broadening the constitutional agenda of the courts. This would seem at least partly due to the financial surplus and communication capabilities generated by economic growth and technological change. Freedom of speech cases, for example, did not appear on the docket of the U.S. Supreme Court until the 1916–1925 period, when the ACLU, along with various leftist political organizations (socialists, syndicalists, and labor unions) had achieved substantial membership bases and resources (see Kairys 1982; Epp 1998). Significant numbers of cases concerning freedom of assembly and public demonstrations started flowing into the courts only in the late 1930s, largely due to the efforts of labor unions, whose organizational capacities and resources had recently been enhanced by federal labor legislation. Later, the formation of the ACLU's Women's Rights Project in 1971 led to a series of successful lawsuits championing women's rights in education and the workplace, as well as in family and reproductive law. Similarly, race relations cases under the constitution's Equal Protection Clause did not become a significant part of the Court's agenda until the 1940s. It was then that the NAACP, growing in financial strength and staff along with the nascent black middle class, mounted a systematic campaign in the courts against official racial segregation (Kluger 1975; Tushnet 2005).

In recent decades, moreover, advocacy organizations modeled on the ACLU or NAACP-LDF have proliferated markedly. These groups rely on private contributions for support and are dedicated to constitutional litigation as a major political strategy (Rabin 1976). The NAACP, for example, is paralleled by the Mexican American Defense and Education Fund, which has brought constitutional challenges against government benefit programs and educational practices that discriminate against Mexican immigrants, and against intrusive immigration law enforcement practices. Lambda Legal, among other organizations, has played a similar role in the pursuit of constitutional litigation on behalf of gays and lesbians. Other advocacy organizations represent more diffuse or specialized interests. Here leadership comes from a new class of "moral entrepreneurs," such as idealistic "public interest lawyers," rather than from the affected groups themselves. These groups' funding is more likely to come from large donors or charitable foundations. In this category one finds, for example, increasing numbers of conservative public-interest law firms. These groups often raise libertarian challenges to welfare state, regulatory, and tax laws, and file amicus curiae briefs in criminal procedure cases, arguing for crime control values (Epstein 1985; Southworth 2005, 2008; Teles 2008).[26]

In addition to this growing phalanx of privately funded advocacy organizations, one might count the governmentally funded lawyers offices that specialize, at least in part, in constitutional litigation, as governments themselves have undertaken legal representation of socially marginal and diffusely organized groups. The steady stream of constitutional cases involving criminal defendants' rights owes a great deal to both Supreme Court rulings and to implementation of legislation, beginning in the early 1960s, expanding indigent criminal defendants' rights to free and competent defense counsel, both at the trial level and on appeal (Casper, Posner 1976: 41–46). Most urban counties now have a public defenders' office specializing in criminal defense, motions for suppression of evidence on grounds of unconstitutional police search practices, and other constitutional claims. Convicted defendants in capital cases regularly have recourse to a lawyer to comb through the trial record seeking evidence of arguably unconstitutional actions.

Similarly, since the mid-1960s, the federal government has financed neighborhood law offices to handle civil cases for poor individuals (see Johnson 1974). Legal Service Corporation lawyers have brought lawsuits challenging debt collection procedures on grounds that they unconstitutionally deny due process to indigent debtors, and they have initiated numerous court cases challenging the constitutionality of the rules and procedures of social welfare agencies and public housing authorities (see generally Lawrence 1990; Davis 1993).

The Civil Rights Division in the federal Department of Justice was established in 1957, succeeding the Civil Rights Section that had been created in 1939, specifically to initiate lawsuits, on constitutional or parallel statutory grounds, against racial discrimination by state and local school administrators and voter-registration officials (McMahon 2004). The Civil Rights Division also regularly intervened in private suits charging discrimination, thereby helping to bring such cases to the higher courts.[27] State and large municipal governments maintain their own offices of lawyers, ready to defend constitutional challenges to their governments' laws, appeal adverse rulings to higher courts, and file *amicus curiae* briefs in support of other states (Morris 1987). In recent decades, state attorneys' general, who often are independently elected and politically partisan, have filed coordinated lawsuits seeking constitutional change (Nolette 2015). In these, as in the other government offices mentioned and in the private advocacy organizations, the opportunity to litigate a case on constitutional grounds typically is regarded by lawyers as the most prestigious form of legal practice.

At the same time, the political benefits of constitutional litigation arguably have increased in certain ways. Because it is sometimes possible to obtain publicity in the mass media simply for filing a novel constitutional claim, political interests who are frustrated in their efforts to win favorable policy decisions in legislatures often are willing to engage in constitutional litigation even if the odds of winning are slim (Coglianese 1998; Provine 1998). Michael McCann (1994) has shown how legal reformers and labor unions were able to transform a single, well-publicized court decision (later revised) into an important weapon in their political campaign to establish "comparable worth" salary schedules that advance gender equality in employment. Likewise, Timothy Lytton (2007, 2008) has explored how litigation designed to expose sexual abuse by Catholic clergy helped to frame subsequent popular accounts of that scandal.

Political Fragmentation

We have argued that American lawyers, judges, and law professors generally promote a particularly flexible, politically driven vision of law. But we have also suggested that in a democratic polity, they could not have succeeded in doing so unless political interest groups, political parties, and political leaders *endorsed* that approach to legal argument and judging. And that is precisely what they have done. Courts and litigation play a large role in American politics because political parties and powerful interest groups, at bottom, want them to do so.

The key to this set of political preferences lies in the political traditions and political structure of the United States. Adopting the typology used by Damaska (1986), the United States blends a historically *reactive* state with a model of *coordinate* political authority.[28] In contrast to the ideal-typical continental European model, in which political authority is both centralized and hierarchically organized, American political authority—

fragmented and limited by its federalist constitution—is dispersed and diffuse.[29] Unlike many European nations, the United States has no national Ministry of Justice or of Education with powers to issue nationwide rules and supervise or replace local personnel. The challenge for the U.S. state has been to coordinate the activities of political and legal authorities at the federal, state, and local levels. In this fragmented political system, the U.S. Constitution, as interpreted by the courts and enforced by litigation, is a powerful tool for extending and implementing uniform national rules or policy changes. Thus, reformers often have pushed for judicial rulings that expand the rights of individuals and minority groups to pursue their grievances against local governments in court, arguing that local policies and practices violate constitutional standards. As noted earlier, in the domain of criminal law, the combination of localized (typically, at the municipal and county level) police and prosecutorial authority encourages lawyers to appeal to the constitution to influence the activities of the thousands of district attorneys and police departments.

Political fragmentation works to encourage constitutional litigation in a variety of ways. Consider the legislative process in Washington. Historically, political party discipline in the United States has been far from perfect. Individual legislators often take their cues from particular constituencies and interest groups, due to several structural features—a tradition of localism, rooted in federalism; the separation of powers between Congress and the Presidency; and decentralized financing of electoral campaigns by individual legislative candidates, who rely on particularistic sources of support. Consequently, presidents and even congressional party majority leaders often exercise only limited and uncertain control over legislators in their own political party. Moreover, due to Senate procedural rules, especially in recent years, a supermajority is required to push politically contentious legislation through that body (Wawro, Schickler 2006). Hence the American legislative process is shot through with "veto points." The consent of key individual legislators (committee chairs, or those strongly committed to particular interest groups or constituencies) often is needed for legislation to move through its complex course from proposal to implementation (e.g., Krehbiel 1998). The opposition of such legislators may make it very difficult to pass measures designed to respond to social or economic change, even if they are popular with a majority of citizens and the president supports them (Hacker 2004).

Confronted with legislative stalemate, reformers often take to the courts. For example, throughout the 1940s and 1950s, because a faction of the Democratic Party effectively blocked all congressional action against racial segregation in local southern school districts, civil rights activists, led by the NAACP, launched a litigation campaign and urged the Supreme

Court to reverse an 1896 precedent and hold that government-mandated apartheid in public schools was unconstitutional. Following their success in *Brown v. Board of Education* [1954], reformers continued to use constitutional arguments in the courts to advance racial integration in school districts throughout the country; to force state legislatures to remedy funding inequalities across locally run and funded public education systems (Reed 1998); to force retrograde state and local prisons and mental institutions to meet national standards (Feeley, Rubin 1998); and to impose constitutional rules, as expanded by federal judges, on state and local police departments and lower courts. Frymer (2003: 484) describes how federal judges forced major labor unions to comply with anti-discrimination standards, concluding, "Civil rights groups used a litigation strategy predicated on their determination that the elected branches were unresponsive and this decision in turn perpetuated its further use."

American institutional fragmentation thereby increases the political role of judiciaries—which in turn increases the political stakes surrounding judicial selection, especially at the federal level, where judges serve for life. Accordingly, political partisans on both sides strive to select judges who will reflect the values of their coalition accurately and for as long as possible—and to block the appointment of judges who will not.[30] Moreover, as Atiyah and Summers (1987) note, fragmentation of political power, coupled with weak political parties and multiple veto points in the legislature, historically has made it more difficult for legislators to reverse judicial decisions, enhancing the autonomy of the judiciary—and enhancing the appeal of constitutional litigation as a mode of advancing and "locking in" the policy preferences of political interests and advocacy groups.

Conclusion

Constitutional litigation is a constant, indeed, an everyday phenomenon in the United States for a variety of reasons. Fragmented political structures create incentives for interest groups to use the courts as avenues for attaining policy goals and ideals. The training and selection process and life experiences of both lawyers and judges incline them to act upon such requests. The reality of constant legal change reinforces and is reinforced by a legal culture that views law, rights, and constitutional litigation as malleable instrumental mechanisms for governance and social engineering. That turbulent, rights-seeking legal culture is the volcanic "steam" that pushes from below, often erupting in constitutional rulings.

Nevertheless, even as constitutional litigation has become more politically salient in Europe (Stone Sweet 2000; Kelemen 2011) and elsewhere

(Kapiszewski, Silverstein, Kagan 2013), the United States in recent years has often been said to be trimming its litigational sails, a shift driven largely by the anti-litigation agenda and political successes of the Republican Party and its allies over the last three decades. The quantitative story of American litigation is no longer one of continuing increase. For the moment, at least, constitutional litigation appears to have roughly plateaued. Certain forms of constitutional litigation, such as habeas corpus petitions by convicted offenders, have even been decreasing in quantity, largely because prisoners tried in state court face legislative restrictions on their capacity to seek redress at the federal level. Conservative majorities on the U.S. Supreme Court have consistently reinterpreted procedural rules so as to limit individual claimants' and social reformers' ability to sue governmental bodies and corporations (Siegel 2006; Staszak 2010; Wasserman, 2012). Conservative Supreme Court rulings have limited judicial remedies seeking racial balance in public schools, as well as voluntary race-based integration policies adopted by politically liberal local school boards.[31]

Yet it is too soon, we think, to see the conservative legal counterattack as a radical change in the dynamics of and incentives for constitutional litigation in the United States, rather than merely an ideological shift in its predominant political valence or thrust. Without a doubt, Republicans have successfully styled themselves an anti-litigation party (Burke 2004). But having learned from the successes of liberal civil rights and environmental groups (Southworth 2005, 2008), conservative groups allied with the Republican Party, as noted earlier in this chapter, have used constitutional litigation to advance their political agenda, and their successes in that regard breed more constitutional litigation.

Through organizational innovations, conservative legal networks and advocacy organizations have created forceful constitutional theories designed to advance conservative causes, built a legal infrastructure to support conservatively oriented constitutional litigation, and worked purposively to shape a judiciary sympathetic to their arguments and values (Teles 2008). Conservative legal advocacy groups have successfully pushed the Court to adopt new constitutional rights, such as an individual right to bear arms, which in turn leads to more constitutional litigation against state and local gun control laws.[32] Business groups, including the U.S. Chamber of Commerce, have also been increasingly successful litigants, sometimes using constitutional arguments. The previously mentioned 2012 Supreme Court opinion concerning the constitutionality of a new national health insurance provision law, while upholding the statute for the most part, articulates new limits on Congress's regulatory powers under the Commerce Clause as well as its powers to use the constitution's "taxing and spending" clause to influence state government policies—limits that invite more constitutional litigation by opponents of governmental regulation and federal power.

As with many issues of substance in American politics, constitutional litigation has not only been politicized, but also polarized. Political activists on both the right and the left seek alternately to limit or expand the political deployment of litigation—and to reshape constitutional legal theory and constitutional interpretation—to advance their interests and values. As in the period between the Civil War and the New Deal, constitutional litigation is a tool not uniquely available to those interested in advancing progressive causes. The standard narrative of postwar constitutional litigation in the United States and elsewhere has been that constitutional courts work to expand individual rights, at least over the long term. The last thirty years of U.S. constitutional development, in contrast, shows that constitutional law is ultimately "up for grabs" politically. Its power can be harnessed by individuals and groups on both the left and the right. Neither side is likely to stop trying to do so.

Robert A. Kagan is Emanuel S. Heller professor of law (emeritus) and professor of political science (emeritus) at the University of California, Berkeley.

Gregory Elinson holds a Ph.D. in political science from the University of California, Berkeley, and a J.D. from Stanford Law School. He is presently working as a law clerk for Judge David J. Barron of the United States Court of Appeals for the First Circuit.

Notes

1. Devins (2010) provides a useful and succinct overview of the variation in state-level judicial selection procedures for state supreme court justices.
2. The estimates in this paragraph were made by the authors, using data provided by the Court Statistics Project of the National Center for the Study of State Courts, available at www.courtstatistics.org. Only 36 states reported data concerning the number of cases formally decided, and only 20 provided data about the number of formal written opinions. According to LaFountain et al. (2010), in 2008, the 14 states reporting the total number of cases decided by their state supreme courts accounted for 3,788 total cases, or an average of approximately 270 per state.
3. This estimate assumes that the caseloads of the fifty state supreme courts are, on average, roughly even, which, although untrue, provides a figure that is relatively easy to understand. In addition, the percentage of decided cases with a full writ-

ten opinion varies significantly by state (LaFountain et al. 2010). One earlier study counted 3,024 instances where a state supreme court considered the constitutionality of a statute between the years 1981 and 1985. This averages out to approximately twelve per state per year (Emmert 1992).

4. In fiscal year 2005–2006, for instance, the California Supreme Court received 5,591 petitions and granted review in only 3 percent of them. In 2005, the New York Court of Appeals "decided 961 motions for leave to appeal in civil cases" and granted only 6.4 percent of them (Eisenberg, Miller 2009: 1459).
5. Another estimate of the possible increase in state-level constitutional litigation is based on a study from the mid-1980s. The authors of that study found that between 1977 and 1986, "state high courts ... rendered at least 217 rights-affirming decisions based upon provisions of their state constitutions—approximately a 131 percent increase in the number of such decisions over the 94 decisions issued during 1950–1977" (Collins, Galie, Kincaid 1986). Of these, 46 were decided in 1985, which the authors indicated was the highest recorded number for any single year to that date.
6. In the 1940–1970 period, for example, the highest proportion of constitutional issues (21 percent of sampled cases) was found in courts (e.g., the California and New Jersey supreme courts) that, like the U.S. Supreme Court, could select their cases from a multitude of petitions for review (Kagan et al. 1977; Kagan et al. 1978; see also Eisenberg, Miller 2009). As LaFountain et al. (2011) point out, however, recent years have seen a slight drop-off in the number of criminal cases in state trial courts, largely because of an overall reduction in crime in the United States.
7. Some scholars have dated some of this attention to an article by Justice William Brennan in the 1977 *Harvard Law Review* in which he called for state courts to "be the guardians of our liberties." As Devins (2010: 1638) writes, "For Brennan, by providing protections 'extending beyond those required by the Supreme Court's interpretation of federal law,' state courts would 'step into the breach' and become the 'font of individual liberties' that the Supreme Court had been during the Warren Court era." State constitutional courts seem to have responded to this call over the past several decades, greatly increasing the number of decisions in which they expand individual rights beyond those available under the U.S. Constitution. In addition, unlike the U.S. Supreme Court, some state courts may provide constitutional advisory opinions to legislators, which gives them additional importance in state-level politics.
8. This estimate is conservative because appellate courts are more likely than district courts to consider constitutional issues.
9. As a report by the Bureau of Justice Statistics on civil rights litigation at the district level noted (Kyckelhahn, Cohen 2008), the total number of civil rights cases filed in federal district court has declined over the past decade, beginning in 2003. The decline in appeals court filings can be traced to the last few years of the 1990s. The decrease in the number of appellate civil rights cases has a number of causes, including statutory modifications, changes in the composition of the federal judiciary, and continuing increases in the expense and difficulty of bringing such cases to trial. Another way to measure the comparative importance of civil rights and criminal cases in the federal court system is to consider the percentage of an individual judge's caseload taken up by such cases. In 2004, one study indicated, almost 24 percent of a federal trial court judge's caseload was spent on the combination of civil rights and criminal cases (Lombard, Krafka 2005).

10. Our guess concerning the number of "serious" constitutional issues is premised on the fact that only 14 percent of court of appeals decisions in 2010 were supported by full, published written opinions, and on the assumption (see Posner 1985) that opinion publication is a marker of "hard issues."
11. One measure of the relationship between criminal and constitutional law is that all three of the federal criminal and all five of the state criminal cases the Court heard in 2010 raised constitutional issues (*Harvard Law Review* 2011).
12. Between 1990 and 1995, for example, of the cases decided by the Supreme Court with full written opinions, the principal issue was one of constitutional law in 49 percent (292 of 595 opinions) (Kreimer 1997).
13. See Strauss (1987) for a discussion of the implications of the limited review of federal appeals court decisions.
14. It is worth noting, however, that the overall volume of cases in the U.S. courts that actually reach adjudication after trial has been steadily declining (Galanter 2004). Only approximately 2 percent of federal civil cases were resolved by trial in 2002. A similarly drastic decline in trial by jury has occurred in state courts.
15. The 2011–2012 Court term suggests that a trend toward somewhat greater unanimity may be returning. See Liptak (2012).
16. In Article I, Section 8 of the U.S. Constitution, the Congress is given the power to "regulate Commerce ... among the several States," in addition to its power to regulate commerce with "foreign Nations" and "Indian Tribes."
17. For example, in *Hammer v. Dagenhart* [1918], the Court struck down a federal child labor law, reasoning that the law unconstitutionally regulated the manufacture of goods, which were, in this case, not inherently immoral (unlike, say, lottery tickets). Because manufacturing was an activity separate from commerce, child labor laws were not properly within the authority of the U.S. Congress.
18. See, e.g., *National Labor Relations Board v. Jones & Laughlin Steel Corporation* [1937]; *United States v. Darby* [1941]; *Wickard v. Filburn* [1942].
19. As is frequently the case, the Court considered Congress's power under the Commerce Clause in conjunction with its authority under the Necessary and Proper Clause of the constitution.
20. This latter principle is known as the "exclusionary rule."
21. The Federal Sentencing Guidelines were established by the Sentencing Reform Act of 1984.
22. Amendments, Article V provides, can be proposed only by a two-thirds vote of both houses of Congress or by two-thirds of the state governments, and adoption requires ratification by three-fourths of the states.
23. Three more of the twenty-seven amendments (the 13th, 14th, and 15th) were enacted by anti-slavery forces in the wake of the North's victory in the Civil War in 1865, while federal troops still occupied southern states. Only three constitutional amendments—the 11th (1795), the first sentence of the 14th (1868), and the 16th (1913, establishing Congress's power to impose income taxes)—were designed to reverse specific Supreme Court decisions
24. Hugo Black had been a trial-court judge in Alabama for a short time before running for and winning election to the U.S. Senate.
25. Article III of the U.S. Constitution ensures that only live cases or controversies between litigants may be brought before the courts. Thus the U.S. Supreme Court—unlike, for example, the French Constitutional Council or the German Federal

Constitutional Court—does not engage in "abstract judicial review" of pending or newly enacted legislation. Nor, does it issue pre-emptive advisory opinions. In addition, many cases are dismissed because they are not yet "ripe" for decision or because the issues they raise are "moot" by the time they reach the Court.

26. Other groups include prisoners' rights groups, a source of a significant number of cases that have led to court orders compelling better medical care, physical accommodations, and due process protections for inmates (Feeley, Rubin 1998); children's rights groups (see Mnookin 1985); the Legal Defense Fund, which consistently challenges death penalty laws and procedures on constitutional grounds (see Meltsner 1973); mental patients' rights organizations, which have won important cases establishing constitutional restrictions against involuntary confinement of the mentally disturbed (Rothman and Rothman 1984; Curtis 1986; Milner 1987); and religiously motivated groups, particularly in areas such as anti-abortion litigation (Wilson 2011).
27. In the 1980s, when the Civil Rights Division leadership was appointed by the Reagan administration, it was also a major source of civil rights claims challenging state and local "affirmative action plans" on grounds that they unconstitutionally discriminate against white males.
28. See Kagan 2001 for a related discussion of American political fragmentation and its implications for the salience of litigation as a mode of governance.
29. However, see Novak (2008) for a critique of the view that the U.S. state is comparatively "weak," as well as a discussion of some of the relevant literature on U.S. state development.
30. As Balkin and Levinson (2006: 506) note, President George W. Bush's nomination of then-White House Counsel Harriet Miers "sank" because members of his conservative base did not believe she would reflect their values if elevated to the bench.
31. *Pasadena City Bd. of Educ. v. Spangler* [1976]; *Missouri v. Jenkins* [1995]; *Parents Involved in Community Schools v. Seattle School District No. 1* [2007].
32. Similarly, Supreme Court decisions limiting governmental affirmative action (or "positive discrimination") programs (*Adarand Constructors, Inc. v. Peña* [1995]; *Gratz v. Bollinger* [2003]) provide precedents enabling white individuals, aided by conservative litigation organizations, to challenge other governmental affirmative action programs. When a conservative majority struck down, on freedom of speech grounds, a Congressional law restricting corporate and other private organizations' independent spending on political campaign advertising (*Citizens United v. Federal Election Commission* [2010]), it stimulated constitutional attacks by corporate and conservative groups on state laws limiting partisan political campaign advertising.

Bibliography

Ackerman, B.A. *We The People: Foundations.* Cambridge, Mass., 1991.

Administrative Office of the United States Courts. *Judicial Business of the United States Courts,* Washington, D.C. 1997. http://www.uscourts.gov/statistics-reports/judicial-business-1997.

Administrative Office of the United States Courts. *Judicial Business of the United States Courts,* Washington, D.C. 2010. http://www.uscourts.gov/statistics-reports/judicial-business-2010.
Atiyah, P.S., Summers, R. *Form and Substance in Anglo-American Law.* Oxford, 1987.
Balkin, J.M., Levinson, S. "Understanding the Constitutional Revolution." *Virginia Law Review,* Vol. 87, 2001, 1045–1109.
Balkin, J.M., Levinson, S. "The Rehnquist Court and Beyond: Revolution, Counter-Revolution, or Mere Chastening of Constitutional Aspirations?" *Fordham Law Review,* Vol. 75, 2006, 489–533.
Barkow, R.E. "Originalists, Politics, and Criminal Law on the Rehnquist Court." *George Washington Law Review,* Vol. 74, 2006, 1043–1077.
Barnett, R.E. "Commandeering the People: Why the National Health Insurance Mandate Is Unconstitutional." *New York University Journal of Law and Liberty,* Vol. 5, 2010, 581–637.
Brace, P., Gann Hall, M., Langer, L. "Placing State Supreme Courts in State Politics." *State Politics and Policy Quarterly,* Vol. 1, 2001, 81–101.
Brace, P., Sims Butler, K. "New Perspectives for the Comparative Study of the Judiciary: The State Supreme Court Project." *The Justice System Journal,* Vol. 22, 2001, 243–262.
Burke, T.F. *Lawyers, Lawsuits, and Legal Rights: The Battle over Litigation in American Society.* Berkeley and Los Angeles, 2004.
Caldeira, G.A., Wright, J.R. "Lobbying for Justice: Organized Interests, Supreme Court Nominations, and the United States Senate." *American Journal of Political Science,* Vol. 42, 1988, 499–523.
Casper, G., Posner, R. *The Workload of the Supreme Court.* Chicago, 1976.
Coglianese, C. "Legal Change at the Margins: Revisiting the Political Disadvantage Theory." Paper presented at Annual Meeting of the Law and Society Association, Aspen, Colorado, 1998.
Collins, R.K.L., Galie, P.J., Kincaid, J. "State High Courts, State Constitutions, and Individual Rights Litigation since 1980: A Judicial Survey." *Publius: The Journal of Federalism,* Vol. 16, 1986, 141–161.
Cordray, M.M., Cordray, R. "The Supreme Court's Plenary Docket." *Washington and Lee Law Review,* Vol. 58, 2001, 737–794.
Cross, F.B., Tiller, E.H. "Judicial Partisanship and Obedience to Legal Doctrine: Whistleblowing on the Federal Courts of Appeals." *Yale Law Journal,* Vol. 107, 1998, 2155–2176.
Curtis, R.W. "The Deinstitutionalization Story." *The Public Interest* 1986 (Fall), 34–49.
Damaska, M.R. *The Faces of Justice and State Authority: A Comparative Approach to the Legal Process.* New Haven, 1986.
Davis, M. *Brutal Need: Lawyers and the Welfare Rights Movement.* New Haven, 1993.
Devins, N. "How State Supreme Courts Take Consequences into Account: Toward a State-Centered Understanding of State Constitutionalism." *Stanford Law Review,* Vol. 62, 2010, 1629–1693.
Eisenberg, T., Miller., G.P. "Reversal, Dissent, and Variability in State Supreme Courts: The Centrality of Jurisdictional Source." *Boston University Law Review,* Vol. 89, 2009, 1451–1503.
Eisenberg, T., Schwab, S. "The Reality of Constitutional Tort Litigation." *Cornell Law Review,* Vol. 72, 1987, 641–695.

Emmert, C.F. "An Integrated Case-Related Model of Judicial Decision Making: Explaining State Supreme Court Decisions in Judicial Review Cases." *The Journal of Politics,* Vol. 54, 1992, 543–552.

Epp, C.R. *The Rights Revolution: Lawyers, Activities, and Supreme Courts in Comparative Perspective.* Chicago, 1998.

Epstein, L. *Conservatives in Court.* Knoxville, 1985.

Epstein, L., Knight, J. "Toward a Strategic Revolution in Judicial Politics: A Look Back, a Look Ahead." *Political Research Quarterly,* Vol. 53, 2000, 625–661.

Epstein, L., Segal, J.A., Spaeth, H.J. "The Norm of Consensus on the U.S. Supreme Court." *American Journal of Political Science,* Vol. 45, 2001, 362–377.

Feeley, M.M., Rubin, E.L. *Judicial Policy Making and the Modern State: How the Courts Reformed America's Prisons.* New York, 1998.

Friedman, L.M. "Courts Over Time: A Survey of Theories and Research." In Boyum, K., Mather, L., eds., *Empirical Theories about Courts.* New York, 1983, 9–52.

Frymer, P. "Acting When Elected Officials Won't: Federal Courts and Civil Rights Enforcement in U.S. Labor Unions, 1935–1985." *American Political Science Review,* Vol. 97, 2003, 483–499.

Galanter, M. "The Vanishing Trial: An Examination of Trials and Related Matters in Federal and State Courts." *Journal of Empirical Legal Studies,* Vol. 1, 2004, 459–570.

Gann Hall, M. "State Supreme Courts in American Democracy: Probing the Myths of Judicial Reform." *American Political Science Review,* Vol. 95, 2001, 315–330.

Gardner, J.A. "The Failed Discourse of State Constitutionalism." *Michigan Law Review,* Vol. 90, 1992, 761–837.

Gibson, J.L. "Challenges to the Impartiality of State Supreme Courts: Legitimacy Theory and 'New-Style' Judicial Campaigns." *American Political Science Review,* Vol. 102, 2008, 59–75.

Graber, M.A. "The Nonmajoritarian Difficulty: Legislative Deference to the Judiciary." *Studies in American Political Development,* Vol. 7, 1993, 35–73.

Grossman, J.B., Epp, C.R. "Agenda Formation on the Policy Active U.S. Supreme Court." In Rogowski, R., Gawron, T., eds., *Constitutional Courts in Comparison: The U.S. Supreme Court and the German Federal Constitutional Court.* New York, Oxford, 2002, 103–124.

Hacker, J.S. "Privatizing Risk Without Privatizing the Welfare State: The Hidden Politics of Social Policy Retrenchment in the United States." *American Political Science Review,* Vol. 98, 2004, 243–260.

Harvard Law Review. "The Supreme Court 1980 Term." Vol. 95, 1981

Harvard Law Review. "The Supreme Court 1984 Term." Vol. 99, 1985.

Harvard Law Review. "The Supreme Court 1986 Term." Vol. 101, 1987.

Harvard Law Review. "The Supreme Court 1990 Term." Vol. 105, 1991.

Harvard Law Review. "The Supreme Court 2010 Term." Vol. 125, 2011. http://cdn.harvardlawreview.org/wp-content/uploads/pdfs/vo125_statistics.pdf.

Hollis-Brusky, A. "Support Structures and Constitutional Change: Teles, Southworth, and the Conservative Legal Movement." *Law and Social Inquiry,* Vol. 36, 2011, 516–530.

Hollis-Brusky, A. *Ideas with Consequences: The Federalist Society and the Conservative Counterrevolution.* New York, 2015.

Howard, J.W., Jr. "Litigation Flow in the Three United States Courts of Appeals." *Law and Society Review,* Vol. 8, 1973, 33–54.

Johnson, E. *Justice and Reform: The Formative Years of the OED Legal Services Program.* New York, 1974.
Kagan, R.A. *Adversarial Legalism: The American Way of Law.* Cambridge, Mass., 2001.
Kagan, R.A. "A Consequential Court: The U.S. Supreme Court in the 20th Century." In Kapiszewski, D., Silverstein, G., Kagan, R.A., eds., *Consequential Courts: Judicial Roles in Global Perspective.* New York, 2013, 199–232.
Kagan, R.A., Cartwright, B., Friedman, L.M., Wheeler, S. "The Business of State Supreme Courts 1870–1970." *Stanford Law Review,* Vol. 30, 1977, 121–156.
Kagan, R.A., Cartwright, B., Friedman, L.M., Wheeler, S. "The Evolution of State Supreme Courts." *Michigan Law Review,* Vol. 76, 1978, 961–1005.
Kagan, R.A., Infelise, B., Detlefsen, R. "American State Supreme Court Justices 1900–1970." *American Bar Foundation Research Journal,* 1984, 371–408.
Kairys, D. "Freedom of Speech." In Kairys, D., ed., *The Politics of Law: A Progressive Critique.* New York, 1982, 237–272.
Kamin, S. *The Death Penalty and the California Supreme Court.* Ph.D. Dissertation, Jurisprudence and Social Policy, University of California, Berkeley, 1999.
Kapiszewski, D., Silverstein, G., Kagan, R.A., eds. *Consequential Courts: Judicial Roles in Global Perspective.* New York, 2013.
Keck, T. "Party, Policy, or Duty: Why Does the Supreme Court Invalidate Federal Statutes?" *American Political Science Review,* Vol. 101, 2007, 321–338.
Kelemen, R.D. *Eurolegalism: The Transformation of Law and Regulation in the European Union.* Cambridge, Mass., 2011.
King, N.J., Cheesman, F.L., II, Ostrom, B.J. "Executive Summary: Habeas Litigation in U.S. District Courts." Vanderbilt University Law School, 2007. https://www.ncjrs.gov/pdffiles1/nij/grants/219558.pdf.
Kluger, R. *Simple Justice: The History of Brown v. Board of Education and Black America's Struggle for Equality.* New York, 1975.
Krafka, C., Cecil, J.S., Lombard, P.A. *Stalking the Increase in the Rate of Federal Civil Appeals.* Washington, D.C., 1995.
Krehbiel, K. *Pivotal Politics: A Theory of U.S. Lawmaking.* Chicago, 1998.
Kreimer, S.F. "Exploring the Dark Matter of Judicial Review: A Constitutional Census of the 1990s." *William and Mary Bill of Rights Journal,* Vol. 5, 1997, 427–526.
Kritzer, H.M., Brace, P., Gann Hall, M., Boyea, B.T. "The Business of State Supreme Courts, Revisited." *Journal of Empirical Legal Studies,* Vol. 4, 2007, 427–439.
Kyckelhahn, T., Cohen, T.H. "Civil Rights Complaints in U.S. District Courts, 1990–2006." *Special Report, Bureau of Justice Statistics,* 2008. http://bjs.ojp.usdoj.gov/content/pub/pdf/crcusdc06.pdf.
LaFountain, R., Schauffler, R., Strickland, S., Bromage, C., Gibson, S., Mason, A. *Examining the Work of State Courts: An Analysis of 2008 State Court Caseloads.* National Center for State Courts, 2010. http://www.courtstatistics.org/~/media/Microsites/Files/CSP/EWSC-2008-Online.ashx.
LaFountain, R., Schauffler, R., Strickland, S., Gibson, S., Mason, A. *Examining the Work of State Courts: An Analysis of 2009 State Court Caseloads.* National Center for State Courts, 2011. http://www.courtstatistics.org/FlashMicrosites/CSP/images/CSP2009.pdf.
Langer, L. *Judicial Review in State Supreme Courts: A Comparative Study.* Albany, 2002.
Lawrence, S. *The Poor in Court: The Legal Service Program and Supreme Court Decision Making.* Princeton, 1990.

Lazarus, R.J. "Advocacy Matters before and within the Supreme Court: Transforming the Court by Transforming the Bar." *Georgetown Law Journal,* Vol. 86, 2008, 1487–1564.
Levinson, S. "Assessing the Supreme Court's Current Caseload: A Question of Law or Politics." *Yale Law Journal Online,* Vol. 119, 2010, 99–111. http://www.yalelawjournal.org/pdf/842_q862jfiz.pdf
Liptak, A.J. "In Supreme Court, Striking Unity on Major Cases." *New York Times,* 30 June 2012. http://www.nytimes.com/2012/07/01/us/supreme-courts-recent-term-a-new-phase.html
Lombard, P., Krafka, C. "2003–2004 District Court Case-Weighting Study." Final Report to the Subcommittee on Judicial Statistics of the Committee on Judicial Resources of the Judicial Conference of the United States, Federal Judicial Center, 2005. http://www.fjc.gov/public/pdf.nsf/lookup/CaseWts0.pdf/$file/CaseWts0.pdf.
Lytton, T.D. "Clergy Sexual Abuse Litigation: The Policymaking Role of Tort Law." *Connecticut Law Review,* Vol. 39, 2007, 809–880.
Lytton, T.D. *Holding Bishops Accountable: How Lawsuits Helped the Catholic Church Confront Clergy Sexual Abuse.* Cambridge, Mass., 2008.
McAdam, D. *Political Process and the Development of Black Insurgency, 1930–1970,* 2nd ed. Chicago, 1999.
McCann, M. *Rights at Work: Pay Equity Reform and the Politics of Legal Mobilization.* Chicago, 1994.
McMahon, K.J. *Reconsidering Roosevelt on Race: How the Presidency Paved the Road to* Brown. Chicago, 2004.
Meltsner, M. *Cruel and Unusual: The Supreme Court and Capital Punishment.* New York, 1973.
Milner, N. "The Right to Refuse Treatment: Four Case Studies in Legal Mobilization." *Law and Society Review,* Vol. 21, 1987, 447–485.
Mnookin, R.H. *In The Interest of Children: Advocacy, Law Reform, and Public Policy.* New York, 1985.
Morris, T. "States Before the U.S. Supreme Court: State Attorneys General as *Amicus Curiae.*" *Judicature,* Vol. 70, 1987, 298–305.
Nolette, P. *Federalism on Trial: State Attorneys General and National Policymaking in Contemporary America.* Lawrence, Kansas, 2015.
Novak, W.J. "The Myth of the 'Weak' American State." *American Historical Review,* Vol. 13, 2008, 752–772.
Olson, M. *The Logic of Collective Action.* Cambridge, Mass., 1965.
Paul, A.M. *The Conservative Crisis and the Rule of Law: Attitudes of Bar and Bench 1887–1895.* Ithaca, 1960.
Peretti, T.J. *In Defense of a Political Court.* Princeton, 1999.
Perry, H.W., Jr. *Deciding to Decide: Agenda Setting in the United States Supreme Court.* Cambridge, Mass., 1991.
Pickerill, J.M., Clayton, C.W. "The Rehnquist Court and the Political Dynamics of Federalism." *Perspectives on Politics,* Vol. 2, 2004, 233–248.
Posner, R.A. "Foreword: A Political Court." *Harvard Law Review,* Vol. 119, 2005, 32–102.
Provine, D. "Raising Race: How Defense Lawyers Made Racism an Issue in Drug Sentencing." Paper presented at Annual Meeting of the Law and Society Association, Aspen, Colorado, 1998.
Rabin, R.I. "Lawyers and Social Change: Perspectives on Public Interest Law." *Stanford Law Review,* Vol. 28, 1976, 207–261.

Reed, D.S. "Twenty-Five Years after *Rodriguez:* School Finance Litigation and the Impact of the New Judicial Federalism." *Law and Society Review,* Vol. 32, 1998, 175–220.
Reynolds, R.S. "Equal Justice Under Law: Post-*Booker,* Should Federal Judges Be Able to Depart from the Federal Sentencing Guidelines to Remedy Disparity between Codefendants' Sentences?" *Columbia Law Review,* Vol. 109, 2009, 538–570.
Richards, M.J., Kritzer, H.M. "Jurisprudential Regimes in Supreme Court Decision Making." *American Political Science Review,* Vol. 96, 2002, 305–320.
Rosen, J.A. "The Unregulated Offensive." *The New York Times Magazine,* 17 April 2005.
Rosen, J.A. "Supreme Court Inc." *The New York Times Magazine,* 16 March 2008.
Rothman, D.J., Rothman, S.M. *The Willowbrook Wars.* New York, 1984.
Sarat, A., Felstiner, W.F. "Law and Strategy in the Divorce Lawyer's Office." *Law and Society Review,* Vol. 20, 1986, 93–134.
Schuck, P.H. *Suing Government: Citizen Remedies for Official Wrongs.* New Haven, 1983.
Segal, J.A., Cover, A.D. "Ideological Values and the Votes of U.S. Supreme Court Justices." *American Political Science Review,* Vol. 83, 1989, 557–565.
Segal, J.A., Spaeth, H. *The Supreme Court and the Attitudinal Model.* New York, 1993.
Segal, J.A., Spaeth, H. *The Supreme Court and the Attitudinal Model Revisited.* New York, 2002.
Siegel, A. "The Court Against the Courts: Hostility to Litigation as an Organizing Theme in the Rehnquist Court's Jurisprudence." *Texas Law Review,* Vol. 84, 2006, 1097–1202.
Silverstein, G. *Law's Allure: How Law Shapes, Constrains, Saves, and Kills Politics.* New York, 2009.
Southworth, A. "Conservative Lawyers and the Contest over the Meaning of 'Public Interest Law.'" *UCLA Law Review,* Vol. 52, 2005, 1223–1278.
Southworth, A. *Lawyers of the Right: Professionalizing the Conservative Coalition.* Chicago, 2008.
Staszak, S. "Institutions, Rulemaking, and the Politics of Judicial Retrenchment." *Studies in American Political Development,* Vol. 24, 2010, 168–189.
Steiker, C.S. "Counter-Revolution in Constitutional Criminal Procedure? Two Audiences, Two Answers." *Michigan Law Review,* Vol. 894, 1996, 2466–2551.
Steiker, C.S. "Things Fall Apart, but the Center Holds: The Supreme Court and the Death Penalty." *New York University Law Review,* Vol. 77, 2002, 1475–1490.
Steiker, C.S., Steiker, J.M.. "Sober Second Thoughts: Reflections on Two Decades of Constitutional Regulation of Capital Punishment." *Harvard Law Review,* Vol. 109, 1995, 355–438.
Stone Sweet, A. *Governing With Judges: Constitutional Politics in Europe.* Oxford, 2000.
Stras, D.R. "The Supreme Court's Gatekeepers: The Role of Law Clerks in the Certiorari Process." *Texas Law Review,* Vol. 85, 2007, 948–997.
Strauss, P.L. "One Hundred Fifty Cases per Year: Some Implications of the Supreme Court's Limited Resources for Judicial Review of Agency Action." *Columbia Law Review,* Vol. 87, 1987, 1093–1136.
Summers, R., Taruffo, M. "Interpretation and Comparative Analysis." In McCormick, D.N., Summers, R., eds., *Interpreting Statutes: A Comparative Study.* Dartmouth, 1991, 461–510.
Tate, C.N., Vallinder, T., eds. *The Global Expansion of Judicial Power.* New York, London, 1995.

Teles, S.M. *The Rise of the Conservative Legal Movement: The Battle for Control of the Law.* Princeton, 2008.

Tushnet, M.V. *The NAACP's Legal Strategy Against Segregated Education, 1925–1950.* Chapel Hill, 2005.

Twiss, B.R. *Lawyers and the Constitution: How Laissez Faire came to the Supreme Court.* Princeton, 1942.

Wasserman, H. "The Roberts Court and the Civil Procedure Revival." *Review of Litigation,* Vol. 31, 2012, 313–352.

Wawro, G.J., Schickler, E. *Filibuster: Obstruction and Lawmaking in the U.S. Senate.* Princeton, 2006.

Williams, R.F. "In the Glare of the Supreme Court: Continuing Methodology and Legitimacy Problems in Independent State Constitutional Rights Adjudication." *Notre Dame Law Review,* Vol. 72, 1997, 1015–1064.

Wilson, J.C. "Sustaining the State: Legal Consciousness and the Construction of Legality in Competing Abortion Activists' Narratives." *Law and Social Inquiry,* Vol. 36, 2011, 455–483.

Wilson, J.Q. *The Politics of Regulation.* New York, 1980.

Wold, J.T., Culver, J.H. "The Defeat of the California Justices: the Campaign, the Electorate, and the Issue of Judicial Accountability." *Judicature,* Vol. 70, 1987, 348–355.

Chapter 2

Access to the German Federal Constitutional Court

Werner Heun

The concept of a constitutional court evokes the picture of one that, in constitutional questions, presides over all others as a supra-appeal court that can be petitioned only after the plaintiff or complainant has passed through numerous other stages of appeal. In the case of the German Federal Constitutional Court, this picture is only partially correct. It is correct in the case of constitutional complaints, but even here, the picture is not complete. A complainant can, under certain circumstances, challenge a law directly without having to go to any other court beforehand. For preliminary rulings or concrete judicial review, according to Article 100 I of the German Basic Law, and for some related procedures, other courts will make the referral. Thus, Article 100 I of the Basic Law inserts another court between citizens and the Federal Constitutional Court. In all other procedures, the Federal Constitutional Court is the court of both first and final resort. These consist of so-called constitutional disputes in the narrow sense, comprising disputes involving the highest organs of the state (art. 93 I 1 of the Basic Law); disputes between the Federation and the federal states or among federal states (arts. 93 I 3; 84 IV 2; 93 I 4; 99 of the Basic Law); election disputes (art. 41 II of the Basic Law); and disputes concerning a possible violation of the Constitution, including forfeiture of basic rights (art. 18 of the Basic Law), the prohibition of political parties (art. 21 II of the Basic Law), the impeachment of the Federal President (art. 61 of the Basic Law), and the impeachment of judges (art. 98 II, V of the Basic Law).

Notes for this chapter begin on page 87.

Thus, access to the Federal Constitutional Court (the Court hereafter) can be fully understood only by differentiating between its various fields of activity. These decisively determine the criteria for access, the Court's control and regulation of access, and the actual mobilization of the Court. Three fundamentally different areas of the Federal Constitutional Court's activity can be identified. First, the Court pronounces upon the above-mentioned constitutional disputes in the narrow sense and on the procedures for the protection of the Constitution. Second, the Court practices judicial review, which can be initiated in various forms and by various parties. Access in this latter area is not regulated uniformly. It includes abstract judicial review (arts. 93 I 2 and 93 I 2a of the Basic Law), also known as abstract norm control; preliminary rulings or concrete judicial review (art. 100 I of the Basic Law), also known as concrete norm control; review of international law (art. 100 II of the Basic Law); submissions from the state constitutional courts (art. 100 III of the Basic Law); applicability of law as federal law (art. 126 of the Basic Law), now almost obsolete; and constitutional complaints by local councils (art. 93 I 4 b of the Basic Law). Third, the Court hears individual complaints concerning the infringement of basic rights of citizens (art. 93 I 4a of the Basic Law), which can also lead to judicial review of parliamentary legislation.

These three areas of activity are not hermetically separated from one another, but rather often overlap. Thus, judicial review may be undertaken in disputes involving the highest organs of the state, disputes between the Federation and the German states, or cases of individual complaints. Nonetheless, access to the Court can be grouped and classified according to the already mentioned areas of activity.

The Criteria for Admission as a Filter for Access

Access to the Court is regulated primarily by the criteria for admission of the different procedural types, although it is not possible to isolate procedural admission questions from problems of substantive constitutional interpretation. Admission is thus the main access filter, the permeability of which varies according to the type of procedure. I shall deal with these in turn.

Constitutional Disputes in the Narrow Sense and Procedures to Protect the Constitution

In the areas of constitutional disputes in the narrow sense and procedures for protecting the Constitution, the access hurdles are low. Parties to a dispute have direct access to the Court without first having to invoke another judicial body. If, for example, the parliamentary group of the Green Party attacks rearmament (*Amtliche Sammlung der Entscheidungen des Bundesverfassungsgerichts* [BVerfGE] 68, 1—*Pershing 2 and Cruise Missile II* case), or individual states consider the State Liability Act to be unconstitutional (BVerfGE 61, 149—*State Liability* case), then they have direct access to the Court as petitioners. As a rule, the only fundamental requirement in these cases is that of a subjective infringement of a (constitutional) legal right (mentioned in art. 64 I of the Federal Constitutional Court Act, and referred to by art. 69 of the Federal Constitutional Court Act). With certain types of procedure, termed objective procedures, even this requirement is not necessary. This applies to those dealing with impeachment, prohibition of political parties, and election disputes. The Federal Constitutional Court is the court of first and last resort in such cases, and settles the dispute between the various highest organs of the state or, if so petitioned, decides objective questions of constitutional law.

Judicial Review

The various forms of judicial review present a different picture. The Court is responsible for decisions concerning the validity of post-constitutional norms as laid down by the Basic Law. The Court's decision-making monopoly is based upon the idea that the validity of a norm should be decided centrally and should generally be binding in order to prevent various courts from reaching different decisions in the context of the concrete application of a norm. Diffuse judicial review does not exist in the case of post-constitutional legislation (see Friesenhahn 1962: 136; see also Schlaich, Korioth 2012: 88). Furthermore, decisions concerning the validity of a norm enacted by the legislature are considered to be of particular importance and are thus conferred to the constitutional judicature, which stands out from the remaining judicature.

Both of these elements led the founders of the Constitution to provide for numerous possibilities for access to the Court (ibid.: 7). Judicial review should be available at all times, but petitions should not overwhelm the Court. For these reasons, the access hurdles depend upon the petitioner. The highest bodies of the state can call directly upon the Court to review a norm and do not have to follow any intermediary stages. They can either use the procedure of abstract judicial review or claim a dispute involving highest organs of the state or a dispute between the Federation and the federal or among federal states. Courts are able to submit norms to the Federal Constitutional Court under more stringent criteria and can do so directly (art. 100 I of the Basic Law). Individual citizens can only aim their constitutional complaint directly at a legislative instrument under exceptional circumstances and by following very strict criteria. Under normal circumstances, they must first follow the regular legal channels; only then can they indirectly trigger judicial review through a constitutional complaint against a judicial decision.

In addition to giving rise to judicial review through constitutional complaints, the majority of judicial reviews are initiated through referral by judges (art. 100 I of the Basic Law). The remaining procedures are, apart from a few important forms of abstract judicial review, quantitatively and qualitatively of minor importance (see Rinken 2002).

In the case of concrete judicial review, two admission criteria limit the courts' access to the Federal Constitutional Court. First, the referring judge must be positively convinced of the unconstitutionality of the legal instrument—mere doubt does not suffice (see, e.g., BVerfGE 68, 337; BVerfGE 68, 352 [358]; BVerfGE 93, 121 [131]—*Tax Assessment II* case; see also Ulsamer (1985) in Maunz et al. n.d., para. 80, n. 21; Pestalozza 1991: 209; Schlaich/Korioth 2012: 117 et seq.). And second, a decision on the constitutionality of a norm must be deemed relevant for the decision at the lower judicial level (see, e.g., BVerfGE 57, 26 [34]; BVerfGE 72, 91; see also Ulsamer 1980: 521; Ulsamer (1985) in Maunz et al. n.d., para. 80, n. 217; Pestalozza 1991: 210 et seq.; Schlaich, Korioth 2012: 123–124). Otherwise all courts, from the local court to the highest federal court, are entitled and compelled to refer, although the judges of the lower courts often have difficulty positively ascertaining the constitutionality of a norm (Heun 1997: 619 et seq.). The Federal Constitutional Court is constantly reminding local courts of this requirement (e.g., BVerfGE 78, 25 [30]; furthermore, the twice rejected attempt of a local court in BVerfGE 77, 364 and BVerfGE 80, 68; see also Schlaich, Korioth 2012: 122). However, it has been noted that the success rate of referring courts correlates with their importance as courts of appeal (see Peters 1976a: 11). Furthermore, a judge is competent to interpret any norm in a way that it is partially constitutional and partially unconstitutional. In this case the norm will not be referred to and decided by the constitutional court.

The hurdle of relevance is more difficult to overcome than that of positive conviction. A decision on the constitutionality of a norm is only relevant if, after all evidentiary possibilities are exhausted, it is certain that the referring court would come to a different conclusion if it applied the norm. The opinion of the referring court is decisive for the evaluation of a norm's relevance unless it is obviously untenable (BVerfGE 66, 226 [231]; BVerfGE 67, 26 [35]; BVerfGE 68, 352 [358]) or no constitutional issue is at stake (BVerfGE 67, 26 [34]; BVerfGE 69, 150 [159]). Over the years the Court has interpreted the question of relevance more restrictively (see

BVerfGE 66, 100; BVerfGE 66, 226; BVerfGE 67, 239; BVerfGE 78, 165 [178]; see Sachs 1985: 1106 with critical comments; Hein 1988: 34). In exceptional circumstances the requirement of relevance can be dispensed with if the "submitted question is of general and fundamental importance for public welfare and thus the decision is urgent" (BVerfGE 47, 146 [151]—*Fast Breeder* case). Through this formula, the Court maintains flexibility in its ability to accept cases. In addition, since 1993, Article 81a Federal Constitutional Court Act has allowed the Court's chambers, each consisting of only three judges, to dismiss certain referrals if they are not admissible.

The referral is up to the judge and not to the parties of the original dispute. Even if a norm is submitted outside the course of normal stages of appeal, access to the Court is not blocked. Parties can still lodge a constitutional complaint against the final decision of the appeal court of last instance.

Constitutional Complaint

In the area of constitutional complaints, two aspects that determine access to the Court have to be considered. These are the criteria of admittance and the procedure for admission.

Admittance Criteria

An individual can, under strict conditions, challenge a legal instrument directly by way of a constitutional complaint. In such cases, the problems of judicial review and questions relating to the admittance of individual basic rights complaints coincide. Generally, initial admission will depend upon the present and direct infringement of a basic right (Schlaich, Korioth 2012: 161). This precondition used to be restricted to constitutional complaints against legislative instruments but is now also being applied in constitutional complaints against judgments (BVerfGE 53, 30 (48)—*Mühlheim-Kärlich* case; BVerfGE 72, 1 (5)—*Age Limit* case; see also Pestalozza 1991: 180; Löwer 2005: 1489–1490; Zuck 2006: 238; Schlaich, Korioth 2012: 172 et seq.). However, a special and precise evaluation of the preconditions is not necessary if the petitioner is affected by individual legal action. The preconditions are then usually deemed to be fulfilled.

The situation is likely to be different, however, in cases of constitutional complaints that are aimed directly at legislative acts. In such cases, as a rule, there will be no direct infringement of basic rights. For this reason, a constitutional complaint against a legislative act is only admissible if an act of execution is not necessary and the law interferes with the petitioner's rights without "requiring for its execution, by law or by administrative practice, a special act, influenced by the will of the executive"(BVerfGE 1,

97 [102]—*Widow's Child Welfare* case; see also for example, BVerfGE 67, 256 [273]—*Investment Aid II* case; BVerfGE 72, 39 [43]; BVerfGE 73, 40 [68]—*Party Finance VI* case, and for a municipal constitutional complaint, BVerfGE 71, 25 [34]; on admission criteria in general see Henning 1981). A classic case of such a situation is direct expropriation through a legislative act. The directness practically replaces the prior exhaustion of legal procedures as a "counterpart to art. 90 II of the Federal Constitutional Court Act" (Schlaich, Korioth 2012: 177). This is because in the case of constitutional complaints against norms, the legal procedures cannot usually be exhausted beforehand, as no legal redress, in the sense of Article 90 II of the Federal Constitutional Court Act, exists against a legislative act—at least not in principle. Thus, the directness evolves out of the idea of subsidiarity. However, aspects of reasonableness can supersede this access criterion (BVerfGE 81, 70 [82]); this applies above all to criminal law (BVerfGE 46, 246 [256]). Comparable cases are those in which the law already leads to dispositions in advance (BVerfGE 43, 291 [386]—*Numerus Clausus IV* case) or the administration lacks any discretion in executing the law (BVerfGE 43, 108 [117]—*Child Tax Allowance* case; BVerfGE 59, 1 [17]), which allows the Court to remain flexible (see also Schlaich, Korioth 2012: 178).

Until the mid 1980s, the submission of a constitutional complaint against a norm was valid if all other procedural requirements were fulfilled and the petitioner was directly affected. The Court has since then departed from this: being directly affected no longer suffices. The admission hurdles became higher when the Court held that "the formal and timely submission of a constitutional complaint of a petitioner, directly and presently affected by a legal norm, can still fail, for the reasons that ... a direct legal course against this legal norm has not yet been exhausted and thus the rule contained in art. 90 II 1 of the Federal Constitutional Court Act has not been fulfilled. The inadmissibility of this constitutional complaint can also follow from the fact that although there is no legal redress directly through a specialist court, the petitioner can, in a justifiable manner, obtain effective legal protection through the prior use of the specialized courts" (BVerfGE 71, 305 [335], see also BVerfGE 74, 69 [74]; BVerfGE 79, 1 [19]; already expounded beforehand by Schenke 1979: 301, 1986: 1451, 1987: 17, who confirms the subsidiarity in all cases of possible incidental judicial review; see also Gerontas 1982: 443; Posser, 1993; Wormke, 1993). In its enthusiasm to stop the flood of constitutional complaints, in this decision the Court, against the wording of the norm in question, introduced a new legal course of action that citizens are obliged to try before launching a constitutional complaint (BVerfGE 70, 35; critical Schenke 1985: 1367; also see Wormke 1993: 124 et seq.; Schenke 1987: 18; opposing, but coming to the same result Henseler 1986: 249; now backtracking BVerfGE 107, 395 [418]).

The limitations of direct challenge of a norm demonstrate that the main obstacle to admission is now the exhaustion of all prior legal procedures, while the condition of infringement of basic rights only prevents complaints launched on behalf of the general public (BVerfGE 60, 360 [370]). The exhaustion of all prior legal procedures according to Article 90 II of the Federal Constitutional Court Act means that the complaint has to be directed against the last legally enforceable judgment of the appeal court of last instance. If a valid legal redress has been omitted or overlooked, the legal process has not been exhausted and access to the Court is therefore cut off (BVerfGE 70, 180 [185/6]; on the exhaustion of legal procedures and subsidiarity see also BVerfGE 63, 45 [58]; BVerfGE 69, 122 [125]; see also Henschel 1984: 165; Lerche 1984: 369; Pestalozza 1991: 185 et seq.; Böhmer 1992: 21 et seq.; Schlaich, Korioth 2012: 168–179). The petitioner must undertake "all that can be reasonably expected of him" (BVerfGE 64, 135 [143]; see also BVerfGE 68, 376 [380]). It is evident from this proviso, however, that the use of legal procedures does not have to be exhausted by the petitioner if such action cannot reasonably be expected of him or her; for example, if the prospect of legal redress is hopeless due to firmly entrenched rulings of the higher courts. This enables the Court, should the situation arise, to gain access quickly to the case and the constitutional problem contained therein.

The purpose of the subsidiarity of constitutional complaints, that is, the exhaustion of remedies, is twofold. First, there is the pressing aspect of relieving the Court. "If a different method exists or existed to remove the infringement of the basic right or to reach practically the same result without having to take recourse to the Federal Constitutional Court" (BVerfGE 63, 45 [58]), then the Court should not concern itself with the matter at all.

The principle of subsidiarity also has the effect of conveying to the court the specialist court's way of looking at a case (BVerfGE 69, 122 [125]; BVerfGE 72, 39 [43]; see also BVerfGE 56, 54 [69]—*Aircraft Noise Control* case). However, this requirement can be dispensed with if the specialized courts cannot give the Federal Constitutional Court their view due to the specialist nature of the matter and tight time limits (BVErfGE 65, 1 [37]—*Census Act* case). In general, it is only through practical application that the meaning of the respective laws can be discovered, which is why direct complaints against a law should be, and must be, the exception. Furthermore, the referring court must prepare the relevant facts in such a way that the Federal Constitutional Court can concentrate exclusively on the constitutional questions.

Through the formula of reasonableness of the diversion to specialized courts—based upon the requirement to exhaust all legal processes—the Court has created an instrument that allows it to react flexibly and at the same time protect itself from an onslaught of cases. In the face of an enormous workload, the Court has directed its inventiveness toward finding "new diversions," despite the fact that the normal course of legal action has ended. Thus the Court demands that petitioners should make counterclaims (*Gegenvorstellungen*) in the specialized courts against decisions that have already been through their final stage of appeal if "failure is not evident from the beginning" (BVerfGE 63, 77 [78]; see also BVerfGE 68, 375 [381]; BVerfGE 70, 180 [185 et seq.]; BVerfGE 73, 322 [325]), despite the fact that a formal means of redress is no longer admissible (see Seetzen 1982: 2342; Weis 1987: 1314; Schlaich, Korioth 2012: 183 et seq.; see also Zuck 1985: 925, who proposes to establish a general "hearing reprimand" [*Anhörungsrüge*] in relation to constitutional issues in the ordinary judicature).

Furthermore, with reference to subsidiarity, the Court demands that the parties' constitutional doubts about a norm must already have been raised in the specialized courts (see BVerfGE 68, 334 [335]; BVerfGE 68, 384 [389]; BVerfGE 72, 84 [88]; BVerfGE 74, 102 [114]—*Educational Rules* case; for criticism of these "hearing reprimands" see Bender 1987, 1988). On the other hand, the Court allows constitutional complaints against final appeal decisions in preliminary proceedings unless the main hearing is deemed capable of resolving the infringement of the basic right in question (BVerfGE 51, 130 [138], see also BVerfGE 53, 30 [52]—*Mühlheim-Kärlich* case; BVerfGE 56, 216 [234]—*Asylum Procedure* case; BVerfGE 62, 117 [143]; BVerfGE 86, 15 [27]). In practice, the *Numerus-Clausus* cases regarding access to higher education were diverted in this way from the Federal Administrative Court, which has no jurisdiction in the preliminary, expedited procedures that were used in these cases. In allowing and then deciding such constitutional complaints, the Federal Constitutional Court acts indeed as a "supra-appeal court" (Schlaich, Korioth 2012: 197). The Federal Constitutional Court can also, under Article 90 II 2 of the Federal Constitutional Court Act, access important cases without having to wait until all legal remedies have been exhausted (see, e.g., BVerfGE 7, 99 [105]—*Broadcasting Time I* case; BVerfGE 19, 268 [273]—*Split Income Church Tax II* case; BVerfGE 62, 117 [144]; BVerfGE 62, 338 [342]; BVerfGE 63, 230 [242]; BVerfGE 86, 15 [24]; BVerfGE 86, 133 [140]—*Detention Period* case; BVerfGE 91, 93 [106]—*Child Allowance* case; Schlaich, Korioth 2012: 187–188). In addition, the court occasionally ignores the barriers set by the admittance criteria with the help of two formal instruments: the transcending of the stake of the dispute, and the use of obiter dicta (Bryde 1982: 171, 365, 371; Schenke 1987: 24).

Moreover, the principle of subsidiarity has attained contours increasingly independent from those of the exhaustion of all legal processes (see Klein 1987: 1306). Having decided many cases, the Court has now withdrawn and has stopped, for example, accepting so-called free rider cases (*Trittbrettverfahren*—BVerfGE 51, 130 [143]; Schlaich, Korioth 2012: 187; for group actions in the area of nuclear law see BVerfGE 53, 30 [52]—*Mühlheim-Kärlich* case; also BVerfGE 54, 173 [190]; BVerfGE 59, 1 [19]; BVerfGE 66, 155 [173, 175]—*Hannover College* case; critical Strietzel 1993: 181/2). The Court has become more restrictive and concentrates on cases concerning fundamental constitutional cases. By putting a new emphasis on the subsidiarity of the constitutional complaint in this way, it retains a high degree of flexibility in its actions (BVerfGE 77, 381 [400]; BVerfGE 78, 290 [301]; BVerfGE 79, 275 [278]; BVerfGE 80, 40 [45]). In recent years the Court has also increasingly required complainants to substantiate the complaint in more and more detail (see Schorkopf 2005: 465 et seq.; now comprehensively with a detailed analysis of the decisions of the Federal Constitutional Court Lange 2012: 26 et seq.). Especially this requirement, which is also applied to referrals according to Article 100 I B.L., gives the Court flexibility in admitting cases (critical Lange 2012: 188 et seq.).

Admission Procedure

The admittance criteria do not stem the flood of constitutional complaints on their own. Every year, 6,000 complaints now arrive at the Court. The chambers, each consisting of three judges, hear more than 5,500 cases each year. However, probably at least a few hundred cases (their number is disputed—see below) are dealt with by secretaries to the president. In the interest of the functioning of the Court, a three-pronged, staggered system of acceptance barriers has been erected to fend off inadmissible, unfounded, or otherwise unsuitable complaints. These barriers are complaint registration, admittance by the chamber, and formal acceptance for decision by the senate.

In essence, the three hurdles can be summarized in one sentence: The constitutional complaint depends upon express admission through the Court (art. 93a of the Federal Constitutional Court Act). This statement makes the procedure seem simpler than it actually is, for in reality it is complicated. Its use by the Court often seems unclear to the petitioner, and the chances for success akin to those in a lottery (Wank 1980: 549; critical are Zuck 1987: 195 and Sailer 1977: 303; for a different view see Benda 1980: 2097; Benda, Klein 2012: 217; Böhmer 1992: 21). The Court's need to have some of its burdens relieved has made the admission procedure the catalyst and focus of at least half of the amendments to the Federal Constitutional Court Act (see Heyde 1981: 233; on the amendment of 2

August 1993 [BGBl. I, 1442] see Pestalozza 1992: 426 et seq.; critical are Wahl, Wieland 1996: 1139 et seq.; Schlaich, Korioth 2012: 181–182). The promotion of the former three-judge committees (*Dreier-Ausschüsse*) to chambers (*Kammern*) and the extension of their competencies were at the centre of the amendment of 1985 (Mirbach 1986: 2096; Ulsamer 1986: 110; Zuck 1986a: 968; 1986b: 2093; Mahrenholz 1987: 1361; *Gesetzentwurf der Bundesregierung*, BT-Drs. 10/2951). In addition a submission fee was introduced, and the fee for misuse upon the rejection of a constitutional complaint was increased. The maximum fee for misuse was €2,600 at the time of writing (art. 34 II of the Federal Constitutional Court Act).

The first acceptance hurdle, which relates to the Rules of Procedure of the Federal Constitutional Court (Geschäftsordnung des Bundesverfassungsgerichts) and the case register, was unaffected by the 1985 amendment. Constitutional complaints that are inadmissible or obviously have no chance of success are not entered into the case register of the senates but only into the "general register" (para. 60 II a Rules of Procedure, see the dispute between Schlink [1984b: 89], Wand [1984: 950], and Schlink [1984a: 2195]; see also Schlaich, Korioth 2012: 182). Furthermore, the decision to enter a case into the general register is taken not by the judges of the chambers but by the secretaries to the president of the Court. Although not judges themselves, they are judicial civil servants and thus fully qualified lawyers. The decision of the secretaries to the president is communicated to the petitioner, who must then, within a certain time period, inform the Court that he or she wishes a judgment on the matter. Only through this expressed desire is the complaint allowed into the actual admission procedure, in other words into the chambers; otherwise, it is treated as closed. Perhaps a quarter of constitutional complaints are not continued and end at this stage (Schlink's [1984b: 90] claim that roughly half the complaints are dismissed at this stage is rejected by Wand [1984: 953], who however does not provide any alternative statistics). Even if one does not consider this practice to be unconstitutional (contrary to Schlink 1984b: 89) on the basis that it is not a judgment on the constitutional complaint, but, in doctrinal terms, merely a "notice of the legal position" (Wand 1984: 952; see also Schlaich, Korioth 2012: 182), this initial control remains problematic, despite the fact that the flood of complaints seems to preclude any other unproblematic alternative. Adopting a procedure similar to the U.S. Supreme Court's would, however, at most be a formal elaboration.

Once the secretaries have passed the complaint on to the president because the petitioner desires a judgment, or because the secretaries to the president are of the opinion that the complaint might be successful, the chambers, formerly the three-judge committees, decide whether or not to accept it. Since their introduction through the first amendment in 1956, the three-judge bodies have been able to decline the admission of a constitutional complaint "if it is not admissible or if for other reasons the likelihood of success is not sufficient" (art. 93a III of the old Federal Constitutional Court Act; see also Zacher 1976: 395; Vitzthum 1984: 293; Zuck 2006: 300). Bryde (1982: 158) remarks correctly that "in practice, the admission procedure of the Federal Constitutional Court plays a role independent of its legal basis." The empirical evidence shows that before the introduction of the admission procedure, Article 24 of the Federal Constitutional Court Act fulfilled the same function (Zacher 1976: 405).

The amendment of 1985 retained the general rule containing the criteria of admission (old art. 93b I 2 of the Federal Constitutional Court Act). To this was added the ability to decline the acceptance of a constitutional complaint on the grounds that the petitioner had not made the advance payment on time (according to the now obsolete art. 34 VI and 93b I 1b of the Federal Constitutional Court Act), or "if it is to be expected that the Senate will not accept the constitutional complaint according to art. 93c" (old art. 93b I 3 of the Federal Constitutional Court Act). The most important change was that the chambers were now—and this above all else justified the name change—empowered by the old Article 93b II of the Federal Constitutional Court Act to grant a constitutional complaint that is obviously well founded due to the Court already having decided upon the relevant constitutional questions. In May 1987, the Court passed its first judgment under this provision (see *Frankfurter Allgemeine Zeitung*, 22 May 1987, p. 5 [Az. 2 BvR 108/87]), and these chamber decisions have steadily increased in importance (see Schlink 1989: 11; Starck 1996: 1041).

The rules were again altered by amendments in 1993. Article 93a II of the current Federal Constitutional Court Act states that a constitutional complaint has to be accepted if it is of general constitutional importance or if it is necessary for the protection of basic rights. The standards have been further tightened by this provision. The chambers are still empowered to grant the constitutional complaint under the aforementioned conditions (art. 93c of the current Federal Constitutional Court Act), and the senate continues to have the exclusive authority to declare a law void or irreconcilable with the Basic Law or with higher federal law.

The only formal caveat to this "floodgate" lies in the requirement that the chambers must make their positive and negative decisions unanimously; otherwise the constitutional complaint advances a step further. A judgment for dismissal cannot be challenged. In other words, it is formally and legally valid (Schlaich, Korioth 2012: 185). The decision does not have to be fully reasoned—referring to the relevant legal aspects suffices. However, this does not prevent the judges from occasionally giving detailed reasoning, which often is also included in the official case reports (see for example BVerfGE 55, 144). Recently the Court has started to publish separate volumes with decisions of the chambers.

After the assessment by the chambers, the relevant senate decides on admissibility. This is the final hurdle before the judgment by the senate. The senate accepts the constitutional complaint if at least three judges hold that the judgment will lead to clarification of a constitutional question, or if the denial of a judgment on the matter will lead to the petitioner suffering "a severe and unavoidable disadvantage" (according to art. 93b 2 in conjunction with 93a II and 93d III 2 of the Federal Constitutional Court Act). The law combines a formal requirement, the vote of three judges, with an alternative, substantive requirement, namely the objective or subjective importance of the issue concerned. Once the chambers have filtered out the majority of complaints, very few fail at this stage. All the same, the senate need not accept even an obviously well-founded constitutional complaint if it is seen as neither objectively nor subjectively of importance (examples are BVerfGE 68, 334; BVerfGE 71, 64; BVerfGE 72, 119 [for the first application of art. 93c 2 of the Federal Constitutional Court Act]; BVerfGE 76, 124; and BVerfGE 77, 125; critical of this result are Vitzthum 1984: 319 and Schlink 1984b: 94; in agreement is Schlaich, Korioth 2012: 187–188).

The whole system of acceptance hurdles and the handling of the admission procedure has been heavily criticized, partly because it is regarded as unconstitutional. Indeed, if one interprets the embedding of the constitutional complaint in the Constitution as a guarantee of individual, subjective legal protection, then one must hold the procedure as a whole to be unconstitutional (among others, Vitzthum 1984: 313 and Schlink 1984b: 93). On the other hand, from an early stage the Court emphasized the dual function of constitutional complaints, which should not only maintain the individual protection of basic rights but should, above and beyond this, safeguard and develop the objective constitutional law (see BVerGE 33, 247 [258]; BVerfGE 45, 63 [74] – *Hameln's Department of Works* case; in detail Schlaich, Korioth 2012: 191–192; Graßhof [2006] in Maunz et al. n.d., para. 93a, n. 30–35). In some cases, the objective aspect can push subjective legal protection into the background. To start with, the legislators knew of the practice and the opinion of the Court when they changed the Constitution by granting the constitutional complaint constitutional status and approving the admission procedure (art. 94 II 2 of the Basic Law). Furthermore, the duty to provide recourse to a court, contained in article 19 IV of the Basic Law, does not extend to the constitutional complaint, which is not an instrument of appeal but a specific mechanism of constitutional law (see Schlaich, Korioth 2012: 151–152, 210; compare also BVerfGE 31; 364 [367] and BVerfGE 49, 329 [340]; Schenke 1987: 16). The other, so-called specialized courts are also already bound to apply and to take into account basic rights by Article 1 III of the Basic Law. The whole idea of the subsidiarity of constitutional complaints is based upon the fact that it is primarily the task of the specialized courts to resolve infringements of the Constitution. The primary task of the Federal Constitutional Court is to guide the other courts toward an optimal realization of the basic rights and, through the treatment of "legal questions of fundamental constitutional importance" (BVerfGE 51, 130 [143]), to enable and extend the development of constitutional law (on the specialist courts' overriding duty to apply the basic rights, see BVerfGE 73, 322 [327]; compare also Schlaich [1981: 122], who draws parallels to the final appeals on points of law [*Revision*], and Schenke [1987: 29], who criticizes these parallels).

The powers of the chambers introduced in 1985 reveal the dual, objective and subjective, function of constitutional complaints. Before 1985 well-founded constitutional complaints had to be heard by the senate and could then fail due to lack of objective or subjective importance; however, the chambers have since been empowered to dismiss the complaint for the same reason in the pre-assessment procedure. Furthermore, constitutional complaints can be decided positively by the chambers so that the senates need not be troubled. The filter of objective and subjective importance is narrowed when the chambers can deal with this aspect beforehand. Generally, the senates are now more able to concentrate on clarifying and developing constitutional law. But the idea of individual legal protection was not neglected: the chambers can still grant the complaint, for example in the case of subjective unimportance, and thus help resolve the individual concern. The amendment of 1985 thus went some way toward alleviating the criticism leveled against the admission procedure without giving up the dual function.

Additionally, the discussion of the constitutionality of the acceptance procedure centers on the question of whether the finding to reject the application for a judgment contains a decision on the matter. The correct interpretation of this procedure is that three judges decline—with binding force—to allow the senate to decide upon the matter, so that the constitutional complaint remains undecided. The introduction of the granting of decisions through the chambers does not alter this interpretation. Decisions of a declining and granting nature are normatively clearly separate from one another. Article 93 b II of the Federal Constitutional Court Act specifically states that the granting decision is equivalent to a decision of the senate and is thus binding according to Article 31 I of the Federal Constitutional Court Act. Only judgments that have the character of legislation as set out in Article 31 II of the Federal Constitutional Court Act remain the prerogative of the senate. The explicit parity of chamber decisions and senate judgments of granting acceptance accentuates the difference of the decision to decline acceptance, where no such parity has been specifically established as a rule of law.

The admission procedure is the most important limitation for individual access. The amendment of 1985 introduced further measures to stem the "flood of complaints." However, these measures, the "abuse" fee that is currently up to €2,600, and the introduction of a submission fee (abolished in 1993) in the event of nonadmission—which the Court could, but did not have to impose—have not played a significant role.[1] The court has been clearly restrained in its application of the fee structure, and the former submission and actual misuse fee are not, in any case, exactly prohibitive. Consequently, they have not caused the number of constitutional complaints to decline significantly. In fact, in 1986 the number of constitutional complaints began to rise, going from 2,935 to 3,693 in 1989, and then to 5,766 in 1995; since 2007 it has exceeded 6,000 (6,477 in 2013) (Statistik des Bundesverfassungsgerichts, Tabelle "Statistik für das Geschäftsjahr 2013, Tabelle A-I-4, http://www.bundesverfassungsgericht.de/DE/Verfahren/Jahresstatistiken/2013/gb2013/A-I-4.html?nn=5493162).

Finally, for the sake of completeness, the possibility of expedited processing of a constitutional complaint has to be mentioned. It is an *a limine* rejection by the senate according to Article 24 of the Federal Constitutional Court Act, which requires prior admittance and thus no longer plays a major role in constitutional complaints. However, for most other types of procedure, it is the only form of quick dismissal. In essence, this form of rejection is already a full decision of the senate with all the consequences of a negative judgment. As of 1993, Article 81a Federal Constitutional Court Act also provides for a quick dismissal of a preliminary ruling request (art. 100 I of the Basic Law). The possibility of a decision for nonadmission of a preliminary ruling request is granted to both the senates and the chambers (Schlaich, Korioth 2012: 128).

Control of Access through Substantive Evaluation and Constitutional Interpretation

Although access to the Court is primarily controlled and defined through the admission criteria, these cannot be isolated from substantive questions (see Heun 2011: 178 et seq.). Often the interpretation of the Constitution and the demarcation of the areas of evaluation determine the acceptability of a petition. The starting point is the necessary subjective infringement of basic rights. The more extensive the sphere of protection granted by a basic right, the stronger the chances of challenging a state measure via a constitutional complaint.

Once the barriers of admission have been overcome, the area to be evaluated determines what the Court can submit to its control. In relation to this, the Court has developed the following rule: "Within the framework of a valid constitutional complaint, the Federal Constitutional Court is no longer limited in its substantive legal evaluation to examining whether one of the reprimanded infringements of basic rights is applicable. Instead, the Court can examine the constitutional harmlessness of a challenged norm from all constitutional aspects" (BVerfGE 53, 366 [390]—*Denominational Hospitals* case; see also BVerfGE 70, 138 [162]). Thus in the case of constitutional complaints by the churches, the guarantees contained in Article 140 of the Basic Law in conjunction with Article 137 of the Weimar Constitution, which do not have the character of a basic right, are used through Article 4 I of the Basic Law (freedom of religion as a basic right) as a yardstick for evaluation (see, e.g., BVerfGE 70, 138 [162]—*Duty of Loyalty* case; Schlaich, Korioth 2012: 150). The design of the admission procedure for constitutional complaints, in which a pre-evaluation of the substantive arguments is carried out, ensures that substantive aspects become a direct instrument of access control. The area of evaluation also influences access indirectly as a consequence of the interpretation of the Constitution, insofar as it determines the success of a petition and thus acts as an incentive or a deterrent for the complainant or petitioner.

In contrast to its desire to channel and ward off the flood of obviously hopeless constitutional complaints, the Court, in relation to the area of evaluation, tries in principle to expand its control competence as far and as generously as possible (see Bryde 1982: 167). This tendency reflects the self-interest of the Court as a participant in the state decision-making process. In principle, the lack of initiative, the admission criteria, and the norm-binding of judicial power demarcate the boundaries. These boundaries are already widely drawn by the Basic Law, given that comprehensive competencies exist, and the norms of the Basic Law are relatively open and indeterminate in the area of basic rights. In fact, as the decisions of the Court are final, binding on the interpretation of the Constitution, and not subordinated to another instance, it largely determines the extent of its control itself. As a consequence of its extralegal, reflexive competence to determine its competence (*Kompetenz-Kompetenz*—see Schlaich, Korioth 2012: 10), it can partially cover up the above-mentioned general limitations of judicial power. In this respect, the leeway of the Court becomes more expansive as the norms become wider, less determinate, and more open. Conversely, this means that norms of the Basic Law that are relatively precise and hardly open to interpretation do not allow much room, through competencies and procedures, for an expanded interpretation (see Schlaich, Korioth 2012: 9 who call this a "dynamic interpretation"; on the aspect of constitutional change see also Heun 1984: 26).

In this respect, the basic rights and general principles of Article 20 of the Basic Law, which need to be concretized, are special cases. It is unsurprising that the Federal Court has increased its control primarily in the area of basic rights. In fact, it has done so to such an extent that the Court is now forced to limit its area of control through other functional aspects. Here again, a large degree of flexibility is a consequence of this opposing tendency.

The most prominent and far-reaching example of an expansion of the area of control is the interpretation of Article 2 I of the Basic Law. Through its famous *Elfes* verdict (BVerfGE 6, 32 [36]), the Court expanded the sphere of protection to a general freedom of action. Through the concept of general freedom of action, the Court is able to protect all imaginable actions or spheres of human freedoms, rather than just those specified and enumerated by legislation. Any burden on a citizen imposed by a measure taken by the state is thus an infringement of basic rights that can be challenged through a constitutional complaint and is open to control by the Federal Constitutional Court. Although commonplace, however, the concept of general freedom of action is not fully accepted (see Hesse 1995: 164 et seq.; Kunig, in v. Münch, Kunig 2012: art. 2, vol. I: 126 et seq.). This dissenting opinion, as issued by Judge Grimm in particular, has caused the critical position to be included in the Federal Constitutional Court (see BVerfGE 80, 137 [164]—*Equestrian* case, as well as the majority opinion in BVerfGE 80, 137 [152]; see also Pieroth 1990: 33).

However, the broad interpretation of the internal thresholds contained in Article 2 I of the Basic Law, which is connected to this expansion of the sphere of protection, has beneficial consequences for the Court in that legal interventions by the state are now fully submitted to review by the Court. This is because every law is seen as an intervention into the protected and all-encompassing sphere of general freedom of action. This intervention is only allowed if the law complies both formally and substantively with the Constitution (BVerfGE 42, 20 [27]—*Public Road Ownership* case).

This principle, which has since been extended to cover all basic rights (e.g., BVerfGE 13, 237 [239]—*Shop Closing II* case, for Article 12 of the Basic Law; BVerfGE 44, 308 [313]—*Quorum* case, for Article 14 of the Basic Law; see also Schlaich, Korioth 2012: 12), means that an individual can challenge any burdensome law as an infringement of basic rights through the constitutional complaint procedure, even if the breach of the Constitution lies exclusively in an infringement of procedural or competency regulations. The relationship between the concrete infringement of the Constitution and the subjective basic right of the complainant is thus paradoxically and doctrinally established. At the same time, it is virtually completely dissolved and disregarded. Consequently, the same idea has to be transferred to all individual actions so that finally all illegal measures contain an infringement of basic rights of the person burdened (Heun 2011: 179; Schlaich, Korioth 2012: 10–11). For this reason any incorrect application of even the normal law by the administration, and especially by the courts, is seen as an infringement of basic rights. The basic rights have become the citizens' entitlement to dispose of any illegal intervention. The instrument for the carrying out of this entitlement is the constitutional complaint.

Through this line of reasoning, the Court submits to its review not only large parts of the allocation of competencies by the Constitution, which would be virtually out of the Court's reach due to the small number of disputes involving highest organs of the state (noted by Bryde 1982: 169), but also the judgments of all courts. The Court (within the framework of constitutional complaints) submits the allocation of competencies to review, at least inasmuch as the legislature is involved. Every Act of Parliament can be directly reviewed, so the regulations concerning federal competencies and legislative procedures often come into play. In relation to court decisions, constitutional law does not set any limits on review by the Constitutional Court.

The Court is able to fine-tune and expand upon the limitations of its area of review outlined above via several additional aspects. Certain "deduced constitutional principles" (Benda 1979: 466) are key here. They derive mainly from the rule of law (*Rechtsstaats-principle*) in conjunction with basic rights, such as the idea of the protection of valid legal expectations (see especially BVerfGE 30, 367 [386]—*Federal Damage Compensation Act* case; 30, 392 [401]—*Berlin Subsidy* case; furthermore BVerfGE 71, 1 [12]; BVerfGE 71, 255 [272]; BVerfGE 72, 175 [196]—*Housing Benefit* case; BVerfGE 72, 200 [242]—*Income Tax Law* case; BVerfGE 72, 302 [322]; see also Kisker, Püttner 1974: 149, 200; Pieroth 1981); the universal principle of proportionality (Grabitz 1973: 568; Schneider 1976: 390; Heun 2011: 195 et seq.); the extension of the area of applicability of basic rights through indirect effect on third-party beneficiaries (since BVerfGE 7, 198 [205]—*Lüth* case; see also Dürig (1975), in Maunz, Dürig n.d., art. 1 III, n. 127 and art. 3 I, n. 505; this subordinates the regular courts to review through the Federal Constitutional Court; see also Kunig, in v. Münch, Kunig 2012, vol. I: 31 et seq.); and the expansion of the protection of the basic rights against indirect (factual) infringements (see BVerfGE 38, 281 [303]—*Employee Chambers* case; BVerfGE 46, 120 [137]—*Direct Call* case; BVerfGE 53, 30 [57]—*Mülheim-Kärlich* case; also important BVerfGE 71, 183 [191]). In addition, individual basic rights are concretized through formulas that are hardly less elastic than the norm text, for example, in relation to Article 3 of the Basic Law (Equality before the Law), where these formulas retain room for decision making. The formulas justify even more abstract levels of argumentation than the basic rights already contain, such as the extension of the basic rights to a system of values (*Wertordnung*), or "decision-making from metaphors" (*Judizieren aus Bildern*—see Bryde 1982: 175 with reference to BVerfGE 40, 296 [301]—*Legislative Pay* case). They generally expand the scope for decision making (Bryde 1982: 174; see also BVerfGE 1, 14 [32]—*Southwest State* case; BVerfGE 7, 198 [205]—*Lüth* case; and finally BVerfGE 73, 261 [269] and the comments in Schwabe 1990; also see Jarass 1985: 363; critical Goerlich 1973; Denninger 1975: 545; see also Denninger 1985: 279).

Of course such universal review, which the Federal Constitutional Court has opened up through its judgments, exceeds all imaginable capacities and transcends the Court's role as a surveyor reviewing the constitutionality of state actions. For these functional reasons, the Federal Constitutional Court has reduced its review. Though the Court has not limited itself in relation to judicial review, as it sees its central role in precisely this area, and the extension of review is quantitatively hardly noticeable, it has reduced its review of other judicial judgments. In this area, the Federal Constitutional Court is in danger of being overwhelmed by the large mass of complaints. Due to the requirement that all prior legal channels be exhausted, the vast majority of constitutional complaints are aimed at final judicial decisions. Furthermore, the Federal Constitutional Court's proprium is in danger of being lost here, as the review of constitutionality will decline into the review of legality unless that is prevented. In order not to become a supreme instance of last appeal (BVerfGE 7, 198 [207]—*Lüth* case; BVerfGE 18, 85 [92]—*Specific Constitutional Law* case), the Federal Constitutional Court invented the formula of "specific constitutional law", which demarcates (and thus limits) its control from that of the specialist courts (as was first hinted at in BVerfGE 1, 418 [420]—*Punishment Law [Hessia]* case, without using the term "specific constitutional law"; identical in substance are BVerfGE 66, 116 [131]—*Wallraff* case; BVerfGE 67, 213 [223]—*Street Theater* case; BVerfGE 68, 226 [230]—*Personal Use I* case; BVerfGE 68, 361 [372]; BVerfGE 71, 162 [177]; BVerfGE 71, 162 [177]; BVerfGE 73, 206 [260]; BVerfGE 73, 261 [269]—*Sit-in I* case; also the important dissenting opinions in BVerfGE 30, 173 [218]—*Mephisto* case and BVerfGE 42, 143 [154]—*Deutschland Magazine* case). The "linguistically unfortunate" formula (Schlaich, Korioth 2012: 197; Bender 1991: 20 et seq.) means that not only must regular law be broken, but above all specific reasons of substantive constitutional law must constitute the infringement of basic rights (see Papier 1976; Steinwedel 1976; Schuppert

1978; Krauss 1987: 75; Schlaich, Korioth 2012: 214). On its own, however, the formula is not very useful.

The Federal Constitutional Court concretizes the formula further in relation to evaluation of a judgment's content, to the extent that a specific constitutional law has been broken if the specialist court has not recognized the relevance of basic rights at all or if it has underestimated the importance of individual basic rights. The breach can occur at two levels or in two steps, namely during the interpretation of the norm and, in addition, during the application of the norm to the concrete case (BVerfGE 30, 173 [188]—*Mephisto* case; for a deficit in attention to basic rights see BVerfGE 43, 130 [137]; BVerfGE 59, 231 [270]; for misjudgment BVerfGE 7, 198 [207]—*Lüth* case; BVerfGE 30, 173 [196]—*Mephisto* case; BVerfGE 42, 143 [148]—*Deutschland Magazine* case; BVerfGE 60, 348 [357]—*Extradition II* case). The Federal Constitutional Court also recognizes a breach of basic rights if the decision is objectively untenable and thus capricious (see BVerfGE 42, 64 [73]—*Compulsory Auction I* case; BVerfGE 52, 131 [157]—*Medical Liability* case; BVerfGE 57, 39 [42]; BVerfGE 58, 163 [167]; BVerfGE 62, 189 [192]; BVerfGE 64, 389 [394]; BVerfGE 71, 202 [204]; critical Schenke 1987: 37), or if it is of the opinion that the boundaries of judicial lawmaking have been overstepped (BVerfGE 22, 114 [121]; BVerfGE 34, 269 [286]—*Soraya* case; BVerfGE 34, 293 [301]; BVerfGE 49, 304 [318]; BVerfGE 54, 224 [234]; BVerfGE 54, 237 [247]; BVerfGE 63, 266 [289]; BVerfGE 65, 182 [194]—*Social Plan* case; BVerfGE 71, 354 [362]).

By this means, the Federal Constitutional Court retains its ability to overrule a judgment in exceptional cases on the basis of a breach of regular law and thus shows itself to be a supreme instance of last appeal in relation to grave miscarriages of justice. (Various commentators talk about a "noncompetence"; see Ossenbühl 1977: 313; Schlaich, Korioth 2012: 223; cf. also Bryde 1982: 313; critiquing Ossenbühl and Schlaich's argument that these judgments are usually correct, at least in their result, Schenke 1987: 55.) The demarcation of the area of review is, in addition, made more flexible by the Federal Constitutional Court's opinion that the limits of review by the constitutional judicature cannot be drawn "rigidly and cannot remain constant" (BVerfGE 18, 85 [93]—*Specific Constitutional Law* case; BVerfGE 54, 129 [135]—*Art Critic* case; BVerfGE 61, 1 [6]—*Campaign Slur* case), and that the intensity of evaluation depends upon the intensity of the infringement of a basic right (BVerfGE 35, 202 [218]—*Lebach* case). In the latter decision, the Court follows the maxim without naming it specifically. However, it refers to it in later judgments (BVerfGE 42, 143 [148]—*Deutschland Magazine* case; BVerfGE 54, 129 [135]—*Art Critic* case; BVerfGE 54, 148 [151]—*Eppler* case; BVerfGE 54, 208 [215]—*Böll* case;

BVerfGE 61, 1 [6]—*Campaign Slur* case; BVerfGE 66, 116 [131]—*Wallraff* case; see also Lincke 1986: 60 et seq.; Krauss 1987: 193).

In comparison to these careful and flexible principles of review of the contents of the judgments of specialized courts, the Federal Constitutional Court evaluates the breach of procedural basic rights virtually without limitations; in other words, it changes over to a "review of the mere legality of the actions of the court" (Schlaich, Korioth 2012: 218; see also the example of BVerfGE 74, 228 [233]; and Krauss 1987: 281; Schmidt-Aßmann 1987). The Court tries to control the burden that results from this through the "specific constitutionally guaranteed extent of legal hearing" (BVerfGE 60, 305 [310]) without it being possible to acknowledge an appropriate restraint in practice.

Finally, all of these differentiated allocation criteria are incomprehensible unless they are seen as an attempt to distribute tasks functionally between the specialized courts and the Federal Constitutional Court. The specialized courts comprehensively decide upon the interpretation of laws and their application. In doing so, they are bound by the basic rights. The Federal Constitutional Court reviews whether the basic rights have been sufficiently taken into account, and it does not hesitate to overrule a particularly grave miscarriage.

This primarily functional delimitation (see Heun 1992: 31 et seq.) of the review of the specialized courts from that of the Federal Constitutional Court needs to be strictly separated from the circumscription of review toward the legislature, which is of a different type (Bryde 1982: 387, also 315, 319). The relationship to the legislature, unlike in the case of the courts, does not concern how far the basic rights affect the rest of the legal system but instead to what extent the norms of the Constitution give the legislature, as an organ of the Constitution, room to maneuver. Functional aspects can only be reverted to in a secondary manner at this stage (Schlaich, Korioth 2012: 23–24). In fact, the workload is immaterial to determining the extent of review in relation to legislative acts (see Gawron, Rogowski 2007: 131–134).

The decision-making capabilities of the Federal Constitutional Court are characterized by numerous means of access and comprehensive review competencies on the one hand, and a differentiated "system of sluices" (Pestalozza 1982: 91) to channel and steer the flood of complaints on the other. The contrast between the far-reaching review competencies and the open access possibilities—the sharp "selection of constitutional complaints" (Zacher 1976: 396)—does not contain a (logical) contradiction. The interaction of the various factors and the flexible determination of the limits of its area of evaluation instead open up a high degree of flexibility and comprehensive access to constitutional disputes for the Court. Review by the constitutional judicature is guaranteed almost without exception but does not prevent the Court from concentrating on important constitutional questions.

Mobilization of the Court

The last part of this chapter provides some empirical evidence and contains a brief discussion of conditions of mobilization of the Federal Constitutional Court (on mobilization of law in general see Black 1973; Blankenburg 1980; on mobilization of the Federal Constitutional Court see Blankenburg, in this volume; see also Peters 1976a: 1, 1976b: 447; Bryde 1982: 154). According to the following data from the General Statistics of the Federal Constitutional Court of 31 December 2013, on that date, 207,615 cases were docketed by the Court. Even more submissions were entered into the general register (in 2013 a total of 9,052 submissions versus 6,477 docketed cases). Of all the docketed cases, 197,033 were constitutional complaints and 3,662 were concrete judicial reviews. In addition, there were 178 abstract and 187 other judicial review procedures according to Articles 100 II, III and 126 of the Basic Law. A further 180 disputes involving the highest organs of the state were commenced. Of the 197,033 constitutional complaints handled by the Court, only 4,640 were successful. This is equivalent to a quota of 2.4 percent. These figures show the obviously undeterred extremely low rate of success of constitutional complaints and their overwhelming weight compared to that of other claims. Apart from this, the raw data require further analysis and explanation in order to convey a more precise picture of the decided cases.

Despite the number of constitutional complaints, against which only concrete judicial reviews can quantitatively stand, constitutional disputes in the narrow sense do not seem to be "an important field of activity for the Federal Constitutional Court" (Bryde 1982: 155; on federal disputes see also Hesse 1989: 728). This could lead one to conclude that the subject of the judgments is primarily the relationship between the state and the citizen and basic rights, whilst relationships between the highest organs of the state, including federal relationships and thus the whole law of government, do not play a significant role. Such a conclusion would give a wrong picture of the decision-making activity of the Court for a number of reasons.

First, as we saw above, the chambers as a rule do not make a judgment on a constitutional complaint so much as they decline to accept it. In this respect, the refusal to accept is equivalent to the denial of certiorari (see Linzer 1979: 1227; on the admission of a case by the U.S. Supreme Court in general see Stern, Gressma 1978: 339 [Certiorari], 374 [Appeals], 1073 [Rules of the US Supreme Court]; see also Hart, Wechsler 1953: 1394; Rohde, Spaeth 1976: 118).

Second, the weight of the decisions is on average completely uneven. The judgment on the dissolution of the Bundestag (BVerfGE 62, 1—*Parliamentary Dissolution* case) is not commensurable with other constitutional complaints, for example regarding the right to a judicial hearing (Art. 103 of the Basic Law). In disputes involving the highest organs of the state and in disputes between the Federation and a state, the Court pronounces upon fundamental questions that are discussed in a wide context within entire norm systems. In comparison to the number of constitutional complaints conducted, the Court's decisions on the corresponding provisions of the Basic Law are tightly meshed (cf., e.g., the extent of comment in the Basic Law Commentary of Leibholz and Rinck, commented on in Bryde 1982: 470). This does not exclude the possibility that in individual cases constitutional complaints will be decided in a similar way and with comparable importance.

Third, the frequency of judgments by the constitutional judicature in the different areas is a function of the openness of the relevant norms. The rules relating to competency and procedure of government afford less room for interpretation, in the majority of cases, than do the open, undetermined basic rights and general principles. In other words, potential conflicts and possibilities for development and interpretation of the Constitution are greatly diminished in the area of the organization of the state. However, the Court's few decisions within this area are of greater importance. On the other hand, in particular the relationships between the parliament and the government are, as a consequence of the parliamentary government system, largely closed to the Federal Constitutional Court, since the conflicts are of a lesser constitutional nature and are often handled on an informal basis. For example, the constitutionally disputed restricted notices (*Sperrvermerke*) on expenditures have not yet been submitted to the Court for judgment, unlike in the United States, where the Supreme Court reviewed municipal budget control and impoundment (*Train v. City of New York,* 420 US 35 [1975]) and the legislative veto (*INS v. Chadha,* 462 US 919 [1983]). Although the parliamentary groups, and thus also the opposition parliamentary groups, are entitled, as organs of the state, to petition the Court and can enforce the rights of Parliament (BVerfGE 68, 1—*Pershing 2 and Cruise Missile II* case; this even applies to individual members of Parliament), they only partially overcome these barriers. Thus many areas remain closed to the constitutional judicature despite the fact that a number of review loopholes have been closed through cases initiated by the Greens (BVerfGE 67, 100—*Flick* case; BVerfGE 68, 1—*Pershing 2 and Cruise Missile II* case [Nachrüstung]; BVerfGE 73, 1—*Political Foundations* case; BVerfGE 73, 40—*Party Finance VI* case: Donations to Political Parties), and the fact that a substantial part of the federal order has been covered again through the case on intergovernmental fiscal relations (BVerfGE 72, 330—*Finance Equalization II* case).

Fourth, the whole area of legislative decisions, including their enactment, has been submitted to the review of the Federal Constitutional Court through numerous cases of judicial review and through the Court's opinion, already mentioned, that formally unconstitutional laws contain an infringement of basic rights. Thus the problem of the Bundestag's capability to make a decision has been raised and decided upon within the context of a constitutional complaint (BVerfGE 44, 308—*Quorum* case; BVerfGE 72, 175 [187]—*Housing Benefit* case).

If we now focus our attention on constitutional complaints, we can categorize the decided cases according to two aspects: the object of the dispute and the reprimanded infringement of basic rights. Due to the requirement of exhaustion of all legal remedies contained in Article 90 II of the Federal Constitutional Court Act, most constitutional complaints are primarily aimed at court judgments. Civil and criminal decisions dominate over those of administrative courts (see Kommers 1976: 174; cf. Bryde 1982: 156). Mistakes by the Court in reviewing civil procedure have been widely criticized (see Gerhardt 1982; Schumann 1983; Stürner 1986). Complaints against the administrative judicature are seemingly often aimed at the norm on which the decision is based (Bryde 1982: 156), so the impression remains that the ordinary judicature is frequently the respondent due to its consideration of basic rights and its handling of procedural rules. Acts of the executive and the administrative courts fade into the background by comparison. In addition, it is evident that the legislature, stimulated by the numerous possibilities of access, is a principal respondent of complaints aimed directly or indirectly at individual norms.

The comparably low quota of challenges to decisions of administrative courts indicates that the administrative judicature applies and incorporates basic rights within the framework of its judgment to a large extent. In administrative courts, the duty of official investigation (*Amtsermittlungsmaxime*) is a factor that likely reduces the number of complaints of infringement of the basic right to a judicial hearing (*rechtliches Gehör*). This observation highlights the Court's lack of opportunities to intervene in the case of a specialized court interpreting basic rights too favorably (see remarks in Bryde 1982: 171, 203). For example, when the Court found a leverage point, in relation to the ownership judgments of the Federal Supreme Court (Bundesgerichtshof, BGH), to interpret the term of "expropriation" in a more restrictive manner (BVerfGE 58, 300—*Groundwater* case), the Bundesgerichtshof was not particularly concerned thereby (see BGH, *Deutsches Verwaltungsblatt* (DVBl) 1982, 950 and BGH, DVBl 1982, 1090; on the competition between the Federal Supreme Court and the Federal Constitutional Court in this area of law see Bryde 1987).

When the cases submitted to the Federal Constitutional Court through constitutional complaints and referral from lower court judges are broken down according to reprimanded infringements of the Constitution, then it becomes plain that in an extraordinarily high number of cases the reprimands involve an infringement of the basic rights of justice, especially the right to a hearing: these cases make up approximately 45 percent of the docketed constitutional complaints (Kommers 1976: 173 for 1967; also mentioned by the government in presenting the draft for the fifth amendment of the Federal Constitutional Court Act, see BT-Drs. 10/2951, p. 6). In this area the Court has, as already mentioned above, not only legally but also factually slipped into the role of a supra-appeal court providing "emergency help" (Schumann 1985: 1134 on BVerfGE 42, 243 [248]) even in minor cases (examples are BVerfGE 67, 199; BVerfGE 69, 141; BVerfGE 70, 215; see also Rüping 1985; Wimmer 1985; and the in-depth dogmatic doctrinal critique by Mauder 1986: 45 et seq.).

The next category is that of reprimands in cases involving infringement of the principle of equality before the law, the overwhelming majority of which concern economic and social matters. Cases that call upon the classic freedoms are relatively few (Kommers 1976: 173). However, the data on the submitted complaints provide only a basic overview of the cases decided by the Court and their impact on the development of constitutional law. The number of cases based upon a basic right again mirrors the number of cases decided, but the selection of constitutional complaints largely equalizes any imbalances. In particular the freedoms contained in Articles 4 and 5 of the Basic Law, which are seldom reprimanded, make up about 6 percent of the successful constitutional complaints (see Bryde 1982: 162). In fact, some of the decisions concerning Article 5 of the Basic Law have taken on a guiding function for other basic rights decisions. This is particularly true regarding the *Lüth* judgment (BVerfGE 7, 198) and the fact that the Court's "theory of reciprocal effect" (*Wechselwirkungstheorie*) was developed in relation to Article 5 of the Basic Law (Münch 2012, vol. 1: 492 et seq.; Heun 2011: 220). The numerous reprimands of Articles 2 I, 3, 20, and 80 of the Basic Law have to be seen in conjunction with the special openness and breadth of these norms. In many judgments the Court has dealt with these norms of the Basic Law without making them more precise, not least in order to retain a high degree of flexibility for itself. In relation to other norms of the Basic Law, however, only a few decisions were necessary to concretize the basic right and ensure its comprehensive application.

Finally, the cases decided can be analyzed according to aspects derived from sociological accounts of the plaintiffs (see Bryde 1982: 157). Such an approach does not, however, contribute greatly toward the characterization of decision-making. The figures Kommers compiled on the complainants for 1967 (Kommers 1976: 171; according to Bryde 1982: 157 these figures are consistent with those in later years) show, first of all, that access to the Court is not occupied disproportionally by lawyers or by business interests, but instead primarily by "normal" citizens. Probably more than half of complaints come from prison inmates or defendants claiming violation of one of the rights granted them by Article 103 of the Basic Law. However, in this area a fundamental decision (BVerfGE 33, 1—*Prisoner's Rights* case) established the important principle of the prerogative of parliamentary legislation in all regulation relevant to basic rights (*Wesentlichkeitstheorie*; see Heun 2011: 111–112). Furthermore, the access possibilities can hardly be termed egalitarian. In particular, the requirement of exhaustion of all stages of appeal implies a transfer of the general obstacles of access to justice to the Court, despite the fact that the typical access barriers such as procedural costs, legal representation, and formal requirements are largely missing at the Federal Constitutional Court level. The starting point of a sociology of plaintiffs is virtually deflated through the selection procedure, the highly flexible control of access, and the Court's own understanding of its function as maintaining and developing the Constitution objectively. This relegates the function of individual legal protection to the background. The Court can, due to its flexible admission procedures, take on a case that statistically does not have much hope of being decided and thus help less privileged interests to be heard (Bryde 1982: 160).

In conclusion, it can be said that in the state-citizen relationship, no field of law will be untilled by the Federal Constitutional Court in the long term (Bryde 1982: 160). The large number of constitutional complaints guarantees that sufficient material from all areas of constitutional law will reach the Court for decision making. Furthermore, all actions of the state that affect individual citizens or societal groups in some way and are questionable constitutionally will at some time be submitted to review by the Court. The constitutional relations of the highest organs of the state remain outside the actual reach of control of the Federal Constitutional Court in individual areas, although even there a gradual increase of control has emerged over time.

Werner Heun is a professor of law and political science at the Faculty of Law of the University of Göttingen.

Notes

1. In 1986 the court demanded 280 prepayments, 691 submission fees, and 65 misuse fees (*Frankfurter Allgemeine Zeitung*, 9 February 1987, p. 4). The numbers for 1989 were 370 prepayments, 886 nonadmission fees, and 34 misuse fees. An exceptional number of misuse fees (66) was demanded in 1999, and in 2011 that number was again high (71); otherwise it is between 20 and 30 (statistic of the Federal Constitutional Court of 31 December 2013, http://www.bundesverfassungsgericht.de/DE/Verfahren/Jahresstatistiken/2013/gb2013/A-VIII-1.html?nn=5493162).

Bibliography

Benda, E. "BVerfG und Gesetzgeber im dritten Jahrzehnt des Grundgesetzes." *Die Öffentliche Verwaltung*, 1979, 465–470.

Benda, E. "Aktuelle Probleme der Praxis des Bundesverfassungsgerichts." *Neue Juristische Wochenschrift*, 1980, 2097–2103.

Benda, E., Klein, E. *Verfassungsprozeßrecht. Ein Lehr- und Handbuch.* Heidelberg, 2012.

Bender, M. "Rügepflichten für Verfassungsverstöße vor den Fachgerichten?" *Archiv des Öffentlichen Rechts*, Vol. 112, 1987, 169–188.

Bender, M. "Vortrag vor den Gerichten und Verfassungsbeschwerde." *Neue Juristische Wochenschrift*, 1988, 808–811.

Bender, M. *Die Befugnis der Bundesverfassungsgerichts zur Überprüfung gerichtlicher Entscheidungen. Zur Bedeutung der Grundrechte für die Rechtsanwendung.* Heidelberg, 1991.

Black, D.J. "The Mobilization of Law." *Journal of Legal Studies*, Vol. 2, 1973, 125–149.

Blankenburg, E. "Mobilisierung von Recht." *Zeitschrift für Rechtssoziologie*, Vol. 1, 1980, 33–64.

Böhmer, A. "Die Subsidiarität der Verfassungsbeschwerde." *Mannheimer Berichte*, no. 40, November 1992, 19–26.

Bryde, B.O. "Der Kampf um die Definition von Artikel 14 GG." In Blankenburg, E., Voigt, R., Gawron, T., Rogowski, R., eds., *Implementation von Gerichtsentscheidungen. Jahrbuch für Rechtssoziologie und Rechtstheorie*, Vol. 11, Opladen, 1987, 384–394.

Bryde, B.O. "Verfassungsentwicklung", Baden-Baden, 1982.

Denninger, E. "Freiheitsordnung – Wertordnung – Pflichtordnung Zur Entwicklung der Grundrechtsjudikatur des Bundesverfassungsgerichts." *Juristenzeitung*, 1975, 545–550.

Denninger, E. "Verfassungsrechtliche Schlüsselbegriffe." In Broda, C., Deutsch, E., Schreiber, H.-L., Vogel, H.-J., eds., *Festschrift für Rudolf Wassermann zum sechzigsten Geburtstag.* Neuwied, 1985, 279–298.

Friesenhahn, E. "Die Verfassungsgerichtsbarkeit in der Bundesrepublik Deutschland." In *Verfassungsgerichtsbarkeit in der Gegenwart. Länderberichte und Rechtsvergleichung.* International Colloquium of the Max Planck Institute for Comparative Public Law and International Law,, Cologne, 1962, 89–197.

Gawron, T., Rogowski, R. *Die Wirkung des Bundesverfassungsgerichts. Rechtssoziologische Analysen.* Baden-Baden, 2007.

Gerhardt, W. "Bundesverfassungsgericht, Grundgesetz und Zivilprozeß, speziell Zwangsvollstreckung." *Zeitschrift für Zivilprozeßrecht,* Vol. 95, 1982, 467–494.

Gerontas, A. "Zur Subsidiarität der Verfassungsbeschwerde gegen ein Gesetz," *Die Öffentliche Verwaltung,* 1982, 440–447.

Gesetzentwurf der Bundesregierung. Entwurf eines Fünften Gesetzes zur Änderung des Gesetzes über das Bundesverfassungsgericht, Bundestagsdrucksache 10/2951. Bonn, 28 February 1985.

Goerlich, H. *Wertordnung und Grundgesetz. Kritik einer Argumentationsfigur des Bundesverfassungsgerichts.* Baden-Baden, 1973.

Grabitz, E. "Der Grundsatz der Verhältnismäßigkeit in der Rechtsprechung des Bundesverfassungsgerichts." *Archiv des Öffentlichen Rechts,* Vol. 98, 1973, 568–616.

Hart, H.M., Jr., Wechsler, H. *The Federal Courts and the Federal System.* Brooklyn, 1953.

Hein, P.E. *Die Unvereinbarerklärung verfassungswidriger Gesetze durch das Bundesverfassungsgericht. Grundlagen, Anwendungsbereich, Rechtsfolgen.* Baden-Baden, 1988.

Henning, S. "Die besonderen Zulässigkeitsvoraussetzungen der Rechtssatz-Verfassungsbeschwerde in der Rechtsprechung des Bundesverfassungsgerichts." Ph.D. dissertation, Göttingen, 1981.

Henschel, J.F. "Rechtswegerschöpfung im Verfahren der Verfassungsbeschwerde." In Zeidler, W. et al., eds., *Festschrift Hans Joachim Faller.* Munich, 1984, 165–172.

Henseler, P. "Rechtsschutz gegen Bebauungspläne in Gesetzesform." *Jura,* 1986, 249–259.

Hesse, K. "Wandlung der Bedeutung des Verfassungsgerichtsbarkeit für die bundesstaatliche Ordnung." In Haller, W., Kölz, A., Müller, G., Thürer, D., eds., *Im Dienst an der Gemeinschaft. Festschrift für Dietrich Schindler zum 65. Geburtstag.* Basel, 1989, 723–731.

Hesse, K. *Grundzüge der Verfassungsrechts der Bundesrepublik Deutschland,* 20th ed. Heidelberg, 1995.

Heun, W. "Die Stellung des Bundespräsidenten im Licht der Vorgänge um die Auflösung des Bundestages." *Archiv des Öffentlichen Rechts,* Vol. 109, 1984, 13–36.

Heun, W. *Funktionell-rechtliche Schranken der Verfassungsgerichtsbarkeit. Reichweite und Grenzen einer dogmatischen Argumentationsfigur.* Baden-Baden, 1992.

Heun, W. "Richtervorlagen in der Rechtsprechung der Bundesverfassungsgerichts. *Archiv des Öffentlichen Rechts,* Vol. 122, 1997, 610–628.

Heun, W. *The Constitution of Germany. A Contextual Analysis.* Oxford, Portland, 2011.

Heyde, W. "Das Bundesverfassungsgericht in der Bewährung." In Grewe, W.G., Rupp, H., Schneider, H., eds., *Europäische Gerichtsbarkeit und nationale Verfassungsgerichtsbarkeit. Festschrift zum 70. Geburtstag von Hans Kutscher.* Baden-Baden, 1981, 229–246.

Jarass, H.D. "Grundrechte als Wertentscheidung bzw. objektivrechtliche Prinzipien in der Rechtsprechung in der Rechtsprechung des Bundesverfassungsgerichts." *Archiv des Öffentlichen Rechts,* Vol. 110, 1985, 363–397.

Kisker, G., Püttner, G. "Vertrauensschutz im Verwaltungsrecht." *Veröffentlichungen der Vereinigung der Deutschen Staatsrechtslehrer,* Vol. 32, 1974, 149–227.

Klein, E. "Subsidiarität der Verfassungsgerichtsbarkeit und Subsidiarität der Verfassungsbeschwerde." In Fürst, W., Herzog, R., Umbach, D., eds., *Festschrift für Wolfgang Zeidler,* Vol. 2. Berlin, 1987, 1305–1323.

Kommers, D.J. *Judicial Politics in West Germany: A Study of the Federal Constitutional Court.* Beverly Hills, 1976.

Krauss, F. *Der Umfang der Prüfung von Zivilurteilen durch das Bundesverfassungsgericht.* Cologne, 1987.

Lange, P. *Darlegungs- und Substantiierungspflichten im Verfassungsbeschwerdeverfahren.* Baden-Baden, 2012.

Lerche, P. "Aspekte verfassungsrechtlicher Subsidiarität in Deutschland und Österreich." In Wilke, D., ed., *Festschrift zum 125 jährigen Bestehen der Juristischen Gesellschaft zu Berlin.* Berlin, 1984, 369–380.

Lincke, D. "Zur Bedeutung der 'Eingriffsintensität' für den Umfang der Nachprüfung gerichtlicher Entscheidungen durch das Bundesverfassungsgericht." *Europäische Grundrechtszeitschrift,* Vol. 13, 1986, 60–73.

Linzer, P. "The Meaning of Certiorari Denied." *Columbia Law Review,* Vol. 79, 1979, 1227–1305.

Löwer, W. "Zuständigkeiten und Verfahren vor dem Bundesverfassungsgericht." In Isensee, J., Kirchhof, P., eds., *Handbuch des Staatsrechts der Bundesrepublik Deutschland,* vol. 3, 3rd ed. Heidelberg, 2005, 1285–1526.

Mahrenholz, E.G. "Kammerbeschlüsse – Nichtannahmegebühren – Neue Institute im Verfassungsbeschwerdeverfahren." In Fürst, W., Herzog, R., Umbach, D., eds., *Festschrift für Wolfgang Zeidler,* vol. 2. Berlin, 1987, 1361–1377.

Mauder, J. *Der Anspruch auf rechtliches Gehör, seine Stellung im System der Grundrechte und seine Auswirkung auf die Abgrenzungsproblematik zwischen Verfassungs- und Fachgerichtsbarkeit.* Munich, 1986.

Maunz, T., Dürig, G. *Grundgesetz. Kommentar,* 8th ed. Munich, n.d., loose-leaf collection.

Maunz, T., Schmidt-Bleibtreu, B., Klein, F., Bethge, H. *Bundesverfassungsgerichtsgesetz. Kommentar.* Munich, n.d., loose-leaf collection.

Mirbach, G. Freiherr v. "Zur Fünften Novelle des BVerfGG." *Neue Juristische Wochenschrift,* 1986, 2096–2097.

Münch, I. von, Kunig, P., eds. *Grundgesetz-Kommentar,* 2 vols, 6th ed. Munich, 2012.

Ossenbühl, F. "Verfassungsgerichtsbarkeit und Fachgerichtsbarkeit." In Stödter, R., Thieme, W., eds., *Hamburg, Deutschland, Europa. Beiträge zum deutschen und europäischen Verfassungs-, Verwaltungs- und Wirtschaftsrecht. Festschrift für Hans Peter Ipsen zum siebzigsten Geburtstag.* Tübingen, 1977, 129–141.

Papier, H.J. "'Spezifisches Verfassungsrecht' und 'einfaches Recht' als Argumentationsformel des Bundesverfassungsgerichts." In Starck, C., ed., *Bundesverfassungsgericht und Grundgesetz. Festgabe aus Anlaß des 25jährigen Bestehens des Bundesverfassungsgerichts,* vol. 1. Tübingen, 1976, 432–457.

Pestalozza, C. *Verfassungsprozeßrecht. Die Verfassungsgerichtsbarkeit des Bundes und der Länder,* 2nd ed. Munich, 1982.

Pestalozza, C. *Verfassungsprozeßrecht. Die Verfassungsgerichtsbarkeit des Bundes und der Länder mit einem Anhang zum Internationalen Rechtsschutz,* 3rd ed. Munich, 1991.

Pestalozza, C. "Änderungen des Bundesverfassungsgerichtsgesetzes." *Deutsches Wirtschaftsrecht,* 1992, 426–432.

Peters, K. "Ergebnisse von Vorlagen nach Art. 100 Abs. 1 GG und einige Überlegungen dazu." *Zeitschrift für Zivilprozeßrecht,* Vol. 89, 1976a, 1–43.

Peters, K. "Die Verfassungsbeschwerde in der amtlichen Sammlung des Bundesverfassungsgerichts." *Monatszeitschrift des Deutschen Rechts,* 1976b, 447–452.

Pieroth, B. *Rückwirkung und Übergangsrecht. Verfassungsrechtliche Maßstäbe für intertemporale Gesetzgebung.* Berlin, 1981.

Pieroth, B. "Der Wert der Auffangfunktion des Artikel 2 Abs. 1 GG." *Archiv des Öffentlichen Rechts,* Vol. 115, 1990, 33–44.

Posser, H. *Die Subsidiarität der Verfassungsbeschwerde.* Berlin, 1993.

Rinken. A. "The Federal Constitutional Court and the German Political System." In Rogowski, R., Gawron, T., eds., *Constitutional Courts in Comparison: The U.S. Supreme Court and the German Federal Constitutional Court.* New York, Oxford, 2002, 55–90.

Rohde, D.W., Spaeth, H.J. *Supreme Court Decision Making.* San Francisco, 1976.

Rüping, H. "Verfassungs- und Verfahrensrecht im Grundsatz des rechtlichen Gehörs." *Neue Zeitschrift für Verwaltungsrecht,* 1985, 304–309.

Sachs, M., "Die konkrete Normenkontrolle – nur ein Instrument zum Schutze subjektiver Grundrechte der Beteiligten?" *Deutsches Verwaltungsblatt,* 1985, 1106–1112.

Sailer, C. "Verfassungsbeschwerde im Zwielicht." *Zeitschrift für Rechtspolitik,* 1977, 303–310.

Schenke, W.R. *Rechtsschutz bei normativem Unrecht.* Berlin, 1979.

Schenke, W.R. "Unmittelbares Betroffensein durch Bebauungsplan – Rechtswegerschöpfung und Rechtsschutz – Normenkontrolle gemäß § 47 Abs 1 Nr 1 VwGO gegen als formelles Gesetz erlassenen Bebauungsplan" (case note). *Deutsches Verwaltungsblatt,* 1985, 1367–1370.

Schenke, W.R. "Die Subsidiarität der Verfassungsbeschwerde gegen Gesetze." *Neue Juristische Wochenschrift,* 1986, 1451–1461.

Schenke, W.R. *Verfassungsgerichtsbarkeit und Fachgerichtsbarkeit.* Heidelberg, 1987.

Schlaich, K. "Verfassungsgerichtsbarkeit im Gefüge der Staatsfunktionen." *Veröffentlichungen der Vereinigung der Deutschen Staatsrechtslehrer,* Vol. 39, 1981, 99–146.

Schlaich, K., Korioth, S. *Das Bundesverfassungsgericht. Stellung, Verfahren, Entscheidungen,* 9th ed. Munich, 2012.

Schlink, B. "Nochmals: Die Vorprüfung der Verfassungsbeschwerde durch die Präsidialräte." *Neue Juristische Wochenschrift,* 1984a, 2195–2196.

Schlink, B. "Zugangshürden zum Verfassungsbeschwerdeverfahren." *Neue Juristische Wochenschrift,* 1984b, 89–94.

Schlink, B. "Die dritte Abhörentscheidung des Bundesverfassungsgerichts." *Neue Juristische Wochenschrift,* 1989, 11–16.

Schmidt-Aßmann, E. "Verfahrensfehler als Verletzung des Art. 103 Abs. 1 GG." *Die Öffentliche Verwaltung,* 1987, 1029–1037.

Schneider, H. "Zur Verhältnismäßigkeitskontrolle, insbesondere bei Gesetzen." In Starck, C., ed., *Bundesverfassungsgericht und Grundgesetz. Festgabe aus Anlass des 25jährigen Bestehens des Bundesverfassungsgerichts,* vol. 2. Tübingen, 1976, 390–404.

Schorkopf, F. "Die prozessuale Steuerung des Verfassungsrechtsschutzes." *Archiv des öffentlichen Rechts,* Vol. 130, 2005, 465–493.

Schumann, E. *Bundesverfassungsgericht, Grundgesetz und Zivilprozeß.* Munich, 1983.

Schumann, E. "Die Wahrung des Grundsatzes des rechtlichen Gehörs – Dauerauftrag für das Bundesverfassungsgericht?" *Neue Juristische Wochenschrift,* 1985, 1134–1140.

Schuppert, G.F. "Zur Nachprüfung gerichtlicher Entscheidungen durch das Bundesverfassungsgericht." *Archiv des Öffentlichen Rechts,* Vol. 103, 1978, 43–69.

Schwabe, J. "Verfassungswidrigkeit des § 90a Abs 2 S 2 HGB—entschädigungsloses Wettbewerbsverbot für einen Handelsvertreter" (case note). *Deutsches Verwaltungsblatt,* 1990, 477–480.

Seetzen, U. "Die Anhörungsrüge kraft Verfassungsrecht." *Neue Juristische Wochenschrift,* 1982, 2337–2344.

Starck, C. "Verfassungsgerichtsbarkeit und Fachgerichte." *Juristenzeitung,* 1996, 1033–1041.

Steinwedel, U. *"Spezifisches Verfassungsrecht" und "einfaches Recht". Der Prüfungsumfang des Bundesverfassungsgerichts bei Verfassungsbeschweren gegen Gerichtsentscheidungen.* Baden-Baden, 1976.

Stern, R.L., Gressma, E. *Supreme Court Practice,* 5th ed. Washington, D.C., 1978.

Strietzel, C. *Die Zulässigkeit von Verfassungsbeschwerden gegen gerichtliche Eilentscheidungen.* Frankfurt/Main, 1993.

Stürner, R. "Die Kontrolle zivilprozessualer Verfahrensfehler durch das Bundesverfassungsgericht." *Juristenzeitung,* 1986, 526–534.

Ulsamer, G. "Zulässigkeitsvoraussetzungen der konkreten Normenkontrollverfahren in der Rechtsprechung des Bundesverfassungsgerichts." *Bayrisches Verwaltungsblatt,* 1980, 519–523.

Ulsamer, G. "Neue gesetzliche Regelungen des Bundesverfassungsgerichts." *Europäische Grundrechtezeitschrift,* Vol 13, 1986, 110–116.

Vitzthum, W. "Das Vorprüfungsverfahren für Verfassungsbeschwerden." In Püttner, G., ed., *Festschrift für Otto Bachof zum 70. Geburtstag am 6. März 1984.* Munich, 1984, 293–320.

Wahl, R., Wieland, J. "Verfassungsrechtssprechung als knappes Gut." *Juristenzeitung,* 1996, 1127–1145.

Wand, W.R. "Befugnisse der Gerichtsverwaltung und Aspekte der Vorprüfung im Verfassungsbeschwerdeverfahren." *Neue Juristische Wochenschrift,* 1984, 950–954.

Wank, R. "Die verfassungsrechtliche Kontrolle der Gesetzesauslegung und Rechtsfortbildung durch die Fachgerichte." *Juristische Schulung,* 1980, 545–553.

Weis, H. "Gegenvorstellungen bei Verletzungen von Verfahrensgrundsätzen" (case note). *Neue Juristische Wochenschrift,* 1987, 1314–1315.

Wimmer, R. "Die Wahrung des Grundsatzes des rechtlichen Gehörs." *Deutsches Verwaltungsblatt,* 1985, 773–780.

Wormke, R. *Die Subsidiarität der Verfassungsbeschwerde.* Berlin, 1993.

Zacher, H.F. "Die Selektion der Verfassungsbeschwerden – Die Siebfunktion der Vorprüfung, des Erfordernisses der Rechtswegerschöpfung und des Kriteriums der unmittelbaren und gegenwärtigen Betroffenheit des Beschwerdeführers." In Starck, C., ed., *Bundesverfassungsgericht und Grundgesetz. Festgabe aus Anlaß des 25jährigen Bestehens des Bundesverfassungsgerichts,* vol. 1. Tübingen, 1976, 396–431.

Zuck, R. "Die Beseitigung groben prozessualen Unrechts." *Juristenzeitung,* 1985, 921–927.

Zuck, R. "Die Fünfte Novelle zum BVerfGG." *Neue Juristische Wochenschrift,* 1986a, 968–971.

Zuck, R. "Die Mißbrauchsgebühr im Verfassungsbeschwerdeverfahren." *Neue Juristische Wochenschrift,* 1986b, 2093–2096.

Zuck, R. "Das Bundesverfassungsgericht als Dritte Kammer." *Zeitschrift für Rechtspolitik,* 1987, 189–195.

Zuck, R. *Das Recht der Verfassungsbeschwerde,* 3rd ed. Munich, 2006.

Chapter 3

Mobilization of the German Federal Constitutional Court

Erhard Blankenburg

Constitutional lawyers like to portray the complaint procedure as an open door through which "anybody" can pass in order to question statutes and institutions of the Federal Republic of Germany. Sending a complaint (even without the help of a lawyer) is easy, as is pointing to some basic constitutional right when people feel seriously violated. Indeed, the text of the Constitution is more general than any statute or regulation. As constitutions in general contain open norms, it is up to the constitutional courts to determine case by case what they mean. Constitutions have gained increased importance in newly established democratic regimes where politics and law have to be institutionalized from scratch. In fact, in postcommunist, postapartheid, and postfascist states, establishing constitutional courts has often been prioritized over organizing ordinary courts to work effectively. The German Federal Constitutional Court was founded with the intention of helping to overcome the perversion of law under the Nazi regime. Similar revolutionary new beginnings led Spain in 1976, postcommunist countries in Central and Eastern Europe, and South Africa in the 1990s to take the German Constitutional Court as a model and to follow its example of an open access complaint procedure.

The specialness of these courts and procedures in the Civil Law tradition is evident in self-confident democracies such as the Scandinavian countries, where no more than a handful of constitutional review cases are filed annually (in the respective supreme courts), or the Netherlands and United Kingdom, which reject any possibility of "constitutional review" (the latter country, as is well known, has never codified a constitution at all). Nevertheless, even they are subject to an international trend of "constitutionalization" of law and politics. Nowadays they are regularly compelled to meet internationally accepted legal standards enshrined, for example, in the European Convention of Human Rights, enforced by the European Court of Human Rights in Strasbourg, or in foundational documents of the European Union, interpreted and enforced by the Court of the European Union in Luxembourg.

The pioneering role of the German Federal Constitutional Court and its open access for a multitude of constitutional complaints will become obvious when we look at the Court's procedures and its attempts to influence mobilization and curb the overwhelming caseload of complaints. In the first part of this chapter, the various roads toward constitutional review are outlined briefly. The succeeding parts contain analyses of the volume and type of the constitutional complainants. Finally, conclusions are drawn about the Court's political role.

The Many Roads toward Constitutional Review

Determining political issues in the light of the Constitution has become a trademark of German politics. The driving force behind this development has been the Federal Constitutional Court at Karlsruhe. Whereas some procedures, such as the "reprimand" or the impeachment procedure, have never been used, four others are key: Privileged access is granted to parties and groups within Parliament as well as the highest organs or branches of the Federal Republic of Germany (disputes involving the highest federal bodies are termed *Organklage*). The federal government, the state governments, and a group of members of Parliament can request constitutional review of statutes (abstract judicial review or abstract norm control—*abstrakte Normenkontrolle.*). Judges of other courts can ask the Court to decide on the constitutionality of provisions in the statutes relevant to their cases (concrete norm control or preliminary ruling—*konkrete Normenkontrolle*). And individual citizens can lodge complaints against any infringements of their basic rights (constitutional complaint—*Verfassungsbeschwerde*). "Anybody" can raise a constitutional complaint—that is, it may be filed by any person alleging that one of his or her basic rights has been infringed by public authority (art. 90 I of the Federal Constitutional Court Act, since 1969 also mentioned in the Constitution in art. 93 I 4a of the Basic Law). Legal action by supranational authorities (such as the European Union, including the Court of the European Union) can be challenged on the grounds that its legal character and principles are not in conformity with the basic guarantees of the German constitution, or that it violates the "constitutional identity" of the Federal Republic. Since this is hard to argue successfully, a more promising strategy is to challenge the legality of German statutes implementing European law and regulations, which happens quite frequently.

The Court's landmark decisions have resulted from diverse issues and political and social conflicts. In the 1950s, the Court ambitiously enlarged its competencies and thereby opened the gates of access for individual complainants. Its extensive interpretation of individual freedom (art. 2 I of the Basic Law) and the right to equal treatment (art. 3 I of the Basic Law) enabled complainants to challenge almost any legal action of the state (see the *Elfes* case—BVerfGE 6, 32). However, the precondition for invoking the Constitutional Court is the exhaustion of all other means of judicial remedy, so most complainants base their claim on a violation of the due process clause (art. 103 of the Basic Law; see Gawron, Rogowski 2007: 97, Tabelle 4-4). This results in the practice of directing most complaints against decisions of other courts (*Urteilsverfassungsbeschwerden*).

Since the 1950s, many opposition groups have mobilized the Constitutional Court to force constitutional decisions ranging from central issues of German democracy down to the banalities of everyday life. In some cases, the parliamentary opposition chose to make use of the abstract judicial review procedure, as when it challenged the crucial issue of rearmament in the 1950s (BVerfGE 1, 281—*European Defence Community* case and BVerfGE 1, 96, cases instigated by the SPD opposition in Parliament), questioned the pension rights of former Nazi civil servants after the Third Reich had ceased to exist (BVerfGE 3, 58—*Civil Servant* case, instigated by the SPD opposition in Parliament plus constitutional complaints by individuals), and tested the incorporation of the Saarland into the Federation (BVerfGE 4, 157—*Saar Treaty* case, instigated by the SPD opposition in Parliament). In other instances, it was the governments of the States that used the abstract judicial review procedure, as in the case of the East-West Treaty between the Federal Republic and the German Democratic Republic (BVerfGE 36, 1—*East-West Basic Treaty* case, instigated by the Bavarian government).

Members of Parliament have regularly used the constitutional complaints procedure to contest central political agreements. In this way they challenged both the opening of relations with Eastern Germany, by questioning the constitutionality of the treaties with the GDR (BVerfGE 40, 141—*East Agreements* case); and the establishment of the European Union, by questioning the constitutionality of the Maastricht Treaty (BVerfGE 89, 155—*Maastricht* case), the latter being a prime example of a strategy reinforcing national sovereignty. More recently the Treaty of Lisbon led to a number of suspense motions, first instigated by a single member of parliament (BVerfGE 123, 267—*Lisbon Treaty* case) and later followed by a formal *Organklage* of the parliamentary group Die Linke, and by constitutional complaints by fifty-three individual members of Parliament as well as a complaint by a few individual citizens. Although these attempts did not succeed in suspending the treaty, they convinced the Court to strengthen the right of parliamentary consent of the Bundestag to the transfer of sovereignty to the European Union. A formal *Organklage* (BVerfGE 130, 318—*European Financial Stability Facility-EFSF* case) and several constitutional complaints were also lodged in 2011 against aid measures for Greece and the euro rescue package, but these attempts failed, and the court saw no violation of the parliament's decision-making powers in budgetary matters.

Many historical decisions of the Court lead to chains of further judgments in which the Court elaborates on its constitutional doctrine. The decision against a television channel controlled by the conservative government of Adenauer in 1961 (BVerfGE 12, 205—*Television I* case, instigated by the government of the city-state of Hamburg) laid the cornerstone for the Court's jurisprudence on the freedom of the press. Similarly, the chain of cases on party financing (BVerfGE 8, 51—*Party Finance II* case, instigated by the government of Hessen; and BVerfGE 20,56—*Party Finance II* case, as well as BVerfGE 73,40—*Party Finance II* case, instigated by various small parties) and abortion (BVerfGE 39, 1—*Abortion I* case; BVerfGE 88, 203—*Abortion II* case) paved the way for constitutional doctrine on the limits of parliamentary and individual self-determination.

The cases demonstrate that almost any sensitive issue in German politics can stimulate a clever lawyer or university professor to translate the political issue into a question of constitutional relevance. They set the pace for series of follow-up claims and have encouraged the provision of special training in preparing constitutional complaints, for instance for prison inmates lodging complaints about violation of basic procedural and treatment rights. Such complaints have little chance of success, but they can gain media attention. For example, this was the case with the challenge to a treaty of the German-speaking countries on an orthographic reform of the German language (BVerfGE 21 June 1996, 1 BvR 1057/96 and 1067/96), instigated by a law professor and his eight-year-old daughter, who had just managed to master the former orthography. Other examples were taxpayers claiming that their fundamental property rights were violated, schoolchildren and their parents claiming that removal of crucifixes from classrooms violated their religious freedom (BVerfGE 93, 1—*Classroom Crucifix II* case), and recipients of welfare payments claiming that the allegedly insufficient living standard provided by state support violated their human dignity. Between 1951 and 2013, the Court received 197,033 complaints, of which only 2.4 percent (4,640 cases) were successful and the overwhelming majority were rejected (Bundesverfassungsgericht, Statistik für das Geschäftsjahr 2013, Tabelle A I 1: Verfahren seit 7. September 1951 bis 31. Dezember 2013"; see also Table 3.1).

Occasionally, organized floods of complaints bring the Court to the center of a political campaign. In 1973, 1,735 taxpayers protested against an

Table 3.1. Number of Admitted Complaints and Their Success Rate, 1987–2013

Year	*Complaints admitted*	*Percent successful*
1987	2,638	3.56
1988	2,975	2.82
1989	3,204	2.72
1990	3,715	17.09
1991	3,452	7.13
1992	3,782	5.55
1993	4,927	5.48
1994	4,901	3.29
1995	4,743	2.93
1996	4,853	2.25
1997	4,663	0.79
1998	4,695	2.15
1999	4,872	2.11
2000	4,884	1.50
2001	4,575	1.95
2002	4,452	2.25
2003	4,499	1.80
2004	5,434	2.19
2005	4,808	2.77
2006	5,876	2.31
2007	6,037	2.45
2008	5,852	1.90
2009	5,911	1.88
2010	6,021	1.71
2011	5,777	1.62
2012	5,327	2.78
2013	6,238	1.46

Source: Bundesverfassungsgericht, "Statistik für das Geschäftsjahr 2013, Tabelle A IV 2: Anteil der stattgegebenen an den entschiedenen Verfassungsbeschwerden pro Jahr seit 1987" at http://www.bundesverfassungsgericht.de/DE/Verfahren/Jahresstatistiken/2013/statistik_2013_node.html;jsessionid=23561FF2CA58326FAF119F4D6B567955.2_cid370.

"economic stability tax" (which explains the peak in constitutional complaints for 1973 displayed in Figure 3.1). Three years later 381 complaints were launched against the federal abortion law, and in 1983 numerous complaints were raised against the general census questionnaires. Although most of these complaints were unsuccessful in the end, they at least raised political awareness, improved chances for further protest, and occasionally, if accompanied by a request for a preliminary injunction, had postponing effects. In the end, it is the media attention and not the chances of success that render mobilizing the Court attractive.

Looking at Figure 3.1, we notice the overriding trend of a steady rise in constitutional complaints. Peaks can largely be explained as single-issue protest against unpopular legislative decisions that lead, with a few years' delay, to a flood of complaints. When such political campaigns ebb, the number of complaints returns to normal levels.

With its popular constitutional complaint procedure, the Court acts in a socio-legal perspective as an ombudsman institution. Furthermore, the Court receives not only formal complaints but also numerous letters in which the staff cannot detect any relevant information on a violation of the constitution. Such communications and trivial constitutional complaints are usually shelved after the first screening. The complainants in these cases normally receive a friendly letter; however, since the procedural reform of 1986 a few are penalized for abuse of constitutional review.

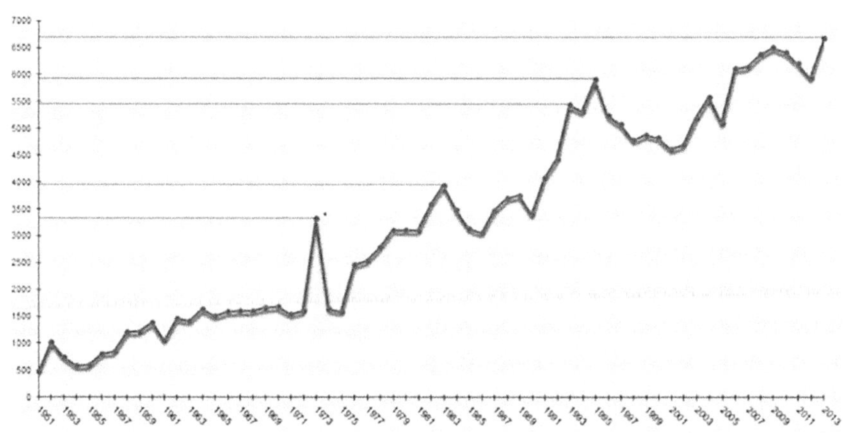

Figure 3.1. Caseload of the Federal Constitutional Court, 7 September 1951–31 December 2013

* decided in so-called parallel procedures.

Source: Bundesverfassungsgericht, "Statistik für das Geschäftsjahr 2013, Tabelle A I 3: Grafische Darstellung der Verfahrenseingänge" at http://www.bundesverfassungsgericht.de/DE/Verfahren/Jahresstatistiken/2013/statistik_2013_node.html;jsessionid=23561FF2CA58326FAF119F4D6B567955.2_cid370.

The precondition that complainants must have exhausted all other legal remedies shapes the selection of issues and the arguments used in mobilizing the Court. Complainants who have gone through several appeal instances are driven by a strong sense of (in)justice when pursuing their concern further at the Constitutional Court, where statistically speaking their chances of success are minimal. The folklore of the Court holds colorful examples of permanent complainers whose "querulous stories" fill the archives. An estimated 10 to 30 percent of all cases belong in this category, depending on the definition of pathological behavior. We have tried to construct a "Q"-index of complaints in a sample of files from 1955 to 1995 (Table 3.2).

Table 3.2. "Querulous" Cases at the Federal Constitutional Court, 1955–1995

1955: 18%
1965: 13%
1975: 11%
1985: 12%
1990: 16%
1995: 12%

Source: Own survey of a "Q"-index (see Blankenburg 1998).

The index presented in Table 3.2 comprises files that contain insulting remarks, unclear writing, confused argumentation, or (frequently occurring) complaints against judges, lawyers and others associated with previous procedures. Our admittedly subjective index shows that over thirty years, a period in which the caseload grew tenfold, the "Q" percentage remained rather constant.

Attempts to Curb the Flood of Constitutional Complaints

While ordinary courts cannot decide to reject a legal conflict that falls into their jurisdiction, the Constitutional Court has the privilege of deciding whether it considers a claim "relevant" for treatment. Since the beginning, the Court has faced ever increasing caseloads and had to find ways of managing it. Over its sixty plus years of operation it has developed a number of procedures for the selection of cases for admittance.

In the first years of its existence, the Court heard all complaints in the First Senate, and every decision was handed down with a written reasoning. However, few cases were accepted. Of all complaints received in 1955, only one was admitted. As early as 1956, when the Court received

686 complaints, concerns about the caseload being too high began to be voiced. The legislature reacted by passing the first amendment of the Federal Constitutional Court Act, which introduced a simplified admittance procedure: three-judge deciding committees (*Dreierausschuss*) could decline to admit a constitutional complaint by unanimous vote. If no agreement was reached between them, then one of the two senates, depending on the scheme dividing jurisdictions, had to decide.

Still, the number of constitutional complaints continued to rise, reaching 1,349 in 1963. In that year an amendment to the Federal Constitutional Court Act enlarged the grounds for admitting a complaint, but at the same time the Court limited its responsibility to review high court decisions to cases that contained a "principally wrong interpretation of a basic right" (the so-called "Heck formula," named after the judge who introduced it in 1964 in BVerfGE 18, 85—*Specific Constitutional Law* case). It remains unclear how effective each such doctrinal change in the admittance procedure was, but the Court managed to master the crisis by taking organizational measures, such as increasing the number of legal assistants per judge to three, and later to four.

Nevertheless, the caseload rose to 1,606 complaints in 1970, which in turn caused the legislature to amend the Federal Constitutional Court Act again in 1971. This amendment allowed the Court to deny admittance if it considered the case "not having sufficient chances of success" (art. 93a III of the Federal Constitutional Court Act, abolished in 1993). The court has the power of to levy a penalty (between €100 and €2,600) for frivolous abuse (art. 34 II of the Federal Constitutional Court Act). According to official court statistics, the average penalty has been around €200 (Bundesverfassungsgericht, "Statistik für das Geschäftsjahr 2013, Tabelle A VIII 1: Missbrauchsgebühren seit 1962").

Nobody was surprised, however, when in spite of ever new admittance rules the caseload continued to rise, reaching 3,828 cases in 1983. Some extreme spikes in the trend were caused by campaigns against the stability tax in 1973, against the regulation of abortion in 1976, and against the population census in 1986. Constitutional complaints subsequently became fashionable, and invoking the Constitutional Court became a means of protest. Since 1990, complaints against asylum decisions have become popular because they help to suspend deportation and have a comparatively high success rate (16 percent in 1990). In the early 1990s, asylum cases, accompanied by demands for preliminary rulings, created a new source of work for the Court. The flood of asylum cases had to be decided summarily in a "parallel procedure." The legislature reacted by amending the constitution in 1993, introducing the new, separate Article 16a of the Basic Law that regulates the right of asylum.

The legislature has several times helped the Court curb the flood of cases by amending the Federal Constitutional Court Act. In 1985 and 1993, the three-judge committees in charge of admitting constitutional complaints were renamed chambers, and the procedure for non-admittance of a complaint was simplified by dropping the requirement to state a reason for rejection. But despite the procedural changes, cases of constitutional complaints continued to rise. After asylum cases peaked in the first half of the 1990s, the caseload of complaints temporarily dropped to 4,499 in 2003, but the following years brought further disillusion with respect to reducing the flood of complaints. By 2013, the docketed caseload of constitutional complaints rose to 6,477. In the same year, 6,369 were admitted for decision making.

Issues of Constitutional Complaints

The issues addressed by constitutional complaints cover a large variety of legal fields. Donald Kommers (1976), in his analysis of party constellations of complaints in the first fifteen years of the Court, identified prison inmates and persons claiming due process in some criminal procedure as the main group of complainants. The second largest group consisted of taxpayers protesting unequal treatment. Neither group has ever diminished in importance, but other types of complaints have accompanied theirs. Table 3.3 lists the numbers of constitutional complaints against judicial decisions, sorted by judicial jurisdictions.

Table 3.3. Constitutional Complaints against Judicial Decisions of Other Courts, 1991–2013

Civil courts	45,349 (39.9%)
Criminal courts	29,827 (26.2%)
Administrative courts	15,210 (13.4%)
Asylum cases	8,689 (7.6%)
Social courts	6,648 (5.8%)
Labor courts	2,869 (2.5%)
Financial courts	3,368 (3.0%)
Others	1,775 (1.6%)
N	113,735 (100%)

Source: Bundesverfassungsgericht, "Statistik für das Geschäftsjahr 2013, Tabelle A IV 4: Verfassungsbeschwerden gegen Gerichtsentscheidungen seit 1991" at http://www.bundesverfassungsgericht.de/DE/Verfahren/Jahresstatistiken/2013/statistik_2013_node.html;jsessionid=23561FF2CA58326FAF119F4D6B567955.2_cid370.

The increase in complaints extends to all legal fields, but some stood out when specific legislative changes had repercussions for the caseload. An example is the increase in the 1980s of due process claims of parties who had been denied appeal in civil courts due to legislative amendments to the procedural codes restricting appeal opportunities in petty cases (Schumann 1983). According to German law, every legal decision deserves at least an opportunity of an appeal de novo (*Berufung*), plus the possibility of a further appeal on legal grounds only (in German: *Revision*). Many attorneys see denial of an appeal after the first instance as a denial of due process, as does the popular sense of justice. The legislature's curbing of the possibility of appeal in petty civil law cases in the 1980s was immediately felt in the Constitutional Court, where complaints claiming denial of justice increased. One survey (Blankenburg 1998) found that about half of all constitutional complaints were directed against a decision of an ordinary court denying appeal, claiming this to be a violation of due process protected under Article 103, section 1 of the Basic Law others combined this with a substantial claim (see Table 3.4). In 1990, 13 percent of all complainants brought a case that had ended in a local court.

Table 3.4. Due Process Complaints (art. 103 sec. 1 Basic Law), 1955–1995

	Of the 50% of all complainants who raised a due process complaint	
in the field of . . . ,	*. . . based their claim on due process alone.*	*. . . combined due process with substantial claims.*
prisons	1%	6%
criminal law process	25%	22%
civil law	14%	21%
civil procedure	28%	15%
others	32%	36%
	100% (N = 98)	100% (N = 198)

Source: Own survey (see Blankenburg 1998).

Considering the many possibilities of appeal in ordinary procedures, launching another complaint after these have been exhausted promises little chance of success. However, we witness in this respect the impact of the involvement of specialized or activist legal representatives. The format and wording of due process complaints often show a professionalism that indicates they were formulated by specialized attorneys. Furthermore, one cannot avoid the impression that some attorneys simply use the last chance of activism to satisfy a client (despite remote chances of success). Their constitutional complaints on behalf of prison inmates and taxpayers show skill in blaming injustice and constructing this on constitutional grounds.

Over the years, the involvement of advocates in filing complaints and representation has increased from 19 percent in 1955 to 38 percent in 1965 and since then has risen to well above 50 percent (Blankenburg 1998). The chances of admittance and success, however, do not increase with lawyer representation. The chances of admittance are small (see Table 3.1), regardless of whether an advocate formulates the complaint or the complainants themselves produce it on a home computer. Furthermore, chances of success vary according to the field of law. In the 1990s, preliminary injunctions of asylum seekers had a high chance of success; by contrast, criminal law complainants had low chances throughout the years, though inmates who complained about the prison regime were somewhat more successful.

Success in approaching the Court and getting a complaint admitted depends on overcoming three hurdles. The first consists of adhering to formal criteria and formulating the claim by addressing an article of the constitution. Quite a number of "letters" that reach the Court are politely redressed by the court administration so that they fit the correct criteria. The next hurdle to admittance is the assessment of the complaint by the constitutional judges' legal assistants, the majority of whom were judges themselves before joining the Constitutional Court. In fact, they are usually experienced judges from the ordinary courts, personally chosen by their respective constitutional judge. Two or three years at the constitutional level is a welcome career opportunity (see also Wieland 2002). Most complaints are rejected at this stage, whereupon the complainant receives a more or less standardized letter. Some rejection letters, however, include careful reasoning, formulated by the judge's team or by one or all three judges of the chamber.

Once the case has passed the sifting stage, a third hurdle is the formal admittance by the chamber and the senate. However, formal admittance does not mean that constitutional complaints are automatically successful. In fact, of the 6,238 formally admitted complaints in 2013, only 91 complaints were finally successful and granted; of these, 75 were granted by chambers and 16 by one of the two senates (Bundesverfassungsgericht, "Statistik für das Geschäftsjahr 2013, Tabelle A IV 1: Erledigungen der letzten fünf Geschäftsjahre "and "Statistik für das Geschäftsjahr 2013, Tabelle A IV 2: Anteil der stattgegebenen an den entschiedenen Verfassungsbeschwerden pro Jahr seit 1987"). As Table 3.5 demonstrates, the overall success of complaints after admittance varies according to areas of law. Furthermore, the table allows realistic prediction of (at least partial) overall success of a complaint, once it has been formally admitted.

Table 3.5. Chances of Admittance and Success of Constitutional Complaints by Area of Law, 1955–1995

	Admittance rate	*Success among those admitted*
Civil law	1.87%	81%
Family law	0.93%	63%
Criminal law	1.14%	70%
Prison regime	2.76%	81%
Administrative law	1.55%	59%
Asylum law	14.56%	98%
Fiscal law	1.99%	50%
Labor law	4.49%	36%
Social insurance	2.27%	22%
Average	2.57%	
N	(346)	(304)

Source: Own survey (see Blankenburg 1998) on the basis of a representative sample of 600. The admittance rate was projected onto the caseload of the entire year; this value was then related to the complaints of the respective field of law of all those admitted. Without "others" we thus end up with N = 346 admitted complaints, of which 304 were decided by the time of the sampling.

The Constitutional Court as a Wailing Wall

There is ample evidence to suggest that the Court has been used as a "Wailing Wall" for general social protest and queries about the lack of due process. But the Court is by no means a model of procedural pedantry itself. Thanks to the Court's official tradition of being "open to all," its mailbag is filled with letters and requests that are hard to categorize. These are first docketed in the general register (*Allgemeine Registersachen*) and, as indicated above, occasionally receive a response with additional information on how to put the case into the proper form of a constitutional complaint. One-third of all general complaint letters usually fulfill the formal requirements once initial mistakes are corrected. In 2013, the Court received 9,052 letters that were entered into the general register. Of these, 3,308 (37%) were later taken over into the register of constitutional complaints (Bundesverfassungsgericht, "Statistik für das Geschäftsjahr 2013, Tabelle D: Übersicht über den Geschäftsanfall im Allgemeinen Register (AR) für die Geschäftsjahre 2003 bis 2013"). Together with those complaints that arrived without formal detriments, this led to a caseload of 6,238 constitutional complaints.

The reasons for selection and the procedures by which the Court works toward its decisions are largely hidden from the public. The admittance procedure is based on written submission, and the decision is taken based on the documents handed in with the complaint. Even when a complaint is admitted, the procedure usually remains document-based, and proof is accepted outside the oral deliberation in the chambers or senates (art. 26 of the Federal Constitutional Court Act). Thus, most decisions are based on evidence submitted in writing. Most decisions are taken without a hearing (Kranenpohl 2010: 100–103). Only in a minority of cases decided by the senates are the parties granted a public hearing. This is probably an important reason why few observers have ever written about the criteria and procedure of nonadmittance of constitutional complaints, despite the rise in publications on every possible issue of substantive constitutional law. Nevertheless, most (but not all) chambers have developed a self-understanding as guardians of individual justice and controllers of the regular courts.

Our interviews with judges of both senates in 1996 revealed that some judges and some chambers follow their own style of guardianship of individual justice (Blankenburg 1998). Some judges issue chains of decisions that aim at a policy of influencing a stricter observation of constitutional rights (e.g., toward prison inmates or asylum seekers). This practice reveals that constitutional judges are not as positivistic as judges in ordinary courts, who are supposed to take statutes by the letter. Constitutional judges' strategies of using petty cases to effect change in the jurisprudence of a field of law meet with considerable critique, but when based on a chain of cases, they are more likely to avoid open conflict and resistance.

Secrecy is often viewed as a necessary condition for granting the Court its substantively wide competence. To complainants and their attorneys, however, the Court behaves like an oracle. Eighty-five percent of decisions not admitted are rejected without any reasoning, so the applied criteria remain secret. It is no wonder that attorneys have complained about the degree of undisclosed discretion (Zuck 1974: 305–307, 1996: 1656–1657, Zuck 1997: 29–30), which turns any initiated complaint into a lottery with indeterminate chances of success.

As a matter of course, a supreme court cannot satisfy all demands to rectify injustice in individual cases. In order to maintain the coherence of its interpretation, it has to remain rather small. In place of guarding individual justice, it has to select a few leading cases and use them to further the policy it deems relevant to protect the constitutionality and consistency of the entire legal system. Following such argumentation, the Commission on the Relief of the Constitutional Court, installed by the Federal Ministry of Justice, recommended in 1998 that the Court be granted full discretion on admittance of constitutional complaints without the need to provide a justification (Bundesministerium der Justiz 1998).

So far, the Federal Constitutional Court lacks full recognition of such wide discretion. Nevertheless, as we have seen, in practice the Court determines the range of its competence by admitting or rejecting complaints, and it can fill in the relevance of constitutional principles with its interpretations of the Constitution. It is able to control regular courts of justice without delving into everyday petty injustice and has kept a watchful eye on the constitutionality of political action at various levels in the Federal Republic of Germany. But if it developed into an agency regulating daily political practice, it would put the acceptance of its decisions, and thereby its own legitimacy as an institution, at risk. In German vernacular these two risks are called the dilemmas of becoming a super-appeal instance of regular courts on the one hand, and a supra-agency controlling politics on the other.

Capture of Politics by the Judiciary?

The Constitutional Court has managed to intervene successfully in central political issues throughout the more than sixty years of its history. At the same time it has kept up an image of being an ombudsman for everyday qualms. However, the Court is not free from conflict instigated by its decision making. Many times it has had to treat follow-up claims when its decisions left room for interpretations and ambiguity. Several times the Court has encountered vehement reaction in the public sphere, in particular in cases in which the Court adopted a—controversial—policy line. On a number of occasions the Court's decisions have initiated symbolic crusades instead of ending political fights. To name only a few examples, its decisions on radical leftists' non-employability in the civil service (*Berufsverbote*), on admittance quotas to universities (*numerus clausus*), and on abortion forced it to deal with a chain of follow-up decisions (see Lamprecht 1996 for controversies on calling soldiers "murderers" and on crucifixes in classrooms). The Court did not resist the temptation to issue judicial orders in response (see Gawron, Rogowski, in this volume), specifying detailed rules and the criteria that would be sufficient for the acceptance of statutory regulations in the future (e.g., the suggestion in 1985 to limit tax-deductible party financing to an amount of DM 100,000 per year, or the definition of conditions under which the Court would consider the regulation of abortion by legislatures or communities and advice centers to be constitutionally tolerable). In consequence, these decisions work as obiter dicta and force the Court to repeatedly evaluate the implementation of its decisions, thereby moving the Court into the center of political action itself.

The Court has stubbornly resisted attempts by diverse opposition groups to instrumentalize it and on many occasions has provided judicial legitimacy to decisions of the legislature, demonstrating an affirmative tendency of government policies. It has entirely invalidated only a few statutes; more often, the Court has defined conditions for their constitutionality. As is true of courts in general, in the end the Constitutional Court's decision leaves the losing party with no chance of support or continuation of the controversy. Its legitimacy rests on its capacity to decide disputes by translating the issue at stake into legal language ending with a noncontested decision (Luhmann 1969). However, a few times the acceptance of a Constitutional Court verdict has been questioned to an extent challenging the legitimacy of the institution as a whole.

The Court's legitimacy is particularly precarious, as it consists of only sixteen judges surrounded by a select halo of professors and other learned experts of constitutional jurisprudence. In fact, about half of the judges have chosen a lifelong career in the judiciary. The Constitution (art. 94 of the Basic Law and art. 4 of the Federal Constitutional Court Act) prescribes that at least three of the eight judges of each senate be recruited from one of the Federal Supreme Courts. The others are found among professors, ministerial bureaucrats, and politicians. Some were judges for part of their previous career. In the 1950s almost half of the constitutional judges still had some experience as attorneys or even as business managers, but these types of background have virtually disappeared over the course of history (see Landfried 1984).

It is apparent that constitutional judges are not recruited to democratically represent all layers of society, but are instead chosen on the basis of their consensus with a professional standard of interpreting the Constitution. The guardian of professional excellence is the federal minister of justice, who administers the nomination lists for judicial candidates (art. 8 of the Federal Constitutional Court Act). These are forwarded for final decision to a committee of the Federal Parliament (50% of the vote) and the representatives of the states (50% of the vote) (regulated by arts. 5–7 of the Federal Constitutional Court Act). Here, political quotas play a decisive role in the recruitment process. In deciding new nominations for the constitutional bench (where judges serve a maximum of twelve years), the majority parties distribute the sixteen judgeships according to middle-of-the-road consensus. Veto positions prevent nomination of outspoken jurists who have aroused the fury of their political opponents. Furthermore, bargaining over the replacement of constitutional judges is a delicate matter in the federal political system of Germany, especially when the majority of federal states are in opposition to the federal government.

The role of the Court has continuously provided increasing legitimacy to the political process. Political discussions in Germany have become used to determining legitimacy in two steps. First, administrative and parliamentary processes decide on controversial policies, and then parliamentary and extraparliamentary opposition groups invoke the Constitutional Court in order to test feasible arguments that may form constitutional restraints. However, such politicization endangers two conditions of the Court's success: compliance with its decisions and the binding force of its future decisions.

Of course the political process anticipates constitutional arguments. Governments and oppositions alike argue with what they suppose to be the interpretation of the Constitutional Court—governments sometimes anxiously, oppositions rather aggressively—often in innovative ways. Even parties and lobbyists get used to checking for any imaginable constitutional argument before thinking about the feasibility of their proposals. This relatively closed club of interpreters of the Constitution is part of a "*Rechtsstaat*" model with a high degree of legal control of policymaking and administrative discretion. Not only implementing agencies at the local or federal level but also political bodies are fixed to statutory and constitutional programs that function as taboos. On the other hand, the Constitutional Court has to anticipate its impact on the political arena, which leads to careful avoidance of decisions that deviate too far from the political and social consensus (Gawron, Rogowski 2007: ch. 6). Controversies are felt to be desirable in politics, but so is the need for an institution that is above all antagonisms and enjoys the authority and legitimacy to end all arguments. In this respect, the Constitutional Court becomes a prisoner of its power of definition: The greater the influence of the Court in political decisions, the more it has to find compromises acceptable to all sides.

Erhard Blankenburg is a professor emeritus of sociology of law at the Faculty of Law of the Vrije Universiteit, Amsterdam.

Bibliography

Blankenburg, E. "Unsinn und Sinn des Annahmeverfahrens bei Verfassungsbeschwerden." *Zeitschrift für Rechtssoziologie*, Vol. 19, 1998, 37–60.

Bundesministerium der Justiz, ed. Bericht der Kommission der Bundesregierung zur Entlastung des Bundesverfassungsgerichts. Bonn, 1998.

Bundesverfassungsgericht. "Statistik für das Geschäftsjahr 2013." http://www.bundesverfassungsgericht.de/DE/Verfahren/Jahresstatistiken/2013/statistik_2013_node.html.

Gawron, T., Rogowski, R. *Die Wirkung des Bundesverfassungsgerichts.* Baden-Baden, 2007.

Kommers, D. *Judicial Politics in West Germany: A Study of the Federal Constitutional Court.* Beverly Hills, 1976.

Kranenpohl, U. *Hinter dem Schleier des Beratungsgeheimnisses. Der Willensbildungs- und Entscheidungsprozess des Bundesverfassungsgerichts.* Wiesbaden, 2010.

Lamprecht, R. *Zur Demontage des Bundesverfassungsgerichts. Beweissicherung und Bestandsaufnahme.* Baden-Baden, 1996.

Landfried, C. *Bundesverfassungsgericht und Gesetzgeber. Wirkungen der Verfassungsrechtsprechung auf parlametarische Willensbildung und soziale Realität.* Baden-Baden, 1984.

Luhmann, N. *Legitimation durch Verfahren.* Neuwied, Darmstadt, 1969.

Schumann, E. *Bundesverfassungsgericht, Grundgesetz und Zivilprozess.* Cologne, 1983.

Wieland, J. "The Role of the Legal Assistants at the German Federal Constiutional Court." In Rogowski, R., Gawron, T., eds., *Constitutional Courts in Comparison: The U.S. Supreme Court and the German Federal Constitutional Court.* New York, Oxford, 2002, 197–207.

Zuck, R. "Der '3. Senat' des Bundesverfassungsgerichts." *Die öffentliche Verwaltung,* Vol. 9, 1974, 305–307.

Zuck, R. "WiMis—Die Gesetzlosen." *Neue Juristische Wochenschrift,* 1996, 1656–1657.

Zuck, R. "Vom Winde verweht: Paragraph 93d BVerfGG und menschliche Schicksale." *Neue Juristische Wochenschrift,* 1997, 29–30.

Part II

Decision Making

Chapter 4

The U.S. Supreme Court's Strategic Decision-Making Process

Timothy R. Johnson and Maron W. Sorenson

The U.S. Supreme Court is but one of three political institutions in the structure of the U.S. federal government. Within this system of separated powers it rules on the constitutionality of some of the nation's most important legal and political issues.[1] Since the turn of the twenty-first century alone, the Court has made decisions that affected the outcome of a presidential election (*Bush v. Gore*), universal health care (*National Federation of Independent Business v. Sebelius*), the rights of homosexuals (*Obergefell v. Hodges*), and the voting rights of minorities (*Shelby County v. Holder*). In making such decisions, the nation's highest court may be considered the most powerful of the three branches of the U.S. federal government.

This may be a controversial position, in view of the powers held by the elected branches at the federal level. Indeed, Congress has clear and important powers explicated in Article I of the U.S. Constitution, such as declaring war, deciding how to raise and spend money, and ratifying all international treaties. At the same time, the president is the nation's chief executive and commander in chief of the military. In short, while the U.S. Supreme Court hears and decides only about seventy-five cases per term, Congress and the executive branch wield their powers on a daily basis. Even so, given the issues on which the Court sets legal policy, it is not a stretch to suggest the justices do indeed wield a great deal of power.

Beyond the debate about the power of each branch, we note that the two elected branches often carry out their jobs in the public eye. Indeed,

Notes for this chapter begin on page 139.

the president is the most visible political figure in the nation, and the work of Congress is covered regularly (at a minimum) by the mass media. In addition, three cable television channels and a radio network (C-SPAN, C-SPAN2, C-SPAN3, and C-SPAN Radio) are devoted to broadcasting floor debates and votes, as well as virtually all committee proceedings, for public viewing. In short, the elected branches enjoy clear power that is (by and large) conducted publicly and transparently on a daily basis.

In contrast, the work of the U.S. Supreme Court is conducted almost completely outside of the public eye, with the exception of one hour set aside for litigants to present oral arguments in most cases it decides, and the public announcement of its decisions.[2] As a result, the Court's decision-making process is largely opaque; the public therefore knows very little about how the justices reach the decisions that affect every part and every citizen of the United States. This chapter seeks to illuminate this process so that scholars, students of the Court, and Court watchers alike can gain a better understanding of how the justices conduct their business and come to terms with some of the most important legal and political decisions in our nation. We begin with a brief summary of our theoretical view of Supreme Court decision-making and then offer a short discussion of the politics surrounding how justices reach the Court. We devote the remainder of the chapter to an examination of the Court's internal decision-making process.

The Strategic Model of Decision Making

We view Supreme Court justices as political actors and strategic decision makers (Gely, Spiller 1990; Eskridge 1991a, 1991b; Ferejohn, Weingast 1992; Cameron 1993; Epstein, Knight 1998), which means their decisions are constrained by a host of factors (Epstein, Knight 1998; Maltzman, Spriggs, Wahlbeck 2000; Johnson 2004; Black, Owens 2012; Black et al. 2012). Specifically, when making decisions, policy-oriented justices must account for the preferences of their immediate colleagues, the preferences of actors beyond the Court, and institutional norms and rules that might affect the decisions that they can make. This section considers the three prongs of this model.[3]

Justices Are Goal-Oriented

An abundance of evidence suggests that Supreme Court justices have many different goals (see, e.g., Levi 1949; Cushman 1929; Baum 1997; Hensley, Smith, Baugh 1997; Epstein, Knight 1998). For example, it has been well documented that some justices seek principled decisions, or decisions that will sustain the Court's legitimacy (see Baum 1997; Walker et al. 1988). Though we agree justices may have many goals, we follow conventional wisdom in the study of judicial politics, which suggests the *main* goal of most Supreme Court justices is the attainment of policy in line with their personal preferences (Maltzman et al. 2000; Segal, Spaeth 2002). As Epstein and Knight (1998: 8) point out, "justices, first and foremost, wish to see their policy preferences etched into law."

The idea that policy is the main goal of Supreme Court justices is neither new nor controversial. Rather, this argument is well grounded in the work of legal realists such as Llewellyn (1931), and Frank (1949), and early judicial behavior scholars such as Pritchett (1948), Murphy (1964), Schubert (1965), and Segal and Spaeth (2002). Scholars have provided empirical support for this argument in several ways, three of which we address here. First, individual justices' voting patterns are very consistent over time. For instance, with the exception of two terms (1974 and 1977) Lewis Powell voted liberally in civil liberties cases no more than 43 percent of the time in any given term. Likewise, William Brennan's liberal support for civil liberties fell below 70 percent in only one term during his Court tenure (1969) (Epstein et al. 1996: 456). This consistency indicates justices pursue specific policy goals and rarely waver from doing so.

Beyond voting patterns, Johnson (2004) indicates that the vast majority of questions justices ask during oral arguments concern policy. After these proceedings, Epstein and Knight (1998: 30–32) demonstrate, almost 50 percent of all remarks made by justices during the Court's conference discussions concern policy, and 65 percent of statements in circulating memoranda during the opinion-writing process address policy considerations. These remarks include statements about legal principles the Court should adopt, courses of action the Court should take, or a justice's beliefs about the content of public policy. Finally, scholars who address the interaction between justices during the opinion-writing process (Murphy 1964; Epstein, Knight 1998; Maltzman et al. 2000) point to justices' bargaining statements during the opinion-writing phase of a case to demonstrate that policy considerations are the driving force behind justices' decisions.

Justices are Strategic

The attitudinal model of Supreme Court decision-making argues that justices are unconstrained in their ability to vote for their most preferred policy outcomes because they enjoy life tenure (Segal, Spaeth 2002). In other words, because justices do not face election or retention, and because they usually do not have higher political ambitions, they can vote for their most preferred outcomes without consequence. In contrast, the strategic model suggests that although they pursue policy goals, justices cannot always make decisions that conform perfectly to their preferences. Rather, because five justices must usually agree on a decision to set precedent, justices must pay particular attention to the preferences, and likely actions, of their immediate colleagues. In short, Supreme Court justices alter their behavior in order to achieve their goals within the context of making decisions by majority rule.

A recent yet rich literature explores the extent and impact of internal bargaining between justices (see, e.g., Epstein et al. 1999; Maltzman et.al. 2000; Johnson et al. 2005; Ringsmuth et al. 2013). These works are progeny of Murphy (1964), who argued that justices are rational actors and act as such when deciding cases. The reason for this is obvious, as Murphy notes: "Since he shares decision making authority with eight other judges, the first problem that a policy oriented justice would confront is that of obtaining at least four, and hopefully eight, additional votes for the results he wants and the kinds of opinions he thinks should be written in cases important to his objectives" (Murphy 1964: 37).

Murphy did not systematically test his theory, but others have done so. For example, in an analysis of Justice Brennan's and Justice Marshall's private papers, Epstein and Knight (1995) demonstrate that over 50 percent of cases in one sample contained one or more bargaining statements between the justices.[4] In a later monograph, Epstein and Knight conclude that "law, as it is generated by the Supreme Court, is the result of short-term strategic interactions among the justices and between the Court and other branches of government" (Epstein, Knight 1998: 18).

Wahlbeck et al. (1998) support these findings in their empirical analysis of opinion circulation on the Court. They find that an opinion goes through more drafts at times of increase in the ideological heterogeneity of a majority coalition, in the number of suggestions given to the opinion writer by other justices, in the number of threats made to the opinion writer, or in the number of times other justices say they are yet unable to join an opinion. This suggests to Wahlbeck et al. that "opinion authors' actions are shaped by the interplay of their own policy preferences and the actions of their colleagues" (Wahlbeck et al. 1998: 312).

Wahlbeck and his colleagues also find evidence that the decision to join a majority opinion is a strategic choice as well (Wahlbeck et al. 1998: 296). Specifically, they demonstrate that the decision to join is determined by how acceptable a majority opinion is to a specific justice, whether that justice can attain concessions from the opinion writer, and the past relationship between the opinion writer and the justice deciding whether to join. Finally, Maltzman et al. (2000) provide evidence that how the chief justice assigns opinions, how justices respond to initial opinion drafts, and how coalitions form are all processes grounded in strategic interaction.[5] This means that the process through which the Court makes decisions is a product of interactions and interdependencies between the justices. If justices simply voted for their most preferred outcomes, there would be no evidence of bargaining and accommodation behind the scenes of the decision-making process.

More recently Black, Schutte, and Johnson (2013) and Johnson et al. (2005) have demonstrated that justices use the rules of the game in a strategic manner. The former analyze how a justice can use threshold issues to keep the Court from deciding a case far from her or his preferred outcome.[6] In addition, Johnson and his colleagues find that chief justices (as well as senior associate justices) can and do manipulate the voting rules during the Court's conference discussions to move a decision closer to their preferred outcomes. Both of these recent works extend and enhance empirically the theoretical concept that justices are strategic political actors.

Justices Account for Institutional Rules

The final tenet of our account suggests that although justices are goal-oriented and consider their colleagues' preferences when making decisions, they must also account for the institutional context within which they decide cases (Danelski 1978; Slotnick 1978; Maltzman, Wahlbeck 1996). By institutions, we mean the rules (either formal or informal) that structure interactions between social actors (Knight 1992). In the context of the Court, legal institutions may constrain a justice's ability to make certain decisions. That is, the "rules of the game" may prevent the justices from always making decisions that equate with their most preferred outcomes. The reason for this is simple: Supreme Court justices comply with institutional rules and norms (like precedent) because the Court must at least have the aura of acting as a legal, nonpolitical, institution (Epstein, Knight 1998; Hoekstra, Johnson, 2003; Black, Owens 2009).

For instance, Knight and Epstein (1996) argue that justices adhere to the norm of respecting precedent. Although their findings are far from general (they analyze only thirteen cases), the evidence is nonetheless compelling. Indeed, if respect for precedent were not a norm, then Knight and Epstein would not have found evidence that the justices frequently discuss past cases in their private deliberations. That the justices make such references to precedents in private memos suggests that they act as if they themselves are constrained to follow these decisions. The question, however, is why the justices feel constrained by precedent. For Knight and

Epstein the answer is simple: "compliance with this norm is necessary to maintain the fundamental legitimacy of the Supreme Court" (Knight, Epstein 1996: 1029). In other words, they argue that if the Court frequently ignored its own legal precedents, then its credibility as a judicial institution might be questioned, and it could potentially lose legitimacy—its main source of power.

Respecting precedent is an informal norm, but the Court must also follow certain formal rules such as those set out in the constitution. Because the constitution gives Congress the power to override Supreme Court decisions, the justices must account for the preferences of Congress when deciding where to set policy in a particular area of law. Other codified rules are found in Article III of the U.S. Constitution; these include the Court's jurisdiction to hear certain cases,[7] the requirement that a party must have standing (*Flast v. Cohen* [1968]) to be heard in the Supreme Court, and that a case must be justiciable before the Court will consider ruling on it.[8]

Nomination and Confirmation

Before considering how strategic justices act when they join the U.S. Supreme Court, it is important to understand the journey they take to reach the nation's highest judicial bench. The reason is intuitive—given that justices are strategic political actors, the process of being nominated and confirmed is itself largely a story about these particular traits. As such, in this section we describe the president's decision to nominate a justice and the Senate's decision to confirm (or reject) the nominee. We turn first to the president's choice and support of a nominee. From there we turn to the Senate's role in the process.

The fundamental tension between the president's power to nominate and the Senate's constitutionally prescribed advice and consent role has led to many nomination showdowns. Examples abound, including the Supreme Court nominations of Robert Bork and Clarence Thomas and, more recently, prolonged battles between the Senate and Presidents Clinton, G.W. Bush, and Obama, over confirmation of nominees to the federal circuit courts of appeals. Despite the ideological and procedural minefield that judicial nominees face in the U.S. Senate, recent history teaches us that presidents usually succeed when they are given the opportunity to nominate someone to the Supreme Court (Cameron, Cover, Segal 1990; Abraham 1999; Yalof 1999; Baum 2013). Indeed, since 1900 only five out of sixty-three Supreme Court nominees have failed to make it through the Senate's confirmation process (Baum 2013: 41).

Because of the magnitude and importance of Supreme Court nominations, as well as the political battles that often ensue over them, political scientists and legal scholars have studied this process generally (Watson, Stookey 1995) and have investigated specific aspects of it, including how presidents choose nominees (Nemacheck, Wahlbeck 1998; Nemacheck 2007), how the ideological relationship between the president and the Senate affects the ideology of the eventual nominee (Moraski, Shipan 1999; Johnson, Roberts 2004), and what drives individual senators' confirmation votes (Segal, Cameron, Cover 1992).

Existing theoretical accounts of Supreme Court nominations and Senate confirmation votes teach scholars a great deal about interactions between the president and the Senate. Most generally, Mackenzie (1981) explores the political exchanges for all executive nominations, while Watson and Stookey (1995) analyze the political process for Supreme Court nominations. More recently, Bell (2002) has investigated the extent to which the increasing activity of interest groups has made the nomination and confirmation process more contentious overall and made it more difficult for presidents to get their nominees confirmed. Other scholars provide systematic evidence that supports these general studies.

Nemacheck and Wahlbeck focus on the initial phase of the process in their analysis of factors that presidents consider when creating short lists of possible nominees. They find that presidents' choices are "related to efforts to reduce uncertainty over the nominee's future behavior on the Court" (Nemacheck, Wahlbeck 1998: 20). More importantly for our study, these authors provide evidence that these choices are strategic because presidents account for the political environment generally and for the way the Senate may react to a nomination specifically. In other words, the ideological relationship between the president, the nominee, and the Senate plays a key role in the president's decision about whom to place on the short list (Nemacheck 2007).

Other theoretical and empirical work explores the president's explicit choice of nominees. This research focuses on the spatial dynamics of the confirmation game and finds that the alignment of the pivotal players (the president, the Senate, and the Court median) along an ideological continuum allows scholars to accurately predict the ideology of a president's chosen nominee (Moraski, Shipan 1999; Johnson, Roberts 2004). Additionally, scholars have learned a great deal about what drives aggregate Senate action on Supreme Court nominees, as well as what drives individual senators' confirmation votes. Binder and Maltzman (2002) suggest that the presence of divided government slows the confirmation process for lower court nominees, while Segal (1987) finds that confirmation battles are as much about partisanship as they are about a struggle between the Senate and the president. Further, Massaro (1990) observes that ideological differences between the nominee and the Senate play a major role in almost all failed nominations. In line with Nemacheck and Wahlbeck's (1998) findings, this is an important point for us because it indicates that the president must consider how the Senate will react to the ideology of a chosen Supreme Court nominee.

Finally, Johnson and Roberts (2004) suggest that presidents can and do take action to support their nominees. In so doing, they clear the way for confirmation, even if the battles with the Senate are not always easy. In fact, when nominees are particularly controversial, presidents are clearly more willing to support them publicly. Table 4.1 corroborates this claim. Its data, which include all public presidential statements about a nominee from Tom Clark through Elena Kagan, demonstrate that those nominees considered the most controversial—including Robert Bork and Clarence Thomas—garner more support from their nominating president. And the result is clear: presidents support their nominees, and that support makes the nominee more likely to win confirmation in the Senate. Indeed, of the nominees in the sample, only three failed to garner the requisite votes to secure confirmation.

Once the president makes a choice, the process turns to the Senate. Scholars have spent a great deal of time analyzing the Senate with regard to Supreme Court nominees. For instance, Cameron et al. (1990) and Segal et al. (1992) use spatial models to analyze individual-level confirmation votes. Their initial findings (Cameron et al. 1990) indicate that a senator's vote is a product of the spatial distance between the nominee and a senator, the nominee's qualifications, and the political strength of the president. Segal et al. (1992) correct for a shortfall in the three colleagues' earlier work by including a measure of interest group involvement in their model. Importantly, they continue to find strong support for the hypothesis that senators' confirmation votes largely depend on the spatial distance between a nominee and the ideology of a senator's constituency.

In general, this literature demonstrates that the ideological relationships between the nominee and the Senate, and the president and the Senate, play a key role in the choices presidents make during the Supreme Court nomination process. Specifically, Nemacheck and Wahlbeck (1998) and Segal (1987) find that presidents consider how the Senate will react to their choice of Supreme Court nominees. Further, Moraski and Shipan (1999), Segal et al. (1992), and Cameron et al. (1990) use spatial models to explore how the ideological relationship between presidents, nominees, and the Senate determines who wins confirmation battles.

Table 4.1. The Frequency of Presidential Political Statements about Supreme Court Nominees

Nominee	*President*	*Qualifications*	*Public Opinion*	*Senate Pressure*
Clark	Truman	0	0	0
Minton	Truman	0	0	1
Warren	Eisenhower	2	0	1
Harlan	Eisenhower	1	0	2
Brennan	Eisenhower	0	0	0
Whittaker	Eisenhower	0	0	0
Stewart	Eisenhower	0	0	0
White	Kennedy	2	0	0
Goldberg	Kennedy	1	0	0
Forts (1)	Johnson	1	1	0
Marshall	Johnson	4	0	0
Fortas (2)	Johnson	2	0	0
Burger	Nixon	3	1	0
Haynsworth	Nixon	8	1	4
Carswell	Nixon	1	0	2
Blackmun	Nixon	0	0	0
Powell	Nixon	3	0	2
Rehnquist (1)	Nixon	3	0	2
Stevens	Ford	2	0	1
O'Connor	Reagan	3	0	0
Scalia	Reagan	10	0	3
Rehnquist (2)	Reagan	10	0	3
Bork	Reagan	28	9	33
Kennedy	Reagan	7	0	5
Souter	Bush	11	2	6
Thomas	Bush	12	12	5
Ginsburg	Clinton	4	1	2
Breyer	Clinton	3	0	0
Total		121	27	72

Source: Johnson, T.R., Roberts, J.M., "Presidential Capital and the Supreme Court Confirmation Process," *Journal of Politics*, Vol. 66(3), 2004, 663–683.

Agenda Setting and the Supreme Court

The U.S. Supreme Court is a passive institution that must wait for cases to come to it. In other words, the justices cannot introduce legislation as members of Congress do.[9] However, as strategic decision makers, justices can do things that encourage litigants to submit cases presenting a particular question or issue area. In this section we briefly discuss the process by which cases are placed on the Court's docket. From there we focus on the key rule that governs agenda setting—the Rule of Four.

The Agenda Setting Process: A Brief Overview

A party who loses in a lower federal court or in a state supreme court (if the case involves a federal question) may appeal to the U.S. Supreme Court.[10] When the appeal, or petition, is submitted, the clerk of the Court provides notice to the respondent (i.e., the winner in the lower court). The respondent has the option to respond, waive the right of response, or do nothing at all. Most respondents choose the first option, whereupon both parties file briefed (written) legal arguments as to why the Court should or should not hear the case.[11] These briefs are then distributed to the justices' chambers for review. Over time there has been a clear increase in the number of petitions submitted to the Court. In fact, Figure 4.1 demonstrates a fivefold increase in the number of petitions submitted between 1935 and

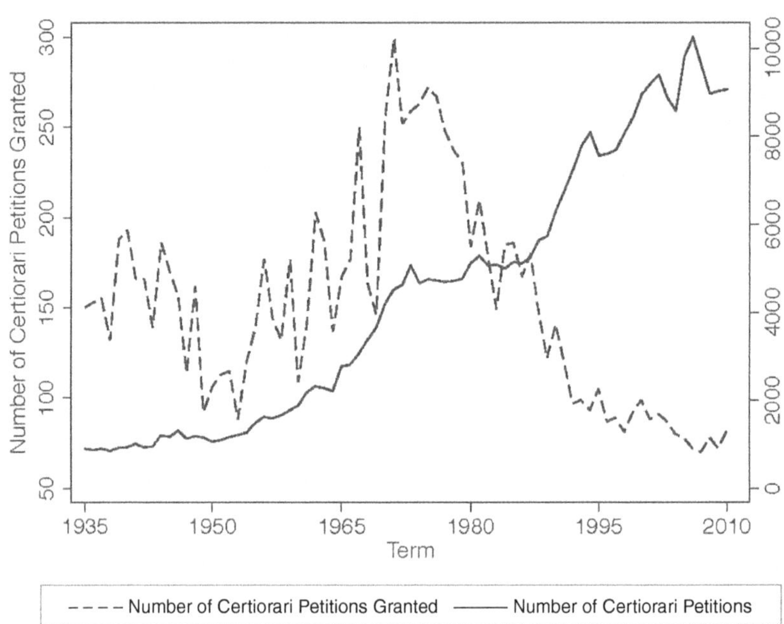

Figure 4.1. Number of Certiorari Petitions Filed and Granted at the U.S. Supreme Court, 1935–2010

Source: Epstein, L., Segal, J.A., Spaeth, H.J., Walker, T.G., *The Supreme Court Compendium*, Washington, 2011.

2010. Meanwhile, the number of cases granted review increased dramatically through the late 1970s but since then has fallen just as precipitously.

Once the parties submit their cert. briefs, the first hurdle to winning review by the Court is making the "discuss list." This list includes all the petitions for review that the justices will discuss and formally vote on during their weekly conference meetings. The chief justice creates the first draft of the discuss list.[12] Any associate justice can add a petition to the chief's list, but may not remove a case already on the list.[13] There is little data on the Court's agenda setting (or cert. process), but the justices are known to discuss a large number of possible cases each term. For instance, over the eight terms from 1986 to 1993 the Court discussed approximately 800 petitions per term (Black, Boyd 2013).

Conference voting at the cert. stage, like voting on case outcomes (see below), is sequential. The justice who places a case on the discuss list speaks first and usually offers a justification for granting a petition review. From there the nine vote on whether to review the case. They do so in descending order of seniority, with the chief justice considered the most senior. It takes four votes to grant review. If four votes are not forthcoming, the Court denies the cert. petition—in other words, the Court will not hear the case. Ultimately, this means the lower court decision remains the law. That said, such a denial does not mean the justices necessarily agree with the lower court decision. Rather, it simply means they could not agree to hear the present case.

The Rule of Four

As we note above, it takes four votes for the Court to hear a case. This important institutional rule is unique because it allows a minority of justices to both set the Court's agenda and change, rather than simply preserve, the status quo.[14] That is, by granting a hearing and by then issuing a ruling on a case from a lower court, the Supreme Court sets national doctrine by either applying the lower court's ruling to the entire country or by reversing the ruling of the lower court altogether. This is an important power for two main reasons. First, it acts as a sharp constraint on majority tyranny at the Court's agenda-setting stage. As Kurland and Hutchinson (1983: 645) put it, "The rule of four is a device which a minority of the Court can impose on the majority a question that the majority does not think it appropriate to address." The potency of this rule is not lost on the justices. As Justice Brennan (1973) put it, choosing cases is "second to none in importance." It also clearly worries at least one former justice: John Paul Stevens (1983: 19) has pointed out that "every case that is granted on the basis of four votes is a case that five members of the Court thought should not be granted. For the most significant work of the Court, it is assumed that the collective judgment of its majority is more reliable than the views of the minority."

The historical record on the Rule of Four is incomplete (Stevens 1983; Revesz, Karlan 1988; O'Brien 1997; Epstein, Knight 1998; Hartnett 2000). We know, however, that it originated sometime after passage of the Evarts Act of 1891. This law established the circuit courts of appeals and codified that no right of appeal to the Supreme Court existed. The result was that the justices had much greater discretion over their appellate docket. As Hartnett (2000: 1657) put it, "thus was born the then revolutionary, but now familiar, principle of discretionary review of federal judgments on writ of certiorari." Although there is evidence justices relied on a minority certiorari rule through the late 1800s and early 1900s, its use did not become public until 1925, when Justice Willis Van Devanter appeared before the House Judiciary Committee during its hearings on the Judges' Bill.[15]

Van Devanter's purpose was to "assure Congress that increased control over its [the Court's] own docket would not lead to arbitrary dismissal of cases" (Robbins 2002). More specifically, to assuage the worry that the Court would reject cases that could be potentially important, Van Devanter explained:

> We always grant petitions when as many as four think that it should be granted and sometimes when as many as three think that way. We proceed upon the theory that, if that number out of nine are impressed with the thought that the case is one that ought to be heard and decided by us, the petition should be granted. (Cited in Robbins 2002: 12)

A decade later, Chief Justice Hughes reiterated Justice Van Devanter's response to the congressional concern that the Court might not take cases important for the law because of the justices' discretion over their docket. In a speech before the American Law Institute, he noted that "we are liberal in the application of our rules and certiorari is always granted if four justices think it should be, and, not infrequently, when three, or even two, justices strongly urge the grant" (Hughes 1937: 459). The point is that for at least the past eighty years, minorities of the justices have controlled the Supreme Court's agenda.

Existing empirical work on the Rule of Four focuses almost exclusively on how it affects the size of the Court's docket each term. For instance, Stevens (1983) argues that the Rule of Four comes into play in about 25 percent of all cases that make the discuss list. He concludes that many of these cases are probably unimportant and should therefore be left off of the plenary docket. O'Brien (1997: 786) obtains similar results in his analysis of Justice Marshall's docket books for the 1990 term. He finds that

22 percent of cases decided during this term were granted certiorari with only four votes.

Perry and Carmichael (1985) take the question of case selection a bit further by testing whether the Rule of Four protects "important" cases. According to their operationalization this does not happen because important cases almost always receive at least five votes for certiorari. The authors point out, however, that the Court should not abandon its long-lasting rule if it is interested in taking "nearly significant" cases.

While Perry and Carmichael suggest the Rule of Four protects somewhat important cases, the normative implication of Stevens's and O'Brien's findings is that the Court should consider abandoning this rule. For Stevens (1983), the quarter of all cases docketed with fewer than five votes presented an additional and unnecessary burden on him and his colleagues. Indeed, Stevens believes the Court should decide only the most important cases, so that the problem of overworked justices could be abated by only taking cases with a majority vote on certiorari.

Beyond the debate between legal scholars and justices, the Rule of Four has drawn scorn from the mass media when its incompatibility with majority rule has come to light in death penalty cases (Liptak 2007). A prisoner sentenced to death needs the vote of a simple majority or five justices to stay or postpone his or her execution, yet the Rule of Four allows a minority of justices to place a prisoner's appeal on the docket. This opens up the possibility that the Court could grant a prisoner's petition to appeal his or her sentence but simultaneously refuse to stay the execution that would, in the legal lexicon, "moot" the case if the prisoner were subsequently executed.

Certainly the normative implications of the Rule of Four are interesting, but this line of inquiry fails to address a fundamental question: why would a minority coalition want to place a case on the docket when five of their colleagues could either vote to "dismiss as improvidently granted" (DIG) on a case at the plenary stage, or simply outvote the minority at the merits stage? After all, on the surface the Rule of Four is incompatible with the rule that a simple majority of justices can vote to dismiss. As such, a preference cycle could exist whereby a case was continually granted and then dismissed (Riker 1988). The literature offers two explanations for why this does not happen on the Court. Regarding DIGs, Epstein and Knight (1998: 120) suggest a norm exists whereby the five justices who voted against certiorari cannot form the five-member coalition to DIG a case. While these scholars point out that this norm can be and has been violated, justices do not often do so. The result, we suspect, is that Rule of Four cases ultimately receive treatment similar to cases granted review with five or more votes.

With respect to the latter point, scholars have offered some answers, albeit not theoretically satisfying ones. For instance, in her analysis of case selection based on Justice Burton's docket sheets, Provine (1980: 157) finds "that the desire to be agreeable and the leadership responsibility felt by chief justices are the primary reasons some justices vote oftener for review in four vote cases than otherwise." She therefore concludes that "the hypothesis that four-vote cases reflect the presence of coalitions seeking review on the merits receives no support in this analysis" (ibid.: 158). This conclusion is based on the fact that the two most frequent members of four-vote certiorari coalitions were Justices Burton and Clark, who both were considered "affable and outgoing in their personal relationships" (ibid.: 156). The point for Provine is that there seems to be nothing strategic about Rule of Four cases, and that the key explanation for justices' joining these minority coalitions is a sense of friendship, a wish to be deferential to their colleagues, or a desire to lead the Court fairly (for chief justices).

The analysis provided by legal scholars is both theoretically and empirically unsatisfying. From a different angle, several political scientists have attempted to systematically analyze the Rule of Four. In his seminal work on Supreme Court agenda setting, Perry (1991) argues that justices do at times engage in strategic behavior during the certiorari stage, and the Rule of Four may encourage such behavior. Perry (1991, 98) also provides evidence that there are times when a coalition of four does not force a case onto the docket because the justices in that coalition know they will surely lose on the merits. This strategy is known as a defensive denial.

Epstein and Knight (1998) go a step further than Perry by providing convincing evidence to support the argument that the Rule of Four can be used for strategic purposes. As they point out: "The Rule of Four invites forward thinking. Policy oriented justices know that if they are to attain their goals they must take those cases they believe will lead to their preferred outcomes and reject those that will not." The key for Epstein and Knight, then, is that justices can use this rule to make "strategic calculations throughout the decision making process" (1998: 121).

In the end, the Court's agenda setting process, and the Rule of Four specifically, demonstrate clearly that the way an agenda is set has a great deal to do with the decisions made by institutions generally and by the U.S Supreme Court specifically. For our purposes, this part of the process fits squarely into the strategic model: policy-minded justices debate and decide which cases to hear, strategy is involved in making such decisions, and an institutional rule (the Rule of Four) is an integral part of the process.

Decision on the Merits: Litigant Briefs

Litigants lucky enough to have a case accepted for review by the Supreme Court submit a second round of briefs. Each brief is meant to convince the justices that a given party should win the case. In this section we briefly discuss the rules surrounding these briefs on the merits. From there we turn to the research that seeks to explain the extent to which written arguments affect the decisions justices make.

The Rules of Supreme Court Briefs

"Rules of the Supreme Court of the United States" is an 83-page document created by the Court that contains, among other things, several sections of detailed information on how to properly file, format, and write a brief. The real paper-shuffling begins once the Court has accepted a case: from this point the petitioner has forty-five days to file a merits brief, and the respondent's brief is required thirty days later. Petitioners are allowed to reply to the respondent's brief, but it must be submitted at least one full week before oral arguments are heard, and no more than thirty days after the respondent's brief is filed. Litigants may request extensions of these time frames, but "an application to extend the time to file a brief on the merits is not favored" (Rule 25.5).

In addition to a rigid time frame, the Court also outlines specifics for the formatting and length of briefs. As dictated by Rule 33, all briefs (merits, response, amicus) are printed on 60-pound paper in booklet format measuring 6 1/8th inches by 9 1/4th inches. These booklets are then bound by saddle stitch or perfect binding, and covered with 65-pound card stock paper of the appropriate color. Merits briefs for both petitioner and respondent are limited to 15,000 words and covered in light blue or red paper, respectively. The petitioner's reply brief is not to exceed 6,000 words, and should have a yellow cover. Each brief may include appendices of unlimited length; however, additional arguments should not appear in these appendices.[16]

One source of briefs not yet discussed is amicus groups. Amici, or friends of the Court, are most often interest groups or established organizations that file a brief in support of either side.[17] Such briefs are limited to 9,000 words, and should "bring to the attention of the Court relevant matter[s] not already brought to its attention by the parties" (Rule 37.1). Although limited in words, there is no limit to the number of separate amicus groups that can file. In the 2012 term, for example, multiple amicus briefs were filed in 67 of the 76 cases granted review. Amicus participation ranged from zero to ninety-seven briefs—the former occurring in only two cases, and the latter supporting *Hollingsworth v. Perry* (2012), one of the term's two same-sex marriage cases.

Finally, Supreme Court rules dictate that forty copies of every single brief (petitioner, respondent, reply, and amicus) be delivered to the Court in hard copy, as per the rules explained above. Considering the hundreds—if not thousands—of pages filed for every case appearing before the Court, such strict rules are necessary to maintain any semblance of order and organization. With so much time, effort, and paper spent on brief writing—and subsequent reading—we next consider the extent to which briefs affect outcomes.

Do Briefs Affect Case Outcomes?

Litigant and amicus briefs serve two broad purposes: to provide information to the Court, and to set the bounds of policy space from which legal opinions can be drawn. The informational nature of briefs is evident, given the pure volume provided to the Court, but what sort of information is contained in these myriad pages? Tables 4.2 and 4.3 offer such insight by presenting a breakdown of issues briefed in a random sample of seventy-five Burger court civil liberties cases. Table 4.2 provides information on cases without amicus participation; note that litigant briefs most often address policy and constitutional issues, which is unsurprising given the description of justices as seekers of policy preferences (Epstein, Knight 1998; Segal, Spaeth 2002). Indeed, these two types of issue dominate litigant briefs and account for over 70 percent of all briefed issues.

Table 4.2. Types of Information Provided to the Supreme Court in Litigant and Amicus Briefs: Cases without Amicus Participation (n = 45 cases)[a]

Issue Area	*Arguments raised in Litigant Briefs*	*% of Briefs*[b]
Constitutional	118	31
Policy	154	40
External Actors	28	7
Precedent	49	13
Threshold	20	5
Facts	16	4
Total	385	100

[a] In the full sample of cases (75), 45 had no amicus participation. Therefore, the main source of information for the justices is the litigants' briefs.

[b] Percentages are rounded to the nearest whole number.

Source: Johnson, T.R., *Oral Arguments and Decision Making on the United States Supreme Court*, Albany, 2004.

Table 4.3 shows a similar trend: when both amicus and litigant participation are taken into consideration, the Court still receives the most information regarding policy and constitutional issues. Note, however, there are clear differences in the types of information provided by each brief. Most specifically, amicus briefs refer more often to precedent and external actors. This is, again, unsurprising because amici are by definition external actors—it makes sense that their briefs would inform the Court on their preferences as well as additional precedent that would support their preferences.

Table 4.3. Types of Information Provided to the Supreme Court in Litigant and Amicus Briefs: Cases with Amicus Participation (n = 30 cases)[a]

	Arguments Raised by			
Issue Area	*Litigant Brief Only*	*Amicus Brief*	*Litigant and Amicus Brief*	*Total*
Constitutional	18 (10%)	15 (9%)	140 (81%)	173 (34%)[b]
Policy	45 (19%)	28 (12%)	159 (69%)	232 (46%)
External Actors	3 (7%)	24 (53%)	18 (40%)	45 (9%)
Precedent	9 (23%)	25 (62%)	6 (15%)	40 (8%)
Threshold	10 (77%)	2 (15%)	1 (8%)	13 (3%)
Facts	1 (50%)	1 (50%)	0 (0%)	2 (0%)
Total	86 (17%)	95 (19%)	324 (64%)	505 (100%)

[a] Thirty cases contained at least one amicus brief.

[b] Percentages in the rightmost column are the total percentage of each issue type raised by the litigants or amici.

Source: Johnson, T.R., *Oral Arguments and Decision Making on the United States Supreme Court*, Albany, 2004.

Next, existing research demonstrates that legal briefs submitted to the Court often set the boundaries of a case by framing the issues for the justices (Lawrence 1990; Wahlbeck 1998). To this end, the legal model of decision-making posits that justices care about the law and are bound to it. Scholarly work in this area agrees. For example, Epstein and Kobylka (1992) examine legal change in the jurisprudence of abortion and death penalty cases. Though they consider factors such as public opinion and a changing political and social environment, they ultimately conclude that "it is the law and legal arguments as framed by legal actors that most clearly influence the content and direction of legal change" (ibid.: 8). Later work by Epstein, Segal, and Johnson (1996) examines briefs and opinions, concluding that the Court follows the doctrine of *sua sponte*—a norm disfavoring issue creation during opinion writing. Finally, Corley (2008) uses plagiarism software to detect when majority opinions "borrow" phrases and sentences from litigant briefs. She finds that the quality of a brief—as defined by the experience of the writing attorney—positively affects the chances a justice will "borrow." Taken together, this line of research suggests that briefs directly impact the decision-making process by providing the Court with valuable information, and by constraining their choice-set by setting policy boundaries. We next consider ways the justices can seek out information rather than simply receive it.

Decisions on the Merits: Oral Arguments

In the Supreme Court's early days, great lawyers such as Daniel Webster, John Calhoun, William Pinkney, and Henry Clay often appeared before the justices. In this time period oral arguments were elaborate oratories, but more importantly, they often provided the justices with their only source of information about a case: briefs were rarely if ever submitted, and outside parties did not submit amicus curiae (friend of the Court) briefs as they do today. Because the justices placed no time limitation on the argument sessions, advocates sometimes spoke for many hours over multiple days. In one case, Davis (1940) points out, Webster and his rival argued for a full ten days. In stark contrast to contemporary arguments, historians suggest the justices rarely interrupted the advocates with questions or comments (compare Warren 1922 with Black et al. 2011).

Hearing arguments over many days was possible because the Court heard so few cases in its early days. However, its rising caseload soon made such indulgences impracticable. In addition, it seems that at some point, the justices could no longer handle such long sessions. As one biographer put it, Chief Justice John Marshall complained of boredom (Beveridge 1929) and Justice Joseph Story found the arguments "excessively prolix and tedious" (Hughes 1928). As a result, in 1849 they instituted Rule 53, which limited each attorney to a two-hour argument (Frankfurter, Landis 1928). At this time the justices also first required written arguments, consisting of an abstract of points and authorities (ibid.). Since 1970, the time allotted for these has been limited to thirty minutes per side.

The modern time constraints on oral arguments may be due to the abundance of information at justices' disposal prior to these open court sessions. Indeed, today they possess litigant briefs (Epstein, Kobylka 1992), amicus curiae briefs (Spriggs, Wahlbeck 1997), briefs on certiorari (Caldeira, Wright 1988), the media (Epstein, Knight 1998), and lower court opinions. Further, unlike in the Court's early days, when the justices were transfixed by the great orators (or put to sleep by boredom), they largely control the argument sessions today. Specifically, one analysis of 347 cases over four recent terms included 43,000 utterances and 1.4 million words spoken by the justices (Black et al. 2011). It seems, then, that in modern cases the justices now speak as much as or more than the attorneys. The question is whether such questioning has any bearing on how the justices decide.

Do Oral Arguments Affect Justices' Decisions?

As with other aspects of the decision-making process, evidence accumulated over the last decade establishes that, generally, oral arguments play an integral role in the Court's decision-making process (Johnson 2004; Wrightsman 2008). For instance, Tables 4.4 and 4.5 show clearly that the justices gather many types of information by asking questions during oral arguments. First, as policy-oriented political actors, justices are clearly concerned with questions of policy. In cases without amici participation, 40 percent of the Court's questions focus on policy, and this figure increases to 43 percent when amici participate. Second, justices spend a great deal of time asking questions about the preferences of actors external to the

Table 4.4. The Focus of the Court's Questions during Oral Arguments by Issue Area and Source of Information: Cases without Amicus Participation (n = 45 cases)

	Oral Argument Questions About		
Issue Area	*Briefed Issues*	*New Issue*[a]	*Total*
Policy	330 (25%)	974 (75%)***	1,304 (40%)
External Actors	37 (3%)	1,122 (97%)***	1,159 (36%)
Precedent	82 (26%)	234 (74%)***	316 (10%)***
Threshold	40 (32%)	86 (68%)***	126 (4%)***
Total	631 (20%)	2,592 (80%)***	3,223 (100%)

[a] New issues are operationalized as those that were not raised in the briefs submitted prior to oral arguments. The Court raises them for the first time during these proceedings.

[b] Percents are in parentheses. They are calculated horizontally for each issue area.

[c] Percentages in the rightmost column are calculated for each issue type raised by the Court.

Note: T-tests in the columns labeled "New Issue" were conducted to determine whether the Court's focus during oral arguments is on new issues, or on issues first raised in the briefs. In Table 4.4. the test is run on the mean number of new questions versus the mean number of questions about briefed issues for each type. In the top half of the table the test is run on the mean number of new questions versus the mean number of questions about briefed issues for each type. In the bottom half of the table the tests are conducted between columns 4 and 5. T-tests were also conducted for the "Total" columns in each half of the table. The tests in this column compare the mean number of policy issues asked about during oral arguments with each of the other issues areas. * = difference is significant at 0.10 level; ** = difference is significant at the 0.01 level; *** = difference is significant at the 0.001 level (two tailed tests).

Source: Johnson, T.R. *Oral Arguments and Decision Making on the United States Supreme Court.* Albany, 2004.

Table 4.5. The Focus of the Court's Questions during Oral Arguments by Issue Area and Source of Information: Cases with Amicus Participation (n = 30 cases)

	Oral Argument Questions About				
Issue Area	*Litigant Brief Only*	*Amicus Brief Only*	*Litigant and Amicus Brief*	*New Issue*[a]	*Total*
Constitutional	18 (8%)	18 (8%)[b]	114 (50%)	78 (34%)	228 (10%)***[c]
Policy	53 (5%)	48 (5%)	232 (23%)	685 (67%)***	1,018 (43%)
External Actors	0 (0%)	10 (1%)	17 (2%)	760 (97%)***	787 (34%)
Precedent	7 (3%)	24 (11%)	4 (2%)	181 (84%)***	216 (9%)***
Threshold	3 (3%)	3 (3%)	1 (1%)	88 (93%)**	95 (4%)***
Total	81 (4%)	81 (4%)	368 (16%)	1,792 (76%)***	2,344 (100%)

[a] New issues are operationalized as those that were not raised in the briefs submitted prior to oral arguments. The Court raises them for the first time during these proceedings.

[b] Percents are in parentheses. They are calculated horizontally for each issue area.

[c] Percentages in the last column are calculated for each issue type raised by the Court.

Note: T-tests in the columns labeled "New Issue" are conducted to determine whether the Court's focus during oral arguments is on new issues, or on issues first raised in the briefs. The test is run on the mean number of new questions versus the mean number of questions about briefed issues for each type. In the bottom half of the table the tests are conducted between columns 4 and 5. T-tests are also conducted in the "Total" columns in each half of the table. The tests in this column compare the mean number of policy issues asked during oral arguments with each of the other issues areas. * = difference is significant at 0.10 level; ** = difference is significant at the 0.01 level; *** = difference is significant at the 0.001 level (two tailed tests).

Source: Johnson, T.R., *Oral Arguments and Decision Making on the United States Supreme Court*, Albany, 2004.

Court. Indeed, 36 percent of questions (1,159) fall into this category when amici are not present in a case (see Table 4.4). When amici participate, this share remains similar at 34 percent (787). Finally, justices raise questions about institutional constraints (precedent and threshold issues) they may face, but these queries are fewer than those about the other issues. Specifically, when amici participate, 13.7 percent of all questions focus on precedent or threshold issues, and 13.2 percent focus on these issues in cases without amici.

Beyond the information provided, there is evidence the quality of oral arguments advanced by attorneys during these proceedings affects justices' votes (Johnson, Wahlbeck, Spriggs 2006). Indeed, even justices predisposed to vote for a particular side (based on their ideological predilections) tend to vote more often for the side that offers better arguments in open court. Finally, there is mounting evidence that during oral arguments, justices foreshadow how they will decide (Shullman 2004; Roberts 2005; Johnson et al. 2009; Black et al. 2012). Such signals emanate from the number of questions justices ask the attorney on a given side of the dispute as well as from the emotive tenor of these questions. When justices give one side a harder time (by asking more questions) or when they ask that side questions using less pleasant language, it is more likely to lose the case.

Conversations with attorneys are not the only discussions justices engage in during oral arguments—they are prone to speak to one another as well. Anecdotally, Wasby, D'Amato, and Metrailer (1977: xviii) argue that "it is not surprising that the judges would use part of the oral argument time for getting across obliquely to their colleagues on the bench arguments regarding the eventual disposition of a case." The same authors conclude elsewhere that "another, less noticed function is that oral argument serves as a means of communication between judges" (Wasby et al. 1976: 418). Recent work corroborates these anecdotal findings. Black et al. (2012) provide systematic evidence that justices speak to (and often speak over) one another, listen to their colleagues' questions and comments, and use the oral arguments to predict the outcome of the case.

Overall, despite the conventional wisdom through the last decade of the twentieth century, scholars have now made clear that the hour-long sessions in open Court can and do affect the decisions justices make. They clearly elicit information from the attorneys that helps them decide. In addition, they make their positions clear in their manner of questioning and also speak to each other through their questions and comments. But what happens once the justices retire to the confines of the Marble Palace? We turn next to this question.

Decisions on the Merits: Conference Discussions

Chief Justice Roberts has publicly said: "We [the Court] are the most transparent branch of government. Everything we do that has an impact is done in public, ... You see our work in public at the Court. Our decisions are out there."[18] Interestingly, the chief's contention rests on the fact that the Court, unlike the elected branches, issues explicit public justifications (in the form of written opinions) for the decisions it makes. The problem with this argument is that the public aspect to which the chief refers is only the end product. With the exception of the oral arguments (see the previous section), the decision-making process occurs behind closed doors in the marble palace. In this section we begin with an overview of the initial part of this process—the justices' conference discussions—and then turn to why these discussions are important for how justices decide.

Behind the Closed Door: The Process of Conference Discussions

During the term the justices sit for oral arguments on Mondays, Tuesdays, and Wednesdays, and hold private conference discussions on Wednesdays and Fridays. These discussions serve two purposes—choosing cases from the discuss list to set for future arguments, and voting on the cases that have already been argued. Here we are more concerned with the latter than the former (see the section on agenda setting for a discussion of the former).

Because the justices meet in conference twice a week, they use Wednesday conferences to discuss the merits (outcomes) of cases heard Mondays and Tuesdays. Friday conferences are therefore reserved for cases argued on Wednesdays.[19] These meetings, held in a conference room that adjoins the chief's chambers, are completely private: nobody is allowed in the room except the justices. If something is needed from outside the room the most junior justice calls to make the request.[20]

When conference begins, the chief justice presents the facts of the first case. From there he offers his personal view of the case and then casts his vote.[21] When the chief is done, the associate justices offer their views and votes in order of seniority. That is, the most senior associate justice presents and votes next, with each justice doing so until the Court's newest member finishes the discussion.[22] Usually the justices have a fairly good idea of how they will vote in the case, but there are times when they are less certain.[23] The justices repeat this process for each case argued during the current week.

The Importance of Conference Discussion and Votes

Scholars have emphasized for decades that conference votes are only the tip of the iceberg in the justices' business (see, e.g., Epstein, Knight 1998). However, the only data normally available to scholars are the conference votes.[24] Because there is so little information about the legal and policy issues the justices discuss during conference, scholars have largely ignored this part of the Court's decision-making process. But despite the paucity of research in this area, there is evidence to suggest the justices discuss the key aspects of cases they decide. Johnson (2004) demonstrates that during conference, the justices clearly pick up on issues briefed by the parties and on issues discussed during oral arguments. More specifically, justices discuss policy options and key precedents during their private conference discussions. Similarly, Knight and Epstein (1996) find that the justices clearly discuss precedent at conference. For them, this suggests the justices believe they are bound by the norm of respecting past decisions. In short, although scholars do not yet have a full picture of what transpires during conference, these studies provide insights that eluded scholars and Court watchers alike until the past decades.

Beyond the discussions about the specific issues they must decide, conference is important because the way the justices vote determines who will ultimately write the majority opinion in a case. A chief justice who votes with the majority at the end of a case discussion is authorized to choose who writes the majority opinion.[25] This prerogative helps the chief justice influence the Court's agenda by selecting either an author whose opinion is close to his (or potentially her) own preferences, or one who will minimize the prospective policy loss if the chief's preferred outcome does not prevail (Epstein, Knight 1998; Maltzman et al. 2000). More specifically, as Maltzman et al. (2000) demonstrate, the justice who assigns the opinion has some power to set the agenda for the majority coalition because the writer gets the first move in the bargaining process. The chief exercises this discretion and guides the opinion toward his (or her) preferred position by assigning it to ideologically proximate justices, especially in important cases. In other words, despite the constraints by norms like equitable distribution of assignments, the chief justice has the power to choose who will articulate the Court's opinion and which lens a case will be decided through.[26]

There is clear evidence chiefs (and sometimes senior associates) act strategically to ensure the opinion assignment power. Johnson et al. (2005) note that Chief Justice Warren Burger was renowned for casting votes at conference that would allow him to control the Court's agenda through opinion assignment. Indeed, Burger often changed his initial votes to join the majority coalition, cast "phony votes" by voting against his preferred position, and sometimes declined to express an initial position at conference (see Woodward, Armstrong 1979; Epstein, Knight 1998). This behavior led one critical justice to point out that "all too damned often the Chief Justice will vote with the majority so as to assign the opinion, and then he ends up in dissent" (Schwartz 1990: 14).

Although many claimed that Burger attempted to manipulate the Court's agenda through opinion assignment, he was probably not the first chief to vote in this manner during conference. Indeed, Murphy (1964) traces sophisticated voting to control opinion writing to John Marshall.

Although short on supporting evidence, some argue that Marshall wrote opinions "even in cases where he dissented" (Schwartz 1993: 152). As Murphy (1964: 84–85) hypothesized of chief justices when they were the first to speak and the last to vote: "Thus, before he finally commits himself, he knows where each Justice stands—at least for the present—and which side will most probably win. If his own views are going to be in the minority, he can vote with the majority and retain the opinion-assigning authority."

Data drawn from the archives of Justice Lewis F. Powell (at Washington and Lee University) illustrate one particular strategy chiefs may use during conference—passing on their chance to cast the initial vote. Table 4.6 presents data on how often each justice passed up on an initial vote in a sample of cases decided during the Burger Court. It is clear that Burger, and then to a lesser extent Rehnquist (who became chief in 1986), passed on their initial vote significantly more often than associate justices did. In fact, Burger was more than twice as likely to pass as any other justice on the bench. Rehnquist is also interesting, as he passed ten times more often once he was elevated to chief. Certainly the senior associate justices (Justice Douglas and then Justice Brennan, in this sample) passed more often

Table 4.6. The Frequency with Which Justices Pass at Conference in a Random Sample of Cases from the 1971–1986 Terms

Justice	*Number of Passes*	*Percent of Conference Votes in which Justice Passed*
Warren Burger	121	11.7%
William Douglas	9	4.8%
William Brennan	18	1.5%
Potter Stewart	30	4.2%
Byron White	11	0.9%
Thurgood Marshall	6	0.5%
Harry Blackmun	6	0.5%
Lewis Powell	13	1.1%
William Rehnquist (as associate justice)	5	0.5%
William Rehnquist (as chief justice)	8	5.2%
John Stevens	11	1.2%
Sandra Day O'Connor	5	1.0%
Antonin Scalia	2	1.3%

Source: Johnson, T.R., Spriggs II, J.F., Wahlbeck, P.J., "Passing and Strategic Voting on the U.S. Supreme Court," *Law and Society Review*, Vol. 39(2), 2005, 349–377.

than their colleagues (with the exception of Justice Stewart) but not nearly as often as the chiefs.

The bottom line for us is that conference is the time when the justices finally speak candidly to one another about a case and cast their preliminary votes. Though scholars have given this part of the Court's decision-making process short shrift, we believe it is quite important and also fits squarely within our theoretical account. That is, justices have to work with their colleagues and deploy their knowledge of opinion assignment rules as they strive to reach consensus.

Decisions on the Merits: Opinion Writing

Once an opinion has been assigned, the writing process might seem straightforward, but this is not always the case. Keeping in mind that a majority-opinion author must write an opinion that pleases at least four other members of the Court, the task is best described as a dynamic and malleable process whereby justices strategically maneuver in an attempt to satisfy their policy preferences (Maltzman et al. 2000). In order to fully explicate the complexities of opinion writing, this section proceeds in three parts. We first provide a simple description of the process. Next, we summarize the two main (and competing) models of opinion writing, which define key actors who influence the final content of the majority opinion. We end the section with a case study of *Gannett v. DePasquale*—an exemplar of the opinion-writing and decision-making process.

Opinion Writing: A Step-by-Step Guide

Due to the volume of work and time constraints the Court faces in the modern era, many justices use their law clerks to draft initial versions of opinions (Wahlbeck, Spriggs, Sigelman 2002; Peppers 2006; Peppers, Zorn 2008). With the clerk's legwork in hand, the opinion author will prepare a first draft, which upon completion is circulated to the Court. At this point, justices are not bound by their stated policy preferences or votes at conference; instead, each has four options: to join the opinion immediately; to suggest some sort of change, via suggestion or threat; to announce an intent to wait before taking any action; or to circulate a concurrence or dissent (Maltzman et al. 2000: 9). Figure 4.2 breaks down how often justices take these specific tacks. Even a cursory glance at Figure 4.2 reveals the modal category is "join."

Figure 4.2 also reveals the myriad options available to a justice who does not immediately join the majority opinion. Note that Threat, Will

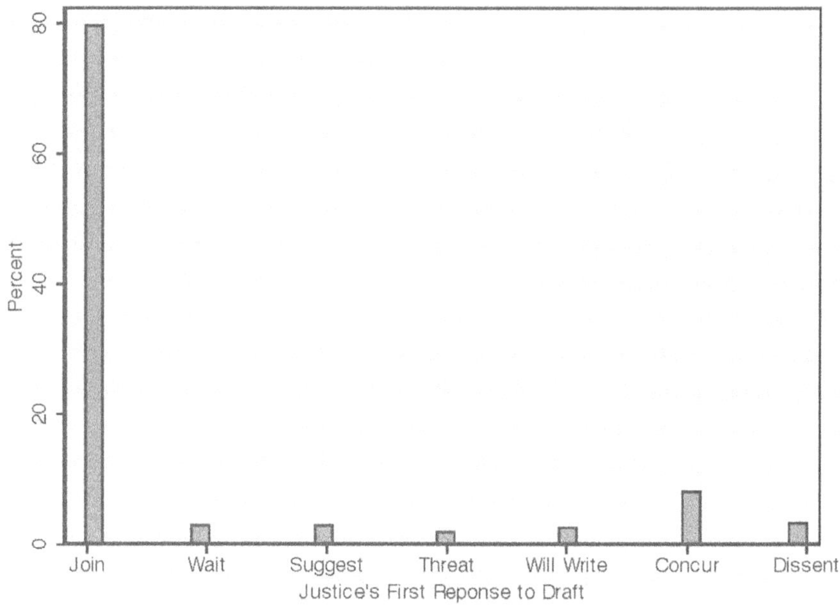

Figure 4.2. Justices' Responses to Initial Majority Opinion Draft Opinions

Source: Maltzman, F., Spriggs II, J.F., Wahlbeck, P.J., *Crafting Law on the Supreme Court: The Collegial Game*, New York, 2000.

Write, Concur, and Dissent all indicate a justice's intention or willingness to circulate a separate opinion, so the majority opinion author takes these indications particularly seriously. In particular, the existence of a well-crafted dissenting opinion has the potential (however small) to steal the majority, especially if it can satisfy the demands of the median justice (Lax, Cameron 2007). Because justices wish to see their policies etched into law, majority-opinion writers seek to mitigate such potential threats. Warding off a dissenting opinion, however, can be difficult. Lax and Cameron (2007) employ models from game theory to demonstrate how the costs of time and effort impact a would-be dissenter. In short, to prevent potential dissenting opinions from gaining traction, a majority-opinion author must craft a sufficiently high-quality opinion that captures the median justice.

No additional effort or response from an opinion's author is necessary when a justice immediately agrees to join the opinion. However, as demonstrated above, gaining the votes of justices who fall into the latter three categories (suggest a change, announce intent to wait, write separately) is a different matter. In these instances, scholars disagree about which justices exert the most influence over the opinion author, and therefore over legal policy.

Opinion-Writing Models

Scholars investigating an author's plight in the struggle to command a majority often model opinion content as a corollary of ideology, pointing to two key players: the Court's median member, and the opinion author her- or himself. The bench median model mirrors legislative models of the median-voter theorem in assuming that policy converges on the median voter—it is, after all, this voter who must be captured in order to gain a majority and thereby create policy (Black 1958). Applied to Supreme Court scholarship, the median justice, as the swing vote, may reject an opinion that falls too far from his or her ideal point. In fact, a majority opinion that does not perfectly satisfy the median justice gives the minority coalition an opportunity to craft such an opinion and capture this essential swing vote (Lax, Cameron 2007). Extensive work by Spriggs and Hansford (2001) provides empirical support for this model. Their findings indicate that, indeed, the Court median exerts influence over the majority opinion.

Beyond the Court median, the opinion author exerts influence on the substantive outcome of a case. This agenda-control model stresses the importance of an opinion author in pulling opinion policy away from the median and closer to his or her own ideal point (Murphy 1964; Rohde 1972; Rohde, Spaeth 1976; Slotnick 1978, 1979; Brenner, Spaeth 1988). Recent work by Bonneau et al. (2007) adds to this body of work by incorporating a legal status quo. In this model, a justice's decision to join an opinion is operationalized as a simple choice between the existing majority opinion and the lower court decision: any justice preferring policy offered in the majority opinion will sign on.

In sum, the rich body of literature on opinion writing provides ample evidence that the opinion author *and* the Court median exert particular influence over opinion content, and therefore policy. This is not to say the other seven justices are moot—to the contrary, the following example demonstrates the impact any single justice can have in this dynamic process.

Opinion Writing as a Dynamic Process

Historical documents available for *Gannett Co. v. DePasquale,* 443 U.S. 368 (1979)—a case involving freedom of the press and courtroom access—offer clear insight into this dynamic process. To begin, the majority opinion was assigned to Justice Blackmun by Justice Brennan, which means that Justices Burger and Stewart were not in the majority when votes were counted at conference, but both Brennan and Blackmun were.[27]

On 4 April, Blackmun circulated a first draft of a majority opinion. The very next day Brennan signed the opinion after making a few minor suggestions, Stewart made known his intention to write a dissenting opinion, White declared he would await Stewart's dissent before signing any opinion, and Stevens attempted to bargain with Blackmun. Specifically, Stevens believed Blackmun's opinion went too far in favor of First Amendment rights (freedom of press), rather than Sixth Amendment rights (right to a speedy and public trial), and was hoping Blackmun would back off from this stance. In the meantime, Marshall joined Blackmun's opinion, and thirteen days later Stevens joined Stewart's dissenting opinion on the exact day it was circulated, noting, "I may add a paragraph of my own." At this point, Blackmun was still two votes shy of commanding a majority.

Despite this deficit, Blackmun responded to Stewart's dissent with, "The dissent merits a mild response. I shall circulate it later today." Blackmun's three-page response highlights the key differences in how each coalition wanted to set policy. Blackmun, along with Brennan and Marshall, wanted to set a clear legal ruling that (1) carried a presumption of open access to trials as implied by the Sixth Amendment, and (2) considered preliminary hearings part of a trial. Stewart, and at this point Stevens, felt the Sixth Amendment's guarantee to a speedy and public trial was meant to protect the *accused*, not the public. Given this choice set, and despite his earlier preference to await Stewart's dissent, White joined Blackmun's opinion, creating a presumptive majority: Blackmun, Brennan, Marshall, White, and Powell. Although Powell had not yet declared any intentions, he had voted with this coalition at conference. Yet this was not how the majority opinion turned out.

On 8 May Chief Burger circulated a dissenting opinion and also declared he would sign on to Stewart's dissent. Rehnquist followed shortly thereafter. The following day, Powell sent a memo to Blackmun expressing doubts about how the majority opinion was taking shape. He too felt the crux of the issue was striking a correct balance between First and Sixth Amendment rights, but saw Blackmun's opinion as tilted too far in favor of the press. Faced with these dichotomous policy choices, Powell eventually joined Stewart's opinion and became the requisite fifth vote to transform that dissent into a majority opinion.

This example highlights two key aspects of the opinion-writing process. First, different justices employed different tactics in attempting to move policy closer to a preferred point. While White (the Court median) held out, some justices directly bargained with Rehnquist and Brennan while others wrote separate opinions. Second, the central debate concerned specific aspects of policy, and not simply a decision to reverse or affirm the lower court's ruling. This idea transcends the traditional liberal-conservative notion of decision-making to reveal a Court concerned with degrees and balancing rather than such simple dichotomizations.

Conclusion

U.S. Supreme Court justices are clearly political actors with policy preferences they seek to etch into federal law. However, their ability to always reach their preferred outcomes is limited by the fact that they do not make decisions in a vacuum and the fact that rules and norms of behavior govern their decision-making process. Despite the Court's uniqueness as an institution, it clearly shares these characteristics with other courts within and beyond the United States.

Timothy R. Johnson is Morse Alumni professor of political science and law at the Department of Political Science of the University of Minnesota, Minneapolis.

Maron W. Sorensen is an assistant professor at the Department of Government and Legal Studies of Bowdoin College, Brunswick, Maine.

Notes

1. It has invoked this power since Chief Justice John Marshall declared such power in *Marbury v. Madison* (1803).
2. Oral arguments and opinion announcements are technically public, but not fully so. The Courtroom holds only 250 seats for spectators, and cameras are not allowed during either proceeding. Today, of course, it is easier to hear what transpires in the Courtroom. Oyez.org makes these sessions available at the end of each week during the Court's term. These audio files can also be found at http://www.supremecourt.gov/.
3. Portions of this section are drawn from Johnson (2004), ch.1.
4. Epstein and Knight (1995: 22) are right to note that this number would probably be higher had they also had access to more than just Brennan and Marshall's papers for this study. Indeed, if they could have seen the private memos sent or received by all the justices who were on the Court during the time period of their sample, their hypothesis may have been supported with even stronger evidence.
5. Other scholars have provided evidence of strategic interaction at almost every stage of the Court's decision-making process, including during the agenda-setting (certiorari) stage (Caldeira, Wright, Zorn 1999), during oral arguments (Johnson 2004), and during conference discussions (Johnson, Spriggs, Wahlbeck 2005).
6. Threshold issues are defined as the requirements from Article III of the U.S. Constitution that there must actually be a case or controversy in order for the Court to decide a case.
7. The exceptions clause in Article III of the U.S. Constitution gives Congress the power to alter the Court's appellate jurisdiction as it sees fit.

8. That a case must be justiciable also stems from the Article III requirement that the Court can only decide cases and controversies. For instance, cases cannot be moot (*DeFunis v. Odegaard* [1974]), and must also be ripe for review (*Longshoremen's Union v. Boyd* [1954]).
9. For instance, at any time a member of Congress may write legislation limiting the right to choose abortion on demand. Though the politics of the House and Senate make it unlikely that any given piece of legislation will be brought to a vote, any member may still attempt to introduce such a law. Justices, however, must wait for a case to be brought to them. Only then may they take up the issue and work toward changing the law or maintaining the status quo.
10. Today almost all appeals come through the Court's certiorari (cert.) process. This legal term means literally "to be informed of, or to be made certain in regard to." The key for the justices is that cert. cases are part of the Court's discretionary docket. In other words, the justices do not have to decide these cases.
11. At this point outside parties may weigh in on whether the Court should take the case. These groups, called amici curiae (friends of the Court) affect the probability the justices will hear a case (see, e.g., Caldeira and Wright 1988).
12. The chief is often considered first among equals (Stevens 2011) but has some power at several points during the Court's decision making process. Creating the initial draft of the discuss list (more generally, being able to mold the Court's possible agenda) is considered one of these powers.
13. Prior to the discuss list the Court actually used a "dead list," which was the opposite of today's practice. The dead list included cases that were not going to be discussed or voted on by the justices. A case that was "dead listed" was automatically denied review by the Court.
14. Very few powers are granted to the minority in the federal government. Beyond the Rule of Four, the key power reserved to a minority is the filibuster in the U.S. Senate (see, e.g., Fang, Johnson, Roberts 2007).
15. In 1916, however, Congress passed a law that the Court interpreted as giving it discretion over whether or not it would hear appeals from state courts that raised federal issues. This was a major change, as Hartnett (2000: 1660) points out: "the Supreme Court produced a fundamental change in the relationship between itself and state courts in constitutional cases—a change far larger than Congress evidently anticipated. As we shall see, this was not the last time that the Court expanded its discretionary control over its caseload beyond that contemplated by Congress."
16. See, e.g., the joint appendix in one of the Court's famous libel cases—*Hustler Magazine v. Falwell* (1988).
17. Note that amici can file in support of a judgment rather than party; however, this is rare.
18. The Chief made this comments during a C-SPAN forum on in cameras in the courtroom. http://www.realclearpolitics.com/video/2011/06/27/chief_justice_roberts_worried_about_impact_of_cameras_in_scotus.html.
19. Note, however, that when the Court is in one of its two-week argument sessions the justices only hold Friday conferences.
20. The most junior justice (today it is Justice Kagan) must also answer the door if anyone knocks. This (semi-onerous task) was the duty of Justice Breyer from 1994 through January of 2006. His tenure as the junior associate justice was one of the longest in history.

21. All votes at conference are preliminary. That is, justices can and do change their votes between conference and the time the Court announces its final decision. Epstein and Knight (1998) demonstrate that at least one justice changes a vote in 50 percent of all cases.
22. From at least the time of John Marshall's tenure on the Court until the 1960s, the discussion of a case at conference started with the chief and concluded with the most junior justice, but voting proceeded in the opposite fashion (see Clark 1959). As Justice Brennan (1960: 402) described: "The junior justice votes first and voting then proceeds up the line to the Chief Justice who votes last." Sometime in the mid 1960s, however, this voting rule changed, and both discussion and voting in a case now proceeds based upon seniority, with the chief both discussing a case and voting first (see Rehnquist 2001: 254).
23. At the time of writing, the justices speak in this order: Chief Justice Roberts, Justice Kennedy, Justice Thomas, Justice Ginsburg, Justice Breyer, Justice Alito, Justice Sotomayor, and Justice Kagan.
24. These notes come from the papers of former justices. Both Justice Blackmun and Justice Brennan left their Court papers to the Library of Congress. Within these papers are docket sheets that note how each justice voted in each case the Court decided during Blackmun or Brennan's tenure on the bench.
25. If the chief is not in the majority, then the senior associate in the majority holds this power.
26. Justices do not specialize in particular areas of the law, and opinions are not assigned based on a justice's perceived expertise in an issue area; however, expertise may affect a chief's choice of assignment. For example, Brenner and Palmer (1988) suggest chiefs may call on colleagues who have more experience writing in a given area of the law. They do so in order to "ensure the smooth and efficient operation of the Court" (Maltzman, Wahlbeck 1996: 427).
27. This deduction is based on the seniority rule of opinion assignment discussed above.

Bibliography

Abraham, H.J. *Justices, Presidents, and Senators.* Lanham, 1999.

Baum, L. *The Puzzle of Judicial Behavior.* Ann Arbor, 1997.

Baum, L. *The Supreme Court,* 11th ed. London, 2013.

Bell, L.C. *Warring Factions: Interest Groups, Money, and the New Politics of Senate Confirmation.* Columbus, 2002.

Beveridge, A.J. *The Life of John Marshall.* Boston, 1929.

Binder, S.A., Maltzman, F. "Senatorial Delay in Confirming Federal Judges, 1947–1998." *American Journal of Political Science,* Vol. 46(1), 2002, 190–199.

Black, D. *The Theory of Committees and Elections.* London, 1958.

Black, R.C., Boyd, C.L. "Selecting the Select Few: The Discuss List and the U.S. Supreme Court's Agenda-Setting Process." *Social Science Quarterly,* Vol. 94(4), 2013, 1124–1144.

Black, R.C., Owens, R.J. "Agenda Setting in the Supreme Court: The Collision of Policy and Jurisprudence." *Journal of Politics,* Vol. 71(3), 2009, 1062–1075.

Black, R.C., Owens, R.J. *The Solicitor General and the United States Supreme Court: Executive Branch Influence and Judicial Decisions.* New York, 2012.

Black, R.C., Schutte, R.A., Johnson, T.R. "Trying to Get What You Want: Heresthetical Maneuvering and U.S. Supreme Court Decision Making." *Political Research Quarterly,* Vol. 66(4), 2013, 819–830.

Black, R.C., Treul, S.A., Johnson, T.R., Goldman, J. "Emotions, Oral Arguments, and Supreme Court Decision Making." *Journal of Politics,* Vol. 73(2), 2011, 572–581.

Black, R.C., Wedeking, J.P., Johnson, T.R. *A Deliberate Dialogue: Oral Arguments and Coalition Formation on the U.S. Supreme Court.* Ann Arbor, 2012.

Bonneau, C.W., Hammond, T.H., Maltzman, F., Wahlbeck, P.J. "Agenda Control, the Median Justice, and the Majority Opinion on the U.S. Supreme Court." *American Journal of Political Science,* Vol. 51(4), 2007, 890–905.

Brennan, W.J. "State Court Decisions and the Supreme Court." *Pennsylvania Bar Association Quarterly,* Vol. 31(June), 1960, 393–407.

Brennan, W.J. "The National Court of Appeals: Another Dissent." *University of Chicago Law Review,* Vol. 40(3), 1973, 473–485.

Brenner, S., Palmer, J. "The Time Taken to Write Opinions as Determinant of Opinion Assignments." *Judicature,* Vol. 72(3), 1988, 179–184.

Brenner, S., Spaeth, H.J. "Majority Opinion Assignments and the Maintenance of the Original Coalition on the Warren Court." *American Journal of Political Science,* Vol. 32(1), 1988, 72–81.

Caldeira, G.A., Wright, J.R. "Organized Interests and Agenda Setting in the U.S. Supreme Court." *American Political Science Review,* Vol. 82(4), 1988, 1109–1127.

Caldeira, G.A., Wright, J.R., Zorn, C.J.W. "Sophisticated Voting and Gate-Keeping in the Supreme Court." *Journal of Law, Economics, and Organization,* Vol. 15(3), 1999, 549–572.

Cameron, C.M. "New Avenues for Modeling Judicial Politics." Presented at the Conference on Political Economy of Public Law, Rochester, N.Y. 15–16 October 1993.

Cameron, C.M., Cover, A.D., Segal, J.A. "Senate Voting on Supreme Court Nominees: A Neoinstitutional Model." *American Political Science Review,* Vol. 84(2), 1990, 525–534.

Clark, T.C. "Internal Operation of the United States Supreme Court." *Judicature,* Vol. 43(1), 1959, 45–51.

Corley, P.C. "The Supreme Court and Opinion Content: The Influence of Parties' Briefs." *Political Research Quarterly,* Vol. 61(3), 2008, 468–478.

Cushman, R.E. "Constitutional Law in 1927–28: The Constitutional Decisions of the Supreme Court of the United States in the October Term, 1927." *American Political Science Review,* Vol. 23(1), 1929, 78–101.

Danelski, D. "The Influence of the Chief Justice in the Decisional Process of the Supreme Court." In Goldman, S., Sarat, A., eds., *American Court Systems: Readings in Judicial Process and Behavior.* San Francisco, 1978, 506–519.

Davis, J.W. "The Argument of an Appeal." *American Bar Association Journal,* Vol. 26, 1940, 895–899.

Epstein, L., Knight J. "Documenting Strategic Interaction on the U.S. Supreme Court." Paper presented at the annual meeting of the American Political Science Association, Chicago, 1995.

Epstein, L., Knight, J. *The Choices Justices Make.* Washington, D.C., 1998.

Epstein, L., Kobylka, J.F. *The Supreme Court and Legal Change: Abortion and the Death Penalty.* Chapel Hill, 1992.

Epstein, L., Segal, J.A., Johnson, T. "The Claim of Issue Creation on the U.S. Supreme Court." *American Political Science Review,* Vol. 90(4), 1996, 845–852.

Epstein, L., Segal, J.A., Spaeth, H.J., Walker, T.G. *The Supreme Court Compendium.* Washington, D.C., 1996.

Epstein, L., Segal, J.A., Spaeth, H.J., Walker, T.G. *The Supreme Court Compendium.* Washington, D.C., 2011.

Eskridge, W.N.. "Overriding Supreme Court Statutory Interpretation Decisions." *Yale Law Journal,* Vol. 101(2), 1991a, 331–455.

Eskridge, W.N. "Reneging on History? Playing the Court/Congress/President Civil Rights Game." *California Law Review,* Vol. 79(3), 1991b, 613–684.

Fang, S., Johnson, T.R., Roberts, J. "The Will of the Minority: The Rule of Four on the United States Supreme Court." Paper presented at the annual meeting of the Midwest Political Science Association, Chicago, 2007.

Ferejohn, J., Weingast, B. "Limitation of Statutes: Strategic Statutory Interpretation." *Georgetown Law Review,* Vol. 80, 1992, 565–587.

Frank, J. *Law and the Modern Mind.* New York, 1949.

Frankfurter, F., Landis, J.M. *The Business of the Supreme Court.* New York, 1928.

Gely, R., Spiller, P.T. "A Rational Choice Theory of Supreme Court Statutory Decisions with Applications to the State Farm and Grove City Cases." *Journal of Law, Economics, and Organization,* Vol. 6(2), 1990, 263–300.

Hartnett, E.A. "Questioning Certiorari: Some Reflections Seventy-Five Years after the Judges' Bill." *Columbia Law Review,* Vol. 100, 2000, 1643–1738.

Hensley, T.R., Smith, C., Baugh, J.A. *The Changing Supreme Court: Constitutional Rights and Liberties.* Minneapolis/St. Paul, 1997.

Hoekstra, V., Johnson, T.R. "Delaying Justice: The Supreme Court's Decision to Hear Rearguments." *Political Research Quarterly,* Vol. 56(3), 2003, 351–360.

Hughes, C.E. *The Supreme Court of the United States.* New York, 1928.

Hughes, C.E. "Reason as Opposed to the Tyranny of Force." Speech Delivered to the American Law Institute in Washington on 6 May 1937, *Vital Speeches of the Day,* Vol. 3(15), 1937, 458–460.

Johnson, T.R. *Oral Arguments and Decision Making on the United States Supreme Court.* Albany, 2004.

Johnson, T.R., Black, R.C., Goldman, J., Treul, S.A. "Inquiring Minds Want to Know: Do Justices Tip Their Hands with Their Questions at Oral Arguments in the U.S. Supreme Court?" *Washington University Journal of Law and Policy,* Vol. 29, 2009, 241–261.

Johnson, T.R., Roberts, J.M. "Presidential Capital and the Supreme Court Confirmation Process." *Journal of Politics,* Vol. 66(3), 2004, 663–683.

Johnson, T.R., Spriggs, J.F., Wahlbeck, P.J. "Passing and Strategic Voting on the U.S. Supreme Court." *Law and Society Review,* Vol. 39(2), 2005, 349–377.

Johnson, T.R., Wahlbeck, P.J., Spriggs, J.F. "The Influence of Oral Argumentation Before the U.S. Supreme Court." *American Political Science Review,* Vol. 100(1), 2006, 99–113.

Knight, J. *Institutions and Social Conflict.* Cambridge, 1992.

Knight, J., Epstein, L. "The Norm of Stare Decisis." *American Journal of Political Science,* Vol. 40(4), 1996, 1018–1035.

Kurland, P.B., Hutchinson, D.J. "The Business of the Supreme Court, O.T. 1982." *University of Chicago Law Review,* Vol. 50(2), 1983, 628–651.

Lawrence, S.E. *The Poor in Court.* Princeton, 1990.

Lax, J.R., Cameron, C.M. "Bargaining and Opinion Assignment on the U.S. Supreme Court." *Journal of Law, Economics, and Organization*, Vol. 23(2), 2007, 276–302.
Levi, E.H. *An Introduction to Legal Reasoning*. Chicago, 1949.
Liptak, A. "Going to Court, but Not in Time to Live." *New York Times*, 8 October 2007.
Llewellyn, K. "Some Realism about Realism: Responding to Dean Pound." *Harvard Law Review*, Vol. 44, 1931, 1222–1237.
Mackenzie, C.G. *The Politics of Presidential Appointments*. New York, 1981.
Maltzman, F., Spriggs, J.F., Wahlbeck, P.J. *Crafting Law on the Supreme Court: The Collegial Game*. New York, 2000.
Maltzman, F., Wahlbeck, P.J. "May It Please the Chief? Opinion Assignments in the Rehnquist Court." *American Journal of Political Science*, Vol. 40(2), 1996, 421–433.
Massaro, J. *Supremely Political*. Albany, 1990.
Moraski, B.J., Shipan, C.R. "The Politics of Supreme Court Nominations: A Theory of Neoinstitutional Constraints and Choices." *American Journal of Political Science*, Vol. 43(4), 1999, 1069–1095.
Murphy, W.F. *Elements of Judicial Strategy*. Chicago, 1964.
Nemacheck, C. *Strategic Selection: Presidential Selection of Supreme Court Justices from Herbert Hoover through George W. Bush*, Charlottesville, 2007.
Nemacheck, C., Wahlbeck, P.J. "The President's Choice of a Supreme Court Nominee." Paper presented at the annual meetings of the Midwest Political Science Association, Chicago, 1998.
O'Brien, D.M. "Join-3 Votes, the Rule of Four, the Cert. Pool, and the Supreme Court's Shrinking Plenary Docket." *Journal of Law and Politics*, Vol. 13, 1997, 779–808.
Peppers, T.C. *Courtiers of the Marble Palace: The Rise and Influence of the Supreme Court Law Clerk*. Stanford, 2006.
Peppers, T.C., Zorn, C. "Law Clerk Influence on Supreme Court Decision Making: An Empirical Assessment." *DePaul Law Review*, Vol. 58 (1), 2008, 51–77.
Perry, H.W., Jr. *Deciding to Decide: Agenda Setting in the United States Supreme Court*. Cambridge, 1991.
Perry, R.C., Carmichael, J.L. "Have Four Vote Certiorari Cases Been Unimportant? Qualitative and Quantitative Tests of Justice Stevens' Argument." *Cumberland Law Review*, Vol. 16, 1985, 419–446.
Pritchett, H.C. *The Roosevelt Court*. New York, 1948.
Provine, D.M. *Case Selection in the United States Supreme Court*. Chicago, 1980.
Rehnquist, W.H. *The Supreme Court*. Revised and updated edition. New York, 2001.
Revesz, R.L., Karlan, P.S. "Nonmajority Rules and the Supreme Court." *University of Pennsylvania Law Review*, Vol. 136(4), 1988, 1067–1133.
Riker, W.H. *Liberalism against Populism: A Confrontation Between the Theory of Democracy and the Theory of Social Choice*. San Francisco, 1982.
Ringsmuth, E.M., Bryan, A.C., Johnson, T.R. "Voting Fluidity and Oral Argument on the US Supreme Court." *Political Research Quarterly*, Vol. 66(2), 2013, 429–440.
Robbins, I.P. "Justice by the Numbers: The Supreme Court and the Rule of Four—Or Is It Five?" *Suffolk University Law Review*, Vol. 36(1), 2002, 1–30.
Roberts, J.G. "Testimony before the Senate Judiciary Committee." *New York Times Online*, 13 September 2005. http://www.nytimes.com/2005/09/13/politics/politicsspecial1/13text-roberts.html.
Rohde, D.W. "Policy Goals, Strategic, Choice and Majority Opinion Assignments in the U.S. Supreme Court." *Midwest Journal of Political Science*, Vol. 16(4), 1972, 652–682.

Rohde, D.W., Spaeth, H.J. *Supreme Court Decision-Making*. San Francisco, 1976.
Schubert, G. *The Judicial Mind: The Attitudes and Ideologies of Supreme Court Justices, 1946–1963*. Evanston, 1965.
Schwartz, B. *The Ascent of Pragmatism: The Burger Court in Action*. Reading, M.A. 1990.
Schwartz, B. *A History of the Supreme Court*. New York, 1993.
Segal, J. "Senate Confirmation of Supreme Court Justices: Partisan and Institutional Politics." *Journal of Politics*, Vol. 49(4), 1987, 998–1015.
Segal, J.A., Cameron, C.M., Cover, A.D. "A Spatial Model of Roll Call Voting: Senators, Constituents, Presidents, and Interest Groups in Supreme Court Confirmations." *American Journal of Political Science*, Vol. 36(1), 1992, 96–121.
Segal, J.A., Spaeth, H.J. *The Supreme Court and the Attitudinal Model Revisited*. New York, 2002.
Shullman, S.L. "The Illusion of Devil's Advocacy: How the Justices of the Supreme Court Foreshadow Their Decisions during Oral Argument." *Journal of Appellate Practice and Process*, Vol. 6(2), 2004, 271–293.
Slotnick, E.E. "The Chief Justices and Self-Assignment of Majority Opinions: A Research Note." *Western Political Quarterly*, Vol. 31(2), 1978, 219–225.
Slotnick, E.E. "Who Speaks for the Court? Majority Opinion Assignment from Taft to Burger." *American Journal of Political Science*, Vol. 23(1), 1979, 60–77.
Spriggs, J.F., Hansford, T.G. "Explaining the Overruling of U.S. Supreme Court Precedent." *Journal of Politics*, Vol. 63(4), 2001, 1091–1111.
Spriggs, J.F., Wahlbeck, P.J. "Amicus Curiae and the Role of Information at the Supreme Court." *Political Research Quarterly*, Vol. 50(2), 1997, 365–386.
Stevens, J.P. "The Life Span of a Judge-Made Rule." *New York University Law Review*, Vol. 58(1), 1983, 1–21.
Stevens, J.P. *Five Chiefs: A Supreme Court Memoir*. New York, 2011.
Wahlbeck, P.J. "The Development of a Legal Rule: The Federal Common Law of Public Nuisance." *Law and Society Review*, Vol. 32, 1998, 613–638.
Wahlbeck, P.J., Spriggs, J.F., Maltzman, F. "Marshaling the Court: Bargaining and Accommodation on the United States Supreme Court." *American Journal of Political Science*, Vol. 42(1), 1998, 294–315.
Wahlbeck, P.J., Spriggs, J.F., Sigelman, L. "Ghostwriters on the Court? A Stylistic Analysis of U.S. Supreme Court Draft Opinions." *American Politics Research*, Vol. 30(2), 2002, 166–192.
Walker, T.G., Epstein L., Dixon, W.J., "On the Mysterious Demise of Consensual Norms in the United States Supreme Court. *Journal of Politics*, Vol. 50(2), 361–389.
Warren, C., *The Supreme Court in United States History*. Boston, 1922.
Wasby, S.L., D'Amato, A.A., Metrailer, R. "The Functions of Oral Arguments in the U.S. Supreme Court." *Quarterly Journal of Speech*, Vol. 62(4), 1976, 410–422.
Wasby, S.L., D'Amato, A.A., Metrailer, R. *Desegregation from Brow to Alexander: An Exploration of Court Strategies*. Carbondale, 1977.
Watson, G.L., Stookey, J.L. *Shaping America: The Politics of Supreme Court Appointments*. New York, 1995.
Woodward, B., Armstrong, S. *The Brethren: Inside the Supreme Court*. New York, 1979.
Wrightsman, L.S. *Oral Arguments before the Supreme Court: An Empirical Approach*. New York, 2008.
Yalof, D.A. *Pursuit of Justices: Presidential Politics and the Selection of Supreme Court Nominees*. Chicago, 1999.

Chapter 5

Decision Making at the German Federal Constitutional Court

Uwe Kranenpohl

The Federal Constitutional Court in the German Political and Legal System

After the introduction of the German constitution in 1949, it took two years to establish the German Federal Constitutional Court due to rather generalized provisions in the Basic Law. Although the constitution mentions the court and sets out some of its competences, decisions on its size, the procedures for electing its judges, and many other issues were left for the first Bundestag to resolve. Not surprisingly, these issues were a source of dispute between government and opposition in the early years of the Federal Republic. Only in 1951 was the Federal Constitutional Court Act (*Bundesverfassungsgerichtsgesetz*) passed, establishing the court (Laufer 1968; Schiffers 1984).

The Federal Constitutional Court is a twin court consisting of two senates of eight judges each. The Bundestag elects half of the judges of each senate by a two-thirds majority for twelve years;[1] the Bundesrat elects the other half under the same conditions.[2] The presidents of the senates also act as President and Vice-President of the Federal Constitutional Court, but in fact, their limited competences mean that each is simply a primus inter pares. Given the size of the senates, a stalemate can emerge; in those cases the court is unable to find a violation of the constitution.

The competences of the Federal Constitutional Court are numerous. The most important types of proceedings are disputes between consti-

Notes for this chapter begin on page 160.

tutional bodies (*Organstreit*), disputes between the Federation and the *Länder* (the individual states), abstract reviews of legislation (initiated by political actors), concrete reviews of legislation (initiated by a court), and constitutional complaints. The tasks are divided between the two senates. In very simple terms, the First Senate deals with fundamental rights, and the Second Senate is responsible for other areas of constitutional law.

Unlike the U.S. Supreme Court, the Federal Constitutional Court is not "the German Supreme Court" but only one of six federal supreme courts (*oberste Bundesgerichte*) established for different areas of law.[3] Thus, in formal terms, the Federal Constitutional Court is "only" a specialized court dealing with constitutional matters. However, from its outset in the 1950s, the court started to enhance its status compared with the other federal supreme courts:

- In 1952—its first year after establishment—the Federal Constitutional Court asserted its independence from all other constitutional organs and therefore a status equal to that of the Bundestag, Bundesrat, and Federal Government (Leibholz 1957).
- In 1957 the Federal Constitutional Court ruled in the *Elfes* case (BVerfGE[4] 6, 32) that formal restrictions on fundamental rights could be challenged as "unconstitutional" by means of a constitutional complaint (and therefore challenged by everybody).
- In the following year, the Federal Constitutional Court held in *Lüth* (BVerfGE 7, 198) that the fundamental rights establish an objective system of values (*objektive Wertordnung*) that not only is effective in constitutional law but also produces a "ripple" effect through all areas of law. Consequently, the court ruled that fundamental rights are not simply defensive rights against the State but can also bind private individuals in their dealings with each other.
- Finally, constitutional complaints may be brought against all actions of public authority. That gives the Federal Constitutional Court the ability to control the judgments of all other courts (and therefore of the other federal supreme courts) as a matter of constitutional affairs. Thus, the court has opened almost all areas of life to its jurisdiction.[5]

As regards the competences of the court, there is general consensus that the Federal Constitutional Court is located at the intersection of law and politics. But there is no consensus (and especially not in the German academic literature) on the characterization of the court's activity between these poles. Most scholars of constitutional law would concede that the cases on which the Federal Constitutional Court rules have political consequences. However, they would also emphasize the nonpolitical nature of the Federal Constitutional Court as a court—and therefore also the nonpolitical character of the decision-making process in the court (Rupp-v. Brünneck 1977: 3–4; Clemens 1995: 16).

In contrast, political scientists often understand the Federal Constitutional Court primarily as a political institution. For these scholars, the central point is the constitutional court's position as a "veto player" in the political process (Tsebelis 2002) because this opens up the chance for the judges to realize their own political preferences (e.g., Hönnige 2007). But the German case is more complicated than that. Admittedly, characterizing the court as a political actor seems reasonable because, in accordance with Article 31 of the Basic Law, its decisions are binding; therefore, the court may actually veto a political decision. At the same time, German constitutional judges follow legal considerations as well as (if not more so than) political ones, with the result that political motives have to remain in the background if they cannot be "transposed" through legal reasoning.

Thus, the function of the Federal Constitutional Court could be described as providing an interface connecting law and politics. Niklas Luhmann (2000: 388–392) characterized the constitution as the "structural coupling" of the political and the legal system. In this context, the essential function of constitutional jurisprudence is "translation," that is, the parties are forced to translate political and social conflicts into the legal code (Gawron, Rogowski 2007: 63–65).

What follows will first more deeply analyze the Federal Constitutional Court as a political actor. The core of this chapter is then a close examination of decision making within the court, especially in relation to its procedural principles and the deliberations in the senates. In the final section, the chapter discusses how the deliberation process affects the case law of the Federal Constitutional Court.

The Federal Constitutional Court as a Political Actor

Konrad Hesse (1995: 278) characterized the function of the Federal Constitutional Court as "*Anteil an der Staatsleitung*" (an element in the State's governance), thus analyzing the co-governance function of the constitutional court in the political system. These steering impulses of the court can be illustrated by three modes of political action: *veto player, reserve legislator,* and *agenda setter* (Kranenpohl 2013b: 259–62).

The description of constitutional courts as *veto players* (Tsebelis 2002) is well known. The designation makes sense because the Federal Constitutional Court can nullify crucial political decisions (see arts. 78; 82(1) and 95(3) of the Federal Constitutional Court Act) and so can act as a political "nuisance."[6] However, in practice, the Karlsruhe court has used this veto relatively restrictively because, under German law, nullification takes effect *ex tunc* and *eo ipso.* Therefore, between 1952 and 1989 the Federal Constitutional Court declared only nine federal laws null and void at large. More often, the court did not reject the entire law, but only parts of it (in 173 cases by 2007).[7] Given the problematic consequences of nullification, it started early on to declare norms simply "incompatible" with the Basic Law (Hein 1988). However, no move by the court to prefer this instrument has been observed.[8]

In addition to its function as a veto player, the court may adopt other modes of political action. When the Federal Constitutional Court does not limit itself to nullification but somehow "creates" new legal norms, it acts as a *reserve legislator.*[9] In these cases, the court uses its competence under Article 35 of the Federal Constitutional Court Act to specify requirements (sometimes very detailed) to the legislators. However, the Karlsruhe court acted in that manner on only thirteen occasions between 1984 and 2001, whereas in 113 cases it nullified a provision or declared it incompatible (Komorowski, Bechtel 2006: 294).

More often, the Federal Constitutional Court finds that although a legislative provision is not unequivocally null and void, some specific interpretations of that provision are. In those cases, the court uses the instrument of "constitutionally compliant interpretations." From 1952 to 1993, it issued such constitutionally compliant interpretations on 193 occasions.[10] This practice is somewhat ambivalent. On the one hand, the court starts from the presumption that the legislators intended to create legislation that is constitutionally compliant but were simply not diligent enough. On the other hand, the "constitutionally compliant interpretation" delivered by the court limits legislators in the future. If the Karlsruhe court has identified the only "correct" interpretation of the provision, there is no further space for legislative activity. Thus, the "constitutionally compliant interpretation" operates in the same manner as a decision where the court openly acts as reserve legislator.

Finally, the Federal Constitutional Court can act as a political *agenda setter.* That role is very clear when the court nullifies a law and sets out requirements for constitutionally compliant legislation. Less dramatically, the court can instead simply appeal for legislative change, which puts the issue on the legislature's agenda all the same. This is particularly the case when the judges tie their judgment to a deadline for new legislation, indicating the "imminent occurrence of an unconstitutional situation" in the near future (Kleuker 1993). Finally, the court can spotlight a specific problem by raising it at the annual "open day."

The possibilities for the Federal Constitutional Court to act politically are ambivalent. It is important to recognize that the court cannot act of its own initiative when operating in the mode of veto player or reserve legislator. For these modes, it is essential that a party bring a case to the court so that it may enter the scene. However, with its rulings in *Elfes* (BVerfGE 6, 32) and *Lüth* (BVerfGE 7, 198), the court also opened up new areas for its jurisdiction. Finally, to manage its workload, it has established strict admissibility thresholds for constitutional complaints. Thus, it can be said that the Federal Constitutional Court acts in a self-referential matter (Rogowski 2013). On the one hand, the immense number of constitutional complaints can lead to an overload and therefore poses a challenge for the court. On the other hand, this large pool of cases opens up possibilities for the court to engage in judicial activism (Gawron, Rogowski 1991: 340). Nonetheless, it should not be overlooked that the court's rules on the admissibility of constitutional complaints are relatively stable and could be changed only in the longer term. Furthermore, a shortage of "appropriate" cases could limit its judicial activism considerably (Katzenstein 1989: 45).

The Federal Constitutional Court as a Decision-Making Body

If the Federal Constitutional Court can be understood as a political actor, it seems also justified to describe it as a political decision-making body. The widest-ranging efforts to analyze decision-making processes have been made by scholars of international relations analyzing the processes of foreign policy-making (Haftendorn 1990). Especially the multidimensional approach of Graham T. Allison (Allison 1969; Allison, Zelikow 1999) has proved useful.[11] I have written elsewhere on the different behavioral assumptions underlying certain approaches to the court's decision-making process (Kranenpohl 2010: 44–64). Particularly productive for the analysis of the court are two of the concepts outlined by Allison: *organizational process* and *governmental politics* (or negotiation game).

From the perspective of organizational process, the Federal Constitutional Court is a complex organization that can manage its workload only through division of labor. In particular, the handling of constitutional complaints is dominated by standard operating procedures (SOPs). In the face of limited resources, SOPs allow the court to accomplish a variety of tasks in an "acceptable" manner. For these purposes, however, it is crucial that SOPs focus the analysis of a case on "standard" and not "exceptional" items. This focus results in an inherent danger of ignoring specific problems, as is illustrated by the *Crucifix* decision (BVerfGE 93, 1). From the perspective of SOPs, this was a "typical" case on matters of religious freedom; consequently, the court followed the precedent established in *Cross in the Courtroom* (BVerfGE 35, 366) and thus overlooked the specific implications of the educational context, causing problems for public acceptance of the ruling.

The organizational process model focuses on aspects characterized by proper administrative procedures, such as allocation of cases to the rapporteur and the case management within his or her department. The model both highlights the various mechanisms that allow the court to work properly and have resources for "extraordinary" cases, and at the same time explains the "misconduct" that occurs when SOPs are used for an exceptional case.

In contrast, the model of governmental politics focuses on situations that are only partially structured by SOPs. From this perspective, a decision results from a "negotiation game." Given the decision-making rules and external factors, these negotiations are aimed either at forming coalitions or at finding an acceptable consensus amongst all "players." The final decision may therefore be a result that none of the players originally intended—more of a collage than a design created on a drawing board.

A player's possible moves are restricted not only by the position of the other players but also by the respective players' resources and existing action channels. Hence, there exists an interface with the organizational process model, since a formal position opens action channels and thus is a strong determinant of a player's options for action and resources (e.g., whether a person has formal responsibility may affect his or her ability to be a player).

Consequently, negotiations are not random but structured by action channels that determine whether a certain actor will face a decision situation and therefore get a chance to take part in the decision game. The judgments issued in *Damages for an Unwanted Child* (BVerfGE 96, 375) demonstrate the potency of action channels. In this case, the First Senate of the Federal Constitutional Court decided that a reference to the plenary of the court was not necessary. This decision was disregarded by the Second Senate, which, relying its own judgment in *Abortion II* (BVerfGE 88, 296), saw fit to issue its own statement on the matter (BVerfGE 96, 409). Outside of some discussions in the media, the statement of the Second Senate had no impact because there was no corresponding action channel to take the case to the plenary.[12]

The Internal Decision-Making Process of the Federal Constitutional Court

Procedural Principles

Like any other court, the Federal Constitutional Court follows clear rules in its proceedings. The principle of division of labor is dominant. It privileges the rapporteur of a case, sometimes described as the "master of the proceedings" (*Herr des Verfahrens*) (Kranenpohl 2009).

First, the court's administrative officials classify the incoming complaints. This is unimportant for most types of proceedings. However, especially for constitutional complaints, it acts as a first filter (Hövel 1990: 172–174). The presidential clerks (*Präsidialräte*)[13] can decide to register complaints in the court's general register (to be dealt with administratively and not by a judge) where these are "manifestly inadmissible" (*offensichtlich unzulässig*) or, having regard to the case law of the court, lack all chance of success (paragraphs 60(2)(a) and 61(1) of the Rules of Procedures of the Federal Constitutional Court [*Geschäftsordnung des Bundesverfassungsgerichts*]).[14] Remarkably, only a third of all complaints pass this filter (BVerfG 2012: Table D).

If a complaint gets past the court administration, the presidential clerks propose a rapporteur with regard to the court's official schedule allocating subject areas to specific judges. Based on this proposal, the president and the vice-president decide which judge is to act as rapporteur and handle the case (para. 20(2) of the Rules of Procedures of the Federal Constitutional Court).[15] The case is then handed to the legal assistants in the judge's own department (*Dezernat*) to work on.

The role of the individual departments (and thus also that of the legal assistants) differs considerably between the judges. An important question in the department is to decide if the matter must be heard by a full senate or not.[16] The two most common types of proceedings (constitutional complaints and concrete judicial review) can be heard by a chamber of three judges under certain conditions:

- the chamber must consider if an application for concrete review is inadmissible (art. 81a of the Federal Constitutional Court Act);
- it decides whether a constitutional complaint fulfills the conditions for a decision of one of the senates (art. 93b of the Federal Constitutional Court Act) or not;
- under certain circumstances a chamber can uphold a constitutional complaint (i.e., decide in favor of the complainant—art. 93c of the Federal Constitutional Court Act).

However, a chamber decision requires unanimity among the three judges. Otherwise, the case must be decided by the senate.

The character of the legal opinion (*Votum*)—and therefore also the role of the legal assistants—differs depending on whether the senate or a chamber decides the case. The senate deliberation (*Entscheidungsberatung*) is the pivotal point of the adjudication process. It focuses on a constructive treatment of both the legal issues and the related political and social questions (Hoffmann-Riem 2006). Therefore, the legal opinions are often very detailed and contain extensive appendixes, including the relevant case law of the Federal Constitutional Court and other courts and the views of legal scholars (para. 23(1) of the Rules of Procedures of the Federal Constitutional Court). The primary purpose of the legal opinion is to inform all members of the senate on the relevant aspects of the case. This allows for intensive deliberations between the judges.

The chambers, in contrast, usually decide by written consensus in lieu of group deliberations, so the legal opinion produced is more of a draft judgment than a deliberation paper. Furthermore, chamber judgments should not be creative; rather, they should comply with stare decisis and avoid mistakes.

Senate deliberations end with a decision amongst the judges on how the case should be decided. Afterwards, the rapporteur and his or her department write the draft judgment. After sending this draft to all members of the senate, the judges meet again in a "proofreading" session (*Leseberatung*) to discuss and revise the text. Finally, the court's administration delivers the judgment.

Obviously, some stages of the decision-making process are dominated by SOPs. In particular, the Federal Constitutional Court uses these procedures to deal with the abundance of constitutional complaints and also to identify the exceptional cases requiring deliberation in the senate. In chamber decisions, the requirement of unanimity and written consensus in lieu of group deliberations encourages the development and operation of SOPs; whereas the senate deliberations clearly focus on a constructive treatment of the issues and are therefore less strongly shaped by SOPs.

Deliberations in the Senate

The legal opinion written by the rapporteur and his or her department is intended primarily to convey the necessary information about the essential aspects of the case to all the judges and thus prepare them for the deliberation process. The legal opinion must satisfy many criteria. It is crucial that the rapporteur refers to the existing case law of the Federal Constitutional Court. In addition, the opinion should not rely solely on legal disciplines, but also mention the relevant academic literature (Hoffmann-Riem 2006: 4). The opinion is thus less a template for the court's decision than an advisory brief that permits a reasonably balanced level of information amongst all the judges and also helps structure the deliberations.

Unlike in the U.S. Supreme Court, where an argumentative style dominates, the main characteristics of the decision-making process in the senates of the Federal Constitutional Court (Kranenpohl 2010: 133–198) are generally deliberation and discursiveness. At the beginning of the senate session, the rapporteur presents her or his legal opinion and its essential points. The following discussions on the opinion can be very controversial, because it is the court's conviction that the senate must evaluate the opinion critically with a view to examining its quality. Overall the session is dominated by problem solving rather than bargaining.

It is critical that the sessions be absolutely confidential—not even the legal assistants are allowed to attend. Wolfgang Hoffmann-Riem, a former judge, describes impressively how this confidentiality creates an atmosphere that generates innovation and "wise decisions" (Hoffmann-Riem 2006: 15–16). In particular, it allows to the judges to deliberate without being publicly labeled a winner or loser. Indeed, it is the senate itself (which ultimately means the losing side) that decides to lift the confidentiality of the discussions and reveal internal dissent by publishing the voting record or even dissenting opinions.

Also important is the strong orientation to consensus at the Federal Constitutional Court, where there is a common belief that consensus is highly desirable, albeit impossible to reach in every case. The court regards consensus as an indicator of "quality," and consensus is also crucial to the deliberation process. Discussions in the senate are continued until all options for a consensus have been considered.[17] However, it is essential that the senate be allowed to rule by majority if there is no chance for unanimity, as otherwise bargaining could take precedence over problem solving and thus destroy the deliberative atmosphere in the sessions.

The senate deliberations form a key element of the decision-making process because this closed-door session has a monopoly over the interpersonal aspects of decision making. Within the Federal Constitutional Court, agreements on voting behavior in the deliberations are considered absolutely unacceptable.[18] To preserve the deliberative character of the discussions, it is essential that the outcome of the process remains unforeseeable for all the judges involved. Therefore, the role of the legal assistants is not so important in the Karlsruhe court. Legal assistants may play significant roles within their own departments (and consequently also in chamber decisions), but their potential for influence ends when the door closes on the judges' deliberations.

Even though its political role is significant, the Federal Constitutional Court acts primarily as a court, for which it is crucial to "transpose" political and social issues into legal ones. This forces the court to adhere to the rules of the legal language game (so as to be compatible with other courts). At the same time, "translation" implies an effect of alienation that permits judges' predispositions to be reviewed. Finally, the legal language game (at least in its German variation) offers considerable scope for controversy. Research on the psychology of groups shows that confrontation with dissent improves the problem-solving capacity of the majority, even if it does not change its position fundamentally (Nemeth 1986: 28, 1992: 100–102).

However, groups that have been in existence for a long time (e.g., the senates of the Federal Constitutional Court) are increasingly at risk of "papering over" conflicts with formulaic compromises (Sader 1998: 235–236). This concern for group cohesion—along with the existing desire to ensure that one's opinion is accepted—may reinforce the tendency toward unanimity. This phenomenon of *groupthink* (Janis 1982) poses considerable danger for highly cohesive groups because their members' efforts to achieve unanimity could drown out their willingness to evaluate alternatives. Groupthink increases the risk of poor decisions because the desire for conformity leads to suppression of critical analyses of the chosen course (Moorhead, Neck 1995: 1130).[19] However, these risks can be reduced when a group works methodically (Janis 1982: 245) as experimental jury decisions have confirmed (Neck, Moorhead 1992: 1088). As regards the decision making process of the court, it is suggested that what dominates is not groupthink but the group interaction pattern of "balanced critical deliberation" (Stern, Sundelius 1997). This is ensured by four factors:

- the primacy of legal reasoning,
- the monopoly of collective deliberation in the decision-making process,
- the absolutely confidential character of the deliberations, and
- the dominance of problem solving over bargaining.

It must be noted that the essential cornerstones of the Federal Constitutional Court's decision-making process are not covered by formal, codified rules. Instead, these norms are transmitted by the organizational culture of the court and internalized by newly elected judges, who experience considerable problems in identifying these norms (Kranenpohl 2010: 440–450). The recruitment process may also have an effect. It is criticized as opaque and seems also to be experienced as such by the "chosen ones" (Kranenpohl 2011, 2013a) who thus demonstrate a strong tendency to follow the informal norms of the court.

The Processing of Constitutional Complaints

In the specific practices of processing constitutional complaints, the primary objective is to pick out the relevant cases. The admissions procedure is particularly important because most complaints fail to clear this hurdle. Meanwhile, it must be recognized that nearly two-thirds of the "key decisions" of the Federal Constitutional Court arise from constitutional complaints, with some one in six resulting from a preliminary ruling or concrete norm control.[20]

Despite the initial sifting carried out by the court administration, a considerable number of constitutional complaints reach the departments. According to the judges, the processing of the complaints in the departments is quite laborious (Kranenpohl 2010: 106). The opinions produced simply for chamber rulings can be very extensive—even where the chamber declines to assess the case on the merits, the opinion may have an appendix totaling one hundred pages (Blankenburg 1998: 213).

But to what extent does the admission process operate as a selection process based on clear categories? Or is it a "lottery" for the complainant (Wank 1980: 549) in which judges take up cases at random? All the judges admit that there are moments of arbitrariness in the admission process because it is not easy to satisfy the open-ended criteria for admission set out in Article 93a(2) of the Federal Constitutional Court Act: "I don't think it will ever be possible to word this provision on admission such that it can be applied to the facts in the same way as a provision of criminal law" (cited from Kranenpohl 2010: 109). Certainly the judges perceive this lack of transparency as a flaw: "Over the years, a 'barbed wire entanglement' of admissibility criteria has been established. This requirement to show both an exhaustion of other remedies and that the complaint is substantiated …! You need excellent arguments to overcome that hurdle" (Kranenpohl 2010: 109).[21] Standardizing the procedure facilitates consistency across the court. In addition, according to the judges, establishing strict formal hurdles is indispensable for a supreme court not subject to supervision. It is the only means of preventing the Federal Constitutional Court from usurping the functions of other authorities, in particular the specialized courts (*Fachgerichtsbarkeit*) (Kranenpohl 2010: 112). Notwithstanding the considerable formal barriers, the procedure allows for a certain leeway in decision making, but not for a system of "case picking."

Formally, the examination of whether the complaint is well founded follows that of admission, but in fact the two issues are interconnected (Lübbe-Wolf 2004: 676–677):

> When is a constitutional complaint sufficiently well founded?[22] Well, that's a value judgment, very much a value judgment. … If you look at a constitutional complaint and see that from various different legal perspectives there is nothing in it, then you are more willing to say: "This doesn't satisfy the requirements for an examination on the merits." Then you're a little stricter on that point, you rely on that, because it's easier. … However, if you get a sense that in other respects the constitutional complaint is well founded and that it deals

> with an important issue, you don't start fussing too much over these requirements. Even though it's the same standard, perhaps you'd say: "Well, let's not look that closely!" That may seem arbitrary to non-lawyers. But where a lawyer has room for interpretation, he makes use of it according to those criteria. (cited from Kranenpohl 2010: 115)

Some judges, meanwhile, regard this discretion with skepticism. Nonetheless, even they admit that the available leeway allows the Federal Constitutional Court to deal with individual circumstances, even if the constitutional complaint is not totally "airtight" in each respect:

> To a layman that might sound as if I am saying that the court acts in an arbitrary and random manner. But it's not like that. All the same, my impression and feeling is that the court operates on the principle *de minimis non curat lex,* if this reduces the workload. It's a question of "should I really take on another senate case? We don't need that right now! It's not exactly important!" (cited from Kranenpohl 2010: 116)

However, the uncertainties in the admission process also open up possibilities for control because rapporteurs' proposals always need consensus in the chamber. Since the criteria for admission are controversial, the SOPs of one judge and that judge's department are repeatedly questioned by colleagues and their departments.

The Impact of the Deliberative Process on the Case Law of the Federal Constitutional Court

Although the relevance of issues of doctrine and method is limited by the Federal Constitutional Court's internal focus on deliberations, these issues should not be ignored out of hand. The ability to perform with legal virtuosity is an important resource for each judge in the negotiation game. Moreover, it is vital that the court's final ruling be "well founded," so that it finds sufficient acceptance within society. Finally, the judgment has to fit within current legal discourses in order to be handled in this framework.

When considering issues of doctrine or method with regard to the Federal Constitutional Court, it has to be noted that contingency plays an important role:

> What the court states on issues of method is not consistent. *In truth the court aims to reach the outcome that appears to it correct.* On the way the court observes basic rules of exegesis or other principles of constitutional interpretation as warning lights, but not as a means of ensuring the correct outcome. They are simply buoys, and do not act as pilots. (Mahrenholz 1990: 60; emphasis in the original)

It should also be noted that whereas clearly structured reasoning for the ruling is not necessary, it does have to be documented that the judgment is not arbitrary. Often it is almost impossible to reconstruct the court's arguments of a prominent ruling: "It is true that a court must demonstrate clearly a deductive process. However, this requirement is satisfied where the judges can at least suggest that their decision is derived from a codified rule of law" (Sobota 1996: 131).

These considerations relating to the overall scheme of the law are not dominant in specific individual deliberations. More important are aspects of the specific case and path dependency resulting from the principle of stare decisis:

> The "judicial doctrine of fundamental rights" emerged more or less as a "by-product". ... You've got a problem, you've got the constitution and you find a way of bringing the two together! For that you need some relatively abstract concepts that sound like doctrine on fundamental rights. That does the trick; you've a solution that appears snappy and convincing. But this doesn't result in real doctrine. (cited from Kranenpohl 2010: 345)

In addition, the Federal Constitutional Court's concept of weighing up the issues is focused on broadening its decision-making scope, given that a strictly doctrinal approach would limit the court and its judges. Weighing allows the court flexibility in adjudication. Inevitably, then, the doctrinal system cannot correct the low standard of legal determination resulting from other methods (Ebsen 1985: 89). The court's requirements for a systematic approach to its own doctrines are less extensive:

> Even if it sounds sometimes as if the court has a particular system in mind, for example, the "value system of the Basic Law," this is not intended as a closed doctrinal system that permits clear and unambiguous legal consequences to be drawn for the interpretation of fundamental rights and for the relationship between those rights (Geiger 1979: 5).

Academic legal literature and the specialist courts are important partners in the judicial discourse of the Federal Constitutional Court as well as an important source of critique. The Association of German Constitutional Law Professors (Vereinigung der Deutschen Staatsrechtslehrer) merits particular mention because prior to their appointment to the court a considerable number of Federal Constitutional Court judges are already members of the association in their capacity as professors of public law (Oppermann 2001).[23] This process of interaction between the court and constitutional law writers is considered very important in the Federal Constitutional Court, particularly because writers and commentators have the task of "cleaning up the doctrine" (Kranenpohl 2010: 274–275).

Overall, the role of doctrine in the court's practice is ambivalent. On the one hand, the Federal Constitutional Court's (quasi-)doctrinal reasoning constitutes a significant factor in explaining its rulings. Doctrinal considerations are also crucial in the internal deliberation process, especially with regard to application of the principle of stare decisis. On the other hand, the judges have a particular interest in using relatively open terminology to give their successors some leeway. However, this desire for flexibility is thwarted when it meets resistance in academic writing and the case law of other courts where schematic considerations are prioritized.

Conclusions

What are the results of applying a social science perspective to the Federal Constitutional Court? First, it must be noted that the court clearly exercises a judicial function. It does not act purely as a political actor but must also be seen as an "exceptional" veto player. Judicial activism is confronted with considerable limits inside the court, making it almost impossible for "activist" judges to follow their personal judicial agenda. These constraints and the enduring internal search for consensus seem to be the most important differences between the Federal Constitutional Court and the U.S. Supreme Court. From the perspective of global history following World War II, constitutional review is a success story, not only in Germany but throughout the democratic world. Yet it has to be recognized that no constitutional court is the same as another. Research on constitutional review needs to go beyond the U.S. Perhaps it is fortunate that the powerful German Federal Constitutional Court exhibits remarkable differences from the U.S. approach. With that in mind, several issues are worth exploring in future research on the Federal Constitutional Court.

In existing research, the most important source of information on the decision-making process of the Federal Constitutional Court has been the judges themselves. But with regard to the day-to-day routine, the focus needs to shift to the departments and the legal assistants working there. Many Federal Constitutional Court judges previously worked as legal assistants, so we have some knowledge of that routine. However, our observations are more impressionistic than systematic. Given that a relatively large number of former assistants now work in other parts of the judiciary, a mixed-methods approach with a standardized survey and complementary semi-structured interviews seems most promising.[24]

Since we have some knowledge of the "manufacturing process" within the Federal Constitutional Court, the texts of the rulings themselves should be investigated more intensively. It is obvious that the reasoning of some judgments focuses on the public (or specific publics) to encourage support or acceptance for the rulings. Analyzing judgments in that regard could prove worthwhile.[25]

Finally, the research should not stop at the U.S. Supreme Court and the German Federal Constitutional Court but has to go further. More comparative research is necessary and should not be limited to national constitutional courts only. It also has to focus on subnational courts (like the supreme courts of the U.S. states or the constitutional courts of the German *Länder*) and the supranational European courts in Luxembourg and Strasbourg.

Uwe Kranenpohl is a professor of political and administrative sciences at the Evangelische Hochschule (EVHN), Nuremberg.

Notes

1. In all cases a judge must retire at the age of 68.
2. Some rules differed somewhat from today's during the first twenty years of the Federal Constitutional Court's existence, but the two-thirds majority as a cornerstone of the electoral procedure was already in force.
3. The other courts are the Federal Court of Justice (Bundesgerichtshof) for civil and criminal cases (also located in Karlsruhe), the Federal Administrative Court (Bundesverwaltungsgericht) in Leipzig, the Federal Labor Court (Bundesarbeitsgericht) in Erfurt, the Federal Social Court (Bundessozialgericht) in Kassel, and the Federal Fiscal Court (Bundesfinanzhof) in Munich.
4. *Entscheidungen des Bundesverfassungsgerichts* = Official Reports of the Rulings of the Federal Constitutional Court.
5. Similarly, in the *Lisbon* case (BVerfGE 89, 155, at p. 171) the Federal Constitutional Court allowed constitutional complaints to be brought against the German ratification of the Treaty of Lisbon, thus securing its ability to control the process of European integration.
6. The criticism is often leveled that the Federal Constitutional Court "knows no bounds" (Jestaedt et al. 2011).
7. The data are taken from the official statistics of the Federal Constitutional Court (Annual Statistics and own counts). Please note that the statistics do not differentiate between primary legislation (statutes) and secondary legislation (regulations, etc.) where only parts of the legislation are nullified. Cf. Kneip (2006) for a policy-oriented analysis.

8. By 2007, only eleven federal laws and 210 individual provisions were declared incompatible.
9. A well-known example of the Federal Constitutional Court's acting as reserve legislator is its decision on the need for parliamentary approval to deploy German armed forces (BVerfGE 108, 34).
10. Since 1994 these are no longer reported in the official statistics. Cf. Wewer (1991: 314 [Table 3]).
11. Allison himself has suggested that his concept "can be applied broadly in arenas beyond foreign affairs" (Allison, Zelikow 1999: 7).
12. Thus Korioth characterizes the behavior of the Second Senate as "odd" (*kurios*) (Schlaich, Korioth 2012: 26, fn. 47).
13. The two *Präsidialräte* assist the president and the vice-president of the Federal Constitutional Court in their functions as chairpersons of a senate.
14. The court informs the complainant of this decision by letter, setting out the complainant's right to request a judicial ruling (par. 61(2) BVerfGGO).
15. If the presidential clerks are in doubt about the correct allocation, the problem is mostly solved informally. As a result, the "committee of six" (art. 14(5) of the Federal Constitutional Court Act) has met on very few occasions since 1952.
16. Only 2 percent of all cases are decided by one of the two senates. In the other cases one of the three chambers of each senate rules as the Federal Constitutional Court.
17. Studies on the American jury system show that the number of unanimous decisions decreases when the jury may decide by majority vote. Under the unanimity rule, discussions are longer and more intense. Even jury members' willingness to change their opinion increases (Nemeth 1977: 53–55).
18. When this commandment is violated, profound conflicts in the Court immediately ensue (Kranenpohl 2010: 490–491).
19. The concept of *group polarization*, which focuses less intensively on crises, describes similar effects (Myers, Lamm 1976).
20. The 209 "key decisions" have been identified using the lists in Grimm, Kirchhof (1993, 95 decisions); Grimm, Kirchhof (1997, 104 decisions); Grimm, Kirchhof, Eichberger (2007, 122 decisions); Menzel (2000, 107 decisions); Säcker (2003, 25 decisions) and Wesel (2004, 76 decisions).
21. Thus, the judges have consistently recognized the need for a proper scheme of touchstones to guarantee some degree of consistency in the procedure (Lübbe-Wolff 2004). On the considerable efforts made within the Federal Constitutional Court see also Kerscher (2004).
22. The examination of the merits is part of the examination of admissibility (Schlaich, Korioth 2012: 153–67).
23. Some also take part in the meetings of professional associations in other areas of law, especially if they are allocated that area under the court's schedule of responsibilities.
24. This would also provide an opportunity to test whether membership of the "Third Senate" (as the legal assistants are humorously known) is really a springboard for further careers, as is often suggested.
25. To accusing the court of a lack of doctrinal rigor (a criticism leveled by certain legal writers) while ignoring its task of "problem-solving" is just as problematic as it is to accuse it of pursuing a political agenda (as some political scientists do) while ignoring the principle of stare decisis.

Bibliography

Allison, G.T. "Conceptual Models and the Cuban Missile Crisis." *American Political Science Review,* Vol. 63(3), 1969, 689–718.

Allison, G., Zelikow, P. *Essence of Decision: Explaining the Cuban Missile Crisis,* 2nd ed. New York, 1999.

Blankenburg, E. "Die Verfassungsbeschwerde – Nebenbühne der Politik und Klagemauer von Bürgern." *Kritische Justiz,* Vol. 31(2), 1998, 203–218.

Bundesverfassungsgericht „Jahresstatistik 2011". http:// http://www.bundesverfassungsgericht.de/DE/Verfahren/Jahresstatistiken/Archiv/2011/gb2011/D.html.

Clemens, T. "Das Bundesverfassungsgericht im Rechts- und Verfassungsstaat: Sein Verhältnis zur Politik und zum einfachen Recht; Entwicklungslinien seiner Rechtsprechung." In Piazolo, M., ed., *Das Bundesverfassungsgericht – Ein Gericht im Schnittpunkt von Recht und Politik.* Mainz, Munich, 1995, 13–31.

Ebsen, I. *Das Bundesverfassungsgericht als Element gesellschaftlicher Selbstregulierung. Eine pluralistische Theorie der Verfassungsgerichtsbarkeit im demokratischen Verfassungsstaat.* Berlin, 1985.

Gawron, T., Rogowski, R. "Drei Seiten des Bundesverfassungsgerichts." In Blanke, B., Wollmann, H., eds., *Die alte Bundesrepublik. Kontinuität und Wandel.* Opladen, 1991, 336–353.

Gawron, T., Rogowski, R. *Die Wirkungen des Bundesverfassungsgerichts – Rechtssoziologische Analysen.* Baden-Baden, 2007.

Geiger, W. *Vom Selbstverständnis des Bundesverfassungsgerichts.* Hanover, 1979.

Grimm, D., Kirchhof, P., eds. *Entscheidungen des Bundesverfassungsgerichts,* 2 vols. Tübingen, 1993.

Grimm, D., Kirchhof, P., eds. *Entscheidungen des Bundesverfassungsgerichts. Studienauswahl,* 2 vols., 2nd ed. Tübingen, 1997.

Grimm, D., Kirchhof, P., Eichberger, M., eds. *Entscheidungen des Bundesverfassungsgerichts. Studienauswahl,* 2 vols., 3rd ed. Tübingen, 2007.

Haftendorn, H. "Zur Theorie außenpolitischer Entscheidungsprozesse." In Rittberger, V., ed., *Theorien der internationalen Beziehungen – Bestandsaufnahme und Forschungsperspektiven.* Opladen, 1990, 401–423.

Hein, P.E. *Die Unvereinbarerklärung verfassungswidriger Gesetze durch das Bundesverfassungsgericht. Grundlagen, Anwendungsbereiche, Rechtsfolgen.* Baden-Baden, 1988.

Hesse, K. *Grundzüge des Verfassungsrechts der Bundesrepublik Deutschland,* 20th ed. Heidelberg, 1995.

Hoffmann-Riem, W. "Die Klugheit der Entscheidung ruht in ihrer Herstellung – selbst bei der Anwendung von Recht." In Scherzberg, A., ed., *Kluges Entscheiden. Disziplinäre Grundlagen und interdisziplinäre Verknüpfungen.* Tübingen, 2006, 3–23.

Hönnige, C. *Verfassungsgericht, Regierung und Opposition. Die vergleichende Analyse eines Spannungsdreiecks.* Wiesbaden, 2007.

Hövel, M. *Zulässigkeits- und Zulassungsprobleme der Verfassungsbeschwerde gegen Gesetze.* Berlin, 1990.

Janis, I.L. *Groupthink: Psychological Studies of Policy Decisions and Fiascoes.* 2nd ed. Boston, 1982.

Jestaedt, M., Lepsius, O., Möllers, C., Schönberger, C. *Das entgrenzte Gericht. Eine kritische Bilanz nach sechzig Jahren Bundesverfassungsgericht.* Frankfurt/Main, 2011.

Katzenstein, D. "Macht und Ohnmacht des Bundesverfassungsgerichts." In Hartwich, H.-H., ed., *Macht und Ohnmacht politischer Institutionen.* Opladen, 1989, 41–56.

Kerscher, H. "Marathonlauf zum Recht. Warum so viele Verfassungsbeschwerden scheitern – eine Richterin kritisiert die vielen Hürden." *Süddeutsche Zeitung,* 10 December 2004, 9.

Kleuker, M. *Gesetzgebungsaufträge des Bundesverfassungsgerichts.* Berlin, 1993.

Kneip, S. "Demokratieimmanente Grenzen der Verfassungsgerichtsbarkeit." In Becker, M., Zimmerling, R., eds., *Politik und Recht.* Wiesbaden, 2006, 259–281.

Komorowski, A., Bechtel, M. "Gesetzgebungs- oder Justizstaat? Zum (Macht-)Verhältnis zwischen Bundesverfassungsgericht und Parlamentsgesetzgeber am Beispiel der aktuellen grundrechtsdogmatischen Entwicklung." In Becker, M., Zimmerling, R., eds., *Politik und Recht.* Wiesbaden, 2006, 282–305.

Kranenpohl, U. "Herr des Verfahrens oder nur Einer unter Acht? Der Einfluss des Berichterstatters in der Rechtsprechungspraxis des Bundesverfassungsgerichts." *Zeitschrift für Rechtssoziologie,* Vol. 30, 2009, 135–163.

Kranenpohl, U. *Hinter dem Schleier des Beratungsgeheimnisses. Der Willensbildungs- und Entscheidungsprozess des Bundesverfassungsgerichtes.* Wiesbaden, 2010.

Kranenpohl, U. "Bewährt oder reformbedürftig? Für und Wider das aktuelle Verfahren der Richterwahl zum Bundesverfassungsgericht." *Zeitschrift für Staats- und Europawissenschaften,* Vol. 9(1), 2011, 78–98.

Kranenpohl, U. "Unter dem 'blauen Himmel'. Das Bundesverfassungsgericht zwischen Formalität und Informalität." In Korte, K.-R., Grunden, T., eds., *Informelles Regieren.* Wiesbaden, 2013a.

Kranenpohl, U. "Verfassungsrechtsprechung: Regieren mit Richtern." In Korte, K.-R., Grunden, T., eds., *Handbuch Regierungsforschung.* Wiesbaden, 2013b, 257–266.

Laufer, H. *Verfassungsgerichtsbarkeit und politischer Prozess. Studien zum Bundesverfassungsgericht der Bundesrepublik Deutschland.* Tübingen, 1968.

Leibholz, G. "Der Status des Bundesverfassungsgerichts. Gutachten, Denkschriften und Stellungnahmen mit einer Einleitung." *Jahrbuch des öffentlichen Rechts der Gegenwart,* Vol. 6, 1957, 109–221.

Lübbe-Wolff, G. "Substantiierung und Subsidiarität der Verfassungsbeschwerde. Die Zulässigkeitsrechtsprechung des Bundesverfassungsgerichts." *Europäische Grundrechte-Zeitschrift,* Vol. 31, 2004, 669–682.

Luhmann, N. *Die Politik der Gesellschaft.* Frankfurt/Main, 2000.

Mahrenholz, E.G. "Probleme der Verfassungsauslegung. Verfassungsinterpretation aus praktischer Sicht." In Schneider, H.-P., Steinberg, R., eds., *Verfassungsrecht zwischen Wissenschaft und Richterkunst. Konrad Hesse zum 70. Geburtstag.* Heidelberg, 1990, 53–65.

Menzel, J., ed., *Verfassungsrechtsprechung. Hundert Entscheidungen des Bundes-verfassungsgerichts in Retrospektive.* Tübingen, 2000.

Moorhead, G., Neck, C.P. "Groupthink und Führung." In Kieser, A., Reber, G., Wunderer, R., eds., *Handwörterbuch der Führung.* Stuttgart, 1995, 1130–1138.

Myers, D.G., Lamm, H. "The Group Polarization Phenomenon." *Psychological Bulletin,* Vol. 83(4), 1976, 602–627.

Neck, C.P., Moorhead, G. "Jury Deliberations in the Trial of *U.S. v. John DeLorean*: A Case Analysis of Groupthink Avoidance and an Enhanced Framework." *Human Relations,* Vol. 45(10), 1992, 1077–1091.

Nemeth, C.J. "Interactions Between Jurors as a Function of Majority vs. Unanimity Decision Rules." *Journal of Applied Social Psychology,* Vol. 7, 1977, 38–59.

Nemeth, C.J. "Differential Contributions of Majority and Minority Influence." *Psychological Review,* Vol. 93(1), 1986, 23–32.

Nemeth, C.J. "Minority Dissent as a Stimulant to Group Performance." In Worchel, S., Wood, W., Simpson, J.A., eds., *Group Process and Productivity.* Newbury Park, CA, London, New Delhi, 1992, 95–111.

Oppermann, T. "Das Bundesverfassungsgericht und die Staatsrechtslehre." In Badura, P., Dreier, H., eds., *Festschrift 50 Jahre Bundesverfassungsgericht,* vol. 1. Tübingen, 2001, 421–460.

Rogowski, R. "Constitutional Courts as Autopoietic Organisations." In Wrase, M., Boulanger, C., eds., *Die Politik des Verfassungsrechts: Interdisziplinäre und vergleichende Perspektiven auf die Rolle und Funktion von Verfassungsgerichten.* Baden-Baden, 2013, 117–131.

Rupp-v. Brünneck, W. "Verfassungsgerichtsbarkeit und gesetzgebende Gewalt. Wechselseitiges Verhältnis zwischen Verfassungsgericht und Parlament." *Archiv des öffentlichen Rechts,* Vol. 102, 1977, 1–26.

Säcker, H. *Das Bundesverfassungsgericht.* Munich, 2003.

Sader, M. *Psychologie der Gruppe.* Weinheim, Munich, 1998.

Schiffers, R., ed. *Grundlegung der Verfassungsgerichtsbarkeit. Das Gesetz über das Bundesverfassungsgericht vom 12. März 1951.* Düsseldorf, 1984.

Schlaich, K., Korioth, S. *Das Bundesverfassungsgericht. Stellung, Verfahren, Entscheidungen,* 9th ed. Munich, 2012.

Sobota, K. "Argumente und stilistische Überzeugungsmittel in Entscheidungen des Bundesverfassungsgerichts. Eine Rhetorik-Analyse auf empirischer Grundlage." *Jahrbuch Rhetorik,* Vol. 15, 1996, 115–136.

Stern, E.K., Sundelius, B. "Understanding Small Group Decision Making in Foreign Policy: Process Diagnosis and Research Procedure." In Hart, P., Stern, E.K., Sundelius, B., eds., *Beyond Groupthink: Political Group Dynamics and Foreign Policy-Making.* Ann Arbor, 1997, 123–150.

Tsebelis, G. *Veto Players: How Political Institutions Work.* New York, 2002.

Wank, R. "Die verfassungsgerichtliche Kontrolle der Gesetzesauslegung und Rechtsfortbildung durch die Fachgerichte." *Juristische Schulung,* Vol. 20, 1980, 545–553.

Wesel, U. *Der Gang nach Karlsruhe. Das Bundesverfassungsgericht in der Geschichte der Bundesrepublik.* Munich, 2004.

Wewer, G. "Das Bundesverfassungsgericht – eine Gegenregierung? Argumente zur Revision einer überkommenen Denkfigur." In Blanke, B., Wollmann, H., eds., *Die alte Bundesrepublik. Kontinuität und Wandel.* Opladen, 1991, 310–335.

Chapter 6

Junior Varsity Judges?

Law Clerks in the Decisional Process of the U.S. Supreme Court

Artemus Ward

The nine justices of the U.S. Supreme Court do not work alone. They are assisted by a group of young attorneys who are intimately involved in each step of the Supreme Court's decisional process. From recommending which issues the Court will address to drafting the opinions issued under the justice's names, the clerks have become central to the Court's operation. As the clerks have taken on more responsibility, critics have suggested that they wield undue influence over the law. To be sure, clerks are expected to make recommendations to their justices and are otherwise working closely with them to craft the law. Still, regardless of the question of undue influence, it is plain that the clerks are firmly entrenched as key participants in the process by which justices make decisions and interpret the U.S. Constitution.

Law Clerks: Sorcerers' Apprentices

Congress has provided funds to allow each justice to hire four law clerks. Because of extra administrative duties, the Chief Justice is allowed five—though Chief Justice Roberts has only chosen to hire four. Each retired justice is allowed a single clerk. The clerks assist the justices with their work, a practice started by Justice Horace Gray in the late nineteenth century (Peppers, Ward 2012). The clerks are recent graduates from top law schools. Though most of the clerks attended Harvard, Yale, Chicago, Columbia, Stanford, Virginia, and Michigan, many other law schools regularly place clerks with the justices. Prior to joining the Court, clerks spend one year clerking for a judge on the U.S. Courts of Appeals, where they gain experience and are recommended by so-called feeder judges who routinely place their clerks at the Supreme Court (Ditslear, Baum 2001). Each justice chooses his or her own clerks, though some delegate the task to trusted confidants. Justice Sotomayor explained what she looks for in potential clerks: "I want smart people but I want people who are good people too. They have to be kind and caring and really smart" (Interview with Justice Sonia Sotomayor 2009). Once at the Court, clerks spend one year working on the cases petitioned to the justices as well as the cases the justices accept. They read petitions, briefs, and lower court opinions; and draft memos, opinions, and other documents to aid their justices in the decision-making process (Peppers 2006). Following their clerkship year, they are highly sought after and typically choose to work in private practice, government, and academia—often commanding salaries far greater than those of the justices they clerked for.

The role of clerks has changed over time. They have taken on an increasing amount of responsibility. Retired Justice John Paul Stevens, who clerked for Justice Wiley Rutledge in 1945, said:

> The clerks have a much larger role in all of the work that goes on. I did very little work on Justice Rutledge's opinions. He wrote them all out in longhand ahead of time and did very little work on comments on other Justices' opinions. We only got one copy of a draft in the chambers, and he would read it, and somebody would send it back and join it—whereas now we all will send at least two copies of a draft opinion around to everyone else because every Justice likes to have his law clerk study the case too before he joins the opinion and see if there are any suggestions that might be helpful to the case. And the clerks now play a much larger role in the entire decisional process than they did when I was a clerk." (Stevens, cited in Garner 2010b: 42)

Do clerks have influence on the decisions the justices make, or do they merely carry out the orders that their justices give them? The justices, for their part, have been adamant that the clerks do not wield power. Justice Elena Kagan remarked, "I know the clerks improve my work [but] they are by no means junior varsity judges" (Kagan 2012b). Justice Stevens said: "I learn from my clerks, to tell you the truth. I'll write something; they'll sometimes rewrite a paragraph, and gee, that sounds a lot better. And I learn a great deal. It's a constant learning process, yes" (cited in Garner 2010b: 50). Research shows that although clerks may not be making the decisions for their justices, they can be influential in terms of the recommendations they make and the opinions they draft (Ward, Weiden

2006; Peppers, Zorn 2008). Clerks are ever present through each stage of the decision-making process and are central to the Court's work.

Deciding to Decide: Agenda Setting

The Court largely *chooses* which cases it wants to formally decide. But it can only choose from among the appeals that litigants ask it to review. Nearly all of these cases come in the form of a petition for a writ of certiorari. The word "certiorari" is Latin for "make certain." Hence, a petition for certiorari—commonly referred to as a "cert petition"—is a request from a litigant asking the Supreme Court to make certain that a lower court decision was correct. Of the nearly 10,000 cases appealed to the Supremes every year, only seventy or so are decided with full written opinions after oral argument.

How can nine justices examine nearly two hundred petitions each week? The answer is that they have a lot of help. Their clerks prepare brief memos on each case, which aids them in deciding which cases should be granted. Stevens explained: "We have to be honest that a lot of the cert petitions we do not actually read. I think we all use clerks to give us an awful lot of help in processing cert petitions. I tend to read the cert petition before I vote to grant, but unless one of my clerks has identified it as a potential grant, I usually will not read the original papers myself" (cited in Garner 2010b: 45).

Each justice employs four law clerks, so there are currently thirty-six clerks who are primarily responsible for reviewing each cert petition the Court receives. The last justice to personally review cert petitions without the aid of his clerks was Justice William Brennan, who retired in 1990. Each of the other justices worked individually with their own clerks to identify meritorious cases. As a result, there were nine chambers independently reviewing each petition. In an effort to save time, a handful of justices started the cert pool in 1973. The plan was that the justices who chose to participate would pool their clerks to divide up the petitions so that each clerk had an equal number of different petitions to review. Instead of the duplication of having nine clerks, one for each justice, review the same petition, that petition would now be reviewed by only a single pool clerk. At first only some of the justices participated in the pool. But over time more and more joined until only one justice operated on his own outside the pool. For many years that was Justice Stevens, whose clerks had to divide up the petitions amongst themselves. Following Stevens' retirement, Justice Samuel Alito chose to operate outside the pool. The justices generally like the fact that at least one justice's chambers operate independently so that there can be a check on the work produced through the cert pool.

Excluding Justice Alito's chambers, there are thirty-two clerks in the pool and sometimes more, when retired justices' clerks participate. As a result, each pool clerk reviews and writes a memo on roughly six cases each week. Justice Alito, like Justice Stevens before him, does not require his clerks to write memos on all of the petitions: if they did, each of his four clerks would be writing nearly fifty memos each week! Instead, they prepare memos only for the cases they think merit discussion.

Which petitions are meritorious? Research reveals that the clerks and the justices look for cues: shortcuts that indicate a case is "worthy" of consideration. The most important cue is conflict among courts. Conflict among two or more courts of appeals is known as a "circuit split," and there can be conflicts between state supreme courts as well. When two or more lower courts have reached different conclusions on the same question, the Supreme Court views its role as that of national arbiter, settling different conclusions reached in different regions of the country and providing clarity in the law. Another important cue is interest-group participation: organized interests file amicus briefs to persuade the Court to hear a case. The justices and clerks view amicus participation as a signal that the case is important. A third cue is that the U.S. government is a party to the dispute. The justices and their clerks pay more attention to cases involving the federal government, particularly those where the government is the petitioner. The Court recognizes that the Office of the Solicitor General—the U.S. government's attorney before the Court—is staffed with highly skilled lawyers with limited resources, so when the solicitor general thinks a case is important enough to ask the justices to review, the Court pays close attention.

Ideology is another cue. The justices and clerks look for cases where lower-court decisions conflict with current Supreme Court ideology. In other words, clerks and justices are thinking about the Court's ultimate vote on the merits when they consider whether a lower-court decision should be granted or not. Justices who are likely to overturn the lower-court result are more likely to grant the case than those who prefer the status quo. Thus ideology is an important cue in the agenda-setting process. Finally, the law matters. Cases that could give the Court an opportunity to a make national pronouncement on an important question of law are often seen as cert-worthy by the justices and their clerks. The chances that the Court will take a case are greatest when two or more cues exist in the same case.

Some justices have their clerks "mark up" the pool memo with their own views and recommendations. The extent to which a pool memo gets marked up varies depending on the quality of the memo and the clerks and justices involved. For example, Justice Harry Blackmun, suspicious of ideological bias, asked his clerks to mark up the pool memo with information about the pool clerk who drafted the memo: the clerk's name, the justice they currently clerked for, the lower court judge they last clerked for, and the law school attended. In-chambers markups of pool memos are thus an important check on pool clerks who might be biased or who might downplay factors important to some justices.

The chief justice and his clerks construct a list of cases they think ought to be discussed and formally voted on in private conference by the nine justices. The other justices may add cases to the "discuss list." Cases not listed by any justice are automatically denied. The vast majority of pool memos recommend denial, making it relatively easy to draw up the discuss list. Jay Wexler, a former clerk to Justice Ruth Bader Ginsburg, said, "I didn't recommend that the Court grant a single one of the 250 or so petitions I worked on" (Wexler 2012). Critics suggest that the clerks are reluctant to recommend grants for fear they might be ostracized for being wrong, particularly if the Court initially grants the petition but later dismisses it as "improvidently granted." Wexler explained that when this happens, "the clerk at fault will feel like a total jackass, and everyone will look funny at the clerk and say things behind the clerk's back. … This is, as you might imagine, the clerk's worst nightmare" (Wexler 2012). Yet both the clerks and the justices know that the vast majority of cert petitions will not be worthy of review. Justice Anthony Kennedy explained: "We've read a lot of other cert petitions, and we know about this issue. And we're walking through familiar terrain. And if there isn't something urgent about the case that is expressed to us at the outset, we know that we're not going to do it" (Kennedy, cited in Garner 2010c: 97).

By tradition, cert is granted if at least four of the justices decide a case deserves to be formally decided on the merits—the so-called Rule of Four. Justice Kagan explained that even though "all of us in the abstract would say we should take more cases," she could not explain why the Court was taking half as many cases as it did when she clerked for Justice Thurgood Marshall in 1987 (Kagan 2012b). Still, she said, she did not believe important cases were being overlooked. On occasion a justice will hedge his or her bet and vote to "join 3," meaning that if three other justices vote to grant the case, that justice will join them as the fourth vote to grant cert. The cert votes are not made public, however, and the Court only announces whether each petition was granted or denied. Sometimes a justice will dissent from a denial of cert and explain why the case should have been granted. Particularly stinging dissents from denials of cert can sometimes prompt justices who initially voted against granting cases to change their positions and vote to accept them.

May It Please the Court: Briefs, Bench Memos, and Oral Argument

Once a case is granted, the Court directs the parties to prepare briefs on the question or questions the justices want to decide. Justice Kagan commented:

> The briefs are your avenue into really important, really challenging legal issues, and that's what makes reading briefs fun. And occasionally, very occasionally, you'll read a brief that is just a masterwork of brief-writing, and you'll just enjoy it for that reason alone. But for the most part reading briefs is interesting because the cases are fascinating, and the legal considerations are fascinating. And the briefs are your way—you know, another way—of trying to figure them out and make sense of them. … The most important thing in a brief is clarity. If there's one thing about brief-writing you could reform, it's confusing briefs—briefs where you're working too hard to try to figure out what the point is and to figure out how the argument goes. There are two really important things about brief-writing. One is you have to know your best arguments. Second, you have to say those arguments clearly. Sometimes it's frustrating, because you'll be reading a brief and there will be good arguments there, but it's just so hard to get them out of this brief. You have to do so much work by yourself or with clerks to do that. It's a disservice to the real arguments that are there. (Kagan 2012a)

Chief Justice John Roberts echoed Kagan's comments: "The quality of briefs varies greatly. We get some excellent briefs; we get a lot of very, very good briefs. And there are some where the first thing you can tell in many of them is that the lawyer really hasn't spent a lot of time on it, to be honest with you" (Roberts, cited in Garner 2010a: 6). Justice Stephen Breyer described his job as one of essentially reading: "Most of what we do is in this enormous stack of briefs. Most of what we do is in memos, briefs, reading" (Breyer 2005).

After the justices receive the legal briefs, they work with their clerks to prepare for oral argument. Former Ginsburg clerk Jay Wexler explained: "All the justices use their clerks differently for this purpose. Most require their clerks to prepare 'bench memos,' papers that range anywhere from three to 50 pages long, which summarize the parties' arguments and offer the clerk's own analysis of the relevant legal issues. Some justices discuss the cases intensely with their clerks; Justice Ginsburg tended to do relatively little of that" (Wexler 2012). Whereas Justice Stevens did not have his clerks do bench memos, he did spend considerable time listening to his clerks: "I always talk to my law clerks. I don't have them write bench memos, but I always review the cases and my thinking about the case both before argument and after argument. I ask them to come in, and we sit down and talk about what happened at the argument. Then I'll talk to them again before and after a conference. I have a lot of conversation with my clerks to get their reaction to a case" (Stevens, cited in Garner 2010b: 47).

Given that the justices have all the information in a case submitted to them in writing, some have questioned whether oral argument matters. Justices often foreshadow their position on the case through their questions and comments. Justice Alito explained how each term he arrives at the first oral argument "filled with hope that this will finally be the term when all of my colleagues see the light of day"—a hope that "begins to fade five or ten minutes into the first case" (Alito 2012). Research shows that the justices pay close attention to their colleagues' questions and statements and use this information to craft opinions during the coalition formation process (Johnson, Black, Wedeking 2012). Meanwhile, Justice Sonia Sotomayor described how seeing a litigant in court can also make a difference: "When you're in your office reading the briefs you understand the voices that they're giving you, but when you see their faces it just reinforces that importance in a way nothing else can" (Sotomayor 2009).

The Court allots thirty minutes for each side in a dispute to orally argue its case. The justices may increase argument time in a particularly complicated case, but this is rare. Over the course of the Court's history, the oral argument time has steadily shrunk from virtually unlimited arguments in the early years to one hour per side as recently as 1969 and half that today. Justice Kennedy explained his frustration with the limited time that he is able to devote to a case: "We have very difficult cases. The amount of time we give is so short that it is cruel. My colleague Justice Breyer and I wish we had more than 30 minutes per side" (Kennedy, cited in Garner 2010c: 88).

Justice Stevens commented on what he expected from attorneys in oral argument: "Be well prepared, of course. Be intellectually honest; don't try and conceal problems that the judges are going to find anyway. And do the best you can to explain why your side should win" (Stevens, cited in Garner 2010b: 48). During oral argument, justices constantly interject questions, often suggested by their clerks, leading to the Court's current reputation of having "a hot bench." Justice Kagan, who served as solicitor general before joining the Court, said that answering questions "was a ton of fun" but was also more difficult than asking them (Kagan 2012b). She defended the system:

> I actually think, for the most part, I think we can overdo it occasionally, and sometimes we do overdue it occasionally. But I think for the most part the hot bench is a good thing. This is a court [where] all nine of us have read the briefs and have read the briefs carefully. For a lawyer to get up and repeat what's in his or her briefs is kind of a waste of time for everybody. It might make the lawyer feel good that she's had a chance to say some things but we really don't

> need that and it doesn't really help us. What does help us is you read a set of briefs and you're going to have some questions about it. You're going to have some times in the briefs where you say 'No, that's wrong' or where you say 'Well I just don't understand that.' In general it's a good thing for arguments to be a place where you can bring all of those questions to the advocates and say 'Convince me of this because right now I'm not convinced' or 'Explain this to me because right now I don't understand this.' Advocates should want that. (Kagan 2012b)

Kagan explained that oral argument is more about the justices talking with each other than it is a series of individual conversations between the justices and an attorney: "Sometimes there's a conversation among the justices that's kind of happening through the lawyer but where the objective is less to ask for the lawyer's views or explanation but more to try to make a point to your colleagues." Justice Kennedy said that sometimes lawyers are not prepared for this: "I think they could understand the dynamic a little bit better. They could understand that when I'm asking a question, I'm sometimes trying to convince my own colleagues, and so they could answer not just me but answer based on what they think the whole Court needs to know to decide the case" (Kennedy, cited in Garner 2010c: 95).

Research shows that oral argument matters. Quality arguments are more likely to win than poor arguments (Johnson 2004). Accordingly, in recent years an elite group of attorneys have come to specialize in Supreme Court oral argument. This "Supreme Court Bar" is largely composed of attorneys who formerly worked in the Office of the Solicitor General or clerked at the Supreme Court. Indeed, it has become routine for former clerks to argue cases before the justices they clerked for. Justice Kagan explained: "They understand what the exercise is about and are extremely good at it. It means we are actually getting answers to our questions" (Kagan, cited in Miller 2012).

Still, a poor argument can win if the justices are either predisposed to ruling that way, or if justices or clerks can marshal persuasive arguments from within the Court *after* oral argument. Justice Stevens related an example:

> I can remember a case when I was a law clerk that I think was argued by an attorney general of one of the states. It was a tax case in which I remember all the law clerks in advance of the argument thought there's no way in the world that this guy could win—and particularly when he made his argument, that there's nothing to it. And he was so bad that the clerks decided they'd better try and research the problem and figure out what arguments might be made on that side of the case, and they came up with arguments he totally omitted, and he won the case. But that doesn't happen very often. (Stevens, cited in Garner 2010b: 49)

Crafting the Law: Voting, Opinion Assignment, and Opinion Writing

The justices meet in their private conference room to discuss the cases in which they have just heard oral argument. Here, the nine are alone—no clerks or secretaries are allowed. The chief begins by stating the facts of the case and his vote. The discussion and remaining votes proceed in order of seniority with the most junior justice speaking and voting last. There is an informal rule that no one should speak twice until everyone has spoken once, and in most cases the discussion ends after each justice has had his or her initial say. But on occasion there is further discussion, as Justice Kagan explained:

> Certainly that's true if you have a fractured Court and then people will try very hard to try to keep talking until some kind of majority emerges. But in other cases too there will be times when people will want to respond to things that another justice has said or want to say "that strikes me as right or wrong or a good understanding or a bad understanding." People will want to debate a little bit often. People will want to raise questions about what each other has said. So sometimes the conversation after the initial go-round can be fairly extensive. And then other times it's like "We've all said what we've said and that about resolves the matter." (Kagan 2012c)

Justice Breyer commented that everyone is actively involved in the process: "The key to that conference is people are saying what they really think. They're not trying to create an impression. And everybody writes down what everybody else says and there is some discussion and it works because we all respect each other as individuals" (Breyer 2005).

The most junior justice is tasked as the official note taker and doorkeeper in case anyone knocks or the justices need something to be brought to them. After her first two years performing this duty, Justice Kagan remarked: "I myself think it's some kind of hazing ritual" (Kagan 2012b). Because she votes last, Kagan explained, she is unable to say anything at conference to influence her colleagues before they vote. Instead, she uses oral argument as the venue to raise issues and make sure her colleagues are aware of how she is thinking about a case: "I do use argument as a way to, not always but sometimes, as a way to sort of float some ideas in hopes that some or one or many of my colleagues hear them" (Kagan 2012c).

The clerks are not allowed in the conference room, so the justices meet with their clerks afterward to review the conference discussion. In this way, the clerks instantly know where the other justices stand on the merits of a case, which can aid them in forming and maintaining coalitions and alliances across chambers. In addition, clerks continue the process of lobbying their justice on the merits of the case—a process that tentatively begins during the cert and oral argument stages. Knowing the details of conference discussion is also important for clerks when they draft opinions for their justices—particularly opinions for the Court, which should reflect the overall will of the majority.

A day or two after conference, opinions are assigned by the chief justice if he is in the majority. If he is not, the opinion is assigned by the most senior justice in the majority. Who writes the opinion is important because if five or more justices agree, the majority opinion is the law of the land. The chief considers a number of factors in assigning opinions. He is concerned with distributing the workload evenly so that each justice writes roughly the same number of majority opinions each term. Chiefs often assign important, landmark cases to themselves to lend the decision additional authority or to build their reputations, or both. In a closely divided case, the opinion is often assigned to a justice with a moderate or tentative position whose vote will constitute a majority—that is, a "swing vote." Some justices become expert in particular areas of the law and are regularly assigned opinions in those cases.

The justice to whom the opinion is assigned directs his or her law clerk to write the first draft of the opinion. The extent of the direction given a clerk depends on the individual justice. Some provide minimal input, while others lay out the key arguments and cases in outline form. Justices revise clerk-written drafts, more or less, depending on both the individual justice's level of engagement in the process and the clerk's skill at opinion writing. Former clerk Jay Wexler (2012) explained: "The clerks usually write a first draft of the opinions that their justice has been assigned to write. Some people find this shocking, but it really is not that big a deal. At least in Justice Ginsburg's chambers, the boss would give us a detailed outline to work from and then, once we turned in our drafts, totally rewrite them. The best you could really hope for as a clerk is to get a little pet phrase or goofy word or other quirky something-or-other into the final opinion." Justice Kennedy described the process in his chambers:

> Right when I hear the opinion's assigned, I'll write out what I think should be the key portions, but then I obviously have to discuss the cases and so forth. I tell my clerk what I want written, but I can't read what the clerk writes until I've read my own. Because the clerk spends a long time on it, and if you're on a scale of 1 to 10, he'll be at level 8. And if I haven't written anything, I'm still at level 1. And I won't know the false starts that the clerk made, or the blind alley, whatever the metaphor is, until I've gone down the blind alley or made the false start myself. There are certain things that you think immediately will be the way to decide the case, but that doesn't work. But you have to almost try them yourself before you understand that. So it's very hard to read someone

else's writing unless you've written something on it before. Then you know why this suggestion is being made. (Kennedy, cited in Garner 2010c: 96)

Justice Kagan said that after she receives a clerk-written draft, she displays it on her computer screen alongside a blank document in which she composes a fresh opinion, using the clerk's draft to orient her in terms of structure and order and to see what does and does not substantively work: "I write all my own opinions. For me it's really important that an opinion sounds like me. I am quite sure that I have had clerks who are better purer writers than I am but it's not the way I write. For me, I don't think through a problem until I write through a problem" (Kagan 2012c). What does a Kagan opinion sound like? She explained that her style is to write as simply as possible, "to be a little bit colloquial, to drop the legalese and express things in the way people would in a normal conversation."

It has become increasingly rare for justices to write their own opinions with little or no clerk input prior to drafting. Newer justices often write their own opinions, and a justice may draft the occasional concurrence or dissent, but clerk-written drafts are the norm. Justice Stevens explained why he endeavored to write his own opinions during his tenure from 1975 to 2010: "I think a judge learns more about a case if he has to put his thoughts down on paper. It helps you think through a case, and when you write it out yourself, you often learn things about the case that you hadn't realized. It's part of the learning process and decisional process that I think is really quite important" (Stevens, cited in Garner 2010b: 42). But research shows that other justices, such as Sandra Day O'Connor and Thurgood Marshall, often issued opinions with few or no changes to what their clerks drafted (Ward, Weiden 2006: 200–236).

Critics suggest that over time, opinions have gotten longer—and therefore more convoluted—because the clerks have taken on the primary drafting responsibility. Justice Stevens agreed: "When a judge writes out an opinion, he can explain what his thinking is and do it in so many words, and that's the end of it, whereas the capable, scholarly law clerks tend to feel they really have to prove everything. And so they will often be much more thorough in their research and their consideration of all the arguments than the judge who just sort of thinks he maybe has to tell the world what motivated his particular actions, so I really think that's part of it" (Stevens, cited in Garner 2010b: 42–43). Clerk-written drafts are read by the other clerks in the chamber, as well as the justice, and revisions are made. When the justice is satisfied with the result, the opinion is circulated to the other justices via written memoranda. Justice Kagan noted: "We communicate by written message. A messenger walks around the corner to deliver them" (Kagan, cited in Miller 2012).

Join Me: Coalition Formation

After the majority opinion author circulates a draft, the clerks from the other chambers review it and, if necessary, suggest changes and make recommendations to their justices. The goal is to achieve as much consensus as possible. Contrary to popular conception, the justices reach unanimity about one-third of the time and reach a high level of agreement more often than not (Corley, Steigerwalt, Ward 2013). Justice Kagan commented: "We agree more than people know and more than we're given credit for. Many of our opinions are unanimous and if they're not unanimous they're 8-1 or 7-2" (Kagan 2012c). If a justice agrees with the majority opinion as written, he or she sends a "join" memo to the opinion author stating "join me" or "I agree." Justices who disagree with the majority opinion send memos to the opinion author requesting changes. The clerk who originally drafted the opinion reviews them and makes recommendations to their justice about what should or should not be changed and why. Justice Alito commented: "What you *want* is a memo saying, 'Perfect! Don't change a word!' What you *get* is, 'if you take this or that [part of the opinion] out, I'll sign'" (Alito 2012). Chief Justice Roberts said: "You have to remember this is a collegial enterprise, and when you're judging authorship, you have to appreciate that compromises are made to get a Court. Somebody says, 'Put in this language' to get a vote. It may not be the language I would have chosen, but I'll do it if I need the vote" (Roberts, cited in Garner 2010a: 33). As a result, majority opinions are the handiwork of multiple clerks and justices.

It is rare for justices to call each other on the phone, let alone walk to each other's chambers to converse face-to-face. Instead, law clerks mine the "clerk network" at lunchtime, in the hallways, and on the basketball court—jokingly referred to as "the highest court of the land"—to ferret out information for their justice on the positions of the other justices. The justices so value information gleaned from the clerk network that they have arranged for a separate law clerk dining area in the Court's cafeteria to facilitate these conversations. In this sense, clerks act as informal ambassadors negotiating and bargaining between chambers.

Justices who are only partially satisfied with the reasoning of the majority opinion but agree with the result may issue their own concurring opinions. Justices who disagree with the majority may write dissenting opinions. As with majority opinions, clerks are primarily responsible for drafting these separate opinions. Justice Kagan explained how writing a dissent and composing a majority opinion are different enterprises: "When you're writing the dissent, even when you expect some other justices to join the dissent, there's an expectation that you can be more yourself.

Sometimes I feel that when I sit down at my computer and I'm writing the dissent and you just have this feeling like 'now I'm being myself' in a way that maybe you're not when you're writing for the Court" (Kagan 2012c).

On occasion, a justice will change his or her mind and switch an initial conference vote during the coalition formation stage. Justice Alito explained: "It's not a change of position by the opinion-writing judge, but it's a change of position by others on the Court. When you read the majority opinion and you read the dissent, and you say, 'Well, the dissent actually seems to be correct,' and then a vote can change. That does happen" (Alito, cited in Smith 2012). He further noted that these switches cause the majority to become the minority about once each term. Justice Breyer said that although the justices can be persuaded to change their minds, it becomes less likely as the case progresses through the Court:

> I'm holding myself open to being persuaded and if I come out of that oral argument and I change my mind, as I do on occasion sometimes, more often than people think, I don't think, oh how stupid I was. I think how great. You see I'm holding myself open. I want to be persuaded, so persuade me. And then we go into the conference. You see it's becoming narrower and narrower. By the time that conference is finished, I say it's tentative but it isn't really so tentative. And by the time people write drafts of opinions and circulate them we change sometimes, once a year, twice a year. (Breyer 2005)

Justice Ginsburg said: "It ain't over 'til it's over. People change their minds about what they thought. So it isn't at all something extraordinary, and that's how it should work. We're in the process of trying to persuade each other and then the public" (Ginsburg, cited in Biskupic 2012).

Even rarer than changing a vote after having read a majority opinion is changing a vote *while* writing a majority opinion. When asked how often this happens, Justice Stevens said: "Not very often, but once in a while it does happen: once every couple of years at the most" (Stevens, cited in Garner 2010b: 43). Justice Scalia remarked that he too has switched his votes: "I have not only done that, I have changed my mind after having been assigned to write the majority opinion. I've written the opinion the other way, it just wouldn't write. There is nothing wrong with that" (Scalia 2012). However, when this happens in landmark cases there can be an unusual amount of scrutiny and press coverage of the switch. For example, in *National Federation of Independent Business v. Sebelius* (2012), journalist Jan Crawford reported that Chief Justice Roberts initially voted with his four conservative colleagues to strike down the Affordable Care Act—popularly known as "Obamacare"—but changed his mind and upheld the law after he and his clerks began working on the majority opinion (Crawford 2012).

Conclusion

In the United States, law clerks are central to the judicial process. In the U.S. Supreme Court, justices vote on cases and provide the intellectual framework for and subsequently edit the opinions drafted by their clerks. Clerks review the thousands of petitions that pour into the Court, recommend which cases to grant, prepare their justices for oral argument, draft opinions, and facilitate negotiations between chambers. In all, the clerks and justices comprise a small group of legal professionals who work together to resolve the nation's most important legal and political controversies. Over a century ago, Justice Louis Brandeis once said that, unlike in the other branches of government, the justices did their own work. Today, the clerks are so completely integrated into the decisional process of the Court that the justices could not do their work without them.

Artemus Ward is a professor of political science at the Department of Political Science, Northern Illinois University, DeKalb.

Bibliography

Alito, S.A. "Justice Alito at RWU Law, Pt.1." *Roger Williams University Law Newsroom,* 14 September 2012. http://law.rwu.edu/story/justice-alito-rwu-law-pt-1.

Biskupic, J. "Exclusive: Justice Ginsburg Shrugs Off Injury." *Reuters,* 8 August 2012. http://www.reuters.com/article/2012/08/09/us-usa-court-ginsburg-idUSBRE87801920120809.

Breyer, S. "Supreme Court Justice Stephen Breyer Interview." *CNN Larry King Live,* 23 November 2005. http://transcripts.cnn.com/TRANSCRIPTS/0511/23/lkl.01.html.

Corley, P.C., Steigerwalt, A., Ward, A. *The Puzzle of Unanimity: Consensus on the U.S. Supreme Court.* Stanford, 2013.

Crawford, J. "Roberts Switched Views to Uphold Health Care Law." *CBSNews.com,* 1 July 2012. http://www.cbsnews.com/8301-3460_162-57464549/roberts-switched-views-to-uphold-health-care-law.

Ditslear, C., Baum, L. "Selection of Law Clerks and Polarization in the U.S. Supreme Court." *Journal of Politics,* Vol. 63(3), 2001, 869–885.

Garner, B.A. "Chief Justice John G. Roberts, Jr." *The Scribes Journal of Legal Writing,* 2010a, 5–40. http://legaltimes.typepad.com/files/garner-transcripts-1.pdf.

Garner, B.A. "Justice John Paul Stevens." *The Scribes Journal of Legal Writing,* 2010b, 41–50. http://legaltimes.typepad.com/files/garner-transcripts-1.pdf.

Garner, B.A. "Justice Anthony M. Kennedy." *The Scribes Journal of Legal Writing,* 2010c, 89–98. http://legaltimes.typepad.com/files/garner-transcripts-1.pdf.

Johnson, T.R. *Oral Arguments and Decision Making on the United States Supreme Court.* Albany, 2004.

Johnson, T.R., Black, R.C., Wedeking, J. *Oral Arguments and Coalition Formation on the U.S. Supreme Court: A Deliberate Dialogue.* Ann Arbor, 2012.

Kagan, E. "Full Transcript of Bryan A. Garner's Interview with Elena Kagan," *ABA Journal,* 1 September 2012a. http://www.abajournal.com/magazine/article/full_transcript_of_bryan_a._garners_interview_with_elena_kagan.

Kagan, E. "Conversation with Supreme Court Justice Elena Kagan." *C-SPAN,* 20 September 2012b. http://www.c-span.org/Events/Conversation-with-Supreme-Court-Justice-Elena-Kagan/10737434240.

Kagan, E. "Justice Kagan Describes Inner Workings of Supreme Court to University of Richmond Audience." *Associated Press, Washington Post,* 20 September 2012c. http://www.washingtonpost.com/local/justice-to-have-discussion-with-richmond-law-school-dean-before-audience-of-students-others/2012/09/20/4cedec3c-02f2-11e2-9132-f2750cd65f97_story.html.

Miller, J. "Supreme Court Justice Elena Kagan Tells U-M Crowd about Serious and Not-So-Serious Workings of the High Court." *AnnArbor.com,* 7 September 2012. http://www.annarbor.com/news/supreme-court-justice-elena-kagan-discusses-the-serious-and-not-so-serious-workings-of-the-high-cour/#.UF8_ho2PU1M.

Peppers, T.C. *Courtiers of the Marble Palace: The Rise and Influence of the Supreme Court Law Clerk.* Stanford, 2006.

Peppers, T.C., Ward, A. *In Chambers: Stories of Supreme Court Law Clerks and Their Justices.* Charlottesville, 2012.

Peppers, T.C., Zorn, C. "Law Clerk Influence on Supreme Court Decision Making: An Empirical Assessment." *DePaul Law Review,* Vol. 51(1), 2008, 51–78.

Scalia, A. "Justice Antonin Scalia on Issues Facing SCOTUS and the Country." *Fox News Sunday,* 29 July 2012. http://www.foxnews.com/on-air/fox-news-sunday/2012/07/29/justice-antonin-scalia-issues-facing-scotus-and-country.

Smith, M.R. "Alito Says Supreme Court Misunderstood by Media." *Associated Press,* 14 September 2012. http://www.boston.com/news/local/rhode-island/2012/09/14/alito-says-supreme-court-misunderstood-media/onnoFr6jnCEhI2c3KDMX9I/story.html.

Sotomayor, S. "Interview with Justice Sonia Sotomayor." *C-SPAN,* 16 September 2009. http://supremecourt.c-span.org/assets/pdf/SSotomayor.pdf.

Ward, A., Weiden, D.L. *Sorcerers' Apprentices: 100 Years of Law Clerks at the United States Supreme Court.* New York, 2006.

Wexler, J. "I Made Clarence Thomas Laugh." *Salon.com,* 18 August 2012. http://www.salon.com/2012/08/18/i_made_clarence_thomas_laugh.

Chapter 7

Legal Assistants at the German Federal Constitutional Court

A "Black Box" of Research?

Otwin Massing

I

Despite the common acknowledgement that the so-called Third Senate of the German Federal Constitutional Court—that is, its legal assistants—cannot be regarded as an independent unit within the Court in Karlsruhe (only para. 13 of the Court's rules of procedure honors legal assistants with a passing mention), the academic literature recounts the judicial activities of the judges' "left hands" (as the legal assistants are bound to follow instructions) in gushing terms. Although the €5 million (roughly $6.76 million) allocated for the legal assistants in the 2013 federal budget is generally perceived as high, assessments of the relevance of their (participatory) judicial function tend to reflect the principle that at some time, and in some way, quantity will influence quality.

However, a problem, which I would like to call the "black box" of the constitutional judicature, is precisely the lack of knowledge of the role of legal assistants, whose contributions to judicial decision-making have been neither deciphered through participant observation nor analyzed from an interdisciplinary point of view in any comprehensive fashion. A crucial part of such research would be to assess the role of the legal assistants in each judge's search for optimal, "objectively consented" (Massing 1989) problem-solving strategies, which the Federal Constitutional Court is supposed to deliver as a bureaucratic institution in an official

Notes for this chapter begin on page 187.

manner. The expectations of the public (parties to disputes and others), which manifest themselves in the demand for cases put before the "stock exchange" of the Court in Karlsruhe, have to be satisfied through the symbolic exchange of institutional "goods" (judgments, decisions, etc.) in order to avoid far-reaching disturbances or imbalances of the "market" (lack of acceptance of decisions, threats to the legal peace, etc.).

The question therefore arises as to when and how the proposed change from quantity to quality occurs, from the legal assistants' "input" as a manpower factor to the "output," that is, the manner and degree of their usefulness in the decision-making process based on the principle of division of labor. The answer requires an assessment of their impact on the realization of a decision whose ultimate purpose, as a final judgment, is to conclude, once and for all, the exchange of interest against law by way of a "just" and lawful collective choice between conflicting rights, and thus to correct the societal imbalance that manifested itself in the dispute submitted to the Federal Constitutional Court.

Neither analytical criticism nor methodical comparison has successfully revealed the role and function of the legal assistants in the constitutional decision-making process (Benda 1980; see also various contributions in Umbach et al. 1984: esp. 213–222 and 357–399; also Landfried 1984: 161 et seq.). This holds true even for the "critically realist" study by Hans Lietzmann (1988) that is characterized by a "blackout" in its theoretical approach when it comes to the judgment factory called the Federal Constitutional Court.

The following remarks provide little more than an outline (one of many possible ones) that might guide research by considering and testing scenarios in a thematic and methodological order, the outcome of which may lead to an independent research program. The primary purpose of presenting areas of inquiry is to uncover paths that transcend an academic discussion that exhausts itself in mere semantic variations on existing and recognized facts (e.g., the repetitive presentation of formally regulated competencies, procedures, and institutionalized relations between the internal and external justice environment) and ultimately engages itself in a theoretically blind, positivistic repetition of reality with uncritical, affirmative tendencies.

II

An empirical examination of the career paths and patterns of the Federal Constitutional Court's "accredited" legal assistants is easy to do and carries the illusion of statistical exactitude. Total number and sex, personal and professional background, length of employment at the Court, remuneration, professional advancement, and the discrepancies in remuneration dependent upon the chosen career path in the hierarchical organization of limited posts, whether in the state or in academia, are well known. Statistically they can be expounded upon with relative ease (see Wieland 2002).

This "precise" information does not, however, say anything about the societal patterns of circulation of a legal or bureaucratic elite whose specialist competence is used both to strengthen the "interior design of power" (*Innenausstattung der Macht,* Glotz 1981), and to increase the efficiency of the administration of justice as a whole by differentiating and distancing it from the societal and political environment. Unless questions are posed about the power or influence of the "perpetrators behind the perpetrators," ironic remarks made about the legal assistants of the Federal Constitutional Court (e.g., "gray eminences," ghost-writers, or vote slaves caught in a dependent, paramilitary-like relationship to "their" judge) quickly become mere flourishes. In fact, the winking, "augural" behavior of all involved points to a conclusion often reached by research into bureaucracy: that as a rule, an objectively founded dependent relationship can only be sustained through symbolic and material compensation, and in any case requires "processing" individually in a compensatory manner. The high degree of personal motivation and career orientation among legal assistants, insofar as they could be surveyed, as well as the occasional fits of elitism and their mirror image—the manifestation of mild cynicism—can be cited as proof of this compensatory effect. If the "basic personality trait" of a lawyer can generally be described as conservatism (a claim supported by much empirical evidence), then maybe one should examine the hypothesis that the personality structure of competent, alert career climbers who have worked at the Court in Karlsruhe may only mirror (or strengthen) that which is expected institutionally and can be labeled as institutionally rewarded "affirmative conformism." Just as it is not possible to reconstruct the genesis of bureaucratic institutions without falling back on the subjects in them as constants and disruptive or dynamic factors, it is also not possible for their character to form without institutional reference. As is known, individuals and their societal relations interact as communicating vessels.

III

The legal assistants at the Federal Constitutional Court can be understood as having dual status. They are *dependents* in that they work according to orders and are essential in relieving the judges' workload, effecting an increase in the judges' standing. Meanwhile, in terms of the *division of labor,* they solipsistically prepare drafts of chamber evaluations, chamber decisions,[1] and the votes of the Senate, but this input is nevertheless absorbed by their judge's function as a solely responsible reporter of the case, or by the judgments of the Senate. Decision making is almost compulsively made to seem a synthesis of a collective will. This occurs at the cost of the "dissolution" of strategic arguments developed by subordinate producers (and precisely because they stem from their subordination), as if these arguments were banished to a telluric, shadowy realm of lowly remunerated ranks. Even in Karlsruhe the *Nibelungen* tragedy of unshakable loyalty can be felt in the form of an exploitative relationship, the difference being that the shining role of the developed constitutional state is magnified through the discretion of the exploited—assuming sensitivity for the machinery of the spectacle.

IV

The anonymity of the Third Senate's work allows the Federal Constitutional Court's practice of "work on the judgment," and work in the judgment factory of justice (Massing 1989), to be described according to the bureaucratic model of line management. During this process the precedence function (or the judgment and responsibility function) of each constitutional judge "covers" the work of his or her staff, no matter what quality and relevance the work may have. Furthermore, the judge's assistant (at the moment each judge has four) is able to use the (empty) title "Member of a Chamber Department," even if this is only by default due to the minimum of personnel. At the same time, the role of the speaker of the legal assistants at the Federal Constitutional Court is already taking on the symbolic character of a "president" of the Third Senate. Of course this role is an organic development, and the title is used ironically. However, apart from planned innovations or conscious restructuring, bureaucracy, as is well known, develops metastatically under pressure to differentiate. If all signs are not illusionary, the beginnings of this process are visible in developments of the Third Senate.

Furthermore, the typical power asymmetries that come into play in the line management relationship necessitate a precarious balancing act to uphold the functioning of the relationship pattern of "loyalty as a social bartering mechanism" (Massing 1987a: 48–74) and to make sure that its emotional life is not prematurely ended. The classical communication structure of "leadership in a collaborative relationship," which is also the basis for the interactions between the assistant and the judge (forming the so-called department [*Dezernat*]) in a chamber; at the moment there are three chambers per Senate), probably cannot prevent the informal development of emotional and argumentative ambivalence, despite a clear hierarchy (dependency upon the allocation of tasks, requirement of support, selection prerogative, and the professional evaluation prerogative of the judge). Although the division of labor between the judge and the assistant makes the work process in "departments," and thus in the judgment factory of the Federal Constitutional Court, more rational and probably more efficient (at least in the context of the use of the important scarce resource of "time"), at the same time its symbiotic system of reliance develops a dynamic of its own. Professional competence and qualification are of (primary) importance, but so are those "secondary characteristics" that have been taught to and internalized by both established and new members of the machinery of justice through their unmistakable intensive socialization. Above all, judges expect reductions in workloads, but they also have an additional expectation as to behavior and loyalty; assistants, meanwhile, see these expected behaviors as obligations on their part. The consequences of the symbiosis should not be way of affective approval, loyalty not only forms undervalued. "By inwardness through the acquisition of values, attitudes, and norms that are pre-established by power and societal rights of disposal, it also creates at the same time conditions for the reinforcement of domination in society through a fixation on its rational or irrational character" (Massing 1987a: 62).

V

This profit relationship of mutuality based upon a division of labor can be "tolerated" in different and differently troublesome ways. A number of hypothetical questions can be formulated in this context. For example, to what extent do the judges deny that the supremacy of their position stems from the power they have to allocate work? Alternatively, to what extent do the judges deny that they depend on the goodwill, willingness to work, and quality of the work of their assistants? Which mechanisms do they use to do so? Do they show their superiority in a cynical way, or do they drown their ambivalent feelings in a show of joviality? Are they secretly plagued by fears in which subjectively the de facto dependency—suspected or recognized—upon the work of others is exorcised symbolically? Does the predetermined, hierarchical, bureaucratic structure, whose representatives they are, resonate in an analogous personality structure? Does this involve the use of a particular ideology of personality, that is, does it manifest itself in an objectively false consciousness? Or are the professional relationships perceived as "normal," evaluated with common sense, and simply seen as commonplace? However, what then does this type of "normality" mean with respect to the perception of atypical relationships?

More importantly, how do the legal assistants react to the objective and subjective ambivalences of the constitutional judges? Is their reaction immediate or delayed? Analogous or opposing? Weakened or strengthened? Showing subservience or latent spite? Which forms of overcompensation occur?

VI

The Court cannot "actively" take up problems and issues arising out of constitutional adjudication. Only through a case (and through those actively participating therein) can the Court officially deal with these issues and problems. The Court's task in doing so is to transform real problems, using its own specific juristic techniques, into its own language in order to enable legal processing. A dilemma arises from this transformation in that the controversial options, the pros and cons of the perception of a problem and the methodology of the problem solving, are determined by the participants or requested by them (and others). However, in hindsight this dilemma proves to be the structural advantage of the Court's judicature. It can be described and understood as the Court's specific location profit (*Lage-Rente*) in the system of separation of powers of the Federal Republic of Germany.

The legal assistants, who are appointed to the Court for a limited period, are also involved in the legal evaluation of the problems brought before the instances of the Federal Constitutional Court—naturally within a framework of formally allocated competencies. However, competence is power to influence (Massing 1987b: 122–123), and this power becomes more uncontrolled the less the contents of the competencies are defined, and the more that the competencies do not themselves prevent automatic expansion or are even immune thereto.

In this context, the sources that the legal assistants include in the synthesized products of the Federal Constitutional Court are of interest mainly from the point of view of *specific selection.* Which sources, internal and external, governmental and nongovernmental, do they use? According to which substantial criteria do they develop the problem outline upon which they base their judgments or submissions? Which precedents do they make use of systematically and which not? And why not? How are insights derived from disused mechanisms of the constitutional judicature applied to new problem constellations and to novel requirements? Does such transfer learning exist at all? In this respect, are the stability-oriented decisions of the Federal Constitutional Court detrimental to the recognition and the consideration of dynamic social changes? Do they even hinder change?

VII

Whatever the answers to such research questions may be, it remains a fact that the Federal Constitutional Court builds its line of reasoning, both in individual and successive cases, at all levels and at all steps of its decision-making process, according to methodically filtered arguments, as a *rationalization of its legal conviction.* The Court deliberates the judgment within its internal circles as a formal compromise and ultimately attempts to make it generalizable in such a way that the decision will command obedience and recognition without the need for qualification.

During the work on legal reasoning, it is vital to develop plausible structures (capture and development of constitutional issues), to sufficiently and argumentatively narrow the tasks thrown up by the processing of the problem, and to transfer these into strict, compelling conclusions. Otherwise, the act of persuasion that culminates in the proposed solution cannot generate—or fabricate—the "contextual objectivity" (Massing 1989) needed to communicate intersubjectively, above and beyond private semantic codes and evidences, the results of this type of "artificial" problem handling (legal reasoning simultaneously as an art and craft) so as to attain unimpeded acceptance of the judgment.

The support required from the legal assistants of the Federal Constitutional Court during this process can be qualified as "decision preparing" rather than "decision conditioning." In other words, it is classifiable as a "position evaluation" (on the categories used here see Carroll 1976). But with certainty it is largely a "decision-justifying" task, in the sense of the constitutionally necessary defense of position that is exclusively incumbent upon the Federal Constitutional Court within the crisis management condominium of the Federal Republic of Germany as a specific *political* prerogative.

Otwin Massing is a professor emeritus of political science at the Faculty of Law of the University of Hannover.

Notes

1. See the sixteen plus volumes of the Kammerentscheidungen des Bundesverfassungsgerichts (BVerfGK). Rüdiger Zuck (2006: 283) even goes so far as to regard the activities of the chambers as the "real BVerfG."

Bibliography

Benda, E. "Aktuelle Probleme des Bundesverfassungsgerichts." *Neue Juristische Wochenschrift*, Vol. 39, 1980, 2097–2103.

Carroll, J.D. "Policy Analysis for Congress: A Review of the Congressional Research Service." In *Congressional Support Agencies: A Compilation of Papers*. Washington, D.C., 1976, pp. 4–30.

Glotz, P. *Die Innenausstattung der Macht. Politisches Tagebuch 1976–1978*. Frankfurt/Main, 1981.

Kranenpohl, U. *Hinter dem Schleier des Beratungsgeheimnisses. Der Willensbildungs- und Entscheidungsprozess des Bundesverfassungsgerichts*. Wiesbaden 2010.

Landfried, C. *Bundesverfassungsgericht und Gesetzgeber. Wirkungen der Verfassungsrechtsprechung auf parlamentarische Willensbildung und soziale Realität*. Baden-Baden, 1984.

Lietzmann, H. *Das Bundesverfassungsgericht. Eine sozialwissenschaftliche Studie*. Opladen, 1988.

Massing, O. *Verflixte Verhältnisse – Über soziale Umwelten des Menschen*. Opladen, 1987a.

Massing, O. "Rechtsstaat und Justizherrschaft." In Massing, O., *Verflixte Verhältnisse – Uber soziale Umwelten des Menschen*. Opladen, 1987b, 114–129.

Massing, O. "Identitat als Mythopoem – Zur politischen Symbolisierungsfunktion verfassungsgerichtlicher Spruchweisheiten." In Voigt, R., ed., *Symbole und Rituale in der Politik*. Opladen, 1989, 235–256.

Umbach, D.C., Urban, R., Fritz, R., Böttcher, H.E., Bargen, J. von, eds. *Das wahre Verfassungsrecht – Zwischen Lust und Leistung. Gedächtnisschrift für F.G. Nagelmann*. Baden-Baden, 1984.

Wieland, J. "The Role of the Legal Assistants at the German Federal Constitutional Court." In Rogowski, R., Gawron, T., eds., *Constitutional Courts in Comparison: The U.S. Supreme Court and the German Federal Constitutional Court*. Oxford, New York, 2002, 197–207.

Zuck, R. "Die wissenschaftlichen Mitarbeiter des Bundesverfassungsgerichts." In Ooyen, R. van, Möllers, M., eds., *Das Bundesverfassungsgericht im politischen System*. Wiesbaden, 2006, 283–292.

Part III

Implementation

Chapter 8

The Implementation of U.S. Supreme Court Decisions

Lawrence Baum

When the United States Supreme Court makes a decision, that decision must be implemented by other public policy makers whose responses are neither automatic nor certain. Since the 1950s, some major Supreme Court decisions have run into highly visible implementation problems that have called attention to the uncertainty and significance of the implementation process. Scholars have done considerable research on the implementation of Supreme Court decisions (see Hall 2011). What we know about this subject is still outweighed by the gaps in that knowledge, but we have learned a good deal about what happens after the Court hands down its decisions. This chapter surveys what we now understand about the implementation of Supreme Court decisions and considers ways of thinking about the implementation process to enhance that understanding.

The Structure of the Implementation Process

At the outset, it is useful to describe the processes by which Supreme Court decisions are implemented. Two kinds of processes should be distinguished.

Responses to Remands

When the Supreme Court reverses or modifies a lower-court decision, the Court ordinarily does not reach a final decision in the case. Rather, it sends back ("remands") the case to the lower court for further consideration in light of the legal rules delineated in the Court's opinion. Because cases come to the Supreme Court primarily from federal courts of appeals and state supreme courts, these are the courts most often called upon to act after a Supreme Court remand. Quite often, these courts return a remanded case to the original trial court for retrial; in other instances, they act on the case themselves.

The amount of leeway that the Supreme Court provides to lower courts with its remands varies considerably. Especially when the degree of leeway is great, the lower court often rules a second time in favor of the party it originally favored—the same one that lost in the Supreme Court (Pacelle, Baum 1992). Such an outcome may be consistent with the Supreme Court's intent, though occasionally there are cases in which a lower court seems to defy the Court by departing from the terms of the opinion that accompanied a remand. One example was a state court decision reinstating a death sentence that the Supreme Court had overturned. When the case returned to the Supreme Court, the justices reversed the state court's decision a second time and pointed out its failure to follow their instructions (*Smith v. Texas,* 550 U.S. 297 [2007])

Responses to remands are an interesting phenomenon that helps to illuminate lower-court judges' attitudes toward the Supreme Court. But ordinarily the final outcome for the litigants in a case decided by the Supreme Court has relatively little impact on national policy. (The Court's decision resolving the 2000 presidential election in *Bush v. Gore,* 531 U.S. 98 [2000] is a noteworthy exception.) Rather, it is a second, much broader implementation process that has significant policy implications.

Application of Doctrine

That process is the application of the Supreme Court's legal doctrines to cases and situations beyond the original case in which those doctrines are established. The rules that govern this application process are somewhat ambiguous. It is generally accepted—though with some reservations and disagreements—that the Court's interpretations of federal law are binding on federal and state judges in any case in which they are relevant. Whether administrators and legislators are bound in the same way is less certain. If the Supreme Court holds that a school practice in one district is illegal, must other school districts eliminate the practice, or can they await a court order directed at them specifically? If the Court overturns one state's law restricting abortion, must other states with similar laws cease enforcing them immediately?

An argument can be made that in such situations, policy makers legitimately can continue their practices until directly ordered to change. But there is a widespread feeling, in both the legal system and society as a whole, that an interpretation of law by the Supreme Court automatically becomes binding on all government agencies to which it is relevant. This feeling is reflected in the practice of putting a Supreme Court decision into effect prior to any direct order to do so. Although this practice is common, however, it is not universal. Students of the judicial process in the United States have sought to determine both the extent to which practices outlawed by the Court in a specific case actually disappear elsewhere and the factors that shape other policy makers' responses to the Court's decisions.

The State of Knowledge on the Implementation of Supreme Court Decisions

Scholars' knowledge about the implementation of Supreme Court decisions is both inconsistent and incomplete. Still, existing research on this process provides a basis for some generalizations about the implementation process, at both the descriptive and explanatory levels.

Description: Patterns of Implementation Behavior

The clearest finding of empirical studies is that implementation in practice is a highly imperfect process. Judges, administrators, and legislators frequently fail to follow the policies mandated by Supreme Court decisions. The most dramatic and best documented examples of these imperfections involve major lines of Court policy that were initiated in the 1950s and 1960s, the period when Earl Warren was chief justice and when the Court substantially expanded protections of civil liberties under the U.S. Constitution.

In *Brown v. Board of Education* (347 U.S. 483 [1954]), the Supreme Court ruled that the systems of separate public schools for black and white students that existed throughout the Southern region of the United States violated the constitutional guarantee of "equal protection of the laws." (The *Brown* decision and its implementation are discussed in Peltason 1971; Kluger 1976; Bullock 1984.) The Court ordered that the schools in that region be desegregated, though it left open the timetable for desegregation. Ten years after the *Brown* decision, the schools of the Deep South—the area most committed to racial segregation—remained almost entirely segregated. This inaction resulted from the behavior of policy makers in all three branches of government.

School administrators in most districts resisted desegregation, with the support of state legislatures and governors who adopted laws and exerted pressure to maintain existing practices. Southern members of Congress gave legitimacy to this resistance with a "Manifesto" supporting it. Federal trial judges in the South, who had the primary judicial responsibility to enforce the *Brown* decision, most often ruled that segregation in a particular school district could continue for the time being rather than requiring immediate action. Not until 1964, when Congress supported the Supreme Court with financial incentives for desegregation, did significant compliance with the Court's decision begin to occur in the Deep South.

In three decisions in 1962 and 1963, the Supreme Court ruled that prayers and other religious observances in public schools violated the constitutional prohibition of an establishment of religion. The first and key decision was *Engel v. Vitale* (370 U.S. 421 [1962]). (Implementation of the school prayer decisions is discussed in Way 1968; Dolbeare, Hammond 1971; Coyle 1995; McGuire 2009.) At the time these practices were widespread, but after the Court's rulings, a high proportion of schools that had these practices—perhaps half—eliminated them. But other schools maintained them, and in many districts this noncompliance was never challenged. Since the 1980s, several state legislatures have enacted laws intended to allow school districts to maintain or resume prayers. Within school districts, noncompliance with the Court's decisions of the 1960s and with more recent Court decisions establishing other limits on school religious observances seems to have increased over time.

During the 1950s and 1960s, the Supreme Court made a number of decisions to safeguard the rights of criminal defendants by regulating police practices. These decisions were reached primarily through interpretation of the constitutional protection of "due process of law." The most significant of these decisions were *Miranda v. Arizona* (384 U.S. 436 [1966]), which required that police officers read certain warnings of rights to suspects prior to questioning them, and *Mapp v. Ohio* (367 U.S. 643 [1961]), which held that evidence obtained through illegal searches could not be admitted in court by the prosecution. (Implementation of these decisions is discussed in Uchida, Bynum 1991; Bradley 1993; Gould, Mastrofski 2004; Leo 2008.) Studies have found incomplete compliance with the *Miranda* requirements and widespread use of illegal searches despite the *Mapp* decision. Noncompliance seems to have declined somewhat over time, but it certainly has not disappeared. For their part, state judges sometimes accept police practices that seem to violate the Supreme Court's rulings.

These histories, along with similar histories for some other major decisions, make it clear that widespread acceptance of an obligation to follow the Supreme Court's legal rulings does not always translate into effective implementation of the Court's policies. Unfortunately, there has been little research on implementation of less controversial Supreme Court decisions and decisions that require more minimal policy changes. However, one study did find that federal administrative agencies comply with Supreme Court decisions that overrule their policies in the great majority of instances (Spriggs 1997).

The second generalization that emerges clearly from the studies is that implementation behavior varies widely. Some of this variation is among decisions. On the whole, for instance, the Supreme Court's rules for police interrogation practices have been carried out more fully than its rules for police searches. In contrast with decisions that met with largely negative responses from officials, rulings from the 1960s to the 1990s that required redrawing of legislative districts generally have been implemented promptly. (The early history of this process is discussed in Baker 1966; Dixon 1968.) That promptness is surprising in light of the massive changes in districting and the concomitant shifts in political power entailed by some of the Court's rulings.

Further, any single Supreme Court decision that requires substantial implementation is likely to receive quite different responses from the various public officials who are responsible for its implementation. School desegregation was minimal in the South, but it came more readily in "Border" states such as Maryland and West Virginia. Though some judges were reluctant to carry out the Supreme Court's decisions expanding the rights of criminal defendants, others applied them enthusiastically—sometimes more enthusiastically than an increasingly conservative Supreme Court desired. Since the 1970s, some state supreme courts have found procedural rights in their state constitutions that the U.S. Supreme Court did not find in the U.S. Constitution (Shaman 2008). This expansion of rights is quite legitimate, since state supreme courts are the highest interpreters of their own constitutions. This pattern of variation indicates that responses to the Court's decisions are not simply the product of their content.

A third generalization concerns differences in the implementation behavior of different kinds of policy makers. There is some evidence that judges tend to respond more positively to the Supreme Court decisions they are called upon to carry out than do administrators and legislators. On school desegregation, for instance, few federal judges adopted the position of explicit noncompliance with *Brown v. Board of Education* that was common among Southern policy makers in the other branches of government.

If this difference does exist, it might have at least two sources. First, judicial implementation of Supreme Court decisions is less likely to involve practical difficulties than is action by legislatures and administrative bodies. Especially at the appellate level, judges often can carry out a decision simply by applying it in their own decisions. In contrast, the other branches of government may have to change existing routines and adopt new programs to implement a decision. This is often true of trial courts as well. When decisions do put heavy administrative demands on trial judges, those judges seem to engage in a degree of noncompliance that is more typical of administrators than of appellate judges. This has been true of the Court's decisions on matters such as discrimination in lawyers' selection of jurors and the provision of lawyers to indigent defendants in misdemeanor cases (see Bogira 2005: 16–17, 67, 157–158, 261).

Second, most judges by their training and activity are highly capable of understanding what a Supreme Court decision requires of them and perceive a strong obligation to follow the Court's lead. The acceptance of this obligation merits emphasis. Lower-court judges depend for their effectiveness on the willingness of litigants and others to obey their decisions, so to deny their obligation to obey Supreme Court rulings might ultimately jeopardize their own authority as well.

Explanation: Accounting for Implementation Behavior

Inevitably, discussion of patterns of implementation leads to consideration of factors that affect this behavior. Here we can take a more systematic view of what is known about explanations for implementation behavior. The forces that affect the implementation process and the ways these forces operate under different circumstances remain uncertain, but some fragments of explanation emerge from the research.

The most important fragment concerns the general sources of variation in implementation behavior. Inadequate implementation may result from problems of three types: communication (officials do not know what they are supposed to do), capability (they are unable to do what is required), and dispositions (they are unwilling to act as required) (see Van Meter, Van Horn 1975: 478–483). If we view these three types of problems as variables, it seems clear that the critical variable in explaining implementation of Supreme Court decisions is dispositions. To be more precise, the extent to which policy makers carry out the Court's decisions is primarily a function of the relationship between the content of those decisions and their self-interest and policy preferences.

The patterns of implementation behavior that scholars have documented support this generalization. The Border states were quicker to desegregate their schools than were the states of the Deep South because policy makers in the Deep South typically favored segregation more strongly and felt heavier pressures to maintain it. Police officers follow the Supreme Court's rulings on questioning of suspects more fully than its rulings on searches because the search rules are more likely to interfere with the task of gathering evidence.

Communication and capability also have an impact. Some implementation problems result from communication weaknesses, such as the ambiguity of the Supreme Court's timetable for school desegregation and the distortion of its criminal procedure decisions that sometimes occurs as those decisions are communicated to police officers. Some decisions run up against capability problems. A good example is the Court's requirement that indigent criminal defendants be supplied with free attorneys in serious cases. Where state and local budgets are severely strained, as they often are after economic downturns, it is effectively impossible to provide the resources needed to meet the Court's mandate fully. It appears, however, that communication and capability have been less important than the dispositions of the policy makers who act as implementers of Supreme Court decisions.

Another fragment of explanation concerns policy makers' attitudes toward the Supreme Court as an institution, as distinct from the Court's decisions. As we have learned over the past few decades, public officials who are negatively disposed toward a ruling often choose not to implement that ruling fully. But empirical studies have shown that even policy makers who disagree with a decision may carry it out faithfully. Certainly the number of school administrators who eliminated school prayers after the Supreme Court held them to be unconstitutional was far greater than the number who approved of the Court's ruling (see Johnson 1967). In explaining this behavior, scholars have pointed to the Supreme Court's authority for other policy makers, authority that creates a perceived obligation to implement the Court's decisions (Petrick 1968: 5–19; Pacelle, Baum 1992). The Court's authority may be less than total, but it appears to be fairly strong for at least some of the people who respond to its decisions. We do not, however, have a clear picture of how the Court's authority affects responses to its decisions.

Beyond the cataloguing of relevant variables, several scholars have offered theoretical frameworks for the analysis of implementation behavior (Canon, Johnson 1999). The dominant framework today, applied primarily to lower-court judges, is rational choice theory in economics (Songer, Segal, Cameron 1994; Lindquist, Haire, Songer 2007; Hall 2009; Kastellec 2011). In this framework, public officials who respond to Supreme Court decisions do so on the basis of their policy goals. Those goals may lead them to deviate from the Court's doctrines, but officials may also comply with the Court's rulings in order to avoid the negative effects of reversal or other action on the policies they favor. This framework gives little if any weight to the Court's authority for judges and other officials.

The Supreme Court's Role in the Implementation of Its Decisions

Supreme Court justices understand the difficulties and uncertainties of implementation. Occasionally they encounter cases in which a litigant claims—often with considerable justification—that one of the Court's decisions was flouted by a lower court. They are also aware of the broader resistance to some of the Court's major decisions.

Knowing of such implementation problems, what can the justices do to reduce them? Clearly, the Supreme Court lacks some important powers that might assist it in controlling the implementation process. Alexander Hamilton argued in the Federalist Papers (Federalist No. 78), the essays written to help secure ratification of the U.S. Constitution, that the judiciary "has no influence over either the sword or the purse" (see Fairfield 1961: 227). With some exceptions, his argument remains accurate. The Supreme Court cannot directly allocate money or deploy force to secure effective implementation of its decisions. The Court lacks other powers that could aid in the implementation process, such as the right to select officials who are responsible for implementation.

Yet the Court does possess means to improve the implementation of its decisions. These means fall into three categories: making decisions in a form that enhances the chances for effective implementation; attacking implementation problems when they occur; and working to create a general climate favoring the implementation of its decisions.

Formulating Decisions

In formulating their decisions, justices can work to improve their clarity. Ambiguity is an obvious source of communication problems. Less obviously, an ambiguous decision can allow some policy makers to claim that they are obeying a decision when in fact they are evading its spirit. This was the case when the Court left uncertain the required timetable for school desegregation. Some lower-court judges argued that they were following the Court's decision as they granted successive delays in desegregation to school districts (Peltason 1971).

Certainly, in some instances justices have worked at achieving clarity in order to ensure that their message is understood. The highly specific language used by Chief Justice Warren in the *Miranda* decision was intended in part to ensure that police officers understood what the Court was asking them to do in their questioning of suspects. But this strategy is not always possible. Language in an opinion may be ambiguous because of disagreements among the justices who subscribed to the opinion. And occasionally the Court is so divided that no opinion musters the support of a majority of justices, thereby leaving the Court's position quite unclear. This was true of *Rapanos v. United States* (547 U.S. 715 [2006]), in which the absence of a majority opinion made it difficult for lower-court judges to ascertain the Court's doctrinal position on protection of wetlands under the Clean Water Act.

Besides improving clarity, justices can use their opinions to try to gain acceptance for the Court's decision among officials who must implement it. This is a common tactic. When the Court struck down a state law making it a criminal offense to desecrate the U.S. flag by burning it, both the majority opinion and a concurring opinion emphasized their authors' reverence for the flag (*Texas v. Johnson*, 491 U.S. 397 [1989]). Those passages undoubtedly were intended to reduce opposition to the ruling. It is not clear, however, that such language has a significant impact on the implementation process. People who strongly disagree with a decision are unlikely to be persuaded by skillful language in the Supreme Court's opinion. Indeed, except for judges, those responsible for implementation may not even read the Court's opinion.

Attacking Implementation Problems

If public officials do not comply voluntarily with the rules of law that the Supreme Court hands down, people who have legal standing can go to court to secure compliance. Ideally, from the Court's perspective, the process would work as follows. Any government practice that is inconsistent with a Supreme Court ruling would be challenged by some litigant, and in ruling on that challenge the Court or a lower court will demand compliance with the Court's ruling. So, if officials in a school district decided not to eliminate religious observances that the Supreme Court had declared unconstitutional, a citizen would bring suit to challenge the district, and either the Supreme Court or a lower court would apply that ruling directly to the district and order it to change its practices. Similarly, a losing party in a lower court who felt that the court had not followed an applicable Supreme Court ruling would appeal the loss, and the Supreme Court or another appellate court would overrule the noncomplying decision.

Moreover, because this process was inevitable, officials usually would follow Supreme Court rulings even before their practices were challenged. By doing so they would avoid the work and expense of defending their practices in court and the embarrassment of an order to change these practices (or, in the case of a lower-court judge, the embarrassment of having a decision reversed). Such reactions might be labeled "anticipatory compliance."

There are several reasons why this ideal process often does not occur in practice. First, the expected challenge to a questionable practice may not arise. The example of school prayer illustrates why this is the case. In a school district that continues to hold prayer exercises, it may be that no citizen disagrees with the practice. Citizens who do disagree still may not bring a challenge for fear of incurring the wrath of those who favor prayers. Indeed, people who challenge government religious practices often receive considerable abuse. The financial costs of a lawsuit challenging the school district and the difficulty of finding an appropriate lawyer to take such a case also deter challenges.

We might not expect this problem to exist in criminal law, because defendants and their lawyers seemingly have strong incentives to challenge noncompliance. But they do not necessarily challenge practices such as searches that appear to be illegal. A defendant may choose to accept a plea bargain prior to trial, which usually means giving up the right to challenge the search. Alternatively, the defense attorney may decide that the best trial strategy involves ignoring the possible illegality of a search; one reason is to avoid a trial judge's potentially negative reaction to motions to exclude evidence obtained through a police search. And despite Supreme Court decisions guaranteeing counsel to indigent defendants, even in the most serious cases defendants often have lawyers who represent them inadequately, allowing illegal practices to go unchallenged (White 2006).

Second, there is no guarantee of anticipatory compliance, in part because challenges to practices that violate Supreme Court decisions may not occur. School administrators might decide to retain prayers because their calculations show that a lawsuit against them is unlikely.

Further, policy makers may accept a possible court sanction as the price of maintaining policies that they prefer. For instance, judges do not like to have their decisions reversed, but reversal is not so damaging that it forces them to follow the Supreme Court's lead. One example is judges on the federal court of appeals for the Ninth Circuit on the West Coast, many of whom have favored more expansive protections of civil liberties than the Supreme Court has in the past few decades. The Supreme Court frequently reverses the Ninth Circuit's pro-liberties decisions and sometimes accompanies those reversals with strong criticism of the lower court (see *Harrington v. Richter,* 178 L. Ed. 2d 624 [2011]; *Cazavos v. Smith,* 181 L. Ed. 2d 311 [2011]). But some Ninth Circuit judges have been willing to accept reversals as the price of deciding cases as they see fit. One judge on that court, when asked whether these reversals bothered him, said, "Not in the slightest! If they want to take away rights, that's their privilege. But I'm not going to help them do it" (Savage 1996).

Legislators and administrators prefer not to have their actions challenged and invalidated in court, but they too may accept this possibility in order to continue policies that they prefer. Indeed, state legislatures sometimes enact laws that directly conflict with Supreme Court decisions on issues such as school prayer and abortion. Legislators' personal convictions and political realities make such laws attractive despite the seeming futility of adopting them. In the field of abortion, some of these laws have been intended to provide the Court with an opportunity to modify its doctrinal positions and thus to allow broader prohibitions of abortion than it has allowed in the past. That has been especially true since 2006, when the Court's membership became more conservative with the appointment of Justice Samuel Alito. After the 2010 and 2014 elections, when Republicans gained majorities in many state legislatures, several states enacted legislation that substantially restricted abortion with the Court in mind.

These imperfections should not be exaggerated. Policies that conflict with Supreme Court decisions are frequently challenged. Further, the possibility that such challenges will occur and that unfavorable court decisions will ensue induces some officials to follow the Supreme Court's lead prior to any direct order to do so. Thus, this feedback process serves as an important force for faithful implementation of decisions.

Creating a Favorable Climate

Supreme Court justices can seek to improve the general climate for their decisions in several ways, but primarily by trying to enhance the Court's standing with other policy makers. Supreme Court justices have a good deal of contact with judges on lower federal courts. Historical evidence indicates that some justices have used this contact to try to create good relations (Murphy 1964: ch. 4). One result might be that lower-court judges are more willing to follow the Supreme Court's lead.

On a less personal level, justices sometimes avoid unpopular decisions in order to maintain the Supreme Court's prestige and limit conflict with other policy makers. Its refusals to hear cases challenging U.S. participation in the Vietnam War (e.g., *Mora v. McNamara*, 389 U.S. 934 [1967]) exemplify the Court's practice of sometimes "ducking" cases that might lead to controversial rulings. Moreover, at times the Court seemingly has refrained from taking certain positions in order to avoid or to defuse conflict with the other branches (Glick 2009). In one example from the late 1950s, several decisions favorable to civil liberties had aroused opposition from conservative members of Congress. When the Court abandoned some of the policies reflected in those decisions, a congressional drive to "punish" the Court died out (Murphy 1962).

More broadly, the Court's decisions reflect an interest in maintaining friendly relations with other policy makers. The Court's reviews of lower-court decisions sometimes offer positive evaluations of the work of the courts under review, even when the Court ultimately overturns a decision. The Court also shows considerable deference toward Congress in both its interpretations of statutes and its constitutional decisions. It is noteworthy that the Court has struck down state and local statutes more than seven times as often as federal statutes (Baum 2016: 160).

One body of scholarship argues that the justices act on a general sensitivity to the political climate, both in government and in the country as a whole. One study concludes that even the introduction of bills threatening action against the Court can make the justices more cautious about overturning federal laws, because such bills reflects weaknesses in the Court's standing with the public (Clark 2011). Some legal scholars argue that the justices are careful not to get too far out of step with the public (Friedman 2009), though others disagree (Pildes 2010).

The Court's caution should not be exaggerated. In contrast with the Vietnam War cases, the Court in recent years has accepted cases on issues as controversial as the constitutional validity of President Obama's health care legislation and of state laws prohibiting same-sex marriage. (Conflicting rulings in the lower federal courts sometimes give the justices little choice but to accept such cases.) And the Court has reached decisions that the justices could predict would arouse strong negative reactions, from the school prayer cases of 1962 and 1963 to the decisions protecting the rights of detainees at Guantánamo between 2004 and 2008. But the Court does show some caution, intended in part to maintain its standing.

It is difficult to evaluate the effectiveness of this and other mechanisms to improve the implementation of Supreme Court decisions. On their face, they seem moderately strong at best. And there is ample evidence that the Court cannot prevent poor implementation of its decisions when conditions are very unfavorable. The history of issues such as school desegregation makes it clear that the Court's powers are limited. Though the array of strategies used by the Court may have a significant cumulative impact on the implementation process, it seems clear that Alexander Hamilton was correct: the Supreme Court is in a weaker position than Congress to secure effective implementation of its decisions.

Implementation and Relationships between Policy Makers

We still have much to learn about the implementation of Supreme Court decisions. At the descriptive level, the limited range of decisions that have been studied needs to be expanded, to give a fuller picture of the overall pattern and of variation in the implementation of decisions. At the explanatory level, more research is required to test hypotheses about the forces that might explain implementation behavior. But existing studies of the implementation process have been sufficient to sketch out a good deal of what occurs in that process. Certainly they have raised some intriguing questions. One set of questions that is central to an understanding of the process concerns the Supreme Court's position in relation to other policy makers. How do government officials perceive the Court, and how does this perception affect their responses to its decisions?

Students of the implementation process often conceive of two important forces that may compete with each other. On the one hand, policy makers respond to Supreme Court decisions largely in terms of their attitudes toward the policies embodied in those decisions, attitudes that frequently are unfavorable. But on the other hand, those policy makers may be drawn to implement Supreme Court decisions faithfully by the hierarchical element of their relationship with the Court, an element based on acceptance of the Court's authority and the possibility of sanctions for failing to follow its lead. This perspective has considerable value as a way of understanding the implementation process. Yet its emphasis on hierarchy in the relationships between the Supreme Court and other policy makers may oversimplify these relationships and obscure some important features of the implementation process. These limitations are perhaps best illustrated by examining the relationship between the Supreme Court and Congress.

This relationship cannot be characterized in simple hierarchical terms. Congress can initiate constitutional amendments to overturn or limit decisions. And in other respects Congress stands in a coequal or even superior legal position to the Court. In statutory interpretation it is Congress that is supreme. To overturn the Supreme Court's reading of a statute, Congress can simply rewrite the statute—as it frequently does (Christiansen, Eskridge 2014; Hausegger, Baum 1998). With some possible limits, it can remove the Court's jurisdiction over a category of cases. Congress holds budgetary power over the Court, including power over salary increases. Congress can even alter the number of justices. Certainly members of Congress do not perceive themselves as subordinates of the Court.

Most of the Court's major decisions involve interpretations of the constitution. Congress cannot override constitutional decisions simply by enacting a new statute, though it can and sometimes does write a new statute with the same goal as the legislation that the Court struck down (Pickerill 2004). Meanwhile Congress, with its full array of powers, can do a great deal to attack constitutional decisions of which it disapproves. Constitutional policies that have evoked widespread congressional disapproval include the Court's limitations on religious observances in public schools, its approval of "busing" to achieve racial desegregation in schools, and its overturning of laws that prohibit desecration of the U.S. flag. Had votes been taken in Congress on the desirability of these decisions, all would have been opposed by large margins.

Yet Congress has done relatively little to overturn or limit these decisions. Over the years, proposals to overturn the school prayer decisions of the 1960s by constitutional amendment were all unsuccessful. On school busing, Congress took some anti-Court actions that were primarily symbolic and had little practical effect. Congress several times came close to proposing a constitutional amendment to overturn the Court's flag desecration rulings, but the Senate never provided the necessary two-thirds majority. Nor has Congress made much use of its powers to attack the Court as an institution. The paucity of such action has been especially striking in recent years, a period in which denunciations of the federal courts—primarily by Republican members of Congress—have been unusually frequent and vigorous (Miller 2009).

How might we explain this record of relative inaction? Part of the answer may lie simply in the difficulty of enacting controversial bills in Congress. Yet something more seems to be involved, in that members of Congress who oppose the Supreme Court's position on particular constitutional issues often vote against proposals to attack the Court over that position. Certainly that is true of flag desecration, for example. As already suggested, that something more cannot be congressional perception of a duty to accept Supreme Court decisions, because no such duty exists legally. (An exception is situations in which the Court issues an order that imposes a legal obligation on Congress.) One important factor may be congressional awareness of broad support for the Supreme Court and for its institutional autonomy among political elites and the general public (Gibson 2007). Public support for the Court declines with overall trust in government, as it has (quite substantially) in recent years, but the Court remains far more popular than Congress. Members of Congress might fear they would incur public disapproval if they actually carried out strong attacks on the Court rather than simply threatening those attacks.

It might also be true that members of Congress operate on the basis of an implicit mutual deference between their institution and the Supreme Court. The Court's sensitivity to congressional powers and prerogatives and its general deference to Congress were noted earlier. This strategy, if that is what it is, may help to deter Congress from attacking the Court. In other words, the two institutions may be involved in a subtle exchange relationship in which both sides act strategically to limit conflict (see Geyh 2006).

There may be another, more mundane force involved. Members of Congress sometimes prefer to evade responsibility for decisions about controversial issues. If Congress defers to the courts, it is judges rather than legislators who will be criticized by those who disagree. Regardless of their own positions on the abortion issue, undoubtedly many members of Congress are pleased that the basic legal rules for abortion are determined by the Court rather than by the legislative branch. In other words, deference to judicial rulings may accord well with the congressional interest in "blame avoidance" (Weaver 1987: 43–47).

Of course, congressional choices about whether to take negative action in response to Supreme Court decisions are not entirely comparable with judges' and administrators' choices to implement or not implement the Court's decisions. In that respect, presidential responses to decisions may provide a better comparison with the responses by the Court's subordinates in the legal system, as the Court's relationship with the presidency--like its relationship with Congress--is one between relative equals rather than one of hierarchy. The relationship is multifaceted (see Segal 1991), but one major aspect is the president's role in implementation of the Court's rulings. In turn, the most interesting aspect of that role is the occasional situation in which presidents are asked to comply with a ruling.

The Court would seem to be in a poor position to demand obedience from the president. Not only does it lack concrete power over the president, but the president's obligation to follow the Court's rulings has been disputed. Indeed, President Franklin Roosevelt twice threatened to disobey prospective decisions by the Court if they went against his policies—though, as it turned out, they did not (Scigliano 1971: 48–49).

Yet two later incidents underlined the Court's capacity to secure presidential obedience. During the Korean War, President Harry Truman ordered seizure of steel mills by the federal government to prevent a union strike that would stop production. The Court ruled that Truman lacked the power to undertake the seizure, and Truman readily complied (*Youngstown Sheet and Tube Co. v. Sawyer,* 343 U.S. 579 [1952]; see Westin 1958). More dramatic was President Richard Nixon's compliance with a Court decision that required him to yield up recordings of conversations in which he had participated (*United States v. Nixon*, 418 U.S. 683 [1974].). Although the evidence in the recordings was highly damaging to his efforts to stay in office—in fact, his resignation followed shortly after the disclosure of that evidence—Nixon obeyed the Court. The main reason apparently was that a refusal to obey would have been perceived as a highly illegitimate act, one that was even more likely than the recordings to ensure that he had to leave office.

In conjunction with the patterns of implementation behavior by judges and administrators, the record of congressional and presidential response to the Court supports several conjectures:

1. Policy makers' legal subordination to the Supreme Court has only limited impact on their responses to the Court's decisions. The relatively positive responses of Congress and presidents, coupled with imperfect compliance by judges and administrators, suggest that acceptance of hierarchy has been overstated as an element in the implementation process. Perhaps we should begin with an assumption that hierarchy plays no role in itself, looking for evidence of its impact rather than assuming it.
2. More than hierarchy, whether policy makers carry out Supreme Court policies with which they disagree depends on what important audiences expect of them (see Baum 2006). Judges are part of a legal community that assesses their performance largely based on their capacity to follow binding rules of law, a capacity gauged in part by their ability to avoid reversals of their decisions. The president is expected to adhere to the rule of law, and failures to do so are highly visible to other elite groups. In contrast, administrative personnel whose activities are not very visible have less reason to implement Supreme Court decisions that they dislike.

   Beyond these general differences among types of policy makers, this conjecture suggests that no particular type responds to Supreme Court decisions in a uniform way. Lower-court judges who are oriented toward the legal community as a whole will feel a relatively strong need to follow the lead of higher courts, while those who identify more with nonlegal audiences may be willing to accept some decline in their legal standing as the cost of pleasing those more relevant audiences. This is one way to interpret the behavior of the Southern federal judges who delayed desegregation: the approval of the Supreme Court and of legal commentators was much less important to them than the approval of their friends and neighbors (Peltason 1971). Similarly, judges on specialized courts, who interact closely with a specialized segment of the bar and a related policy community, may be more interested in pleasing those specialists than in securing affirmance of their rulings by higher courts.
3. The intensity of interaction between a set of policy makers and the Supreme Court helps to determine their responses to the Court's de-

cisions. Abstract obligations to follow the lead of a distant legal authority may have little meaning in practice. A state trial judge whose decisions are never reviewed by the Supreme Court and who never encounters Supreme Court justices may not feel a strong inclination to carry out the Court's decisions, but the same judge may be far more willing to implement decisions of an appellate court that reviews the judge's decisions directly.

In contrast, the institutional interactions between the Supreme Court and the president, Congress, and lower federal courts are likely to be salient to both sides. The relationships that grow from these interactions may lead to mutual deference. The Supreme Court exhibits some reluctance to strike down statutes adopted by Congress; by the same token, Congress exhibits some reluctance to use its powers against the Court. As a general rule, then, we might posit that Supreme Court decisions are implemented more effectively within the federal government than in state and local governments.

These conjectures point to some issues that emerge when hierarchy is deemphasized as an element in the implementation process. Whatever we ultimately learn about the relationships between the Supreme Court and the policy makers who respond to its decisions, it seems useful to consider these relationships in broad and open terms. In this way, we can gain a fuller sense of the complex process by which other public policy-makers decide how to respond to the Supreme Court decisions they encounter. In turn, that process is critical to the Court's impact on public policy and the life of the nation.

Lawrence Baum is a professor emeritus of political science at the Department of Political Science of Ohio State University, Columbus.

Bibliography

Baker, G.E. *The Reapportionment Revolution: Representation, Political Power, and the Supreme Court.* New York, 1966.
Baum, L. *Judges and Their Audiences: A Perspective on Judicial Behavior.* Princeton, 2006.
Baum, L. *The Supreme Court,* 12th ed. Washington, D.C., 2016.
Bogira, S. *Courtroom 302: A Year Behind the Scenes in an American Criminal Courthouse.* New York, 2005.
Bradley, C.M. *The Failure of the Criminal Procedure Revolution.* Philadelphia, 1993.

Bullock, C.S., III. "Equal Education Opportunity." In Bullock, C.S., III, Lamb, C.M., *Implementation of Civil Rights Policy*. Monterey, 1984, 55–92.

Canon, B.C., Johnson, C.A. *Judicial Politics: Implementation and Impact,* Washington, D.C., 1999.

Christiansen, M.R., Eskridge, W.N., Jr. "Congressional Overrides of Supreme Court Statutory Decisions, 1967-2011." *Texas Law Review,* Vol. 92(6), 2014, 1317–1541.

Clark, T.S. *The Limits of Judicial Independence*. New York, 2011.

Coyle, P. "Prayer Pendulum." *American Bar Association Journal,* Vol. 81(1), 1995, 62–66.

Dixon, R.G., Jr. *Democratic Representation: Reapportionment in Law and Politics*. New York, 1968.

Dolbeare, K.M., Hammond, P.E. *The School Prayer Decisions: From Court Policy to Local Practice*. Chicago, 1971.

Fairfield, R.P., ed. *The Federalist Papers*. Garden City, N.Y., 1961.

Friedman, B. *The Will of the People: How Public Opinion Has Influenced the Supreme Court and Shaped the Meaning of the Constitution*. New York, 2009.

Geyh, C.G. *When Courts and Congress Collide: The Struggle for Control of America's Judicial System*. Ann Arbor, 2006.

Gibson, J.L. "The Legitimacy of the U.S. Supreme Court in a Polarized Polity." *Journal of Empirical Legal Studies,* Vol. 4(3), 2007, 507–538.

Glick, D. "Conditional Strategic Retreat: The Court's Concession in the 1935 Gold Clause Cases." *Journal of Politics,* Vol. 71(3), 2009, 800–816.

Gould, J.B., Mastrofski, S.D. "Suspect Searches: Assessing Police Behavior under the U.S. Constitution." *Criminology and Public Policy,* Vol. 3(3), 2004, 315–362.

Hall, M. "Experimental Justice: Random Judicial Assignment and the Partisan Process of Supreme Court Review." *American Politics Research,* Vol. 37(2), 2009, 195–226.

Hall, M.E.K. *The Nature of Supreme Court Power*. New York, 2011.

Hausegger, L., Baum, L. "Behind the Scenes: The Supreme Court and Congress in Statutory Interpretation." In Weisberg, H.F., Patterson, S.C., eds., *Great Theatre: The American Congress in Action*. New York, 1998, 224–247.

Johnson, R.M. *The Dynamics of Compliance. Supreme Court Decision-Making from a New Perspective*. Evanston, 1967.

Kastellec, J.P. "Hierarchical and Collegial Politics on the U.S. Courts of Appeals." *Journal of Politics,* Vol. 73(2), 2011, 345–361.

Kluger, R. *Simple Justice*. New York, 1976.

Leo, R.A. *Police Interrogation and American Justice*. Cambridge, 2008.

Lindquist, S.A., Haire, S.B., Songer, D.F. "Supreme Court Auditing of the U.S. Courts of Appeals: An Organizational Perspective." *Journal of Public Administration Research and Theory,* Vol. 17(4), 2007, 607–624.

McGuire, K.T. "Public Schools, Religious Establishments, and the U.S. Supreme Court: An Examination of Policy Compliance." *American Politics Research,* Vol. 37(1), 2009, 50–74.

Miller, M.C. *The View of the Courts From the Hill: Interactions Between Congress and the Federal Judiciary*. Charlottesville, 2009.

Murphy, W.F. *Congress and the Court*. Chicago, 1962.

Murphy, W.F. *Elements of Judicial Strategy*. Chicago, 1964.

Pacelle, R.L., Jr., Baum, L. "Supreme Court Authority in the Judiciary: A Study of Remands." *American Politics Quarterly,* Vol. 20(2), 1992, 169–191.

Peltason, J.W. *Fifty-Eight Lonely Men: Southern Federal Judges and School Desegregation*, 2nd ed. Urbana, 1971.
Petrick, M.J. "The Supreme Court and Authority Acceptance." *Western Political Quarterly*, Vol. 21(1), 1968, 5–19.
Pickerill, J.M. *Constitutional Deliberation in Congress: The Impact of Judicial Review in a Separate System*. Durham, N.C., 2004.
Pildes, R.H. "Is the Supreme Court a 'Majoritarian' Institution?" *Supreme Court Review*, 2010, 103–158.
Savage, D. "Crusading Liberal Judge Keeps High Court Busy." *Los Angeles Times*, 3 March 1996, A3.
Scigliano, R. *The Supreme Court and the Presidency*. New York, 1971.
Segal, J.A. "Courts, Executives, and Legislatures." In Gates, J.B., Johnson, C.A., eds., *The American Courts: A Critical Assessment*. Washington, D.C., 1991, 373–393.
Shaman, J.M. *Equality and Liberty in the Golden Age of State Constitutional Law*. New York, 2008.
Songer, D.R., Segal, J.A., Cameron, C.M. "The Hierarchy of Justice: Testing a Principal Agent Model of Supreme Court–Circuit Court Interactions." *American Journal of Political Science*, Vol. 38(3), 1994, 673–696.
Spriggs, J.F., II. "Explaining Federal Bureaucratic Compliance with Supreme Court Opinions." *Political Research Quarterly*, Vol. 50(3), 1997, 567–593.
Uchida, C.B., Bynum, T.S. "Search Warrants, Motions to Suppress and 'Lost Cases': The Effects of the Exclusionary Rule in Seven Jurisdictions." *Journal of Criminal Law and Criminology*, Vol. 81(4), 1991, 1034–1066.
Van Meter, D.S., Van Horn, C.E. "The Policy Implementation Process: A Conceptual Framework." *Administration & Society*, Vol. 6(4), 1975, 445–488.
Way, H.F., Jr. "Survey Research on Judicial Decisions: The Prayer and Bible Reading Cases." *Western Political Quarterly*, Vol. 21(2), 1968, 189–205.
Weaver, R.K. "The Politics of Blame." *Brookings Review*, Vol. 5(2), 1987, 43–47.
Westin, A.F. *The Anatomy of a Constitutional Law Case*. New York, 1958.
White, W.S. *Litigating in the Shadow of Death: Defense Attorneys in Capital Cases*. Ann Arbor, 2006.

Chapter 9

Implementation of German Federal Constitutional Court Decisions

Judicial Orders and the Federal Legislature

Thomas Gawron and Ralf Rogowski

In contrast to the long-standing and elaborate research on the impact of U.S. Supreme Court decisions (see Baum, in this volume, and the pathbreaking studies by Wasby 1970; Becker, Feeley 1973; and Johnson, Canon 1998), study of the impact and implementation of Federal Constitutional Court decisions is still underdeveloped in Germany. Constitutional lawyers who focus on the legal rather than the political or social aspects dominate the discussion of postjudicial processes. Political and social scientists have only recently begun to develop research designs for the study of judicial implementation (Gawron, Rogowski 2007; Höland 2011; Ooyen, Möllers 2015).

This chapter starts with an overview of the existing research on the impact of the Federal Constitutional Court and then presents empirical insights into the Court's control density regarding the output of the German Federal legislature. The chapter proceeds by offering a research design for assessing the Federal Constitutional Court's decisions as implementation programs. In its final sections it provides an analysis of the unique, peculiar instrument for influencing the German legislature, namely, judicial orders.

Notes for this chapter begin on page 223.

Existing Research on Impact and Implementation of Federal Constitutional Court Decisions

German constitutional lawyers traditionally discuss aspects of impact or implementation of Federal Constitutional Court decisions under the heading of procedural constitutional law. The legal account assumes that constitutional court decisions are more or less self-enforcing and generally are complied with. A further assumption is that the Court possesses a favorable reputation or strong authority, which also applies to its decisions (see Schlaich, Korioth 2012, 364–367).

Legal aspects of enforcement or implementation are regulated by the Federal Constitutional Court Act, which states that the decisions of the Court are automatically "binding upon Federal and Land constitutional organs as well as on all courts and authorities" (art. 31 I of the Federal Constitutional Court Act). Decisions on the constitutionality of statutes "have the force of law" (art. 31 II of the Federal Constitutional Court Act) and the same legal status as parliamentary acts. Furthermore, the Court "may state by whom the decision is to be executed" (art. 35 of the Federal Constitutional Court Act). It is known that the Court has hardly ever used its powers to issue specific executive orders (see Klein 1983: 443), although it has used them in a controversial manner to impose interim legislative solutions (in particular the two abortion decisions in BverfGE 39, 1 et seq.—*Abortion I* case and BverfGE 88, 203 et seq.—*Abortion II* case; see also the analysis in Kommers, Miller 2012: 374–94, esp. 385).

However, although the Court's verdicts are binding by law, it is well known that not all decisions affect the legislature and other constitutional bodies in the same way. The plain statutory terms outlining the legal effects of decisions and the Court's powers to influence those decisions' execution do not capture their real impact or the processes of implementation. Furthermore, the Court lacks a special enforcement agency and is thus dependent on other public authorities to implement its decisions. These bodies operate with significant autonomy. Like other forms of regulation, judicial decisions must reconcile with the views of the implementing bodies. Their original aims and intended effects are often not, or are only partially, achieved. Independent organizations and actors determine the implementation and execution of laws and decisions. Knowledge of their mode of operation is vital to an understanding of the implementation process (see Pressman, Wildavsky 1973 and Bardach, Kagan 1982 on general aspects of implementation).

Thus, in order to understand the implementation of Federal Constitutional Court decisions, it is necessary to transcend the legal account. An important first step is to assess the political function of the court. Like other political program makers, the Federal Constitutional Court, in authoritatively concretizing the abstract constitution by way of judicial interpretation, creates programmatic guidelines for other constitutional organs as well as for administrations, courts, and organized interests. Judgments of the Court are generally similar in structure to political programs. They can also be divided into symbolic and instrumental programs (a distinction originally introduced by Gusfield 1972) containing both arguments of a general nature as well as specific advice for policy makers and administrative agencies.

Given the importance of the Court's political role, it is remarkable that German postwar political science and social science have, all told, generated few empirical findings on the topic. Political science research in particular has resorted mostly to qualitative accounts of the Court's role. Early studies assessed the Court's influence by analyzing in rather normative terms its position within the political system (Laufer 1968) and by presenting data on the awareness, support, and compliance of elite political institutions (see Kommers 1976: ch. 7 on the impact of the Court). Later studies engaged in policy analysis (Stüwe 1997; Lhotta 2003; Vanberg 2005; Hönnige 2007; Lembcke 2007) and counted, for example, the number of legislative acts reviewed by the Court (Beyme 1988; Wever 1991; Kneip 2009). Newer studies analyze the role of the Court in the political process and its influence on the political system (see empirical contributions in Wrase, Boulanger 2013 and Ooyen, Möllers 2015). In the tradition of critical theory and neo-Marxism, a number of studies have criticized the Federal Constitutional Court's practice of decision making. They argue that the Court adheres to a model of constitutional law that contrasts sharply with social reality in Germany and has a negative influence on social change (Massing 1976; Hase, Ladeur 1980; Preuß 1987; Lietzmann 1988).

However, these analyses can hardly be called implementation studies, as the latter analyze the processes that occur after the Court has delivered its decision. The implementation perspective views judicial decisions not only as solutions for past conflicts but as programs for future policies (Blankenburg et al. 1987). Implementation research understands judicial implementation as a form of policy implementation and compares judicial programs to legislative acts (see Baum 1981), as both consist of programs that guide implementation processes. Furthermore, it treats implementation as a temporal process characterized by a certain degree of autonomy.

Hard empirical evidence on the implementation processes of Federal Constitutional Court decisions is rare. A few studies have analyzed the addressees of decisions (Dopatka 1982), the stifling impact of the Federal

Constitutional Court on decision-making of the Federal Parliament (Landfried 1984), the impact of the Federal Constitutional Court on societal self-regulation (Ebsen 1985), implementation via communication between the Federal Constitutional Court and other courts (Gawron, Rogowski 2007: ch. 4), and the impact of Federal Constitutional Court decisions on the administrative system (Gawron 2013).

To comprehensively study the impact of the Court, we have suggested in previous research that effects of the Court should be distinguished according to their addressees and arenas of implementation (Gawron, Rogowski 2007: ch. 3). With respect to Federal Constitutional Court decisions, five main addressees and arenas of implementation should be distinguished: the legislative, the judicial, the administrative, that involving associations and political parties, and the private arena involving establishments and citizens.

In this chapter we focus on the first arena: the legislature. After briefly comparing judicial review with other activities of the Court, we examine the extent to which the Court has reviewed federal statutes and declared them null and void or incompatible with the Basic Law. Among the devices available to the Court for declaring objections to norms, the so-called judicial order (*Gesetzgebungsauftrag*) is unique. We analyze this particular instrument, with which the Court directly intervenes in legislative processes. From an implementation perspective, it is remarkable how the government handles the judicial orders and, in particular, how specific departments in federal ministries act as implementation agents monitoring the legislative response to judicial orders of the Court. This will be the focus of the last part of our analysis.

The Control of the Legislature by the Federal Constitutional Court

The Federal Constitutional Court has a variety of procedures at its disposal. It deals with election disputes as well as procedures for impeachment of the federal president. It acts as an arbitrator in disputes between the federation and the states or between the states themselves. It can be called upon by anyone who claims to have been damaged by an act of the state or has been denied one or more basic rights (constitutional complaint). And, finally, the Court has extensive competencies and unique powers of judicial review of legislation. Of special importance in this context are the procedures of "abstract" judicial review according to Article 93 I 2 of the Basic Law, and "concrete" judicial review or preliminary ruling by way of judicial referral according to Article 100 I 1 of the Basic

Law (see Heun, in this volume). Statistically they seem to be insignificant, since "abstract" judicial review accounts for only 0.1 percent and "concrete" judicial review for about 2.5 percent of the caseload, in comparison to the constitutional complaints that constitute more than 95 percent (see Statistik des Bundesverfassungsgerichts, Tabelle "Statistik für das Geschäftsjahr 2013, A I 5: Plenar- /Senats- / Kammerentscheidungen" http://www.bundesverfassungsgericht.de/DE/Verfahren/Jahresstatistiken/2014/gb2014/A-I-5.html). However, the two forms of judicial review are far more influential in the Court's decision-making practice than the statistic suggests. Whereas less than 3 percent of all constitutional complaints are admitted (see Heun and Blankenburg, both in this volume), 65 percent of the judicial review applications are granted a full hearing (Peters 1976b).

By definition, judicial review controls the statutory output of the legislature. However, in order to assess the real control density[1] of the Court, those constitutional complaints that either aim directly at legislative acts as the source of violation of a basic right or indirectly lead to questioning the constitutionality of a norm have to be added to the cases brought under the two special procedures for judicial review, that is, "abstract" and "concrete" judicial review. Of all decided constitutional complaints published in the official register, almost 30 percent are directly or indirectly concerned with reviewing a legal norm (Peters 1976b).

In order to establish the density of control exercised by the Federal Constitutional Court over the federal legislature, it is necessary to assess, first, the percentage of federal acts overturned by the Court. In the first sixteen parliamentary terms, from 1949 to 2009, the German federal legislature passed 7,036 acts of Parliament (in accordance with arts. 77 and 78 of the Basic Law [excluding statutory orders]). Of these, 306 or 4.4 percent were declared totally or partially void (142) or totally or partially incompatible (184) with the Basic Law by the Federal Constitutional Court (see Table 9.1).

However, the real control density of the Court can be determined only by taking all statutes handled by the Court into consideration. In previous research based on published decisions for the period 1951–1987, we calculated that in this period the Court had reviewed (i.e., controlled) 505 acts, or 12.6 percent of all acts passed by the federal legislature. Comparing this number of federal acts reviewed by the Federal Constitutional Court (505) with the number of acts declared void or incompatible with the Basic Law (175) shows that every third act controlled by the Court is declared wholly or partly unconstitutional. For the period 1951–2011, Sascha Kneip (in this volume) found that "the Federal Constitutional Court declared 640 federal and state laws (or specific norms within these laws) unconstitutional in whole or in part."

Table 9.1. Invalidated German Federal Statutes, 1949–2009

		Number of federal statutes declared unconstitutional		
Parliamentary terms	*Number of federal statutes enacted*	*Total*	*Void or partially void*	*Incompatible or partially incompatible*
1949–1953	545	31	26	5
1953–1957	507	34	22	12
1957–1961	424	26	19	7
1961–1965	427	20	7	13
1965–1969	453	22	7	15
1969–1972	335	8	3	5
1972–1976	516	36	14	22
1976–1980	354	14	6	8
1980–1983	139	16	5	11
1983–1987	320	13	3	10
1987–1991	369	19	8	11
1991–1994	507	26	7	19
1994–1998	565	18	5	13
1998–2002	559	12	7	5
2002–2005	400	7	2	5
2005–2009	616	4	1	3
	7036	306	142	164

Sources: *Datenhandbuch zur Geschichte des Deutschen Bundestages 1949 bis 1999: Gesamtausgabe* 2000 and *Datenhandbuch zur Geschichte des Deutschen Bundestages 1990 bis 2010: Ergänzungsband* 2011, and own calculations.

Decisions of the Federal Constitutional Court as Implementation Programs

Understanding judicial decisions as programs (see Gawron, Rogowski 1990) makes it possible to distinguish the instrumental from the symbolic part of the decision. The instrumental part guides implementation processes by determining the condition of its execution. The Court has a number of instruments at hand to influence the implementation of decisions invalidating legislative acts. These consist of declarations of legislative acts being null and void or incompatible with the constitution, judicial orders directed at the federal legislature, and imposition of an obligation to interpret an act only in conformity with the constitutional interpretation of the Court. Most of these instruments are a result of legal innovations introduced by the Court itself (see Ipsen 1983).

In the early days the Court had to declare each act it found to be unconstitutional automatically null and void. However, serious consequences arose because an act declared void loses its applicability retrospectively from the moment of its coming into force. Not only the legislative act declared void but also those legal acts that are based on the rejected norm become invalid. "Everybody is weary of such total annihilation, which disappoints the confidence of citizen" (Pestalozza 1982: 175 [translation R.R.]). In particular, administrations are faced with serious problems because they not only lose a legislative program on which they can base future administrative acts, but their past acts also become invalid.

The declaration that an act is void leads, in many cases, to social consequences not intended by the Court. Constitutional objections in tax and welfare law, for example, are concerned with privileges of particular groups that infringe upon the rights of those not privileged. However, the constitutional objections lead to the paradoxical situation that a declaration of null and void would in fact disadvantage those who are so far also entitled to gain certain rights, so now it is the constitutional beneficiaries who suffer an infringement of their basic right to equality before the law ("unequal denial of benefit"—BVerfGE 25, 101 (111); see also BverfGE 33, 349).

In this situation the Court introduced the distinction between null and void, on the one hand, and incompatible norm, on the other, in order to limit the negative retrospective effects (BVerfGE 28, 227; see also Benda 1979). The federal legislature eventually recognized this distinction between declarations of null and void and of incompatibility, introduced *praeter legem* by the Court, in the 1970 reform of the Federal Constitutional Court Act (amendment of art. 31 of the Federal Constitutional Court Act). By holding that a norm or a statute is (merely) incompatible with the Basic Law, the Court avoids a legal vacuum and calls upon the legislature to correct only the norm rejected by the Court. The legislature is left with numerous possibilities to resolve the state of unconstitutionality (see also BVerfGE 55, 100 (112) and Hein 1988).

By becoming able to call directly upon the legislature to overcome the unconstitutional situation, the Court refined its control competency in a remarkable manner. The declaration of incompatibility is a sophisticated instrument for influencing the implementation of its decision by the legislature. On the one hand, the Court respects the circumstances of parliamentary legislation, but on the other hand it exerts pressure on the legislative process. However, within its relationship to the legislature it extended its programming capacity by becoming able to call upon the federal legislature to behave like an implementation actor. The notice of unconstitutionality, through which the legislature is called upon to "fix matters," enables the Court to exercise further control over the implementation process, which would not be possible in the case of a null and void declaration.

Judicial orders are an even farther-reaching instrument for influencing the legislature (see Kleuker 1993). They demand corrective legislative action from the legislature, usually setting a deadline and occasionally directing the legislature to adopt a specific solution. In legal writings, judicial orders are often called "admonitory decisions" (*Appellentscheidungen*—Rupp-von Brünneck 1972; see also Badura 1982; Schulte 1988). The Court introduced them in order to issue guidelines for legislative actions. The Court empowered itself with judicial orders to overcome situations in which an unconstitutional but unvoided law leads to a stalemate between the Court and the legislature. Judicial orders are also used when the Court, for reasons of prudence, abstains from a declaration of unconstitutionality but indicates that the law will be declared constitutional for only a limited period. Upon a declaration of "still constitutional" (*noch verfassungsmäßige Rechtslage* in German constitutional law parlance; see Pestalozza 1976), the Court issues a warning that it will render the law in question unconstitutional in the future unless the legislature acts to reform it. "By resorting to this procedure, the court keeps the constitutional dialogue going and furnishes parliament with a flexibility it needs to work out creative solutions to the problem under scrutiny" (Kommers, Miller 2012: 37).

We can identify the gradual expansion of the use of the declarations the Court undertakes in its judgments as attempts to create judicial programs that can exercise some control over post-judicial processes. With its declarations of "void," "incompatible," and "still constitutional," which all can be combined with judicial orders in the form of appeals, proposals for specific solutions, and the setting of time limits, the Court has created a canon of control instruments with which it can react flexibly to each individual case and at the same time influence the implementation process.

Judicial Orders

Judicial orders dominate in judgments that declare a norm incompatible with the Basic Law. The "soft" instrument of a declaration of incompatibility is sharpened by judicial orders that require the legislature always to take action to "repair" the norm in question in the light of the Court's directives (on judicial orders as "a duty to repair" see Steinberg 1987). However, the reasoning of judicial orders shows that the Court rarely provides explicit instructions. It might suggest or encourage the legislature to consider certain aspects for the required amendment. Nevertheless, judicial orders also protect the autonomy of the legislative process and create possibilities for "implementation games" (Bardach 1977).

The Processing of Judicial Orders by the Federal Government

Although addressed abstractly to the federal legislature, judicial orders are processed not by the federal parliament, but by the federal government (Heyde 1984). Within the federal government, the ministry that was in charge of the invalidated legislation is responsible for processing a judicial order. In fact, the same ministerial departments that were originally responsible for drafting the unconstitutional legislation also handle the judicial orders. However, there is one major difference: the Federal Ministry of Justice exerts control over the implementation of judicial orders.

The procedural code on drafting legislation provides that the Federal Ministry of Justice monitors legal and constitutional conformity of all bills proposed by the federal government (section 46 I of the *Gemeinsame Geschäftsordnung der Bundesministerien*). In the case of judicial orders, there used to be a particular mechanism of internal control in the federal government. Between 1979 and 1991, the Federal Ministry of Justice administered an official internal list of pending "Judicial Orders in Judgments of the Federal Constitutional Court."[2] Within the Federal Ministry of Justice, the constitutional law department was in charge of compiling this list. We found in our research that the list was prepared from the transcripts sent to the ministry immediately after the pronouncement of the judgment and was distributed to the ministries in charge of the legislative redrafting every six months (Gawron, Rogowski 2007: 138–139).

The list indicated which judicial orders were and were not yet completed. It distinguished judicial orders deriving from declarations of null and void from declarations of incompatibility and judgments in which the constitutionality of a norm was upheld. Furthermore, it registered the time limits for implementation, special appeals, and any other suggestions contained in the Court's judgments. In particular, the list included information on (1) the judicial reference number and/or the citation of the judgment in the official case report of the Federal Constitutional Court; (2) the Act or the norm that was invalidated; (3) in keywords, the legal advice and the main thrust of the Federal Constitutional Court decision; and (4) the method by which to resolve the issue.

In compiling the list, the Federal Ministry of Justice used pragmatic criteria to determine whether a judicial order existed. It did not distinguish whether the order was contained in the tenor of the judgment, in its legal reasoning, or in obiter dicta. The ministry understood any concrete proposal for future legislative action mentioned by the Court as a judicial order. Of the 63 judgments in which the Federal Ministry of Justice found judicial orders, 39 contained declarations of incompatibility, 15 were declarations of null and void, and 9 were declarations of "still constitutional."

Forty-seven judicial orders had been fully executed by 1991. The duration of the execution of a judicial varied between ten years and a few months (Gawron, Rogowski 2007: 140).

Policy Areas of Judicial Orders

The political content of decisions with judicial orders can be ascertained by analyzing the ministerial responsibilities in dealing with them. On the list compiled by the Federal Ministry of Justice, more than half of the orders dealt with issues falling in the domains of the departments of Justice, and Labor and Social Affairs (19 and 14 judicial orders respectively out of 63). Furthermore, if one looks at the policy areas, it becomes clear that a large number of decisions with judicial orders concerned social policy issues like divorce, social security, labor law, and health and safety. A significant number of decisions with judicial orders dealt with the legal status of civil servants, tax consultants and lawyers. Another noteworthy group of decisions with judicial orders involved political matters such as census law, the legal status of local government parties, or the financing of political parties. Furthermore, the constitutional law provision on which constitutional objections in judgments with judicial orders were based was, in the majority of the decisions, Article 3 of the Basic Law, guaranteeing the right of equality before the law and equal treatment.

In analyzing the political content of judgments with judicial orders, it becomes apparent that many judgments dealt with interventionist welfare policies that grant special rights to a particular group. Those who felt disadvantaged by such positive discrimination mobilized the Court. The cases pitted groups such as university professors against college professors, civil service pensioners against ordinary pensioners, widowers against widows, househusbands against housewives, those divorced before 1977 against those divorced after 1977, transsexuals under 25 years of age against transsexuals over 25 years of age. In most of these cases, the Court saw itself as an arbiter that had to balance aspects of positive and reversed discrimination.

However, it is not immediately apparent why the Court prefers to sanction its judicial policy with judicial orders in these types of cases. One explanation might be the complexity of policy making in the arena of social politics, where the Court co-operates with a dense set of actors. These include the various social ministries, welfare organizations, trade unions, and employer associations. In Germany, stable inter-organizational networks characterize this arena. Policies result from continuous negotiations within these corporatist networks. Indeed, the networks provide the background for perpetual new games. To some extent, they make it easy for the Court to become a participant in the games. In the end, however, powerful interest groups control this arena and watch over the dispensation of justice.

The Impact of Judicial Orders upon Legislation

Judgments with judicial orders have both profound immediate and long-lasting effects upon legislation. They often require a rearrangement of interests in the affected political field. They strengthen the bureaucratic control of legislation. In general, they limit the political room for maneuver and thus contribute to a tendency of petrification of policy making.

Judgments of the Federal Constitutional Court with judicial orders have immediate effects on the government. Although the primary addressee of these judgments is the legislature, normally represented by the parliament, it is in fact the federal government and in particular the responsible departments that have to deal with judicial orders. The judgments reflect the different addressees by distinguishing symbolic and instrumental parts. The symbolic parts of the decision aim at the legislature, and the instrumental parts at ministerial bureaucracy. Judicial orders are particular devices contained in the instrumental parts of the decision that target the secondary addressees of the judgments as the main actors in their implementation. But in order to be effective, judicial orders have to be clear. If they consist merely of an admonition of a possible unconstitutionality, the internal mechanism of legislative drafting may ignore the constitutional demand.

Furthermore, judicial orders create effects beyond the particular legislative act in question. They can function as externally induced means of strengthening internal procedural control within the organizational frame of the federal government. The control of constitutional compliance is hereby of utmost importance. Paragraph 45 I of the *Gemeinsame Geschäftsordnung der Bundesministerien* stipulates that all legislative drafts have to be assessed by the Ministry of Justice and the Ministry of the Interior in terms of their compliance with constitutional requirements. The aim of this provision is to anticipate and prevent rejection by Karlsruhe and the possibility of further judicial orders. The constitutional law departments of the Federal Ministry of Justice and the Interior are, in a sense, permanent participants in the legislative process within the federal government. They even play a role outside the government, for example, when they are asked to compile a report for a committee of the federal parliament.

The constitutional control of proposed legislation gives the constitutional law departments special importance and an untouchable competence (Seibert 1984). They interpret the judgments of the Federal Constitutional Court for other departments within their ministry. Through a precise exegesis of the reasoning, they undertake, to a certain extent, an "authentic constitutional interpretation" (Dreier 1976: 42) and clarify the "will" of the Federal Constitutional Court for other ministerial actors. The interpretation can be limited to highlighting important passages of the reasoning. In cases of unclear or ambiguous formulation, the room for interpretation increases. Implementation problems that could occur through unclear formulation by the Court are minimized in this first stage of interpretation. As the constitutional law departments have detailed knowledge of the previous judicial activity of the Federal Constitutional Court, the interpretation can be undertaken with reference to established lines of judicial decision-making.

As clarifiers of the possible intention of the decisions of the Federal Constitutional Court, the constitutional law departments become external collaborators of the Court that operate as highly qualified implementation agents of the judiciary in Karlsruhe. During our interviews in the constitutional law department at the Federal Ministry of Justice, we encountered many civil servants who were former legal assistants in the Federal Constitutional Court. The function of evaluating the likelihood that planned legislation will be challenged in constitutional procedures ensures that the constitutional law departments enjoy a high degree of autonomy within the government. However, there is also a risk that constitutional scrutiny of proposed legislation will lead to further bureaucratization of the legislative process. In strengthening constitutional monitoring of prospective legislation, judicial orders foster depoliticization and further juridification of the legislative process.

Conclusion

The relationship between the Federal Constitutional Court and the German political system is dynamic and sometimes conflictual, but most often functional. Analyses of the relationship reveal how the administration of justice influences the legislative process—in other words, the impact of law on politics—and how the appointments of particular judges represent attempts at political control of the Court, or in other words the impact of politics on law. Indeed, it has been argued that the juridification of politics by an "unbounded court" (Jestaedt et al. 2011) and the reversed process of politicization of justice are dangers in Germany (Lamprecht, Malanowski 1979; Wesel 2004: 359–372). Implementation research can inform this debate with empirically based accounts of the relationship between the Federal Constitutional Court and the federal legislature, analyzing the actual juridification and politicization processes in the concrete implementation of constitutional adjudication by the legislature.

Our analysis of judicial orders issued by the Federal Constitutional Court and their implementation by the German legislature exemplifies both a politicization of the Court and a juridification of politics. Judicial orders are an important indicator of the Federal Constitutional Court's general responsiveness toward the legislative process. A procedural responsiveness operates with formalized procedural prerequisites and encourages the juridification of legislating. Judicial orders are often of a technical nature and aim at the "correction" of mistakes in the procedural process of legislating. However, they create a danger of bureaucratic encroachment on political processes. In conjunction with the directly binding effect of the judgment of the Federal Constitutional Court, the instrument of judicial orders demonstrates what German legal theorists call the "increasing rule of law" or the juridification of the legislative process.

Thus the switch from the mere declaration of void to an active exertion of influence on legislation through judicial orders and other procedural instruments, actively promoted by the Court, gives cause to question the function of the Federal Constitutional Court in relation to the legislature. The selective shaping of politics and the control of procedures undertaken by the Court via judicial orders mark a transfer from negative to positive participation in the legislative process. This has led, on the part of the legislature, to a strengthening of ministerial bureaucracy and of the gatekeeping function of the legal and especially the constitutional law departments in federal ministries. There is no doubt that the Court intends the higher degree of bureaucratic control over the legislature to ensure smooth implementation of its decisions. It achieves this partly by making its decision-making process more flexible, thereby enabling increased responsiveness to the conditions of implementation in the legislative process. However, the extent to which the Court's preference for a higher degree of legislative adoption of quasi-judicial procedural regulation is feasible, and indeed desirable, remains to be seen.

Thomas Gawron is a lecturer in law at the Hochschule für Technik und Wirtschaft (HTW), Berlin.

Ralf Rogowski is a professor of law and director of the Law and Sociology program at the School of Law of the University of Warwick, Coventry.

Notes

1. Our quantitative account of control density of judicial review differs from the normative understanding adopted in academic legal writing. The latter is concerned with the intensity with which the Court is allowed to control legislative acts. See Schlaich, Korioth 2012: 196–197 and 354–358. See also Chryssogonos 1987: 179–203.
2. The list was a response to criticisms that the former president of the Federal Constitutional Court, Ernst Benda uttered at one of the many official meetings with leading representatives (in this case, the swearing in of a new federal president). He criticized the slow implementation of judicial orders at the end of the 1970s.

Bibliography

Badura, P. "Die verfassungsgerichtliche Pflicht des gesetzgebenden Parlaments zur Nachbesserung von Gesetzen." In Müller, G., et al., eds., *Staatsorganisation und Staatsfunktionen im Wandel : Festschrift für Kurt Eichenberger zum 60. Geburtstag*. Basel, 1982, 481–492.

Bardach, E. *The Implementation Game. What Happens after a Bill Becomes a Law.* Cambridge, 1977.

Bardach, E., Kagan, R.A. *Going by the Book: The Problem of Regulatory Unreasonableness.* Philadelphia, 1982.

Baum, L. "Comparing the Implementation of Legislative and Judicial Politics." In Sabatier, P., Mazmanian, O.A., eds., *Effective Policy Implementation.* Lexington, MA, 1981, 39–92.

Becker, T.L., Feeley, M.M., eds. *The Impact of Supreme Court Decisions.* 2nd ed. New York, 1973.

Benda, E. *Grundrechtswidrige Gesetze. Ein Beitrag zu den Ursachen verfassungsgerichtlicher Beanstandung.* Baden-Baden, 1979.

Beyme, K. von. "Verfassungsgerichtsbarkeit und Policy Analysis." In Beyme, K. von, ed., *Der Vergleich in der Politikwissenschaft*. Munich, 1988, 369–395.

Blankenburg, E., Voigt, R.; Gawron, T., Rogowski, R., eds. *Implementation von Gerichtsentscheidungen. Jahrbuch für Rechtssoziologie und Rechtstheorie*, Vol. 11. Opladen, 1987.

Chryssogonos, K. *Verfassungsgerichtsbarkeit und Gesetzgebung. Zur Methode der Verfassungsinterpretation bei der Normenkontrolle.* Berlin, 1987.

Datenhandbuch zur Geschichte des Deutschen Bundestages 1949 bis 1999: Gesamtausgabe. Compiled by P. Schindler. Baden-Baden, 2000.

Datenhandbuch zur Geschichte des Deutschen Bundestages 1990 bis 2010: Ergänzungsband. Compiled by M.F. Feldkamp. Baden-Baden, 2011.

Dopatka, F.-W. *Das Bundesverfassungsgericht und seine Umwelt. Zur Analyse der Entwicklung des Bundesverfassungsgerichts und der adressatenspezifischen Bezüge seiner Rechtsprechung.* Berlin, 1982.

Dreier, R. "Zur Problematik und Situation der Verfassungsinterpretation." In Dreier, R., Schwegmann, F., eds., *Probleme der Verfassungsinterpretation. Dokumentation einer Kontroverse.* Baden-Baden, 1976, 13–47.

Ebsen, I. *Das Bundesverfassungsgericht als Element gesellschaftlicher Selbstregulierung. Eine pluralistische Thorie der Verfassungsgerichtsbarkeit im demokratischen Verfassungsstaat.* Berlin, 1985.

Gawron, T. "Das ferne Gericht – Wirkungsanalysen zum Verhältnis zwischen Bundesverfassungsgericht und Verwaltungsbehörde." In Wrase, M., Boulanger, C., eds., *Die Politik des Verfassungsrechts. Interdisziplinäre und vergleichende Perspektiven auf die Rolle und Funktion von Verfassungsgerichten.* Baden-Baden, 2013, 216–240.

Gawron, T., Rogowski, R. "Implementation von Programmen des Bundesverfassungsgerichts." In Raiser, T., Voigt, R., eds., *Durchsetzung und Wirkung von Rechtsentscheidungen. Die Bedeutung der Implementations- und Wirkungsforschung für die Rechtswissenschaft.* Baden-Baden, 1990, 226–239.

Gawron, T., Rogowski, R. *Die Wirkung des Bundesverfassungsgerichts. Rechtssziologische Analysen.* Baden-Baden, 2007.

Gusfield, J.R. *Symbolic Crusade: Status Politics and the American Temperance Movement,* 3rd ed. Urbana, 1972.

Hase, F., Ladeur, K.H. *Verfassungsgerichtsbarkeit und politisches System.* Frankfurt/Main, 1980.

Hein, P.E. *Die Unvereinbarerklärung verfassungswidriger Gesetze durch das Bundesverfassungsgericht. Grundlagen, Anwendungsbereich, Rechtsfolgen.* Baden-Baden, 1988.

Heyde, W. "Gesetzgeberische Konsequenzen aus der Verfassungswidrigerklärung von Normen." In Zeidler, W., Maunz, T., Roellecke, G., eds., *Festschrift für Hans Joachim Faller.* Munich, 1984, 53–62.

Höland, A. "Which Effects Do Courts Have?" In Papendorf, K., Machura, S., Andnaes, K., eds., *Understanding Law in Society.* Berlion, Zürich, 2011, 160–180.

Hönnige, C. *Verfassungsgericht, Regierung und Opposition. Die vergleichende Analyse eines Spannungsdreiecks.* Wiesbaden, 2007.

Ipsen, J. *Rechtsfolgen der Verfassungswidrigkeit von Norm und Einzelakt.* Baden-Baden, 1983.

Jestaedt, M., Lepsius, O., Möllers, C., Schönberger, C. *Das entgrenzte Gericht.* Frankfurt/Main, 2011.

Johnson, C.A., Canon, B.C. *Judicial Policies: Implementation and Impact,* 2nd ed. Washington, D.C., 1998.

Klein, E. "Verfassungsprozeßrecht – Versuch einer Systematik anhand der Rechtsprechung des Bundesverfassungsgerichts." *Archiv des öffentlichen Rechts,* Vol. 108, 1983, 410–444 and 561–624.

Kleuker, A. *Gesetzgebungsaufträge des Bundesverfassungsgerichts.* Berlin, 1993.

Kneip, S. *Verfassungsgerichte als demokratische Akteure. Der Beitrag des Bundesverfassungsgerichts zur Qualität der bundesdeutschen Demokratie.* Baden-Baden, 2009.

Kommers, D.P. *Judicial Politics in West Germany: A Study of the Federal Constitutional Court.* Beverly Hills, London, 1976.

Kommers, D.P., Miller, R.A. *The Constitutional Jurisprudence of the Federal Republic of Germany,* 3rd ed. Durham, London, 2012.

Lamprecht, R., Malanowski, W., eds. *Richter machen Politik. Auftrag und Anspruch des Bundesverfassungsgerichts.* Frankfurt/Main, 1979.

Landfried, C. *Bundesverfassungsgericht und Gesetzgeber. Wirkungen der Verfassungsrechtsprechung auf parlamentarische Willensbildung und soziale Realität.* Baden-Baden, 1984.

Laufer, H. *Verfassungsgerichtsbarkeit und politischer Prozeß. Studien zum Bundesverfassungsgericht der Bundesrepublik Deutschland.* Tübingen, 1968.

Lembcke, O. *Hüter der Verfassung. Eine institutionentheoretische Studie zur Autorität des Bundesverfassungsgerichts.* Tübingen 2007.

Lhotta, R. "Das Bundesverfassungsgericht als politischer Akteur: Plädoyer für eine neoinstitutionalistische Ergänzung der Forschung." *Schweizerische Zeitschrift für Politikwissenschaft,* Vol. 9(3), 2003, 142–153.

Lietzmann, H. *Das Bundesverfassungsgericht. Eine sozialwissenschaftliche Studie über Wertordnung, dissenting votes und funktionale Genese.* Opladen, 1988.

Massing, O. "Das Bundesverfassungsgericht als Instrument sozialer Kontrolle." In Tohidipur, N., ed., *Verfassung, Verfassungsgerichtsbarkeit, Politik.* Frankfurt/Main, 1976, 30–91.

Ooyen, R.C. van, Möllers, M.H.W., eds. *Handbuch Bundesverfassungsgericht im politischen System,* 2nd ed. Wiesbaden, 2015.

Pestalozza, C. "'Noch verfassungsmäßige' und 'bloß verfassungswidrige' Rechtslagen. Zur Feststellung und kooperativen Beseitigung verfassungsimperfekter Zustände." In Starck, C., et al., eds., *Bundesverfassungsgericht und Grundgesetz. Festgabe aus Anlaß des 25jährigen Bestehens des Bundesverfassungsgerichts,* vol. 1. Tübingen, 1976, 519–567.

Pestalozza, C. *Verfassungsprozeßrecht. Die Verfassungsgerichtsbarkeit des Bundes und der Länder,* 2nd ed. Munich, 1982.

Peters, K. "Ergebnisse von Vorlagen nach Art. 100 Abs. 1 GG und einige Überlegungen dazu." *Zeitschrift für Zivilprozeß,* Vol. 89, 1976a, 1–43.

Peters, K. "Die Verfassungsbeschwerde in der amtlichen Sammlung des Bundesverfassungsgerichts." *Monatschrift des Deutschen Rechts,* 1976b, 447–452.

Pressman, J., Wildavsky, A. *Implementation: How Great Expectations in Washington Are Dashed in Oakland; Or, Why It's Amazing that Federal Programs Work at All.* Berkeley, 1973.

Preuß, U.K. "Aus dem Geist des Konsenses: die Rechtsprechung des Bundesverfassungsgerichts." *Merkur,* Vol. 41, 1987, 1–12.

Rupp-von Brünneck, W. "Admonitory Functions of the Constitutional Court." *American Journal of Comparative Law,* Vol. 22, 1972, 387–403.

Schlaich, K., Korioth, S. *Das Bundesverfassungsgericht. Stellung, Verfahren, Entscheidungen,* 9th ed. Munich, 2012.

Schulte, B. "Appellentscheidungen des Bundesverfassungsgerichts." *Deutsches Verwaltungsblatt,* Vol. 103, 1988, 1200–1206.

Seibert, H. "Prüfung der Verfassungsmäßigkeit." In Bundesakademie für öffentliche Verwaltung, ed., *Praxis der Gesetzgebung.* Regensburg, 1984, 81–99.

Steinberg, R. "Verfassungsgerichtliche Kontrolle der 'Nachbesserungspflicht' des Gesetzgebers." *Der Staat,* Vol. 26, 1987, 161–186.

Stüwe, K. *Die Opposition im Bundestag und das Bundesverfassungsgericht.* Baden-Baden, 1997.

Vanberg, G. *The Politics of Constitutional Review in Germany.* Cambridge, 2005.

Wasby, S. *The Impact of the United States Supreme Court: Some Perspectives.* Homewood, 1970.

Wesel, U. *Der Gang nach Karlsruhe. Das Bundesverfassungsgericht in der Geschichte der Bundesrepublik.* Munich, 2004.

Wever, G. "Das Bundesverfassungsgericht: Eine Gegenregierung?" In Blanke, B., Wollmann, H., eds., *Die alte Bundesrepublik. Kontinuität und Wandel.* Opladen, 1991, 310–335.

Wrase, M., Boulanger, C., eds. *Die Politik des Verfassungsrechts. Interdisziplinäre und vergleichende Perspektiven auf die Rolle und Funktion von Verfassungsgerichten.* Baden-Baden, 2013.

Part IV

Comparative Perspectives

Chapter 10

The U.S. Supreme Court and the German Federal Constitutional Court

Selection, Nomination, and Election of Justices

Klaus Stüwe

Introduction

The process by which justices of constitutional courts are selected and appointed is more than just a question of mechanics. Given the far-reaching jurisdiction of constitutional courts, it is of upmost importance that they maintain public recognition and authority. Both the objectivity with which a court is able to operate and the general acceptance of its decisions are highly dependent on how the appointment of justices is regulated. Therefore, the method by which justices are elected plays a crucial role in defining the integrity of a constitutional court (Triepel 1929: 27).

In regulating the appointment of justices, what criteria need to be considered so that the effectiveness of a constitutional court can be guaranteed? First, in a democratic system it is self-evident that the justices must have democratic legitimization. Second, unilateral political influence in the election of justices should be minimized as much as possible. Third, the selection process should lead to highly qualified judges. Finally, suitable federal representation should be achieved in federal states such as the United States and Germany.

These criteria, referred to as the "magic square of the appointment of justices" (Laufer 1968: 207), are actually difficult to meet simultaneously. In democratic systems, which are characterized by majority decision, it is practically impossible to achieve democratic legitimization without involving political parties. Therefore, the possibility of partial, politically motivated influences always exists. Try to expel the influence of political parties, and the democratic legitimization suffers. The need for democratic legitimization can also cause the candidates' juristic qualifications to be reduced to secondary importance. As for the criterion of federal representation, unilateral influence is not to be discounted. For these reasons, a perfected process for the selection of justices is unachievable. No procedure would meet all of these desired criteria in equal measure. When it comes to the constitutional and lawful regulation of the appointment of justices, the only realistic goal can be to meet the above-mentioned requirements as well as it is possible.

The respective procedures for appointing justices to the U.S. Supreme Court and the German Federal Constitutional Court pursue this goal using very different methods. The following chapter will present how the selection and nomination of justices in each country are designed judicially and how the processes transpire in the political practice.

The Appointment Procedure for Constitutional Judges

U.S. Supreme Court

Richard Neustadt, one of the most influential political scientists in the U.S., at one point labeled the United States' political system as "a government of separated institutions sharing powers" (Neustadt 1991: 29). Even the nomination of the U.S. Supreme Court Justices follows this pattern: executive and legislative branches cannot individually appoint justices, but rather must work in cooperation with one another.

The U.S. Constitution's description of the nomination process for U.S. Supreme Court Justices is a matter of just a few words. Art. II 2 of the U.S. Constitution reads: "The president … shall nominate, and by and with the Advice and Consent of the Senate, shall appoint … Judges of the Supreme Court." Hence, both the executive branch and the legislative branch are participants in a mandatory three-step procedure. The first step is the nomination of a candidate by the president. The phrasing "consent of the Senate" means that a second step consisting of the Senate's approval must take place before the third step, in which the justice is appointed by the president. The question of what exactly the term "advice" means in this portion of the constitution is contested. Some political scientists interpret this provision to mean that the Senate has the right to recommend a candidate to the president before the official nomination (Ferling 1974: 66). Others proceed on the assumption that the Senate's contribution of "advice and consent" is limited to the endorsement or rejection of a candidate already nominated by the president (Harris 1968: 34). Since the founding of the U.S. Supreme Court in 1789, a total of 160 nominations by the president have been forwarded to the Senate (see Table 10.1). Of these, 124 candidates have been endorsed by the Senate (seven of which declined the appointment). Altogether, twelve candidates have been rejected by the Senate.

In political practice, the appointment procedure stipulated by the constitution has been supplemented by several intermediary steps. Although according to the constitution only the president and the Senate are participants in the process of appointing justices, the Senate Judiciary Committee has also played an important role since its founding in 1816. Even before the Civil War, more than two-thirds of the nominations up to that point had been made at the advice of the Senate committee, which currently consists of eighteen members. In 1868 the Senate decided that nominations made by the president must automatically be transferred to the Senate Judiciary Committee for deliberation. In the nineteenth century deliberations took place behind closed doors. In 1925 Harlan F. Stone became the first candidate required to face a personal questioning by the panel. Such a personal hearing has been conducted for all candidates since 1955. This process was first televised in 1981 with the questioning of Sandra Day O'Connor.

In the nineteenth century the Senate Judiciary Committee generally required just a few days to deliberate over the nomination of justices. In the past decades, however, this process has become more and more drawn out. Since the 1960s, the following procedure has been established: First, the panel undertakes its own investigation of the nominated individual. Following this is the public hearing, in which the committee members personally interview the candidate. Sometimes the interviews extend over multiple days, particularly in cases where the nomination is controversial. Since 1992, at least one session of the hearing has taken place out of the public eye, to allow for the discussion of confidential topics.

Following the questioning of candidates, statements are obtained from other individuals and institutions. In accordance with a tradition that has developed over the last several decades, a recommendation from the American Bar Association (ABA), the most powerful consortium of law-

Table 10.1. U.S. Supreme Court Nominations, 1789–Present

Nominations	*Confirmed*	*Rejected*	*Postponed*	*Withdrawn*	*Declined*	*No action*
160	117	12	3	11	7	10

This table lists only nominations officially submitted to the Senate. It does not include nominations announced but never officially submitted (such as that of Douglas Ginsburg in 1987).

Source: Official webpage of the U.S. Senate: http://www.senate.gov/pagelayout/reference/nominations/reverseNominations.htm#official.

yers and judges, is held in particularly high esteem. The ABA's Standing Committee on the Federal Judiciary evaluates the nominee's personal qualifications and pronounces her or him "well qualified," "qualified," or "not qualified." The results of this evaluation are read before the Senate Committee by the chairman of the ABA.

Usually in the week following the hearings, the Judiciary Committee meets one last time to vote on the recommended resolution, to be presented at the Senate's plenary session. The resulting recommendation can be positive (in favor of the candidate) or negative (against him or her). It is also theoretically possible to not announce a recommendation of any kind as a way to prevent a vote in the Senate; however, this has occurred only eight times since the founding of the Senate Judiciary Committee (Rutkus 2010: 32). Of the 160 recommended resolutions, seven have been negative, the last of which was in 1987 against Robert H. Bork.

The next step takes place in the plenary session of the Senate, which is always open to the public and since 1986 has also been televised. The proceedings begin when the majority leader, after consultation with the minority leader, moves for the nomination deliberation. It has long been the custom that the majority leader requests the senators' unanimous consent (Stüwe 2013: 83) to begin the deliberation. If the senators are not able to agree, then an opposing minority might try to delay or impede the deliberation with the help of a filibuster, an extremely long speech. This type of blockade was most recently employed in 2006 during the nomination of Samuel A. Alito; however, the decision to start the consultation was finally reached.

Once the Senate agrees to deliberate a nomination, the debate over the candidate begins. Through their speeches the senators evaluate the candidate from highly diverse perspectives. Usually up for discussion are the professional qualifications of the nominee and his or her personal aptitude, but additionally and perhaps most importantly the focus is on his or her juristic philosophy. Is the nominee a conservative or a liberal jurist? Does he or she operate under an interpretation of the constitution categorized as "originalism" or under an interpretation categorized by the concept "living constitution"?

In addition to the fundamental unanimous consent to begin, the members can also take the opportunity to agree to a certain limit on the period of deliberation. In the case of highly contested candidates who are rejected by a minority of the senators, the risk of a filibuster arises once again if the senators did not agree beforehand on a time limit for the deliberation period. In practice, however, it comes to this extremely rarely. Conversely, the nominee's advocates have the option to vote for the closure of the debate with a three-fifths majority (sixty senators).

When the debate within the Senate is over, the presiding officer calls for a vote. Since 1967 the senators have voted by roll call, in which a simple majority is all that is required to approve a nomination. Only in cases of highly contentious candidates are the rulings narrowly decided. In most cases the senators vote for the nomination by a large majority. Only a few justices, like Samuel A. Alito in 2005 or Clarence Thomas in 1991, have been approved by only very small margins (see Table 10.2).

Table 10.2. Nominations to the U.S. Supreme Court, 1981–Present

Nominee	*Date received in Senate*	*President*	*Judiciary Committee final vote*	*Senate final action*
Elena Kagan	10 May 2010	Barack Obama	reported favorably (13–6)	confirmed (63–37)
Sonia Sotomayor	1 June 2009	Barack Obama	reported favorably (13–6)	confirmed (68–31)
Samuel A. Alito	10 November 2005	George W. Bush	reported favorably (10–8)	confirmed (58–42)
Harriet E. Miers	7 October 2005	George W. Bush	no vote taken	withdrawn
John G. Roberts	6 September 2005	George W. Bush	reported favorably (13–5)	confirmed (78–22)
John G. Roberts	29 July 2005	George W. Bush	no vote taken	withdrawn
Stephen G. Breyer	17 May 1994	Bill Clinton	reported favorably (18–0)	confirmed (87–9)
Ruth Bader Ginsberg	22 June 1993	Bill Clinton	reported favorably (18–0)	confirmed (96–3)
Clarence Thomas	8 July 1991	George H. W. Bush	reported without recommendation (13–1)	confirmed (52–48)
David H. Souter	25 July 1990	George H. W. Bush	reported favorably (13–1)	confirmed (90–9)
Anthony M. Kennedy	30 November 1987	Ronald Reagan	reported favorably (14–0)	confirmed (97–0)
Robert H. Bork	7 July 1987	Ronald Reagan	reported unfavorably (9–5)	rejected (42–58)
Antonin Scalia	24 June 1986	Ronald Reagan	reported favorably (19–0)	confirmed (98–0)
William H. Rehnquist	20 June 1986	Ronald Reagan	reported favorably (13–5)	confirmed (65–33)
Sandra Day O'Connor	9 August 1981	Ronald Reagan	reported favorably (17–1)	confirmed (99–0)

Source: Rutkus, D.S., Bearden, M. "Supreme Court Nominations, 1789–2010: Actions by the Senate, the Judiciary Committee, and the President," *Congressional Research Service* 7-5700, RL33225, Washington, D.C., 2010, pp. 37–42.

Now and then a nomination is in fact rejected by the Senate. Even George Washington experienced this. A heated public dispute broke out when the first president of the United States nominated John Rutledge as chief justice in 1795. Opponents of Rutledge accused him in the media of lacking competence, and in the end the Senate rejected his nomination. However, rejections occur relatively infrequently: altogether the Senate has rejected just twelve candidates, most recently (in 1987) Robert Bork, who was considered very conservative.

When the Senate has approved the nomination of a candidate, the secretary of the Senate issues a "resolution of confirmation" and forwards it to the White House. The president then signs a written document, the so-called commission, which enables the official appointment of the candidate to the position of justice. Finally, the Department of Justice furnishes the commission with a date of appointment (determined according to the day on which the president signed the document) as well as the seal of the Justice Department. The certificate of appointment is then delivered to the new Supreme Court Justice.

The nomination process concludes with the swearing-in. Unlike federal political officials, the Supreme Court Justices must recite two official oaths: a judicial oath, required by the Judiciary Act of 1789; as well as a constitutional oath, required by art. VI of the U.S. Constitution. Both oaths are received by the chief justice. The judicial oath has always normally been recited in an intimate setting opposite the new fellow justices in the Supreme Court building, whereas the reciting of the constitutional oath takes place in a public ceremony attended by numerous politicians, officials, friends and family members. Ever since the appointment of Antonin Scalia and William Rehnquist under President Ronald Reagan in 1981, the newly appointed justices have recited their constitutional oaths in front of running television cameras at the White House. However, Sonia Sotomayor (2009) and Elena Kagan (2010) broke with this tradition and recited both official oaths in the Supreme Court building.

The appointment is for life. According to the will of the Founding Fathers, this unlimited term of office, ending only with resignation or death, is intended to strengthen judicial independence: justices need never make decisions based on a desire to be reelected. Many Supreme Court Justices therefore have decades of experience: the longest tenure to date is that of William O. Douglas, who spent over thirty-six years in office from 1939 to 1975.

German Federal Constitutional Court

Unlike in the United States, the election of judges to the Federal Constitutional Court in the Federal Republic of Germany's parliamentary system is a matter for the legislative branch alone. Art. 94 I 2 of the Basic Law dictates there be an election for the members of the Federal Constitutional Court: "half the members of the Federal Constitutional Court shall be elected by the Bundestag and half by the Bundesrat." The Basic Law does not provide further specifications; instead, art. 94 II communicates that the configuration of the election process is described more clearly in a simple federal law. This Federal Constitutional Court Act (*Bundesverfassungsgerichtsgesetz*) came into effect in 1951 after lengthy debate in the German Federal Parliament (Stüwe 1997: 55–58). As the Federal Constitutional Court is made up of two senates, each composed of eight judges, the Federal Constitutional Court Act makes the statement originating in the Basic Law concrete, first of all by saying that half of each senate is to be elected by the Bundestag, the other half by the Bundesrat. Responsibility for electing the president and vice president of the Federal Constitutional Court, who preside over both senates, alternates between the Bundestag and the Bundesrat.

Until 2015, the election procedure was regulated differently depending on the electoral body. The Bundesrat, in accordance with section 7 of the Federal Constitutional Court Act, elects judges during the plenary sessions, thus directly. But until 2015 the Bundestag, in contrast, followed an indirect electoral procedure in accordance with section 6 of the Federal Constitutional Court Act, in which the authority to elect was assigned to an election committee specifically designed for this purpose. The election committee was comprised of twelve delegates elected by the Bundestag in accordance with the proportional representation regulation. Under section 6 II of the Federal Constitutional Court Act, only parliamentary groups (*Fraktionen*) could submit lists of proposed candidates for the committee. Multiple groups could present a communal list, which results in excluding individual delegates or even whole groups that still were smaller than a *Fraktion* from their right to make recommendations.

In accordance with the d'Hondt highest averages method, the number of candidates to be considered from each list was calculated based on the total number of votes for each recommendation. In this way, the election committee could be differentiated from the installation of the remaining committees. For these other committees, the relative strength of the *Fraktion* was essential according to section 12 of the German Bundestag's standing orders. However, the composition of the election committee could vary from those regulations if the number of submitted votes did not correspond to the group's representative proportion in the Bundestag. For this reason, the minor parliamentary groups were especially anxious to have as many members as possible present at the Bundestag's plenary session where the lists of recommendations were voted on. They did not always succeed. In 1987, the Green Party (Die Grünen) failed to have any representation in the election committee because too few Green Party delegates took part in the vote (see Table 10.3). And in the 13th parliamentary term, the SPD had to give up a potential additional seat on the election committee for the same reason.

The electors were elected for one parliamentary term and could not be dismissed. When a member retired, the next person on the list took his or her place. The committee did not have a chairperson. The oldest member called it to order and conducted the nonpublic election committee sessions. Anonymous voting was not a stipulation. In practice, voting occurred via a simple show of hands.

The Bundestag's policy of electing judges not in a plenary session but rather indirectly, through a special election committee, has always been disputed in the fields of political science, constitutional doctrine, and even politics. In the deliberation over the Federal Constitutional Court Act, two motives were associated with the implementation of the indirect election. First, it should prevent the occurrence of public debates over the candidates up for the position of judge, thus upholding the applicants' personal privacy. This objective was strengthened by section 6 IV of the Federal Constitutional Court Act, which bound the election committee members to maintain confidentiality. This obligation to maintain confidentiality extended to candidates' personal circumstances as well as their political convictions (Ruppert 2005: 212). Second, the assessment of the applicants' professional and personal qualities should not become a matter of public political arguments between parties. It was also assumed that the process of finding candidates could be carried out more objectively in a small committee than in a plenary session of the six hundred plus members of the German Bundestag.

In every legislative period since 1987, the Bündnis '90/Die Grünen parliamentary group has introduced a bill to abolish the indirect electoral process. Even the President of the Bundestag Norbert Lammert suggested in a 2012 newspaper interview that the Federal Constitutional Court Justices should be elected by *all* members of the Bundestag. However, in 2012 the Federal Constitutional Court itself judged the indirect election of Federal Justices in the German Bundestag (*Bundesverfassungsrichterwahl*—BVerfGE 131, 230) to be constitutional.

In 2015, however, all parliamentary groups in the Bundestag introduced a bill (BT-Drs. 18/2737) that eventually will lead to direct election of judges in plenary sessions of the Bundestag. This will correspond to the situation in the Bundesrat, whose sixty-nine members have always voted in plenary session on the Federal Constitutional Court Justices. Although there is no obligation to maintain confidentiality, in practice there has never been a public discussion about the candidates in the Bundesrat. In fact, the fed-

Table 10.3. Membership in the Electoral Committee of the Bundestag, 1990–present

Parliamentary term	*CDU/CSU*	*SPD*	*FDP*	*B'90/Grüne*	*PDS/Linke*
18. (2013–2017)	6	4	–	1	1
17. (2009–2013)	5	3	2	1	1
16. (2005–2009)	5	4	1	1	1
15. (2002–2005)	5	5	1	1	–
14. (1998–2002)	4	6	1	1	–
13. (1994–1998)	6	4	1	1	–
12. (1990–1994)	6	5	1	–	–

Source: Deutscher Bundestag, *Amtliches Handbuch des Deutschen Bundestages*. Berlin (loose-leaf publication, 1990–2015).

eral state government representatives' conferences take place beforehand and are not public. To prepare for the election, commissions composed of the sixteen ministers of justice (Justizminister) are created in some cases (Ruppert 2005: 216); in other cases informal arrangements are made between heads of state governments. In neither case is there elucidation of exactly what reasoning led to the selection of a particular candidate. A consolidated recommendation is then presented to the Bundesrat's plenary session. The voting in the plenary session traditionally occurs without dispute and in most cases is even unanimous.

The high frequency of consensual decisions in the election of judges can be explained by an institutional constraint: the law regarding the Federal Constitutional Court requires that the judges of the Federal Constitutional Court be elected with a two-thirds majority both in the Bundesrat and in the Bundestag's electoral committee. This qualified majority requirement creates a need for all participants in the vote to agree on a single candidate before the actual election. This need for agreement concerns first and foremost the political parties. As in all political bodies of the Federal Republic of Germany, parties are the prevailing actors in both the Bundestag election committee and the Bundesrat. As a single party alone is very unlikely to achieve a two-thirds majority in the Bundestag and Bundesrat, the parties have to try to step away from their ideological and programmatic positions in order to reach an agreement—or more precisely, the parties that are able and willing to come together to substantiate the two-thirds majority have to find a way to reach agreement.

Except at times of grand coalitions, in practice the compulsory two-thirds majority has worked to prevent the respective government majorities from pushing a judge through against the will of the opposition. The opposition parties conveniently have a blocking minority. The record of parliamentary consultations on the corresponding regulations shows that this was absolutely intentional. By avoiding a unilateral staffing of the Court by the government, legislators hoped to gain the public's highest possible respect for the court. For this reason the first version of the Federal Constitutional Court Act actually allowed for a three-fourths majority, which in 1956 was reduced to the two-thirds majority that still applies today.

Since the founding of the Federal Republic, only the two large parties—the CDU/CSU and SPD—have been in a position to together create a two-thirds majority in both electoral bodies: these parties supply the members of the electoral committee and lead the federal state governments represented in the Bundesrat. Not even a "coalition" of one of these two big parties together with a smaller party has ever been able to reach the required majority. Therefore the CDU/CSU and SPD are each always dependent on the vote of the other during the selection of candidates. The two parties are therefore on equal footing when it comes to participation in the election of judges.

As a practical consequence, the system of proportional representation that has been evolving since the beginning guarantees the CDU/CSU and SPD the nominating power for a certain number of judges' posts. When a position becomes vacant, the party that has the right of nomination for that position can name a replacement candidate. If the other parties indicate their approval, then the matter is settled. If the other parties object, then the party must make a new recommendation. If there are multiple positions to be filled, then the CDU/CSU and SPD agree on an entire list, or packet. For the offices of the president and vice president of the Federal Constitutional Court, the right to appoint alternates has been established.

Certain points of this fundamental arrangement between the CDU/CSU and SPD have been further refined over the course of time. Theoretically, provided they could agree, the two parties could have built a duopoly for the election of judges that would not necessarily depend on the compliance of smaller parties. From the outset, however, it has been standard practice that the smaller parties of a government coalition are likewise allowed to make recommendations for the replacement of a judge. Thus, when the CDU/CSU and FDP were in a coalition, the former ceded the nomination of a candidate to the latter. The SPD also later took on this custom. With the creation of the red-green coalition, a more far-reaching agreement in 1998 between the coalition partners bound the SPD and the Green Party with a coalition contract: "the coalition groups will vote unanimously in the Bundestag and in all Bundestag bodies"—including the election committee. Hence, the smaller coalition partners were effectively involved in the selection of candidates to be named by the SPD. The CDU/CSU-FDP coalition contracts took on this formulation in 2009.

Due to the party agreements of the 1950s and 1960s, the Federal Constitutional Court's First Senate consisted mostly of judges recommended by the SPD, and the judges of the Second Senate had primarily been nominated by CDU/CSU. For this reason the senates were referred to as the "red" and "black" senates. Later, a balance of party politics was established within the senates so that today, half of the senate judges are nominated on the basis of a CDU/CSU recommendation and half on the basis of an SPD recommendation. Due to the solicited coalition agreement, judges who were recommended by FDP and the Green Party can also be found in the First Senate (see Table 10.4).

How do the parties reach consensus regarding which candidate to nominate for the position of justice? This is achieved via confidential arrangements in a task force that is nowhere legally grounded. Who belongs to this task force regularly remains undisclosed. In years past this unofficial council has in most cases consisted of four people, two each from the SPD and CDU/CSU. The federal dimension is also considered: two people come from the Bundestag and two from the Bundesrat. If the larger

Table 10.4. Judges of the Federal Constitutional Court in 2016, by Nominating Parties

Judge	*Year elected*	*Electoral body*	*Nominating party*
First Senate			
Baer, Susanne	2011	Bundestag	B'90/Grüne
Britz, Gabriele	2011	Bundesrat	SPD
Kirchhof, Ferdinand	2010	Bundestag	CDU/CSU
Paulus, Andreas L.	2010	Bundestag	FDP
Schluckebier, Wilhelm	2010	Bundestag	CDU/CSU
Masing, Johannes	2008	Bundesrat	SPD
Eichberger, Michael	2006	Bundesrat	CDU/CSU
Gaier, Reinhard	2004	Bundesrat	SPD
Second Senate			
Maidowski, Ulrich	2014	Bundestag	SPD
König, Doris	2014	Bundestag	SPD
Kessal-Wulf, Sibylle	2011	Bundesrat	CDU/CSU
Müller, Peter	2011	Bundesrat	CDU/CSU
Hermanns, Monika	2010	Bundestag	SPD
Huber, Peter M.	2008	Bundestag	CDU/CSU
Voßkuhle, Andreas	2008	Bundesrat	SPD
Landau, Herbert	2005	Bundesrat	CDU/CSU

Source: http://www.bundesverfassungsgericht.de/DE/Richter/richter_node.html.

government party is entitled to the right of nomination, then the federal chancellor, chosen by that party, may also voice his or her opinion.

The names of the candidates for judge are also treated as classified information (Ley 1985: 188)—any premature release of names to the public occurs only through indiscretion. This is especially the case when one side recommends a candidate who, for whatever reason, is found unacceptable by the other side. Only when the informal task force has agreed on a comprehensive package are the names made public. Thus the task force effectively constitutes the actual decision-making body, while the two legally authorized election bodies only formally carry out the election. Even so, in 2010 the Bundestag parliamentary groups were for the first time given the possibility to hear the candidate and to be able to form an impression. A public hearing does not take place as it does in the United States.

The subsequent election of judges is merely a formality. One is elected as a judge when eight votes, that is, a two-thirds majority of the committee members, are in his or her favor. Should a judge's replacement not be identified within two months of the expiration of the previous judge's term of office or his or her retirement, then in accordance with section 7 of the Federal Constitutional Court Act the Federal Constitutional Court suggests three candidates from which the (former) election committee or the Bundesrat can elect a single candidate. However, this has not yet happened. Meanwhile, as the foregoing indicates, the decision making behind the election of applicants remains concealed from the general public. There are no accessible written records and no verifiable statements that could make the parties' arrangements concrete.

The elected judges are appointed by the president of the German Federal Republic as stipulated by art. 60 of the Basic Law and section 10 of the Federal Constitutional Court Act. The appointment is merely a formal act—the president is not permitted to scrutinize the decision made by the electoral bodies. The certificate of appointment of an elected judge must bear the signature of the federal chancellor or the federal minister. Upon entering office, newly appointed judges take an oath before the President of the Federal Republic of Germany, committing as judges to faithfully observe the German constitution at all times and to diligently fulfill their judicial duties. The formal ceremony normally takes place in front of invited guests at the official residence of the federal president.

Criteria for Selecting and Evaluating a Nominee

The question of which criteria the Federal Constitutional Court should use to select judges has a legal dimension and a political dimension. It must first be ascertained whether the constitution or other laws make definite, formal provisions. As the judges are nominated and confirmed by political bodies, it is also interesting to consider what political motives play a role in the process. What personal qualifications does a U.S. Supreme Court Justice or a Federal Constitutional Court judge have to exhibit?

Legal Provisions

Unlike in the United States, in Germany a number of concrete legal provisions have to be taken into account during the selection of Federal Constitutional Court Justices. The Basic Law itself provides only two pieces of information. First, art. 94 II 1 of the Basic Law provides that "the Federal Constitutional Court shall consist of federal judges and other members." Apart from the reference to an undefined number of federal judges, the constitution thereby leaves open whether the Federal Constitutional Court can be staffed with people who lack the qualifications for judicial office. In fact, in 1948/49 during the parliamentary council's consultation regarding the Basic Law, there was a certain attempt to fill the bench with lay judges (Schlaich, Korioth 2012: 28). In 1951, though, with the adoption of the Federal Constitutional Court Act, was it decided to appoint only trained lawyers to the position of judge. All candidates for the position of judge must meet the qualifications for judicial office by successfully passing both the First Legal Examination and the Second State Examination. For those living in the former East Germany, a diploma in law is also an accepted qualification.

Second, art. 94 I 3 of the Basic Law applies a strict incompatibility mandate to the justices: "They may not be members of the Bundestag, of the Bundesrat, of the Federal Government, or of any of the corresponding bodies of a Land." Their appointment excludes them from these political entities, insofar as they previously belonged to any of them. The Federal Constitutional Court Act additionally stipulates that the justices must exercise their functions on a full-time basis. A second occupation is not permitted, except in the case of professors, who have the privilege to continue to teach at a university. However, "the function of Federal Constitutional Court Justice takes precedent over the function of professor." These strict incompatibility rules are intended to strengthen the justices' autonomy.

What is more, the Federal Constitutional Court Act defines additional qualifying criteria for judicial office and further specifies the role of election bodies (the Bundesrat and the election committee). According to section 3 I of the Federal Constitutional Court Act, Federal Constitutional Court judges must be at least forty years old. Section 4 III of the Federal Constitutional Court Act furthermore states that a justice can remain in office only until the end of his or her 68th birthday, which can be interpreted as the setting of an age limit of sixty-eight. According to section 3 I of the Federal Constitutional Court Act, a candidate for judge must be eligible for election to the German Bundestag and must put into writing that he or she will become a member of the Federal Constitutional Court.

Three judges in each senate must be elected from among the judges of the five supreme federal courts. This ensures that the Federal Constitutional Court has members with many years of judicial experience at its disposal (BVerfGE 65, 157). In practice, the Bundestag elects two federal judges, and the Bundesrat elects one federal judge to each senate. This goes back to an arrangement between the CDU/CSU and SPD that began with the election of justices in 1971 (Fromme 2000: 2977).

The Federal Constitutional Court Act stipulates in section 8 that the federal minister of justice must keep two lists of names. The first list contains the names of federal judges who meet the requirements for Federal Constitutional Court judgeship. The second list records the names of all individuals who have been recommended for office by either a Bundestag faction, the federal government, or a federal state government. These individuals too must meet the formal qualifications required of this post. Both lists of recommendations are made open to the public. The Ministry of Justice is obligated to forward both lists to the President of the Bundestag and to the Bundesrat at least one week prior to the election of a justice. That said, the significance of these lists is rather minimal. The names of federal judges who are also formally qualified for the Federal Constitutional Court are identifiable without the help of the first list. And the election bodies are in no way bound to the second list, making it readily renounceable. In practice, therefore, the list of recommendations has no more significance than a nonbinding suggestion (Gusy 1989: 1627).

Whereas the prerequisites for judicial office within the German Federal Constitutional Court are very explicitly defined, the U.S. Constitution does not stipulate any particular technical qualifications for federal judges or, therefore, for justices of the U.S. Supreme Court. Even in common federal law there are no regulations regarding justices' qualifications. Unlike in German legislation, no age limits, be they minimum or maximum, are included. Candidates are not even officially required to have a law degree. It is thus no surprise that justices without law degrees have been appointed over and over in the history of the U.S. Supreme Court. In fact, 38 of 112 justices in 2011 had not received any formal university degree in the field of law. The most notable example was James F. Byrnes, later Secretary of State, who served as a justice in 1941 and 1942 without ever having gone to college. Justice Stanley Forman Reed was the last individual without a law degree to become a justice (1938–1957).

Despite the significant variance in the legislation on the professional and personal conditions for qualification, in practice there are actually many parallels between the Supreme Court and the Federal Constitutional Court. Though there is no official regulation regarding minimum age, no justice under the age of forty has been elected to the U.S. Supreme Court since 1852. (The last such justice was Edward A. Bradford, who was thirty-eight at the time of his appointment.) In actuality, there is also conformity regarding the professional qualifications: all members of the Supreme Court, even those without law degrees, have worked as attorneys, and therefore gained juridical experience, prior to their appointment.

Over time, a degree from one of the United States' most prestigious law schools has in fact become one of the most important prerequisites for nomination. Of the thirteen justices appointed since 1981, six studied at Harvard Law School and three others studied at Yale Law School. Someone without any juridical experience would certainly fail to make it through the hearing procedure. Early on in the ABA's confirmation procedure, the assessment of the nominees' professional qualifications alone serves as a significant filter. In addition, a judicial layperson would be challenged to even try to answer the numerous questions posed in the hearings of the Senate Judiciary Committee.

With that said, a comparison of the biographies of Federal Constitutional Court judges and U.S. Supreme Court Justices reveals many similarities, despite the variation in formal regulations: "On the American side, the Supreme Court is staffed, for example, in addition to a former president, with multiple former governors, senators, cabinet members, law professors and a large portion of judges who already served on federal courts" (Kau 2007: 171). Likewise, on the German side there are two former minister-presidents (Ministerpräsidenten), multiple federal and state ministers, members of Parliament, officials in the federal and state ministries, and law professors, as well as former federal judges.

Political Motives

Particularly in the U.S.—although also within the formal regulations regarding the qualifications for the position of justice in Germany—the actors who take part in the justice appointment procedure have a considerable amount of leeway in the selection of candidates for the bench. Ultimately, certain motives are always the decisive factors determining precisely which individuals are appointed to either constitutional court.

Despite differences in judicial appointment methodology, the same motives have priority in the United States and Germany. Nominating the professionally best qualified candidates is in everyone's best interest. If a U.S.

president selects a candidate with dubious professional qualifications, the individual has virtually no chance of winning the Senate's approval. On the other hand, by proposing a convincing candidate who is proven as a jurist and has studied at one of the country's top universities, the president demonstrates a capacity to appoint applicants with the highest professional qualifications. Such a recommendation improves the likelihood of gaining the Senate's approval for said candidate while also sending a strong political signal to voters: the president is presenting himself as a competent leader.

In Germany too, a candidate's professional qualifications play a significant role. Indeed, the law stipulates that only trained lawyers may be elected to the Federal Constitutional Court, and three judges in each senate must be elected from among the judges of the five supreme federal courts. As is the case in the United States, in Germany a proven expert gains the approval of other parties more readily than a less qualified candidate. Because of this, members of the Federal Constitutional Court have always been distinguished legal experts. In the search for suitable candidates, efforts are made to ensure that the justices of the Federal Constitutional Court are familiar with the most important fields of law. Thus many candidates are experts in specific fields of law, for example, constitutional law, administrative law, domestic relations law, labor law, tax law, and so on. In terms of the professional and educational backgrounds of its members, the court represents the "full spectrum of legal expertise" (Hartmann 2013: 221).

Compared to the United States, parties that recommend candidates receive less attention from the public. In Germany candidates are not nominated by a single person, but rather by an unofficial committee whose members are entirely unknown to the public. Additionally, the election of justices receives much less public attention than in the United States. However, the question of juristic qualification plays a role, as was evident in the 2011 example of the former minister-president of Saarland, Peter Müller, whom the CDU/CSU recommended for the Federal Constitutional Court. Müller had in fact studied law, but his professional experience was primarily as a politician. Consequently, it was publicly questioned, especially by the SPD but also by members of his own party, whether he really was highly qualified for the bench. The weekly newspaper *Die Zeit* expressed this critique in a nutshell: "Never before has someone become a candidate for the position of justice in Karlsruhe who is so intimately entangled in Berlin politics, who is so involved in party politics and who is so unversed in constitutional law as Müller" (Welfing 2011: 48). In the end, despite these objections, Müller was elected.

In both countries, a candidate's personal integrity is an important selection criterion, as an especially high level of integrity is expected of judges. Candidates whose integrity comes into question have very poor prospects of being nominated. Along these lines, a bipartisan Commission on Judicial Selection in the United States explained in 1996 that the ideal justice has "a personality that is evenhanded, unbiased, impartial, courteous yet firm, and dedicated to a process, not a result" (Miller Center of Public Affairs 1996: 10). It would certainly be embarrassing if, in the course of the appointment process, the suspicion arose that a candidate might be guilty of moral misconduct. During the candidacy of Clarence Thomas in 1991, when he was accused of having sexually harassed a former colleague, the hearing turned into a media frenzy. The Senate approved Thomas with just 52 votes for and 48 against, the closest outcome for a justice in the twentieth century. To avoid such difficulties, the recommending party preemptively verifies potential candidates' moral integrity. For example, it was reported that shortly after the 2000 election outcome was known, President George W. Bush's staff "began putting together a list of potential nominees and conducting extensive background research on them" (Greenburg 2007: 241).

Recently, more effort has been put into nominating females to become constitutional justices. Women have always been underrepresented in both the U.S. Supreme Court and the Federal Constitutional Court. In the over 220 years of the Supreme Court's existence, only four women have been appointed as justices: Sandra Day O'Connor (1981–2005), Ruth Bader Ginsburg (1993–present), Sonia Sotomayor (2009–present), and Elena Kagan (2010–present). President Barack Obama deliberately recommended the latter two to strengthen the ratio of women to men in the Court. The Supreme Court currently consists of six male and three female judges. The number of female justices in the Federal Constitutional Court has also gradually risen. Until the 1970s, at most one woman if any was selected per senate; now there are two women in the First Senate and three in the Second.

However, strategic motives are the most important factor in the selection of candidates for justice. In both the U.S. and Germany, every judicial selection is also a political decision. All of the actors who take part in the selection process come from the political sphere, and every judicial appointment has political consequences. As the political parties decisively shape the political process, the selection of constitutional justices unavoidably has a dimension of party politics. In both countries it is effectively members of political parties who decide who is appointed to the constitutional court.

Considerations of party politics therefore always play a role when a seat on the bench of the U.S. or German constitutional court needs to be filled. No U.S. president would recommend a candidate whose political position was completely different from his or her own. When making a nomination, the president is looking to install a candidate—should the individual also be approved by the Senate—who, in the administration of justice, follows a line that is consistent with the president's own ideological stance. "Especially in the last 25 years, Republican presidents have tried to substantially influence the development of the administration of justice by electing specific justices" (Hiesel 2010: 178). The Senate is generally able to block the appointment of too-extreme candidates, but many presidents nevertheless can and want to influence the court politically through their choice of candidates. It was in this spirit that President Lyndon B. Johnson (1963–1969) nominated Thurgood Marshall, the first African-American Supreme Court Justice, in 1976. Richard Nixon (1969–1974) used his four nominations to create a conservative counterpoint to the liberal administration of justice of the 1960s (McMahon 2011: 251ff.). Through their recommendations, U.S. presidents can also show special consideration for particular voting blocs from which political support may be forthcoming. For instance, in 2009 President Obama appointed Sonia Sotomayor, a woman and the first justice of Hispanic origin.

However, this does not always work out for the president. Some justices' decision-making tendencies do not develop in the way the nominating president anticipated (Epstein et al. 2007: 1483). A famous example is that of Chief Justice Earl Warren: although President Dwight D. Eisenhower had hoped he would make conservative decisions, he instead became one of the most liberal justices in the history of the Supreme Court—hence Eisenhower's later reference to this appointment as "the biggest damn fool mistake I ever made" (Urofski 2001: 264).

But it is not only the president who has political motives. The deliberation processes in the Judiciary Committee and the Senate's plenary sessions are also very strongly shaped by political considerations. Especially during phases of divided government, senators take extra pains to ensure that the candidate nominated by the president does not represent extreme political positions. To this end, a background investigation is preemptively conducted. The commission even factors in the confidential FBI files kept on the applicants. Each candidate must also answer an extensive written questionnaire that thoroughly queries the nominee on his or her professional career up to that point, publications, membership in organizations, and political engagement, among other fields of interest. The answers serve as the basis for the public hearings, in which party members question the candidates intensely.

As soon as the name of a nominee is known, public debate commences. The candidate's qualifications are discussed, as is what her or his appointment would mean for the future of the Supreme Court. This public debate is predominantly led by political commentators on television, in the print media, and increasingly, in recent years, online; as well as by interest groups actively working for or against a candidate (Rutkus 2010: 26).

Because the hearings are public and since 1981 even televised, this phase is also of great political significance. In the case of a non-consensus candidate—one who does not receive the approval of both political parties—the hearing is an opportunity to bring the candidate's political philosophy to light, helping undecided senators form their opinion of a candidate. Other senators use their questions as a way to work toward a general approval or rejection of the candidate. Still others apparently use the questions to communicate their values to the candidate in the hope of influencing how he or she will later operate in the court (Wermiel 1993: 141). Incidentally, all candidates are well prepared for the hearings: to improve the chances of its chosen nominees, the White House provides them with a considerable amount of information. Sometimes simulated hearings are conducted to train the candidate.

When the Judiciary Committee's work is complete, the debate in the Senate's plenary session becomes very strongly dominated by political questions: "In recent decades, the senate debate on virtually every Supreme Court nomination has focused to some extent on the nominee's judicial philosophy, ideology, constitutional values, or known positions on specific legal controversies" (Rutkus 2010: 39). The senators are of course well aware that every new justice has the potential to alter the majority situation in the Supreme Court and therefore its judicial practice. The public hearings also offer the senators the chance to distinguish themselves politically by supporting or objecting to a particular candidate.

Political positions become clear during the vote on a nominee, if not before. It is true that candidates are seldom rejected (see Table 10.1), but consensual decisions are just as infrequent. The Senate last reached a completely unanimous vote in 1987, when President Ronald Reagan nominated Justice Anthony M. Kennedy. All candidates since then have received between three (Ruth Bader Ginsberg) and forty-eight (Clarence Thomas) votes against their appointment.

A candidate's party-political position also plays a central role in the staffing of the Federal Constitutional Court. In order to avoid unilateral government-party influence, the Federal Constitutional Court Act adopted in 1951 stipulated that to be accepted, a candidate for judge requires approval of a two-thirds majority vote. In the past this two-thirds majority in actuality meant that the largest party in opposition always possessed veto power over the judicial vote. For this reason the two large parties were forced to come to an agreement.

The system of proportional representation that developed out of this situation led to the two large parties today having a balanced right to make nominations. In the Second Senate, the SPD and the CDU/CSU take turns nominating four justices. In the First Senate, the government coalition partners are taken into consideration: the SPD and CDU/CSU each nominate three candidates, while another candidate is recommended by Bündnis '90/Die Grünen and one more by the FDP. The system of proportional representation consequently leads to a neutralization of party politics (Stüwe 1997: 140). All of the parties represented in the German Bundestag—except for Die Linke—take part in proportional representation: "the motto is: two left-wing, two right-wing" (Lamprecht 1996: 70).

The result of this informal arrangement is that the SPD and CDU/CSU are each able to fill half of the Senate with candidates who support their political program. In fact, the justices appointed in the first decade of the Federal Constitutional Court's existence were primarily members of these two parties. As of 1975 candidates without any party attachment began increasingly to be elected as justices: initially there was just one, but since the 1980s there have been two unaffiliated justices in each senate (Frank 1987: 163–165). Nowadays the original relationship has reversed itself: only two to three justices currently in office are former members of a political party. Despite this, the recommending parties of course still make sure that the candidates they propose have political positions that are at least similar to their own. As in the United States, the justices are expected to shape the administration of justice in the German courts according to their own basic political preference. However, a correlation between justices' party alignment and the results of the administration of justice is relatively unlikely (Bryde 1998: 496).

The large parties' ability to veto a candidate during the election of federal constitutional justices usually prevents the election of candidates with all-too-extreme party-political positions. The recommended individuals can obviously favor one political party only so far as the other party can be expected to put up with it. This is easy to empirically support: there has never been a constitutional judge who was previously a high-ranking official of any political party. It is indeed true that before their election, some judges were high-ranking public officials: Gebhard Müller (CDU), for example, was minister-president of Baden-Württemberg; Peter Müller (CDU), minister-president of Saarland; Ernst Benda (CDU), federal minister of the interior; Ernst Gottfried Mahrenholz (SPD), minister of cultural affairs in Lower Saxony; Roman Herzog (CDU), minister of cultural affairs and the interior in Baden-Württemberg; Peter M. Huber, minister of the interior in the Free State of Thuringia; Hans Hugo Klein (CDU), parliamentary secretary of state to the minister of justice; Jutta Limbach (SPD), Berlin senator of justice. However, none of them could be called an outspoken party leader before his or her appointment.

For this reason they were electable by those from the other side of the political spectrum. By contrast, candidates who distinguish themselves primarily as party politicians have practically no chance of being accepted by the opposing party. This has occasionally caused a political tug-of-war between the parties. For instance, in 1993 the CDU/CSU managed to block the election of SPD politician Herta Däubler-Gmelin to the vice presidency of Karlsruhe. As a member of the SPD Federal Executive Board, Ms. Däubler-Gmelin had held a prominent political function for many years. In 2008 the CDU prevented the election of Horst Dreier, a professor of constitutional law recommended by the SPD for the judgeship in the Federal Constitutional Court because his perspective on the protection of human life was unacceptable to them: in the National German Ethics Council, Dreier had presented his belief that embryos are not to be considered bearers of human dignity.

Nevertheless, the election of Federal Constitutional Court judges is not a highly political matter. Unlike in the United States, the decisions are made behind closed doors in an informal process and no public hearing is conducted, so the public normally takes little notice of them. In the United States, the nine Supreme Court Justices possess a relatively high degree of recognition, but the sixteen justices of the German Federal Constitutional Court remain unknown in Germany even after their appointment. Only the president of the Federal Constitutional Court, who outwardly represents the constitutional body, enjoys somewhat more public attention.

Conclusion

There is no perfected procedure for appointing federal constitutional justices. In both the United States and Germany the procedures are able to fairly well satisfy the criteria of the "magic square of justice appointment" (Laufer 1968: 207). In both cases the justices are (indirectly) democratically legitimated, unilateral influence of political parties is largely avoided, the candidates' professional qualifications are given appropriate consideration, and the federal dimension is brought to bear in the procedure of appointment.

In both countries, the political parties play a central role in the appointment procedure. Not only legal but also political motives shape the process. Indeed, in both cases the institutional regulations see to it that justices are appointed only when the two major parties are able to reach a consensus. The justices of the Supreme Court and of the Federal Constitutional Court are therefore not merely unilateral candidates of the executive branch. In both the United States and Germany, the respective opposition parties effectively possess a veto when it comes to staffing the constitutional court.

Due to these parallels, it is not surprising that the profiles of justices appointed to the two courts also exhibit significant similarities. In both countries constitutional justices are above all distinguished by their considerable professional expertise, and candidates with extreme legal philosophical or partisan positions have very remote chances of being appointed to the constitutional court. This strengthens the status and the acceptance of both courts within their respective political systems. The Federal Constitutional Court has long received better evaluations in surveys than the political entities of the Bundestag and the federal government (*Bundesregierung*). For many decades the approval rating of the U.S. Supreme Court has been similarly stable and considerably higher than for other branches of government. At the end of the 1960s it reached an all-time high of 66 percent. The dramatic decrease in people's satisfaction with the Supreme Court in the last few years (down to approximately 44 percent) is likely due to several contentious decisions such as the Citizens United Case, which in 2010 allowed unlimited campaign spending by corporations and unions, and the Affordable Care Act decision of 2012, which validated the Obama administration's health care reform.

Significant variance, however, is found in the details of the two appointment procedures. The most important difference is that in Germany, both houses of the legislature elect constitutional justices, whereas in the United States it is the president and the Senate that have to collaborate. The appointment procedure in the U.S. is highly political; after the president nominates a candidate, the public becomes intimately involved in the proceedings. Above all it is the public hearings in the Senate that boost the numbers of citizens concerning themselves with the personal qualifications of candidates for the position of justice. In contrast, the selection of candidates in Germany takes place behind closed doors and rests in the hands of a small circle of party politicians.

Both procedures have advantages and disadvantages. A positive aspect of the U.S. model is that it allows for a high degree of transparency. Opening the public hearings and the vote in the Senate to the public guarantees wide public discussion of the professional and personal qualifications of candidates for the bench. A disadvantage that must therefore also be acknowledged is that individual candidates are subject to being discredited and can even face defamation.

By contrast, the German procedure guarantees that candidates are not publicly injured. However, this comes at a high price: the public is practically excluded from the appointment procedure. In addition, and contrary to what is written in the Basic Law, until 2015 half of the justices were not elected by the German Bundestag's plenary session, but rather by an election committee. Many political scientists and lawyers justifiably critiqued this procedure (Bröhmer 2004: 257). Although the Federal Constitutional Court deemed the indirect election procedure itself constitutional (BvC 2/10), the key decision regarding the composition of the highest German court should not be exercised by a committee, but rather by plenary session of the German Bundestag. Therefore, the 2015 reform of the Federal Constitutional Court Act, which introduced direct election of the judges by the Bundestag, made sense and was long overdue. It would similarly be sensible for the candidates to be required to present themselves in a hearing before the elected bodies. To avoid negative consequences for the applicant, these hearings could be conducted away from the public, unlike the procedure in the United States.

Incidentally, in Germany public interest in the work of the Federal Constitutional Court—and likewise in the election of justices—has distinctly risen in the past few years. Upon the fortieth anniversary of the Federal Constitutional Court in 1991 it was lamented that "very little is publicized about the election that just took place" (Ley 1991: 420), but today the media report on the Federal Constitutional Court much more extensively. The election of judges unquestionably resonates noticeably with the public, especially when a party presents a candidate the other party does not want to accept. Nevertheless, this still does not compare with the excitement that accompanies some judicial nominations in the United States.

Klaus Stüwe is a professor of comparative political science at the Department of History and Social Sciences of the Katholische Universität Eichstätt-Ingolstadt (KU).

Bibliography

American Bar Association. "Selecting Supreme Court Justices: A Dialogue." *Focus on Law Studies,* Vol. 20(2), 2005, 1–17. http://www.americanbar.org/content/dam/aba/publishing/focus_on_law_studies/publiced_focus_spring05.authcheckdam.pdf.

Billing, W. *Das Problem der Richterwahl zum Bundesverfassungsgericht: ein Beitrag zum Thema 'Politik und Verfassungsgerichtsbarkeit'*. Berlin, 1969.
Bröhmer, J. *Transparenz als Verfassungsprinzip: Grundgesetz und Europäische Union*. Tübingen, 2004.
Bryde, B.-O. "Die Verfassungsgerichtsbarkeit in der Rechtssoziologie." In Brand, J., Strempel, D., eds., *Soziologie des Rechts. Festschrift für Erhard Blankenburg zum 60. Geburtstag*. Baden-Baden, 1998, 491–504.
Epstein, L., Martin, A.D., Quinn, K.M., Segal, J.A. "Ideological Drift Among Supreme Court Justices: Who, When, and How Important?" *Northwestern University Law Review*, Vol. 101(4), 2007, 1483–1542.
Ferling, J. "The Senate and Federal Judges: The Intent of the Founding Fathers." *Capitol Studies*, Vol. 2(Winter), 1974, 57–70.
Frank, H. "Die 'neutralen' Richter des Bundesverfassungsgerichts." In Fürst, W., Herzog, R., Umbach, C., eds., *Festschrift für Wolfgang Zeidler*. Berlin, 1987, 163–174.
Fromme, F.K. "Verfassungsrichterwahl." *Neue Juristische Wochenschrift*, 2000, 2977–2978.
Greenburg, J. C. *Supreme Conflict: The Inside Story of the Struggle for Control of the United States Supreme Court*. New York, 2007.
Gusy, C. "Der Bundestag als Wahlorgan, Gesetzgeber und Prozesspartei im Verhältnis zum Bundesverfassungsgericht." In Schneider, H.P., Zeh, W., eds., *Parlamentsrecht und Parlamentspraxis. Ein Handbuch*. Berlin, New York, 1989, 1619–1656.
Harris, J.P. *The Advice and Consent of the Senate: A Study of the Confirmation of Appointments by the United States Senate*. Berkeley, 1953 (reprint New York, 1968).
Hartmann, J. *Das politische System der BRD im Kontext*. Wiesbaden, 2013.
Hiesel, M. "Rechtsprechungskorrektur durch Richterernennung? Über den Einfluss von Präsidenten auf die Entwicklung der Rechtsprechung des US Supreme Court durch die Ernennung neuer Richter." *Zeitschrift für öffentliches Recht*, Vol. 65, 2010, 177–202.
Kau, M. *United States Supreme Court und Bundesverfassungsgericht*. Berlin, 2007, 157–182.
Lamprecht, R. *Vom Mythos der Unabhängigkeit. Über das Dasein und Sosein der deutschen Richter*, 2nd ed. Baden-Baden, 1996.
Laufer, H. *Verfassungsgerichtsbarkeit und politischer Prozeß*. Tübingen, 1968.
Ley, R. "Die personellen Veränderungen des Bundesverfassungsgerichts im Jahre 1983." *Zeitschrift für Parlamentsfragen*, Vol. 16(2), 1985, 188–205.
Ley, R. "Die Wahl der Mitglieder des Bundesverfassungsgerichtes. Eine Dokumentation anlässlich des 40jährigen Bestehens." *Zeitschrift für Parlamentsfragen*, Vol. 22(3), 1991, 420–449.
McMahon, K. J. *Nixons's Court. His Challenge to Political Liberalism and its Political Consequences*. Chicago, 2011.
Miller Center of Public Affairs *Improving the Process of Appointing Federal Judges: A Report of the Miller Center Commission on the Selection of Federal Judges*. Charlottesville, VA, 1996.
Neustadt, R. *Presidential Power and the Modern Presidents: The Politics of Leadership from Roosevelt to Reagan*. New York, 1991.
Ruppert, S. "Das Wahlverfahren der Bundesverfassungsrichter im Bundestag." In Umbach, D.C., Clemens, T., Dollinger, F.-W., eds., *Bundesverfassungsgerichtsgesetz. Mitarbeiterkommentar*, 2nd ed. Heidelberg, 2005, 207–216.

Rutkus, D.S. "Supreme Court Appointment Process: Roles of the President, Judiciary Committee, and Senate." *Congressional Research Service 7-5700,* RL31989. Washington, D.C., 2010.

Rutkus, D.S., Bearden, M. "Supreme Court Nominations, 1789–2010: Actions by the Senate, the Judiciary Committee, and the President," *Congressional Research Service* 7-5700, RL33225, Washington, D.C., 2010.

Rutkus, D.S., et al. *Supreme Court Nominations.* Alexandria, 2010.

Schlaich, K., Korioth, S. *Das Bundesverfassungsgericht – Stellung, Verfahren, Entscheidungen,* 9th ed. Munich, 2012.

Stüwe, K. *Die Opposition im Bundestag und das Bundesverfassungsgericht.* Baden-Baden, 1997.

Stüwe, K. *USA.* Schwalbach, 2013.

Triepel, H. "Wesen und Entwicklung der Staatsgerichtsbarkeit." *Veröffentlichungen der Vereinigung der Deutschen Staatsrechtslehrer,* Vol. 5, 1929, 2–28.

Urofski, M.I., *The Warren Court. Justices, Rulings and Legacy.* Santa Barbara, CA, 2001.

Wefing, H. "Richter unter Verdacht. Warum Peter Müller nicht nach Karlsruhe gehen sollte." *Die Zeit* 48, 24 November 2011.

Wermiel, S.J. "Confirming the Constitution: The Role of the Senate Judiciary Committee." *Law and Contemporary Problems,* Vol. 56(4), 1993, 121–144.

Chapter 11

The Impact of the German Federal Constitutional Court on the Consolidation and Quality of Democracy

Sascha Kneip

Introduction

It seems to be a commonly shared conviction that constitutional courts have become powerful (co-)players in democratic governance (see, e.g., Waltman, Holland 1988; Vallinder 1995; Stone Sweet 2000; Epstein, Knight, Shvetsova 2001; Guarnieri, Pederzoli 2002; Ginsburg 2003; Koopmans 2003; Sandler, Schoenbrod 2003; Epstein, Knight 2004; Scheppele 2005; Horowitz 2006; Romeu 2006). The twentieth century therefore should be regarded not only as an age of democratization, but also as a period of constitutionalization of politics (Elster, Slagstad 1993; Henkin 1994; Holmes 1995; Bellamy 1996; Alexander 1998; Hilbink 2008). Until the 1920s, only a handful of countries had established "diffuse" or "specialized" constitutional jurisdiction. Today, almost every democratic society in the world features some sort of constitutional court, the U.S. Supreme Court and the German Federal Constitutional Court being only the most prominent (and perhaps most successful) representatives of these two types of constitutional jurisdiction. The limitation of democratic politics through constitutional and fundamental rights has become part of the self-image of modern democracies, as has the institution of constitutional courts as safeguards of these fundamental rights. Even the "mother of

Notes for this chapter begin on page 278.

parliamentary sovereignty," the United Kingdom, established a Supreme Court in 2009. It still has no authority to review parliamentary decisions but nevertheless checks (and sanctions) executive acts by the standards of (constitutional) law.[1] In short, constitutional courts and constitutional judicial review of legislative and executive acts are integral parts of today's established democracies.

However, the sheer empirical existence of constitutional courts in democratic settings does not have to be accompanied by a normative or actual acceptance of their activities. Neither politicians nor scientists necessarily share the view that constitutional courts are essential actors for and in democracies. Both normative and empirical studies on democracy have found broad skepticism toward the status, function, and role of constitutional courts. While parts of the normative theory of democracy (and of normative legal theory) occasionally regard legal constraints on democratic processes quite critically (e.g., Maus 1992, 2004, 2005; Waldron 1999, 2006), empirically oriented research sometimes suspects that constitutional courts intervene too much in the sphere of politics. Opponents of strong constitutionalism claim that the shift of decision-making procedures from directly elected parliaments to (at best) indirectly elected judges is weakening democratic governance. Binding decisions, they argue, are no longer made by legitimate representatives, but by a handful of judges. "Governing with Judges" (Stone Sweet 2000) has, in this view, turned into "Government by Judges" (see Tushnet 1999, 2008; Sandler, Schoenbrod 2003; Hirschl 2007).

It is beyond dispute that constitutional courts can limit the scope of political action. The records of the U.S. Supreme Court and the German Federal Constitutional Court surely shine a light on this. Courts have the ability to curtail the power of political actors, and they sometimes act as (conditional) veto players (Tsebelis 2002). Indeed, the mere possibility that a legal issue can be referred to a constitutional court limits political actors' policy options in the first place. But this simple fact does not tell us much about the actual role of courts in democracies, about the way courts are acting in the process of democratic governance, or about the impact courts have on the functioning of democratic systems. Is the strong institutional position of constitutional courts "good" or "bad" for democracies? Do courts contribute to the functioning of democracy or spoil democratic self-governance? Can courts play a decisive role in the establishment of democratic governance at all? The answers are empirically rather unclear.

This chapter addresses these issues by looking at the Federal Constitutional Court. It proceeds in three sections. First, it shows why the German Federal Constitutional Court, as a comparatively strong and independent court, is a perfect example with which to analyze the given questions.

The second section provides some general remarks on the relationship between constitutional courts and democratization, and links these perceptions to empirical insights about how the Court supported the consolidation of German democracy after 1945. Third, the issue of democratic quality and constitutional jurisdiction is addressed via an empirical examination of the Court's contribution to the quality of German democracy. A short summary will conclude the chapter.

The Federal Constitutional Court: Powerful, Independent—and Enormously Popular

Constitutional courts can have an impact on politics and society—and thus on the quality of a democratic system—only if they meet three conditions: they have to be institutionally (and actually) powerful, independent from politics, and popular among the population. The Federal Constitutional Court fulfills all three criteria.

The Federal Constitutional Court is eminently powerful in comparison to most other constitutional or high courts of the world. Formal powers of a constitutional court are usually measured by assessing a court's formal competencies and its openness to access (see, e.g., Ginsburg 2003: 34ff.). Regarding formal competencies, the Federal Constitutional Court possesses almost all possible powers of a constitutional court. It is, for example, entitled to hear cases of abstract and concrete judicial review; it adjudicates constitutional complaints by citizens; it has final authority in constitutional disputes between government institutions; it delivers decisions in cases of objective constitutional protection (it decides, e.g., on the impeachment of the Federal President and high judges and on party-ban proceedings, and furthermore has the final say in electoral complaint cases); and it has the competence to review supranational and transnational law by the standards of the German constitution (for further competences of the Court, see Brünneck 1988, 1992). In principle, there is no issue or topic that could not be subject to the constitutional jurisdiction of the Federal Constitutional Court.

This is more or less also true for the U.S. Supreme Court. Its original procedures deal primarily with federal litigation and other questions of horizontal and vertical authority, but as the highest court of appeal it also handles all kinds of other issues. At least two features distinguish the German from the U.S. court: the Supreme Court does not hear abstract judicial review cases, and access to the court differs significantly.

The Federal Constitutional Court belongs—at least institutionally—among the most "open" courts of the world. This openness is due to a comparatively large number of authorized petitioners in conjunction with relatively low thresholds for legal proceedings. Depending on the procedure, potential applicants include the executives of federal and state governments, the federal legislature (or one-quarter of its members), ordinary courts, parties, associations, and citizens. Most important for openness of access to the Court is certainly that citizens can file constitutional complaints (and particularly that they can file direct constitutional complaints against court decisions). This distinguishes the German from the U.S. case: German citizens have the right to approach the Federal Constitutional Court directly whenever they think their constitutional rights have been curtailed (and when it is unreasonable for them to go through official channels). Furthermore, in principle the Court has to decide on every complaint that reaches it—review of a case is basically not a matter left to judicial discretion but an individual right that cannot be openly ignored. Although the success rate of complaints is not substantially higher in Germany than in the United States (2.5% approximately), court access itself seems to be significantly broader.

But there is more to the possibility of constitutional complaint than just the extension of court access. From the perspective of democratic theory, the most eminent feature of constitutional complaints is that they enable each citizen to supervise political decisions that are taken in his or her name. In other words, the institutionalization of constitutional complaints turns every citizen into a potential litigant and "controller" of democratic politics, as long as he or she can prove that state action curtails his or her constitutional rights. This strengthens not only the power of the citizens in the democratic process, but also (and perhaps above all) the power of the constitutional court itself, by way of its frequent involvement in constitutional disputes. Finally, the additional opportunity to file complaints against court decisions highlights the fact that citizens in a democracy should have standing against executive and judicial actions as well as legislative decisions. This opportunity has resulted in a substantial expansion of fundamental rights protection by constitutional jurisdiction. This specific design of constitutional complaints sets the Federal Constitutional Court apart from other constitutional courts of the world, including the Supreme Court of the United States.

However, formal judicial powers do not necessarily make a court a strong and active player in democratic governance. A court that never uses its formal powers is as weak as a court that lacks these powers from the very beginning. To turn formal power into actual power, two other features have to be added: empirical legitimacy and a proactive role orientation of a court.

With regard to empirical legitimacy, the Federal Constitutional Court is very highly trusted by the German population. In August 2012, an opinion poll by the Allensbach Institute recorded that 75 percent of German citizens were satisfied or highly satisfied with the way the court in Karlsruhe was ruling (Köcher 2012). This trust rate—incredibly high even by German standards—may have been a product of the hotly debated Euro bailout of the European Union and the Court's long-awaited decision on this issue in the summer of 2012. But this high level is anything but an outlier: since the early 1980s, the trust rates measured for the Court have constantly ranged between 60 and 70 percent and thus have been much higher than those for the legislature, the executive, or the political parties in the same period (see, e.g., the data in Vanberg 2005: 98; Vorländer, Brodocz 2006; Kneip 2009: 198ff.). In other words, the "political" actors of German democracy are much less trusted by German citizens than is the Federal Constitutional Court, which makes it actually impossible for them to ignore or openly foil the Court's decisions. The Court, on the other hand, can build on its high empirical legitimacy in order to turn formal powers into actual power and does not run a risk of being informally overruled by the political branches.

This high empirical legitimacy is rather unique among constitutional courts. Even the U.S. Supreme Court has significantly lost empirical legitimacy in the last couple of years, as recent polls have shown. The approval rate of the Supreme Court dropped from 62 percent in 2000 to 46 percent in the summer of 2012.[2] While the U.S. Supreme Court seems to be regarded more and more as a "political" player, the Federal Constitutional Court has obviously succeeded much better in presenting itself as a neutral, nonpolitical body that does a pretty good job in German democracy.

This perception of the Court and its rulings is due to the third feature that is important for the strength of the Federal Constitutional Court in German politics: its institutional independence from politics. Empirically, institutional independence can be measured indirectly by the inclusiveness of the election process of judges, and directly by the sitting judges' isolation from political pressure. In both respects, the German institutional system grants the Court a high level of independence. More precisely, three institutional features provide for this strong judicial independence: the concrete selection process of the Federal Constitutional Court judges, the rules on the term in office, and the self-authorization as a constitutional body established by the Court itself in 1952.

Concerning the selection process, the German constitutional system is one of the few systems in the world in which a two-thirds majority in both houses of parliament is required to appoint a judge to the constitutional court. This threshold means that both major parties, the Social Democrats (SPD) and the Christian Democrats (CDU/CSU), have to agree on candidates, so that each thus holds a de facto right to veto undesired candidates. As a result of this institutional (and consociational) arrangement, no openly biased or poorly qualified person has a chance to become a sitting judge of the constitutional court. In the more than sixty years of its existence, and perhaps with the exception of a small period in the 1970s, the Court has almost always been considered rather impartial and nonpartisan, even though the selection process has always been controlled by the two major political players.

The rules on the term in office also secure the judges' strong independence. Federal Constitutional Court judges are elected for twelve years, and since 1970 judges have been prohibited from re-election. This ensures that a judge does not feel forced to rule in favor of a specific party or majority whose support she or he might need in order to be re-elected. Also, the judges cannot be recalled. The twelve-year term without the possibility of re-election thus ensures that judges are sufficiently independent without turning them into godlike judges with life tenure.

Finally, the so-called "Statusdenkschrift" (status memorandum) issued by the Court in 1952 was a unique declaration of independence. With it, the Court declared itself a constitutional body with equal rights and standing, thus disentangling itself from the authority of the Ministry of Justice, with which it had been associated before. No longer subject to administrative supervision, it was, as an autonomous constitutional body, equipped with an independent budget within the federal budget. Thus, since the early 1950s, it has not been possible to politically discipline the Court through financial incentives or penalties. Together with the consensus-oriented selection of judges and the institutional arrangements that protect judges from political pressure (and in conjunction with the high legitimacy accorded the Court by the German population), this ensures that the Federal Constitutional Court has operated, and now operates, with strong institutional and actual independence.

Actual Interventions by the Federal Constitutional Court over Time

The Federal Constitutional Court is and always has been a court with the formal prerequisites and capabilities to influence the way (German) democracy is developing. But what about its actual interventions? Have formal and actual strength, institutional independence, and high empirical legitimacy led the Court to intervene more frequently in politics? In other words, has the strong position of the Court in the German governmental system led to stronger tendencies of "judicialization" in Germany? The answer is yes and no.

First of all, it is a fact that every year the Karlsruhe court receives more complaints than it did the prior year. Until the end of the 1950s, fewer than 1,000 litigations per term had to be decided by the Federal Constitutional Court. Nowadays, the Court has to adjudge between 6,000 and 6,500 complaints per year (see the annual statistics of the Federal Constitutional Court at http://www.bundesverfassungsgericht.de/EN/Verfahren/Jahresstatistiken/jahresstatistiken_node.html)—roughly as many cases as the U.S. Supreme Court receives each term. But as already discussed above: The U.S. Supreme Court is more or less free not to hear all these cases. Actually it only deals with approximately eighty cases per year,[3] whereas the Federal Constitutional Court at least formally has to decide on all complaints brought to it. This alone has made the Federal Constitutional Court a stronger player in German politics over the years, as it is quite frequently involved in constitutional disputes.

But the absolute number of complaints reaching Karlsruhe is just one side of the story. The more important question is what the Court makes of it. How often does the Federal Constitutional Court actually intervene in politics? How often does it declare legislative norms unconstitutional and/or void?

Once again, the absolute number of interventions is quite remarkable. Between 1951 and 2011 the Federal Constitutional Court declared 640 federal and state laws (or specific norms within these laws) unconstitutional in whole or in part. Statistically, this is an average of 10.6 constitutional objections per year. The U.S. Supreme Court, on the other hand, has overruled "only" about 1,500 laws since the year 1803, an average of 7.2 annulments per year. The distinctions become even more obvious when one compares the records of both courts between 1990 and 2011: in this period, the U.S. Supreme Court declared 5.1 laws per year unconstitutional, while the Federal Constitutional Court annulled 11.1 norms per year (see the Supreme Court Database at http://scdb.wustl.edu/index.php and, for Germany, the numbers at http://www.bundesverfassungsgericht.de/EN/Verfahren/Jahresstatistiken/jahresstatistiken_node.html). In the last twenty-one years, the annulment rate of the Federal Constitutional Court has thus almost doubled that of the Supreme Court.

Still, the absolute numbers of cases and annulments do not tell the full story. A third factor has to be taken into account: the number of confirmations of norms. High numbers of annulments tell us little about a possible "judicialization" of politics until they are contrasted with the number of norm approvals. A closer look at the proportion of annulments in comparison to norm approvals over time reveals an interesting pattern. First of all, the balance of annulments shows great variation over time (see Figure 11.1). From the 1950s to the mid 1970s Germany's constitutional court con-

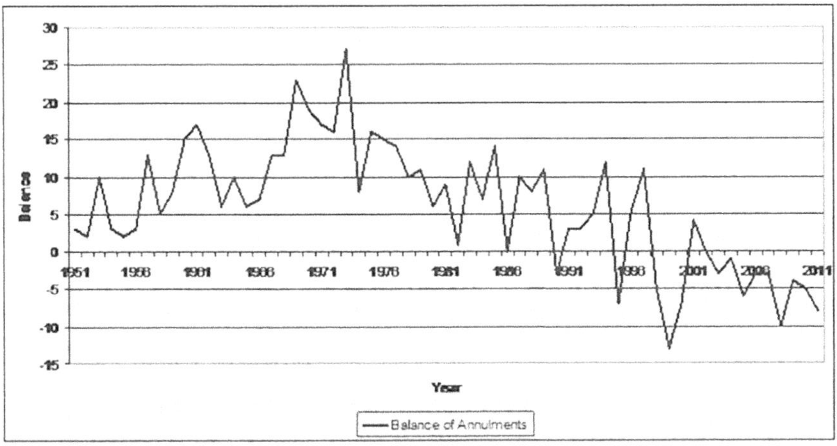

Figure 11.1. Balance of Annulments and Approvals by the Federal Constitutional Court, 1951–2011

Source: Own calculations, based on the official statistics of the Federal Constitutional Court. See http://www.bundesverfassungsgericht.de/EN/Verfahren/Jahresstatistiken/jahresstatistiken_node.html.

firmed many more norms per year than it annulled. The balance reached its positive peak in 1973, when the Court approved thirty-three norms but declared only six norms unconstitutional and/or void. But even more interestingly, the balance shifted toward the zero line from the mid 1970s to the mid 1990s: the Court still approved more norms per year than it annulled, but the ratio became distinctly lower. At the end of the 1990s this trend clearly intensified, and since 2003 the balance between norm approvals and norm annulments has been clearly negative, meaning that the Court has declared more norms per year unconstitutional than consistent with the constitutional provisions.

As becomes apparent from Figure 11.1, an observable trend of judicialization has gained strength in Germany since the mid 1990s. The Federal Constitutional Court obviously interferes more often with politics than in the previous years and decades. There are several possible reasons for this. The Court itself could have become more active in its judicial interventions; or it could have changed its general line of jurisdiction over time, inevitably—all other factors remaining constant—leading to higher annulment rates because political actors counted on interpretations other than the ones ultimately favored by the Court. But upon a closer look at the relevant decisions the Court handed down after the year 2000, an alternative explanation seems to be more reasonable: the Court has more often interfered in politics because more and more laws that indeed are unconstitutional have been contested in Karlsruhe. This leads us to ask whether and how extensively constitutional jurisdiction is related to the quality of democratic governance—and to what extent the German Constitutional Court has had (and still has) an impact on the development of German democracy.

The Federal Constitutional Court's Impact on the Consolidation and Quality of German Democracy

Analysis of the impact of the Federal Constitutional Court on German democracy requires that two different periods be distinguished: the consolidation period shortly after democratization, and the period of regular democratic governance after consolidation had taken place. The following discussion will first treat the general role of (constitutional) courts in both periods and then empirically investigate the actual record of the Federal Constitutional Court.

Courts, Democratic Consolidation, and the Quality of Democracy

Analyzing the record of the Federal Constitutional Court with respect to German democracy requires some preliminary remarks on the general role of courts in the consolidation and enhancement of democracy. The theoretical discussion here will provide the yardstick for the subsequent empirical analysis.

The process of democratization of a political system can be divided into three stages (see for the following, e.g., Merkel 2010: 93ff): the end of the autocratic regime, the institutionalization of the new democratic regime, and the consolidation of democracy. The second and the third phases of democratization are of interest for the issues covered here. The way new democratic structures are built during the institutionalization period depends on the constellation of actors and their interests and power resources. Electoral systems and party systems have to be established, the main features of the new system of government designed, the accreditation of associations and civil society actors regulated, and so on. Above all, central constitutional institutions and actors such as the government, the parliament, and the judiciary have to be established. The most important step here is the drafting of a new constitution (or else the modification and adaptation of the old constitution). The new constitution turns ad hoc patterns of political behavior in the time of regime transformation into legally secured norms and structures. Thus, it produces reliability of expectations between the relevant actors and commits them to structures and norms that formerly were diffuse and ambiguous. With the new constitution as the basis of all legitimate governmental and societal action, the transition from autocratic to democratic rule can actually be carried out (Merkel 2010: 94).

The third stage of democratization, the consolidation of democracy, describes the complex process of the stabilization of democratic governance. The literature on consolidation draws a distinction between constitutional, representative, behavioral, and civil society consolidation (ibid.: 111–112). Whereas constitutional consolidation mainly refers to the establishment and acceptance of the key constitutional institutions, representative consolidation means the implementation of territorial and functional interest representation by parties and interest groups (ibid.: 112). The third type, behavior consolidation, aims above all at acceptance of the new democratic rules by central elites and groups that are not directly associated with the political system (e.g., "informal" political actors such as the military, financial capital, entrepreneurs, or radical [militant] groups). Finally, consolidation of civil society refers to what is probably the most protracted process: the creation of a democratic civic culture as a "socio-cultural foundation" (ibid.) of democracy. In an ideal-typical perspective, complete consolidation of a crisis-resistant democracy can be expected only when all four levels of consolidation are firmly established.

What functions does a constitutional court fulfill during the consolidation of a new democracy? Can it at all affect the consolidation of democratic governance in the early years of democratization? These questions can be addressed both theoretically and empirically.

In theory, constitutional courts can affect all four levels of democratic consolidation (see Figure 11.2). Most obviously, this is the case for the institutional consolidation of the constitution itself. A newly implemented constitution—like any constitution—largely consists of legal norms that have to be interpreted; only very rarely is their regulatory content clear from the outset. Usually, fundamental rights tend to conflict and have to be weighed against each other; competencies of individual and collective actors have to be defined; and demarcation problems between different federal levels have to be addressed. In short, constitutional norms do not unfold their content and their binding force by themselves; rather, they depend on authoritative interpretation by constitutional courts. Moreover, a constitution can produce binding effects only when its rules are perceived as fair and just and the constitutional order is able to solve political and social conflicts effectively at the same time. If this is the case—that is, if the new constitutional order can ensure social and political inclusion, institutional efficiency, and political effectiveness (see Merkel 2010: 116)—then the likelihood of its acceptance by political elites and citizens increases.

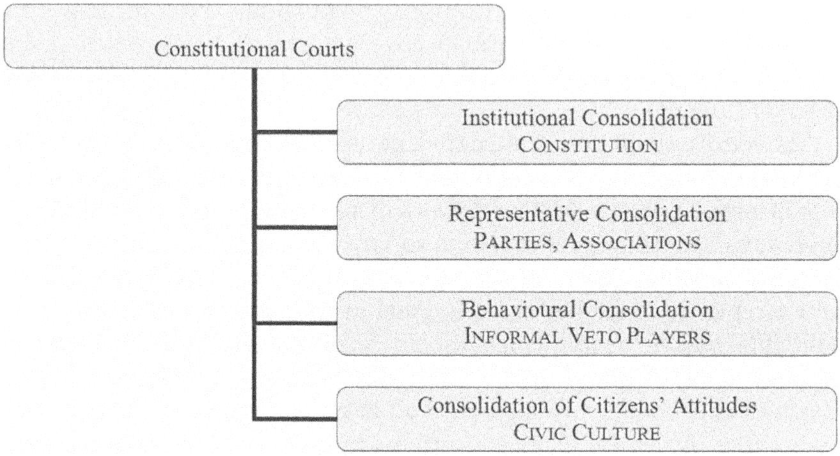

Figure 11.2. Constitutional Courts and the Levels of Democratic Consolidation

Source: Modified figure, taken from Merkel, W., *Systemtransformation. Eine Einführung in die Theorie und Empirie der Transformationsforschung*, 2nd ed., Wiesbaden, 2010: 111.

A constitutional court as "guardian" and ultimately authoritative interpreter of a constitution can (at least in theory) contribute effectively to this end (see Kelsen 1931 for an early account).

At the level of representative consolidation, constitutional courts can affect the consolidation process as well, for example, when they are involved in the process of designing the electoral system, the party system, or the organizational system. If no specific electoral system is prescribed by the constitution or the interpretation of the election rules is under dispute between the actors involved, it often falls to constitutional courts to resolve these conflicts—such as disputes about the admission of parties to election or the validity of specific electoral thresholds—at the constitutional level. The same applies to the consolidation of the party system, especially at the beginning of a consolidation period. How to deal with parties from the old system (or their successors), how to constitute rules for party financing that are in line with the constitution, and how to design rules for formal party accountability are questions that regularly have to be clarified by constitutional courts. This is vitally important for every young democracy because the interpretation of party laws strongly affects the consolidation of the political system at the representative level. The same applies to the level of functional representation, as constitutional adjudication can also affect whether and how trade unions, employers' associations, or environmental and cultural associations can be established; how easily they can develop; and how successful organized societal interests can be aggregated.

Furthermore, constitutional courts can directly or indirectly affect the consolidation of the behavior of informal political actors (the military, big landowners, militant groups, etc.). When constitutional courts constitutionally limit privileges and prerogatives of potential veto actors at the outset of the consolidation process, a faster consolidation becomes more likely. Courts may directly influence the further course of consolidation when, for example, they restrict the role and powers of the military or constrain unjustified prerogatives of large landowners in line with the norms of the new constitution. The more stable these new rules are from the beginning of the consolidation of democracy, the more informal veto players will adapt to them—and the more these players will show behavior compliant with democracy (Merkel 2010: 123). If political elites, together with the constitutional court, succeed in establishing a consensus on the acceptance of the fundamental rules of democracy, the likelihood that this will have a positive impact on veto players like the military increases tremendously.

The most implicit impact of constitutional jurisdiction is manifested at the level of citizens' attitudes and behavior. The longer a society has been governed autocratically, the more likely its citizens are, at the beginning of democratization, to adhere to the role of passive subjects instead of becoming active members of a participatory culture (for the concept of political [civic] culture see Almond, Verba 1963). For the medium-term consolidation of democracy, however, participatory attitudes in the population are needed to support democracy from below and to immunize it against a relapse into autocratic conditions. Participation here does not just refer to the political process in the strict sense, but includes participation in rule-of-law procedures. It might, for example, be a sign of evolving civic culture values when citizens start to file claims for their individual rights against the political and administrative branches. Such behavior considerably increases the chances of democratic consolidation. In addition to appropriate institutional rules (e.g., specific litigation rights or the possibility of filing a constitutional complaint), constitutional jurisdiction can positively influence the likelihood of democratic consolidation by strengthening the "rule-of-law culture" in politics, administration, and the judiciary.

Constitutional courts therefore can principally affect all four levels of consolidation of a young democracy. But what about the influence of constitutional courts on the development and quality of a democratic system after consolidation has taken place? To answer this question, one has first to define what "quality" of democracy means and how it can be measured. The so-called "Democracy Barometer" (Bühlmann et al. 2012; see also http://www.democracybarometer.org/concept_en.html) offers an approach to measuring the quality of democracy. Using a medium-range model of democracy, this approach tries to capture qualitative differences between established democracies. The three constituent principles of democracy—*freedom, equality,* and *control*—are divided into nine basic functions for this purpose.[4]

Regarding the impact of constitutional courts on the quality of democracy, these specific functions of the Democracy Barometer are of particular interest for the analysis at hand. The democratic principle of freedom has the components *individual liberties, rule of law,* and *public sphere*; the principle of equality is described by *participation, transparency,* and *representation*; and the principle of control is defined by the functions *mutual constraints, competition,* and *governmental capability* (Bühlmann et al. 2012: 9ff.). Each of these functions is further divided into (sub-)components, which are then measured by 100 indicators. The basic idea is simple: the higher the values for the measured functions, components, and indicators, the higher the quality of the democratic system. The manifestation of the rule of law function, for example, is measured by the presence of de facto equality before the law as well as the quality and independence of the judiciary. The higher the scores of both components, the higher the democratic quality of this evaluated function. Figure 11.3 illustrates the particular components of the quality measurement of the Democracy Barometer.

Principle	Function	Components
Liberty	Individual Liberties	Right to Physical Integrity
		Right of Self-Determination
	Rule of Law	Equality before the Law
		Quality of the Judiciary
	Public Sphere	Freedom of Association
		Freedom of Expression
Equality	Participation	Equal Opportunity to Participate
		Effective Participation
	Transparency	Absence of secrecy
		Freedom of Information
	Representation	Substantive Representation
		Descriptive Representation
Control	Mutual Constraints	Relations between executive and legislature
		Control Mechanisms (Federalism, Const. Courts)
	Competition	Degree of Contestation
		Openness of Contestation
	Governmental Capability	Resources
		Factors of effective implementation

Figure 11.3. Components of the Quality of Democratic Governance

Source: Modified Figure, taken from Bühlmann, M., Merkel, W., Müller, L., Giebler, H., Weßels, B. "Demokratiebarometer – ein neues Instrument zur Messung von Demokratiequalität," *Zeitschrift für Vergleichende Politikwissenschaft,* Vol. 6 (1), Supplement, 2012: 123.

For most of the nine functions and their components it is reasonable to assume that constitutional courts do (or at least can) have an impact on their empirical value. In constitutional democracies, decisions by constitutional or other high courts on individual freedoms are as common as constitutional court decisions that affect the content of the freedom of expression, the transparency of government action, the quality of the judicial system, the configuration of electoral representation, the extent of political (party) competition, or the relationship between different democratic institutions. Constitutional courts thus can—at least in principle—influence all key quality components of democratic governance. They usually deal with all nine democratic functions distinguished here and are thus central actors when it comes to analyzing the quality of established democratic systems of government. Yet the empirical question remains: How often and how successfully do constitutional courts in fact influence the quality of a democratic system? And how is the record of the German Federal Constitutional Court in this respect? These issues are addressed in the next section together with the question of the Court's impact on democratic consolidation in Germany.

The Empirical Impact of the Federal Constitutional Court on the Consolidation of German Democracy

Given the questions discussed here, the Federal Constitutional Court is a suitable object of study for two main reasons. First, the Court is often regarded as one of the central, most important factors in the democratic development of the Federal Republic of Germany since 1945 (see, e.g., Wesel 1996, 2004; Bryde 2006); furthermore, since 1989, the Federal Constitutional Court has been regarded as a "role model" for the emerging courts in the young democracies of Central and Eastern Europe (see, e.g., Beyme 2006). However, no detailed empirical examination of those courts' output during the early years of democratization has yet been delivered. It therefore seems worthwhile to look more closely at the Court's performance in the first years of democratization. Second, not only is the Federal Constitutional Court one of the most prominent contemporary examples of a strong constitutional court in terms of its institutional strength, independence, and legitimacy (see the discussion above and Kneip 2007, 2008), but the Court has also been a rather strong and independent body right from the start of its operation in 1952. Nearly all its current institutional capabilities and features were already laid down in institutional rules by the early 1950s (namely, in the German Basic Law [*Grundgesetz*] and the Federal Constitutional Court Act). What we do not know, however, is how popular the Court was during the first ten years of democratic consolidation: no empirical data is available concerning German citizens' support for the work of the Court in the 1950s (only in the mid 1970s did such data become available).

The extent to which the strong institutional powers and high level of independence of the Federal Constitutional Court found expression in its judgments at the beginning of democratic consolidation is analyzed here by looking at all decisions rendered by the Court in the first ten years of its existence. More precisely, the empirical analysis rests on all published decisions of the Court from 9 September 1951 to 17 May 1961 (this corresponds to all decisions published in the official law reports of the Federal Constitutional Court [BVerfGE], vols. 1–12). These 413 decisions were examined with regard to, first, the level of democratic consolidation that was affected by the respective decisions, and second, the democratic function that they supported (for the respective criteria, see the previous section).[5]

Regarding the relevant consolidation levels associated with the 413 decisions, the resulting picture confirms the suspicions above. As Figure 11.4 illustrates, the bulk of the decisions concern the level of institutional consolidation. This is not really surprising, since constitutional courts deal above all with the interpretation of the constitution and the functioning of the legal system understood as an institutional structure. By interpreting ambiguous legal and constitutional standards, defining specific interpretative approaches, and setting down concrete constitutional procedures, the Court indeed supported German democratic consolidation at this consolidation level. For example, early on the Court used a variety of (rejected) constitutional complaints to define the nature and function of the right to constitutional complaint and to clarify the requirements and procedures of concrete judicial review cases. Other cases related to the institutional consolidation of the German rule-of-law system dealt, for example, with the specification of procedural law, due process questions (art. 103 I of the Basic Law), and the right to a fair trial (art. 101 I of the Basic Law).

The support for institutional consolidation has also been expanded to the consolidation of the parliamentary and the federal system of government. For example, the Court ruled on the competencies of the federal and the state parliaments in legislative procedures, on the provisions of the Bundestag's rules of procedure, on the rights and duties of representatives and delegates vis-à-vis parliament and government, and on jurisdictional disputes at both the federal and the *Länder* level. Furthermore, the Court very early stepped into the field of voting rights and electoral issues, where it ruled on the admission of referendums, the constitutionality of electoral laws, and complaints regarding scrutiny of elections. Finally, the Court decided important cases concerning the burdens of war, especially the then controversial question of whether civil servants of the old regime

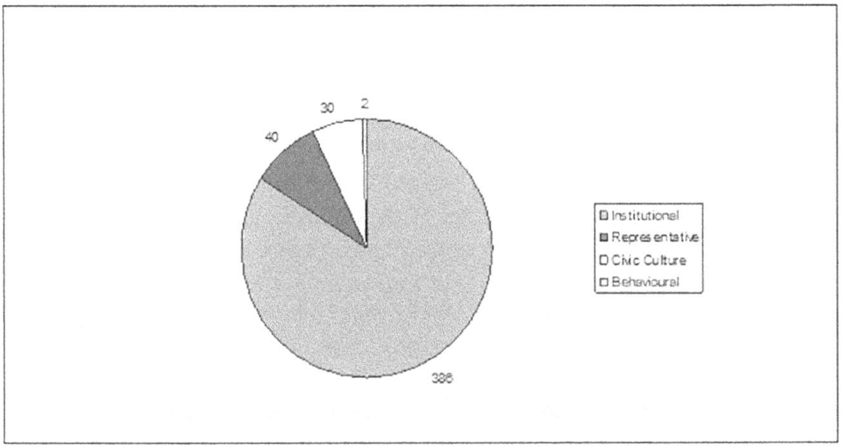

Figure 11.4. Decisions of the Federal Constitutional Court according to Levels of Democratic Consolidation, 1951–1961

Source: Own calculations, based on law reports of the Federal Constitutional Court, vols. 1–12 (BVerfGE 1–12).

were still to be held in office (G-131-law) and whether norms established during the Nazi regime remained in force.

The Court's involvement in questions of representative consolidation was much more indirect. This was most obvious in the two party-ban cases during this period. The Court first banned the Sozialistische Reichspartei (SRP), a successor to the Nazi Party, and later the Communist Party of Germany (KPD). With both bans the Court directly influenced the consolidation of the German party system in the 1950s. In addition, the Court engaged in questions of the constitutionality of electoral laws, the admission of parties to run for elections, and party financing. In this respect, the Court at least indirectly defined the roles and actual chances of political parties in the political process, the stabilization of party competition, and the establishment of the whole party system.

Even more indirect—and in fact much weaker—was the Court's impact on levels of behavioral and civic consolidation. As already suggested theoretically, a direct impact of the Court can hardly be demonstrated here. Only if one considers former Nazi officials and civil servants, members of the armed forces, members of the SRP or KPD, and former industrialists (who tried to sue in Karlsruhe in several instances in the first years of consolidation) as informal veto players can a few examples be found where the Constitutional Court might have influenced the behavioral consolidation of these veto players. However, the problem of informal veto players did not occur to an extent comparable to that in other young democracies, since after the total defeat of Nazi Germany in 1945 the young Federal Republic was occupied by the victorious powers of World War II and thus was only semi-sovereign under the occupation statute until 1955.

As for consolidation of the civic culture, in some important early decisions the Court directly and indirectly addressed citizens' attitudes toward democracy, for example in the aforementioned party-ban cases and in decisions on the right to petition, freedom of movement, and especially freedom of speech. It is hard to prove empirically how influential these decisions have been for the development of the civic culture of German society, but it does not seem entirely implausible to argue that these decisions indirectly influenced the emerging participatory civic culture in the young Federal Republic of Germany in the late 1950s and early 1960s. Still, the most formative influence on the civic culture was most likely the sheer existence of the constitutional court itself, and the institutional ability to approach the Court with constitutional complaints.

The variance in the Court's decisions with regard to the different levels of consolidation is obviously somewhat limited. But if attention shifts away from the levels of consolidation and toward the different functions of democracy, much more variance can be discovered. Figure 11.5 illustrates that in the first ten years of democratic consolidation, rule of law in a strict sense was the main democratic area affected by the decisions of the Federal Constitutional Court; however, it also shows a comparatively wide spread of decisions across different democratic functions. In addi-

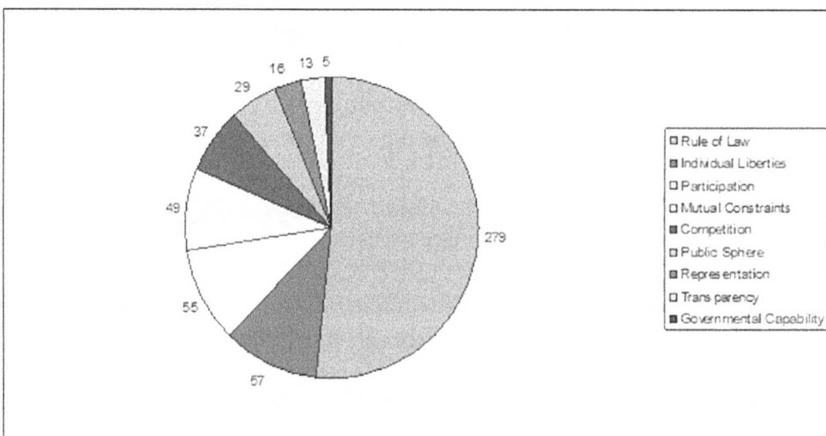

Figure 11.5. Decisions of the Federal Constitutional Court according to Democratic Functions, 1951–1961

Source: Own calculations, based on law reports of the Federal Constitutional Court, vols. 1–12 (BVerfGE 1–12).

tion to matters of the rule of law in a strict sense, matters of individual liberties, participation, horizontal accountability and mutual constraints, competition, and the public sphere were especially affected by the constitutional jurisdiction in the first decade after democratization.

The Federal Constitutional Court's decisions concerning the rule of law in a strict sense included, for example, judgments on due process (arts. 101 and 103 of the Basic Law), on the general functions of constitutional complaints and concrete judicial review processes, on procedural law, on the continuation of laws established before 1945, and on the prohibition of retroactive legislation. Quite often, the Court also incidentally specified the requirements of judicial procedures while deciding all kinds of different matters. This is one reason for the large share of the rule-of-law category in the analysis presented here. The second largest category, individual liberties, is closely connected to the rule-of-law issue and cannot always be reasonably differentiated from it. To some extent, core issues of the rule of law were touched here as well—for example, in matters of extraditions of German citizens, the interpretation of the code of criminal procedure, and the validity in the area of West Germany of punitive sentences issued by courts in the Soviet Zone, aka East Germany—but we find also decisions concerning classical fundamental (individual) rights such as the freedom of movement; the treatment of prisoners; parents' rights; the protection of marriage and family; the criminalization of homosexuality; freedom of action, of occupation, and of religion; conscientious objection, and asylum and amnesty issues.

Characteristic decisions in the field of the democratic function of participation focused, for example, on the legal admissibility of popular petitions and referendums, on the right to vote, on the right of political parties to run for office, and on party financing. All these decisions directly or indirectly affected citizens' and parties' opportunities for political participation.

The relatively high number of decisions on horizontal and vertical accountability and mutual constraints in the first ten years of the operation of the Federal Constitutional Court is quite striking. Here, the Court was involved in a series of federal-state conflicts from the very beginning, and it delivered several landmark decisions on disputes between different political organs, the relationship between the executive and the legislative branch at the federal level, the rights of political groups and members of Parliament against the Bundestag as a collective organ, and the constitutionality of the rules of procedure of the Bundestag itself. The Court's involvement in the repeated conflicts about the separation of power does not seem to have especially hurt the standing of the Court. On the contrary, the Court was able to position itself as a neutral actor at a very early stage and then present itself as ruling impartially on the justified (and unjustified) complaints of different kinds of actors at all federal levels.

Decisions of the Court that are associated with the democratic function of competition are often congruent with those of the category participation and concern mainly issues that directly or indirectly affect the competition between parties. These decisions include those mentioned above on the constitutionality of electoral laws, the party-ban cases, and other kinds of party-law cases (e.g., decisions on the Political Parties Act) that affected parties' opportunities to run in elections. Finally, important decisions on the democratic "public sphere" function also included the aforementioned party-ban cases (which in fact dealt with the issue of impairment of freedom of association) as well as rulings on the freedom of association, on various state-level press laws, on the public broadcasting service, and on the freedom of expression in general.

One might summarize by saying that the Federal Constitutional Court thus mainly established, defined, and clarified the rule-of-law system of the Federal Republic of Germany in the first ten years of democratization. It also was an active player in the area of electoral and party laws, helped to clarify important fundamental rights such as the freedom of speech (BVerfGE 7, 198—*Lüth* case) and the freedom of action (BVerfGE 6, 32—*Elfes* case), practiced a judicial form of dealing with the past, and at an early stage defined the spheres of competence of the federal and state governments on the one hand and those of the different democratic federal-level powers on the other. In other words, it put its mark on the institutional consolidation of the Federal Republic in the first decade after democratization.

Although this is far from self-evident in a fragile institutional environment, from the beginning the Court did not spare political bodies from conflicts such as the now famous case on the rearmament of the German forces ("Wiederbewaffnung," BVerfGE 2, 79), or the case of a public-service broadcasting station run by the federal government that the Court declared unconstitutional ("Deutschland-Fernsehen," BVerfGE 12, 45). In these decisions the Court proved its de facto independence from politics—and incidentally also established and strengthened its own position as *the* guardian of the German constitution within the constitutional system. The Court benefited from the absence of partisan divisions within the Court in these crucial questions (which was likely to have strengthened its position against politics significantly). Furthermore, the Court was wise enough not to deliver one-sided verdicts in favor of specific political actors or federal levels. This probably helped the Court to establish and maintain the perception that it is the only neutral actor in a sea of political interests.

Has the Federal Constitutional Court been a flawless consolidator? Reviewing the more than four hundred decisions of the first decade, only two groups of issues blur the extremely positive picture: The first is the rather strange—from today's perspective—decision concerning male homosexuality as a punishable offense (BVerfGE 6, 389). In this decision, the Court did not adequately fulfill its constitutional function to protect the free development of personality and the freedom of action. Instead, it referred to an undefined "moral law" behind the then criminal sanction of homosexual practices. Certainly this decision did not affect the consolidation of German democracy, but it essentially turned citizens under the threat of this penalty into second-class citizens whose rights had been fundamentally curtailed.

The second group of dysfunctional but much more ambivalent decisions relates to the two party bans of the SRP and the KPD. From the perspective of democratic theory, a party ban is a deep intervention into political competition and an obstacle to the democratic process. In an ideal democratic world, positions of power are awarded after political competition between different organized interests and free, equal, secret elections have taken place. Meaningful elections depend on political competition that is organized in a plural manner, that is, different interests and ideas have to be fed into the contest. The exclusion of certain interests, for whatever reason, inherently violates this core democratic principle. Thus, the task of the Constitutional Court would actually be to protect the openness of the democratic competition—and not to dismiss certain aggregated interests from this process. At the same time, with the two party bans the Court effectively advanced the consolidation of the representative system of German democracy and strengthened the unconsolidated party system by excluding two (more or less) relevant anti-system parties from the democratic process. From the normative standpoint of democratic theory, one may assess these early decisions rather critically; however, they surely did not harm the consolidation of the German party system in the 1950s.

Overall, the Federal Constitutional Court effectively supported the consolidation of the young German democracy in the early years of the Federal Republic. It helped to establish a functioning rule-of-law system, expanded individual freedoms and fundamental rights, marked democratic spheres of competences, and thus helped to make the (federal) democratic process work. Based on strong institutional resources and (carved-out) independence, the Court succeeded in helping German democracy consolidate as well as actively and sustainably supporting the core functions of democratic governance.

Furthermore, in these early years the Court also laid the foundations for its strong position in the German system of governance. The de facto power and independence of the Court, like the extremely high empirical legitimacy it enjoys today, is rooted in these first ten successful years of operation. But what can be said about the Court's overall impact on the quality of German democracy? This question is briefly addressed in the final part of the chapter.

The Federal Constitutional Court and the Quality of German Democracy

Analysis of the functional and dysfunctional aspects of the Court's judgments from 1951 onward suggests that the Court has significantly strengthened the quality of German democracy (see Kneip 2009: 309–337). An investigation of all officially published decisions between 1951 and 2005—in all 1,297 decisions (67 abstract judicial reviews, 588 concrete judicial reviews, and 642 constitutional complaints)—has shown that the vast majority of these decisions can be categorized as beneficial to democracy. Only 82 of the investigated decisions proved to be dysfunctional (according to the standards applied here).[6] This means that only 6 percent of all decisions the Court delivered between 1951 and 2005 can be labeled "dysfunctional" on the basis of liberal democratic theory.

The data highlights three major findings. First, it shows that the German Constitutional Court is indeed deeply involved in German politics. Being consistently engaged in constitutional disputes, it is an important player in democratic governance. Second, however, it is noticeable that in most cases the Court—although institutionally strong and independent—is far from being a strong veto player in German politics. In two-thirds of the cases observed here, the Court examined the laws without challenging them and without declaring norms to be unconstitutional. The third important observation is that in most cases the Court correctly intervened in the playing field of the legislature ("functional intervention") because a parliamentary majority had violated constitutional rights, norms, or procedures. From time to time, the Court invalidated norms wrongfully (and thus exceeded its democratic powers), but in a much larger number of cases it sanctioned violations of constitutional norms and principles correctly and hence supported liberal democratic governance. As already discussed in the previous section, this was especially true of the consolidation period of German democracy. Figure 11.6 indicates once again that until the end of the 1960s, the Court delivered only very few dysfunctional decisions and proved to be an important player for the consolidation of German democracy (see also Bryde 2006). This also holds true in varying degrees for the period after 1970.

In its more than sixty-year history, the Court issued only a few rulings that did not sufficiently protect the German constitution, its citizens, or German democracy on the whole. Among these "dysfunctional" judgments was the confirmed discrimination against homosexual citizens in the 1950s, 1960s, and 1970s. The (sometimes too submissive) approval of

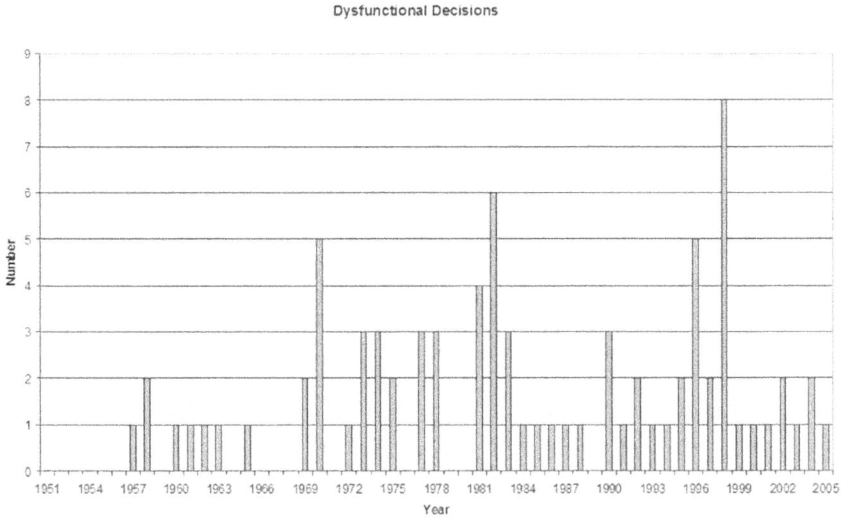

Figure 11.6. Dysfunctional Decisions of the Federal Constitutional Court: Abstract and Concrete Judicial Reviews and Constitutional Complaints, 1951–2005

Source: Kneip, S., *Verfassungsgerichte als demokratische Akteure. Der Beitrag des Bundesverfassungsgerichts zur Qualität der bundesdeutschen Demokratie,* Baden-Baden, 2009, 318.

anti-terror laws in the 1970s (at the time of left-wing terrorism by the Rote Armee Fraktion [RAF]) may also be considered dysfunctional from the perspective of liberal democratic theory and strictly applied rule-of-law principles. Additionally, in the 1980s and 1990s the Court clearly overstepped its competencies in a (small) number of decisions in the area of social, fiscal, and financial policy, where the Court decided on issues that are clearly—according to the Court's own principles—the prerogative of the legislature. Overall, however, very few dysfunctional judgments can be found in the law reports of the Federal Constitutional Court. Indeed, the vast majority of the judgments of the Karlsruhe court can be regarded as milestones of a democratic and liberal constitutional development, and many of them have been exemplary in international comparison. In particular the Court's judicature on fundamental rights has increased the democratic quality of the Federal Republic significantly, and it is no coincidence that the Court's jurisprudence on basic rights created a model for post-1990 constitutional courts in Central and Eastern Europe (Schwartz 2000; Beyme 2006).

One obvious example of the Court's functional behavior is its jurisdiction in cases of homeland security policies. Since the beginning of the 1990s, and once again after the terrorist attacks of 9/11, the political discourse about stricter policies on internal security led to a large number of federal and state laws that significantly restricted civil rights and liberties. The Federal Constitutional Court, often because of complaints of ordinary citizens, ruled on many of these laws—a federal law on acoustic surveillance (*Großer Lauschangriff*) and federal and state law-and-order acts restricting secrecy of telecommunication; the federal law on aviation security and state laws regulating the automatic recording of car license plates and online searches and reconnaissance via the Internet; and the EU-driven federal law on data preservation and on the European Arrest Warrant, to name but a few. In all these cases, federal and state legislatures introduced significant restrictions on core liberal democratic values, including civil rights, horizontal accountability, and checks and balances. The Federal Constitutional Court invariably declared these laws unconstitutional in whole or in part. Through these interventions the Court protected core principles of liberal democratic governance. It thus acted in a functional mode and demonstrated that strong judicial powers not only theoretically increase the quality of democracy, but actually increased it with functional interventions.

This rather positive assessment of the Court's record can of course claim validity only as long as "democracy" is understood as a "liberal, constitutional democracy" that institutionalizes individual fundamental rights and protects these rights from illegitimate interference by political or societal majorities. If, by contrast, democracy were defined simply as "electoral democracy" of mere majority rule without constitutional constraints, the assessment of the Court's record would of course be quite different (see Kneip 2009: 284–347 for details). But regardless of the model of democracy that is applied, it is beyond doubt that the German Federal Constitutional Court has exerted—and still exerts—a huge influence on politics (and policies) of the Federal Republic. Only in part can the institutional features discussed above explain the Court's position, which is exceptionally strong, even in international comparison. But what then does explain it?

One important but sometimes underestimated factor seems to be the specific role orientation of the German Court as a collective organ. The strong institutional facilities discussed above are necessary but certainly not sufficient to ensure the Court's strong role in the political life of German democracy. These institutional features have to be joined by the Court's will to actually make use of them—and this "will" derives directly from the self-perception of the Court and its judges. So, what is the "role" of the Court in German democracy? Does the Court see itself as the "guardian of the constitution" in the sense of Hans Kelsen (Kelsen 1931)? Is it a mere referee in constitutional conflicts, a special kind of dispute settlement body, or even an educator of the politicians and the masses?

From the perspective of democratic theory, the Federal Constitutional Court may be best described as the guardian of the written constitution and its unwritten principles, for two reasons: its great skill at conflict resolution and extraordinary ability to handle conflicts with the executive and the legislative branches; and its distinct judicature on fundamental rights and principles. Both characteristics distinguish the Federal Constitutional Court from many other constitutional courts in the world. This seems to be also the case in comparison with the other strong constitutional court of the Western world, the U.S. Supreme Court. Traditionally the U.S. Supreme Court has been more reserved in limiting the power of the executive (especially in times of war and crisis) or constraining the rights of Congress. In response to the anti-terrorism legislation after 9/11, for example, both courts show refined distinctions in their reluctance to interfere with executive (or legislative) prerogatives. However, given the influence of the free adoption procedure of the Supreme Court, the protection of fundamental rights seems to be considerably weaker in the U.S. than in the German case.[7]

All in all, the image of a "guardian of the constitution" suits the actual role of the Court in German democracy quite well. It reflects the Court's contributions during the consolidation period as well as its status in today's democratic life in Germany. Whether this standing will endure in times of an "ever closer" European multilevel system of constitutional courts is an important but open question. Anyhow, hopes run high that a future European system of constitutional control will maintain the level of quality that the jurisdiction of the Court has reached in the last decades.

Conclusion

This chapter has above all identified three things. First, it tried to highlight the plausibility of constitutional courts potentially being key players in consolidation processes of young democracies and show that they can help improve the quality of democratic systems of government. Second, it specified the (institutional) conditions under which constitutional courts can turn theoretical impact into real influence. And third, it empirically examined the actual impact of the Court on the consolidation and contemporary quality of German democracy.

Regarding the first two objectives, the essay argued that constitutional courts have the ability to influence all four levels of democratic consolidation as well as the different democratic functions defined above. Constitutional courts are thus not only central actors in already established and consolidated democracies, but also major (potential) players in times of democratic consolidation. To actually use its potential impact, however, a court requires an institutional environment that equips it with sufficient levels of competence and independence. If a given court is also able to generate empirical legitimacy among the citizens of a democratic society, and if it regards itself as a "guardian of the constitution," the probability increases that that court will be able to supply vital support to a society's democratic development.

In the case of the Federal Republic of Germany it has been shown empirically that the Federal Constitutional Court in fact exerted influence on all four levels of democratic consolidation and across all nine democratic functions during the first ten years of its existence. However, significant differences emerge with regard to the distribution of this influence. In the 1950s, the Court especially supported the institutional consolidation of the young German democracy, but the representative and the behavioral levels of consolidation were affected to a much lesser extent. As for how democratic functions were affected, the Court addressed above all the rule-of-law function, the validity of norms of individual freedom, and participation and power control issues. Thus the Court first and foremost strengthened the rule-of-law components of liberal democracy while at the same time broadening individual freedom and especially the participatory elements of the democratic process. In the period subsequent to democratic consolidation, the record of the Court has been considerably supportive of democracy as well, for the Court has acted in a markedly functional way with respect to democratic governance. In the sixty plus years of the Court's history, only a few rulings have not sufficiently protected the German constitution, its citizens and residents, or German democracy on the whole. Therefore it can be argued that not only did the Federal Constitutional Court have an effective impact on the consolidation of German democracy after 1945, but that it was also one of the key factors in the overall success of the second German democracy.

Dr. Sascha Kneip is a research fellow of the Democracy and Democratization research unit at the Berlin Social Science Center (WZB).

Notes

1. The informal commitment of UK politics to fundamental rights and rule-of-law standards has increasingly transformed into a more institutionalized form of judicial review.

Especially the UK Human Rights Act, implemented in 2000, laid the foundation for a system of constitutional control whose effects have become gradually visible since then (see Kavanagh 2009). Moreover, it should not be forgotten that the UK—as well as the Netherlands, Switzerland, and other examples of democratic countries without a clearly defined constitutional jurisdiction—has already been integrated into a European multilevel constitutional court system and is therefore subject to the jurisdiction of the European Court of Justice and the European Court of Human Rights. The assumption that democratic governance is not at all constrained by rule-of-law institutions no longer corresponds to the European reality.

2. See http://www.gallup.com/poll/4732/supreme-court.aspx. The average approval rate for the U.S. Supreme Court was about 54 percent between 2000 and 2012, with a high of 62 percent in the years 2000 and 2001 and a low of 42 percent in 2005. In 2005, in fact, more people disapproved than approved of the way the U.S. Supreme Court was doing its job.
3. Confronted with almost 8,000 litigations per year, the U.S. Supreme Court thus deals "only" with 1 percent of all complaints that are addressed to it. See http://www.supremecourt.gov/publicinfo/year-end/2011year-endreport.pdf.
4. The underlying model of democracy is also a medium-range model. It goes beyond minimalist conceptions of democracy, but without referring to maximalist, normatively charged positions. It is thus in principle universally applicable to all societies at all times.
5. The assignment of a decision to a given level of consolidation of democracy and the affected democratic function was usually done by looking at the syllabus of the decision, or otherwise with reference to the entire text of a decision. Multiple counts of a judgment were possible if multiple levels or functions were affected by the judgment, so the sum of the individual categories is higher than the number of the analyzed 413 decisions. E.g., the early decision concerning the "Southwest State" (Vol. 1, 14), contains no fewer than thirty-nine guiding principles concerning four different democratic functions.
6. "Functional" and "dysfunctional" decisions were categorized using a four-stage test, taking into account the concrete norms of the German constitution, a theoretical distinction between functional and dysfunctional decisions of courts in the light of liberal democratic theory, the respective justifications provided by legislators and the Federal Constitutional Court in the concrete cases brought to the bench, and the criteria the court itself applies in constant jurisdiction (controlling of evidence, plausibility, and content). The data was coded as follows: Court decisions based on a clear and undisputed norm of the German constitution were coded functional per se. If the underlying norm of the respective decision had to be interpreted by the Court (which was almost always the case), it was analyzed whether the Court intervened in the core regimes of democratic governance or rather dealt with policy questions. If the Court referred to core principles of democracy and/or core principles of the rule of law (e.g., equality before the law, principle of proportionality, prohibition of arbitrariness, etc.), the decision was coded functional. Otherwise it was coded dysfunctional. See Kneip (2009: 313–337) for more details.
7. At least, a litigant's chance that his or her case will be heard by the Court is today somewhat lower in the United States than in Germany. This does of course not mean that the protection of fundamental rights is less pronounced in the U.S. legal system. The diffuse system of constitutional jurisdiction (the "American model") delivers at least as much control density as do systems of specialized constitutional control (the "European model"). Only protection by the Supreme Court itself seems to be quantitatively and

qualitatively less comprehensive from the perspective of the individual citizen, given the significantly lower chance of being heard by the Court at all.

Bibliography

Alexander, L., ed. *Constitutionalism: Philosophical Foundations.* Cambridge, 1998.

Almond, G.A., Verba, S. *The Civic Culture.* Princeton, 1963.

Bellamy, R., ed. *Constitutionalism, Democracy and Sovereignty: American and European Perspectives.* Aldershot, 1996.

Beyme, K. "The German Constitutional Court: A Model For New Democracies?" In Ergül, O., ed., *Democracy and the Judiciary.* Ankara, 2006, 67–100.

Brünneck, A. "Constitutional Review and Legislation in Western Democracies." In Landfried, C., ed., *Constitutional Review and Legislation: An International Comparison.* Baden-Baden, 1988, 219–262.

Brünneck, A. *Verfassungsgerichtsbarkeit in den westlichen Demokratien.* Baden-Baden, 1992.

Bryde, B.-O. "Der Beitrag des Bundesverfassungsgerichts zur Demokratisierung der Bundesrepublik." In van Ooyen, R., Möllers, M., eds., *Das Bundesverfassungsgericht im politischen Prozess.* Wiesbaden, 2006, 321–331.

Bühlmann, M., Merkel, W., Müller, L., Giebler, H., Weßels, B. "Demokratiebarometer – ein neues Instrument zur Messung von Demokratiequalität." *Zeitschrift für Vergleichende Politikwissenschaft,* Vol. 6(1), Supplement, 2012, 115–159.

BVerfGE, *Entscheidungen des Bundesverfassungsgerichts.* Tübingen, 1952 et seq.

Elster, J., Slagstad, R., eds. *Constitutionalism and Democracy.* Cambridge, 1993.

Epstein, L., Knight, J. "Courts and Judges." In Sarat, A., ed., *The Blackwell Companion to Law and Society.* Oxford, 2004, 170–194.

Epstein, L., Knight, J., Shvetsova, O. "The Role of Constitutional Courts in the Establishment and Maintenance of Democratic Systems of Government." *Law and Society Review,* Vol. 35(1), 2001, 117–163.

Ginsburg, T. *Judicial Review in New Democracies: Constitutional Courts in Asian Cases.* Cambridge, 2003.

Guarnieri, C., Pederzoli, P. *The Power of Judges: A Comparative Study of Courts and Democracy.* Oxford, 2002.

Henkin, L. "A New Birth of Constitutionalism: Genetic Influences and Genetic Defects." In Rosenfeld, M., ed., *Constitutionalism, Identity, Difference, and Legitimacy.* Durham, 1994, 39–53.

Hilbink, L. "Assessing the New Constitutionalism." *Comparative Politics,* Vol. 40(2), 2008, 227–245.

Hirschl, R. *Towards Juristocracy: The Origins and Consequences of the New Constitutionalism.* Cambridge, 2007.

Holmes, S. "Constitutionalism." In Lipset, S.M., ed., *The Encyclopedia of Democracy.* London, 1995, 299–306.

Horowitz, D.L. "Constitutional Courts: A Primer for Decision Makers." *Journal of Democracy* Vol. 17(4), 2006, 125–137.

Kavanagh, A. *Constitutional Review under the UK Human Rights Act.* Cambridge, 2009.

Kelsen, H. "Wer soll Hüter der Verfassung sein?" *Die Justiz,* Vol. 6, 1931, 576–628.

Kneip, S. "Starke und schwache Verfassungsgerichte: Gibt es eine optimale Verfassungsgerichtsbarkeit für die Demokratie?" In Kropp, S., Lauth, H.J., eds., *Gewalten-*

teilung und Demokratie. Konzepte und Probleme der 'horizontal accountability' im interregionalen Vergleich. Baden-Baden, 2007, 91–109.

Kneip, S. "Verfassungsgerichtsbarkeit im Vergleich." In Gabriel, O.W., Kropp, S., eds., *Die EU-Staaten im Vergleich.* Wiesbaden, 2008, 631–655.

Kneip, S. *Verfassungsgerichte als demokratische Akteure. Der Beitrag des Bundesverfassungsgerichts zur Qualität der bundesdeutschen Demokratie.* Baden-Baden, 2009.

Köcher, R. "Das Bollwerk." *Frankfurter Allgemeine Zeitung,* 21 August 2012.

Koopmans, T. *Courts and Political Institutions: A Comparative View.* Cambridge, 2003.

Maus, I. *Zur Aufklärung der Demokratietheorie. Rechts- und demokratietheoretische Überlegungen im Anschluß an Kant.* Frankfurt/Main, 1992.

Maus, I. "Vom Rechtsstaat zum Verfassungsstaat. Zur Kritik juridischer Demokratieverhinderung." *Blätter für deutsche und internationale Politik,* Vol. 49(7), 2004, 835–850.

Maus, I. "Zur Ideengeschichte der Gewaltenteilung und der Funktionsweise der Justiz." In Hitzel-Cassagne, T., Schmidt, T., eds., *Demokratie in Europa und europäische Demokratien. Festschrift für Heidrun Abromeit.* Wiesbaden, 2005, 224–262.

Merkel, W. *Systemtransformation. Eine Einführung in die Theorie und Empirie der Transformationsforschung,* 2nd ed. Wiesbaden, 2010.

Romeu, F.R. "The Establishment of Constitutional Courts: A Study of 128 Democratic Constitutions." *Review of Law and Economics,* Vol. 2(1), 2006, 104–135.

Sandler, R., Schoenbrod, D. *Democracy by Decree: What Happens When Courts Run Government.* New Haven, 2003.

Scheppele, K.L. "Democracy by Judiciary: Or, why Courts Can be More Democratic than Parliament." In Czarnota, A., Krygier, M., Sadurski, W., eds., *Rethinking the Rule of Law after Communism.* Budapest, New York, 2005, 25–60.

Schwartz, H. *The Struggle for Constitutional Justice in Post-Communist Europe.* Chicago, 2000.

Stone Sweet, A. *Governing with Judges: Constitutional Politics in Europe.* Oxford, 2000.

Tsebelis, G. *Veto Players: How Political Institutions Work.* Princeton, 2002.

Tushnet, M. *Taking the Constitution Away from the Courts.* Princeton, 1999.

Tushnet, M. *Weak Courts, Strong Rights: Judicial Review and Social Welfare Rights in Comparative Constitutional Law.* Princeton, Oxford, 2008.

Vallinder, T. "When the Courts Go Marching In." In Tate, C.N., Vallinder, T., eds., *The Global Expansion of Judicial Power.* New York, London, 1995, 13–26.

Vanberg, G. *The Politics of Constitutional Review in Germany.* Cambridge, 2005.

Vorländer, H., Brodocz, A. "Das Vertrauen in das Bundesverfassungsgericht. Ergebnisse einer repräsentativen Bevölkerungsumfrage." In Vorländer, H., ed., *Die Deutungsmacht der Verfassungsgerichtsbarkeit.* Wiesbaden, 2006, 259–295.

Waldron, J. *Law and Disagreement.* Oxford, 1999.

Waldron, J. "The Core of the Case Against Judicial Review." *Yale Law Journal,* Vol. 115(6), 2006, 1346–1406.

Waltman, J.L., Holland, K.M., eds. *The Political Role of Law Courts in Modern Democracies.* New York, 1988.

Wesel, U. *Die Hüter der Verfassung. Das Bundesverfassungsgericht: seine Geschichte, seine Leistungen und seine Krisen.* Frankfurt/Main, 1996.

Wesel, U. *Der Gang nach Karlsruhe. Das Bundesverfassungsgericht in der Geschichte der Bundesrepublik.* Munich, 2004.

Chapter 12

Constitutional Courts in Changing Political Systems

Hans J. Lietzmann

Any comparison of the development of the U.S. Supreme Court and the German Federal Constitutional Court encounters precipitous obstacles. The difficulties do not lie in a lack of similarities to be found in their judgments, or in their place within the political pattern. Rather, it is on the level of the courts' "habitual" disposition that a number of parallels can be discovered—which is why (particularly in the constitutional and public law literature, with their emphatic manner of a continuing search for comparability) statements of symmetry, simultaneity, and parallelism are made repeatedly. As a rule, however, these prove to be untenable and more in the spirit of mutual harmonization (resulting in a fear to develop something individually) than actual academic assessment of the matter. Indeed, I am of the conviction that the fact that the U.S. constitutional court was established in the eighteenth century and that of the Federal Republic of Germany in the twentieth century renders any comparison implausible, even if similar structures of competence could be found in both countries. Problems of historical simultaneity and nonsimultaneity of political institutions arise emphatically.

However, and precisely because of the historical difference, the possibility of comparison cannot be excluded. Perhaps due to the differences in the historical development of the courts, a decoding of the courts' focus, hidden behind the mantle of national specificity, can be undertaken. It can be supported in a number of ways.

The Supreme Court, as the older and more traditional of the courts but also as the more restructured, is said to have changed itself, its judgments, and its legal and political standards in various ways over the years. This unspectacular process of "amendment" of the "political government" allows a number of conclusions to be drawn from a historical perspective, conclusions concerning the possibility of continuity below the level of change. These conclusions hinge upon the following questions. Is there a golden thread of motivation, a self-understanding of function, or even an objective allocation of roles, requiring that a different political stance be taken at different times, in order to ensure the continuity and symmetry of a particular political purpose under altered circumstances? Does the maintenance of a fixed aim under changing conditions thus require a changed political judicature?

The decision making of the Supreme Court can be divided into three general periods exercising a particular, including external, stringency (see Lerner 1933; Miller 1968; Frankenberg, Rödel 1981: 237 et seq.; O'Brien 1986). Essentially this refers to the judgments of the Supreme Court from the time of its conception in 1789 until about the mid nineteenth century; the period after this until about 1930; and the final period from the time of the New Deal until the present day (see also Rehnquist 1986 and the criticism by Rau 1996).

The first phase of judicial politics in the United States can be summarized as the attempt to stringently enforce the national market, following the guidelines of central government and avoiding the Balkanizing tendencies among the individual states. The interest-specific motivation for this was undoubtedly the stabilization of political and economic relations in order to develop commercial capital. The abolition of the individual states' protective import taxes and the nationalization of various forms of commercial transport reflected the desire for commercial capitalistic expansion to new markets. Stabilization of the market economy, nationalization of product distribution, and reduction of the commercial privileges of England formed the political and economic emphasis, as capitalist forms of production were still in an evolutionary stage at this time in the United States (see also the interesting idea of Meuschel 1981: 15 et seq. and 57 et seq.). The Court did not take up the development of universal freedom and equality, which could have been considered in the context of the paternalist, slave-oriented economy.

In the mid nineteenth century the political and economic priorities changed, as commerce faced an expansion crisis (partly due to restrictions imposed by the European market) and capital investment in national enterprises increased (Ernst 1976: 176; Meuschel 1981: 97). The investment of capital in new areas of industrial production, which had to finance the regeneration of trade routes and the production of goods, also created new orientation points with respect to the legal hypotheses upon which politics were based.

Therefore, in the second half of the nineteenth century the nationalization of the economy and the expansion of its operational radius were not as high on the agenda as the intensification and mechanization of the production process in order to increase the profitability of previously antiquated factories. The opponents of this new political orientation, which the Supreme Court also adopted, was thus no longer a rear guard composed of small farmers and slaveholders whose patriarchy the market economy had to overcome. Instead, industrialists and investors had to combat resistance from cottage industries and small manufacturers, who were victims of the Court's legal and institutional creations under the politics of laissez-faire (e.g., its recognition of corporations as carriers of individual rights). The investment capriciousness, speculation profit, and concentration of power that evolved from commercial capital into production capital was safeguarded by the judicature, while at the same time state controls and nationalization were viewed as an unacceptable intrusion into society and subjected to restrictions. Thus the Supreme Court presented itself, under these changed circumstances, as the "authoritative faculty of political economy" (Commons 1924: 7). Directly and indirectly, it served to minimize capital risks (Miller 1968: 26), even though this created policies and legal instruments diametrically opposed to those of the Court's precedence (Mendelson 1956: 125).

Interestingly, the Court acted in the absence of any particular desire for legitimacy expressed by the Supreme Court's contemplative public or legitimacy pressure felt by the Court itself. Instead, the Court gained competencies in the interpretation of central areas of political and economic legislation. Judicial review blatantly dominated the economic areas with its anti-interventionist perspective.

The collapse of the policy of uncoordinated expansion and intensification of capital production culminated in the Wall Street crash, directly bankrupting many economic centers as well as the politics of the Supreme Court. The necessity of central state intervention as a foundation for stability (in states with an advanced capitalistic production) became conspicuous. Even if the question of the significance of the reappointments Roosevelt made within the Supreme Court is ignored, it can be noted that the Court handed over the global economic determination to the executive and legislative, and restricted itself to "constitutional politics" in the narrow sense.

The Supreme Court accepted the New Deal legislation and proceeded to focus on "political culture" by turning its attention to the question of freedom of speech and to regulations relating to the freedom of the press. From the construction of the foundations of political power, the Court arrived at the internal design of the same. Having lost its fight on the battleground of the political economy, the Court withdrew to the sidelines of political morality. But by regulating political rules of behavior and the continual (re-)creation of a political culture neglected by a national government focused on new central coordination, the Supreme Court returned to the political stage. The Court was not necessarily weakened by this move, as is evident in the fact that it can be credited with positive developments of the political system, in particular when it demanded a partial reintegration of the "good life" (Roelofs 1979: 96). By appointing itself the defender of interests not sufficiently taken into account in the economic sphere, and by enabling minorities to have a course of action, the Court provided complainants with an addressee and at the same time left the populace with the impression of "freedom of democracy."

If one is trying to establish a link between the policies of the Supreme Court over the last two hundred years and the policy strategies of the German Federal Constitutional Court, then the latest phase of U.S. judicial policy is of course the most relevant. The orientation of judicial activities to topics such as freedom of speech and assembly, the dignity of men and women, and the putative values of the constitution—in short, the manifestation of the traditional civil-democratic rhetoric—is formative for both courts. However, this comparison can also contain the genesis of the orientation, that is, the process of evolution and of historical growth, which allows conclusions to be drawn on the developmental factors of this policy of justice.

As had occurred in the United States of the 1930s, in the post–World War II Federal Republic of Germany the political economy constituted itself in total independence from the constitutional judicature. The parameters of state intervention and economic laissez-faire were determined in different places—in the state and federal parliaments, in the ministries, by corporate committees, and by the Allies—not just by the judicature. The economy organized itself through other, more just, political avenues. It no longer needed the judicature as a corrective of contrary political strategies.

Instead, the constitutional judicature was understood as (and understood itself to be) a meaningful element of an increasingly harsh world. Here the institution of a "just state" (*Gerechtigkeitsstaat*), as Adolf Arndt called it (cited in Laufer 1968: 133), was being formed as a holistic and culturally satisfying element of a corporate structured government. The constitutional courts (as a department of political power in both the United States and the Federal Republic of Germany) organized the social and cultural mortar, which, promising communicative happiness, contributed to reuniting the people with an environment that had become independent of them.

Of course, it is not possible to completely institutionalize independent spheres of economic and "cultural" politics, and the modern constitutional courts will in due course also be confronted with questions of economic relevance, in particular in the area of the admissibility of state intervention into freedom of enterprise (see Lietzmann 1988: 165 et seq.; Landfried 1992: 50 et seq.). However, contrary to earlier judicial policy, the constitutional courts legitimized the executive branch's prerogative to organize the political-economic field. Limitations upon the freedom of occupation, investment-controlling taxation, and many other parameters of economic policy were confirmed through the courts' submission to the terms of reference of the executive branch, even to the point of allowing the executive to dictate the criteria. Yet this did not always have to occur in the express form of an actual transfer of arguments, or in the offensive strategy of the "political question doctrine." The inconspicuous effectiveness of the non-acceptance policy in relation to cases submitted is unsurpassable, particularly in this context. On the other hand, by transporting the economic action paradigm to the level of constitutional law, constitutional courts gained a constitutional policy surplus.

But despite their involvement in even peripheral areas of economic policy, the constitutional courts were always aware that they should not acquire too succinct a profile in these matters. Instead they drew their images from the lucid territories of the civil freedom of communication and the attached disposition of free civil provenance (see also Haltern 1997).

The constitutional judicature's habitual commitment to the patriarchal granting of civil freedoms to a world that "in principle" is not prepared for them seems in any case to be—in the United States after 1930 as in the Federal Republic of Germany—the decisive component of an appropriate understanding of their politics. Wholly in the spirit of Pierre Bourdieu (1977), the gestures with which they compose their judgments seem to be more important than the concrete decision they reach. Within the judicial disposition of a free and unhindered (by practical constraints) middle-class mentality, a kernel of hope is articulated. This hope is the basis of a sentimental, "heroic" middle-class mentality whose fruition, though awaited to no avail in the daily trudge, makes the daily mundaneness bearable. Thus the constitutional courts and their dispositions suggest an already attained level of "the good life" (Habermas 1981: 548; also see Habermas 1968: 62 and 68). They represent the societal ideal, the final realization to which both the German and American social orders aspire. The imagination of a comprehensive freeing of the spirit, of equality, and of harmony, remains the heroic fiction of both cultures. Here a national specification of the various "civic cultures" could be applied (on heroism, compare Schlaffer 1989 and Michel 1959).

The habitual realization of this fiction, symbolized by the constitutional values and the personification of the constitutional courts, denies the most decisive factor: both constitutional values and constitutional courts, whether American or German, can uphold their disposition and societal fiction only in the form of a radical asceticism toward precisely the things that determine and organize the reality of life in both countries and societies—namely, questions of current economic production and distribution. The asceticism toward these spheres both decisively determines their existence and furnishes their reputation; and their reputation makes the societal fiction plausible. This fiction of free socialization is the focus of symbolic politics, which uses constitutional courts as diversifying departments of an all-encompassing "political government." As a matter of routine, reference must be made to Murray Edelman (1964) at this stage. However, the discussion has progressed (as many will know).

Even as the constitutional courts in both countries function in this respect as "cathedrals" of the symbolic politics, they neglect central coordination roles that are also (and have been) expected of them; the central state's coordination of legal regulations with the demands of practice; and the coordination of political-legal criteria in the interpretation and execution of undefined statutory norms (see also Frankenberg 1996; Lietzmann 1998). These and similar matters are daily political tasks that must be solved in one form or another by a political institution. The Supreme Court was established for this purpose alone and played that role for almost 150 years. Under the current political structures, however, such coordination roles seem mainly to be fulfilled purely according to executive-state rationality and effectiveness. The aura of (in old-European and constitutional-euphemistic terms) "eroticism" of the state—the aura emblematized by the Basic Law in Germany and the constitutional fathers in the United States—can be dispersed only with great difficulty through such themes. The crude parameters of current politics are immune to societal integration through constitutional emotionality. For these parameters, all emphatic constitutional adjudication is excluded as a political medium.

A gulf is thus developing between the institutionalized expectations—the political-legal obligations demanded of the constitutional judicature—and the political-cultural integration tasks that the two courts have become accustomed to performing over the last fifty and thirty years respectively. On the one hand, increasingly more areas of society are becoming dominated by purely functional system requirements, and their management can no longer be represented by recognizable criteria of symbolic politics. Habermas (1987 Vol. 2: 370 et seq.) suitably characterizes this process as "colonization" but incorrectly identifies an extensive autonomy of the "system" and "lifeworld" (see also Lietzmann 1988: 261 et seq.). On the other hand, and precisely because of the increasing de-poetization of the lifeworld, the instances of symbolic politics come under increasing pressure (Haltern 1997; Guggenberger 1998: 222; Lietzmann 1998).

To satisfy both political desires, one must square the circle. From a political point of view, strategies to reduce the differences between the two obligations are thus desperately needed to keep *both* function demands from remaining unfulfilled (in other words, unsatisfactorily realized for the political actors as well).

In the case of the United States at the turn of the nineteenth century and then in particular as a consequence of the New Deal, we could recognize the Supreme Court's decisive orientation away from the demands of system-wide economic coordination and toward the integration of society under a "civil religion." While the executive undertook to steer the quasi-business processes, the Supreme Court organized the political soul—that is, the political-cultural framework (Volcansek 1992: 117; Dauses 1994: 228; Shapiro, Stone 1994; Sander 1998: 113).

After a development phase in central state and foreign politics in the Federal Republic of Germany, on the other hand, the role of the Court of Justice of the European Union (CJEU) comes into view. In relation to everyday problems, the CJEU appears to be a practical, organized body operating on the basis of totally un-aura-like criteria that take over the necessary coordinating tasks in legal and political business matters. In the juridical politics of the CJEU, nothing remains of the old European constitutional rhetoric (see, however, Höreth 2008, 67–73, who demonstrates how national constitutional principles influence the CJEU's development of general principles of union law). Everything orients itself to the newest European market economy, giving the habitual appearance of a judicial practice oriented to everyday politics. It is a coordinating body of legal-economic realpolitik that is above all unencumbered by the ornamental paraphernalia of symbolic politics.

In this respect, the CJEU deals with business while the Federal Constitutional Court produces the nation-state aura. The dispute as to which has supremacy in questions of the interpretation of basic rights thus has institutional as well as political-cultural consequences. These lie in the clear distribution of functions, division of application, and presentation of the power of justice. The constitutional values, which, in their hidden form of real political application—particularly in the economically determined areas (to be regulated primarily at the European level)—can no longer be presented and represented through politically integrated gain, find their representative medium in the Federal Constitutional Court. In their undetermined but still individual freedom–establishing form, however, they have at the same time lost all meaning for the political mainstream. The relevant organ for the mainstream is the functional and efficient CJEU, which is also free of all traditional and cultural ties. Thus the judges of the CJEU orient their decisions to realpolitik, the economy, and the executive, while the Federal Constitutional Court boasts commonplace sentimental decisions. Systemic structure and political culture seek to complement each other. Meanwhile, in the United States the division seems to lie mainly between the Supreme Court and the direct centers of the executive. In these differences, each system attains plausibility for its area. Neither can claim greater functionality or terseness.

The fact that the commonplace of a generalized disposition of official political culture in Germany and the United States is focused on the oracle of a supreme judicature deserves attention. Political morals obtain legal status. Herein lies the main parallel of the European and the American (and not just the official) political cultures.

Hans J. Lietzmann is the Jean-Monnet professor for European studies at the Department of Political Science of the Bergische Universität, Wuppertal.

Bibliography

Bourdieu, P. *Outline of a Theory of Practice.* Cambridge, 1977.

Commons, J.R. *Legal Foundations of Capitalism.* New York, 1924.

Dauses, M.A. "Die Rolle des EuGH als Verfassungsgerichtshof." *Integration,* Vol. 17(4), 1994, 215–229.

Edelman, M.J. *The Symbolic Uses of Politics.* Urbana, 1964.

Ernst, J. "Ideology and Economic Interpretation of the Revolution." In Young, A.F., ed., *The American Revolution: Explorations in the History of American Radicalism.* Dekalb, 1976, 160–185.

Frankenberg, G. "Verfassungsgerichtsbarkeit und Zivilgesellschaft." *Kritische Justiz,* Vol. 29(1), 1996, 1–14.

Frankenberg, G., Rödel, U. *Von der Volkssouveränität zum Minderheitenschutz.* Frankfurt, 1981.

Guggenberger, B. "Zwischen Konsens und Konflikt. Das Bundesverfassungsgericht und die Zukunftsfähigkeit der Gesellschaft." In Guggenberger, B., Würtenberger, Th., eds., *Hüter der Verfassung oder Lenker der Politik? Das Bundesverfassungsgericht im Widerstreit.* Baden-Baden, 1998, 202–232.

Habermas, J. *Technik und Wissenschaft als 'Ideologie'.* Frankfurt, 1968.

Habermas, J. *Theory of Communicative Action, Volume 2: Lifeworld and System: A Critique of Functionalist Reason,* Boston, 1987.

Höreth, M., *Die Selbstautorisierung des Agenten: Der Europäische Gerichtshof im Vergleich zum U.S. Supreme Court,* Baden-Baden 2008.

Haltern, U. "Integration als Mythos." *Jahrbuch für Öffentliches Recht,* Vol. 45, 1997, 31–88.
Landfried, C. "Judicial Policy-Making in Germany: The Federal Constitutional Court." *West European Politics,* Vol. 15(3), 1992, 50–67.
Laufer, H. *Verfassungsgerichtsbarkeit und politischer Prozeß. Studien zum Bundesverfassungsgericht der Bundesrepublik Deutschland.* Tübingen, 1968.
Lerner, M. "The Supreme Court and American Capitalism." *Yale Law Journal,* Vol. 42(5), 1933, 668–701.
Lietzmann, H.J. *Das Bundesverfassungsgericht – Eine soziologische Studie.* Opladen, 1988.
Lietzmann, H.J. "'Reflexiver Konstitutionalismus' und Demokratie. Die moderne Gesellschaft überholt die Verfassungsrechtsprechung." In Guggenberger, B., Würtenberger, Th., eds., *Hüter der Verfassung oder Lenker der Politik? Das Bundesverfassungsgericht im Widerstreit.* Baden-Baden, 1998, 233–261.
Mendelson, W. "Missing Link in the Evolution of Due Process." *Vanderbilt Law Review,* Vol. 10(1), 1956, 125–37.
Meuschel, S. *Kapitalismus oder Sklaverei.* Frankfurt 1981.
Michel, K.M. "Gefühl als Ware – Zur Phänomenologie des Kitsches." *Neue deutsche Hefte,* Vol. 57, 1959, 31–48.
Miller, A. *The Supreme Court and the American Capitalism.* New York, 1968.
O'Brien, D. *Storm Center: The Supreme Court in American Politics.* New York, London, 1986.
Rau, C. *Grenzen in der Rechtsprechung des United Supreme Court und des Bundesverfassungsgerichts.* Berlin, 1996.
Rehnquist, W.H. "The Changing Role of the Supreme Court." *Florida State University Law Review,* Vol. 14(1), 1986, 1–14.
Roelofs, J. "The Warren Court and Corporate Capitalism." *Telos,* Vol. 39(Spring), 1979, 94–112.
Sander, G.G. *Der Europäische Gerichtshof als Förderer und Hüter der Integration.* Berlin, 1998.
Schlaffer, H. *The Bourgeois as Hero.* Cambridge, 1989.
Shapiro, M., Stone, A. "The New Constitutional Politics of Europe." *Comparative Political Studies,* Vol. 26(4), 1994, 397–420.
Volcansek, M.L. "The European Court of Justice: Supranational Policy Making." *West European Politics,* Vol. 15(3), 1992, 109–121.

Index

H

I

www.ingramcontent.com/pod-product-compliance
Ingram Content Group UK Ltd.
Pitfield, Milton Keynes, MK11 3LW, UK
UKHW021836100926
8556IPUK00004B/376

9 781785 332739